The Decameron of Giovanni Boccaccio

Giovanni Boccaccio

THE

DECAMERON

OF

GIOVANNI BOCCACCIO

INCLUDING

FORTY OF ITS HUNDRED NOVELS

WITH AN INTRODUCTION BY HENRY MORLEY

LL.D., PROFESSOR OF ENGLISH LITERATURE AT
UNIVERSITY COLLEGE, LONDON

LONDON

GEORGE ROUTLEDGE AND SONS

BROADWAY, LUDGATE HILL

NEW YORK: 9 LAFAYETTE PLACE

1884

INTRODUCTION.

GIOVANNI BOCCACCIO was born, if not at Paris, on a little family estate, by the market town of Certaldo, nineteen miles from Florence, in the year 1313. He was the last born of the three Patriarchs of Modern Literature, having been nine years younger than Petrarch, and forty-eight years younger than Dante, who died in 1321, when Boccaccio was a child eight years old. Boccaccio's father was a prosperous Florentine merchant, his mother a Parisian lady, and he was their illegitimate son, of whom his father took due care.

Boccaccio's bent was, from early childhood, towards Literature. In France he received some part of his early education. He was apprenticed to a merchant for six years, and showed no aptitude for trade. He then lost nearly another six years in making it evident to his father that he had as little aptitude for canon law. Canon law was abandoned, and trade taken up again. Then having learned Greek, he partly earned a living as Greek copyist, but being settled in Naples, where King Robert of Anjou held his Court, he blossomed into praises of a Maria, who was natural daughter to King Robert, and who, like Boccaccio, had a French mother. Maria was the Fiammetta for whom he told in prose the tale of Florio and Blanchefleur, his "Filocopo," and in verse the story of Palamon and Arcite, as his "Teseide." Boccaccio's "Teseide" was the first poem in modern Europe that told a tale of love and chivalry straight through in clear music, without allegorical admixture. The octave rime that he chose for its stanza he used again, and through his example it became in Italy the favourite measure for heroic poems. From Boccaccio's "Teseide," Chaucer took his "Knight's Tale."

At the age of about twenty-eight, Boccaccio was recalled by his father to Florence, and he there wrote, in prose mixed with verse, his "Ameto," on the subduing power of love. This was a piece that had much influence on the development of pastoral.

At the age of thirty-one, in 1344—King Robert having died in 1342—Boccaccio returned to Naples; there he remained until 1350, when his father died. He was free to use his genius as he would, and was foremost poet and scholar at the Court of King Robert's granddaughter, Giovanna. Giovanna succeeded her grandfather at the age of nineteen, and was married to Andreas, the brother of the King of Hungary. Because Andreas wished to advance Hungarians in Naples, and for other reasons, there was a conspiracy against Giovanna's husband, in which the Queen herself was suspected of chief part. He was assassinated in 1345, and Giovanna soon afterwards took for second husband the murderer of her first. The brother of Andreas was Louis of Anjou, King of Hungary, then a youth of nineteen. He marched upon Naples to take vengeance, and Boccaccio was with the Court of Giovanna in her flight and in her return. The Pope inquired into the accusation against the Queen, and declared her no accomplice in the murder.

It was to please this Queen that Boccaccio collected the stories afterwards set in the framework of "The Decameron." During his second stay in Naples, Boccaccio wrote also, again in octave rime, his "Filostrato." The fame of this poem made Troilus and Cressida the love story of the Italians. It was Englished by Chaucer as his "Troilus and Cressida," with changes that put into it a sense of purity and honour, little known then at the Court of Naples.

The genius of Boccaccio has reproduced the Italian life of his time; but he was himself scholar as well as poet, a preserver and transcriber of MSS., a friend of learned men, a student of Greek, enthusiastic in devotion to Dante, warm in friendship and open in admiration towards Petrarch. His own kindly nature took no very deep stain from the corrupt life about him. "The Decameron," chiefly or wholly produced in Naples at the Court of Giovanna, was first given to the public in 1353, and by repeated copying was quickly spread through Europe. In the year 1360, Boccaccio left Florence for Certaldo, where, in the following year, he received a prophecy of his approaching death from a Carthusian monk of Sienna, who brought it from the deathbed of another of his order, the holy Father Petroni, attested by the revelation of a secret which Boccaccio believed to have been known only to himself. He entered the Church in 1362 under the influence of this monastic warning, but he lived until 1375, employed sometimes by the Republic of Florence, envoy once from Florence to the Court of Brandenburgh, and once to the Pope Innocent VI. at Avignon, but seeking no worldly advancement ; although always poor, still happiest among his books and busy with his pen. In the induction to the fourth day of the Decameron (p. 118), Boccaccio replied for himself in the right manly tone to those who took compassion on him for his poverty.

Among the books written by Boccaccio in Latin was one, "De Casibus Illustrium Virorum," a recital in prose form, with poetic feeling, of the fates of men, from Adam downward, who had fallen from their high prosperity. This was turned afterwards into a French poem by Laurent de Premierfait, and through the French by John Lydgate into his poem of "The Falls of Princes," which afterwards also suggested the production of "The Mirror for Magistrates," and its growth by gradual addition in the days of Queen Elizabeth.

On the 23rd of October 1373, Boccaccio delivered the first of the lectures founded at Florence for the study of Dante. His health was then failing. In those days, when he also was dying, Petrarch read for the first time his friend's "Decameron." He liked the last novel so well, the tale of Patient Griselda (which, he said, none had been able to read without tears), that he translated it into a Latin spiritual myth, "De Obedientia et Fide Uxoria," with the lesson which Chaucer repeated when he took Petrarch's version as the original of his own "Clerke's Tale : —

> " For sith a woman was so patient
> Unto a mortal man, well more us ought
> Receiven all in gree that God us sent."

Petrarch sent his version of Griselda to his friend Boccaccio with the last letter he ever wrote. He died a few weeks afterwards on the 18th of July 1374. The death of Boccaccio followed on the 21st of December 1375.

Petrarch's delay in reading "The Decameron" was due probably to the fact that Boccaccio, who seems to have destroyed his own MS. of it after he had received the warning from the dying Carthusian, had withdrawn his interest from the book, while Petrarch's attention was drawn rather to the Latin writings of his friend; for by his Latin works each hoped especially to live. Nevertheless, "The Decameron," with its hundred novels, told by a man of genius with a rare gift for story-telling, in clear natural language that laid the foundation of Italian prose, was the book of its age throughout the European world of fashion. It mirrored the life of its time, and attacked corruptions of the Church while sharing the corruptions of the world. It was a great cause, also, of story-telling in others. Sequences of tales connected by a thread of imaginary incidents became numerous. In our own country, Chaucer's masterpiece, "The Canterbury Tales," as well as his friend Gower's "Confessio Amantis," owed their existence and some part of their character to the example set. Boccaccio had gathered his stories from many sources, very many out of France; but his way of telling them made old tales new, and "The Decameron" remains to this day a storehouse of material for poetic treatment.

The third novel of the first day is the source of the plot of Lessing's "Nathan the Wise;" Shakespeare's "Cymbeline" is founded on the ninth novel of the second day. The third novel of the third day suggested Molière's "Ecole des Maris," and Otway's "Soldier's Fortune." The ninth novel of that day is the source of Shakespeare's "All's Well that Ends Well." In the fourth day, the first novel has been reproduced in many forms. It is the original of Dryden's "Sigismunda and Guiscardo," and theme of pictures by Correggio and Hogarth. From the fifth novel of that day Keats took his poem of "The Pot of Basil." On the first novel of the fifth day Dryden founded his poem of "Cymon and Iphigenia," and Sir Frederick Leighton his picture exhibited at the Royal Academy in 1884. The eighth novel of the fifth day was versified by Dryden in his "Theodora and Honoria," and the ninth is the source of Lord Tennyson's play of "The Falcon." The tenth novel of the sixth day was formally censured by the Council of Trent for its satire upon fraudulent relics. The ninth novel of the seventh day suggested Chaucer's "Merchant's Tale," and, through that, Pope's "January and May," while the first novel of the eighth day is the original of Chaucer's "Shipman's Tale;" the sixth of the ninth day suggested Chaucer's "Reeve's Tale," and the fifth of the tenth day is Chaucer's "Franklin's Tale." The eighth novel of the tenth day is the story of "Titus and Gisippus," which was told again by Sir Thomas Eliot in his "Governour;" and the tenth of the tenth day, the last story in the book, is of the patience of Griselda, taken by Chaucer as the foundation of his "Clerke's Tale," not directly, but, as has been said, through the spiritual rendering by Petrarch.

The "Black Death" that swept through Europe in 1348-9 was the most terrible of the five pestilences of the fourteenth century. It had its origin in Asia, was in Cyprus, which it almost depopulated, in Sicily, Marseilles, where it is said to have killed 16,000 in one month, and entered some Italian seaports, in 1347. In January 1348 it appeared in Avignon; in the beginning of April it reached Florence. It did not touch England until August, and was not in London until three months later. It reached Sweden in November 1349, and spread along the northern countries into Russia, but did not appear in Russia until 1351. Fourteenth-century statistics need correction. It was said that there died of the plague in Florence 60,000, in Vienna 100,000, in Avignon 60,000, in Paris 50,000, in London 100,000, in Norwich 51,100 ; of Minorites in Italy 3,000 ; of Franciscan Friars in Germany 124,434. It has been argued by a modern writer that in Europe alone this plague must have destroyed 25,000,000 of inhabitants. At Paris, when 500 a day were dying in the Hôtel Dieu, new volunteers were, it is said, always ready to replace the Sisters of Charity who died at their posts. The age had its unnamed heroes whose fame spread only in Heaven.

Boccaccio's opening to "The Decameron" is the most famous account of this great pestilence. No translations reproduce fairly the charms of style ; but of all translations of early Italian writers the least congenial are those made in the eighteenth century by men whose theory of writing was based on a reaction against Italian influence. For that reason, and because the first · complete translation of "The Decameron," which was made in the reign of James the First, was first published in 1620 and reached its fifth edition in 1684, is now a scarce book, I have chosen to give "The Decameron" from that translation, only restoring names to their Italian form, and making a few trivial corrections. Its first edition was entered in the registers of the Stationers' Company on the 22nd of March 1619 (New Style, 1620), when it must have received the license of the Bishop of London's chaplain. But in the margin there is inscribed against this entry, "recalled by my lord of Canterburyes comand." The objection of the Archbishop of Canterbury was, however, overcome. The book was provided with a little spiritual armour (here put off), in the shape of a short moral placed after the title of each tale, but the whole was fairly translated, with the omission only of one tale of Dioneo's and substitution of a worthier, and with here and there a little Englishing of dishonest into honest love. These purifying touches are always very light, and sometimes only perceptible by their effect. In one novel, however, the seventh of the third day, a bolder touch by the old translator, who there ventures to change a couple of relationships, has enabled me to include in this collection a good story that must otherwise have been omitted. His purifying touch even adds comic effect to the novel of the Nightingale.

The whole framework of "The Decameron" is here given, with forty of its tales, including all the best. Ten more might have been given, none of them important ; but the book gains much by omission of the other fifty. Indeed, the novels of "The Decameron" illustrate in their own way the saying, drawn from Hesiod, that sometimes the half is greater than the whole.

H. M.

July 1884.

THE DECAMERON

OF

MESSER GIOVANNI BOCCACCIO.

———◦◦◦———

THE FIRST DAY.

INDUCTION.

Wherein, after the demonstration made by the author upon what occasion it
happened, that the persons (of whom we shall speak hereafter) should thus
meet together to make so quaint a narration of novels, he declareth unto you
that they first begin to devise and confer under the government of Madam
Pampinea, and of such matters as may be most pleasing to them all.

GRACIOUS ladies, so often as I consider with myself, and observe
respectively, how naturally you are inclined to compassion, as
many times do I acknowledge that this present work of mine will, in
your judgment, appear to have but a harsh and offensive beginning
in regard of the mournful remembrance it beareth at the very
entrance of the last pestilential mortality, universally hurtful to all
that beheld it, or otherwise came to knowledge of it. But for all that
I desire it may not be so dreadful to you, to hinder your further
proceeding in reading, as if none were to look thereon but with sighs
and tears. For I could rather wish that so fearful a beginning
should seem but as a high and steepy hill appears to them that
attempt to travel far on foot, and ascending the same with some difficulty, come afterward to walk upon a goodly even plain, which causeth
the more contentment in them because the attaining thereto was
hard and painful. For even as pleasures are cut off by grief and
anguish, so sorrows cease by joy's most sweet and happy arriving.

After this brief molestation—brief, I say, because it is contained
within small compass of writing—immediately followed the most
sweet and pleasant taste of pleasure, whereof before I made promise to you ; which peradventure could not be expected by such
a beginning, if promise stood not thereunto engaged. And, indeed,
if I could well have conveyed you to the centre of my desire by
any other way than so rude and rocky a passage as this is, I would
gladly have done it ; but because without this narration we could

not demonstrate the occasion how and wherefore the matters happened which you shall read in the ensuing discourses, I must set them down even as constrained thereto by mere necessity, in writing, after this manner.

The year of our blessed Saviour's Incarnation, 1348, that memorable mortality happened in the excellent city, far beyond all the rest in Italy ; which plague, by operation of the superior bodies, or rather for our enormous iniquities, by the just anger of God was sent upon us mortals. Some few years before, it took beginning in the eastern parts, sweeping thence an innumerable quantity of living souls, extending itself afterward from place to place westward, until it seized on the said city, where neither human skill nor Providence could use any prevention, notwithstanding it was cleansed of many annoyances by diligent officers thereto deputed, besides prohibition of all the sickly persons' entrance, and all possible provision daily used for conservation of such as were in health, with incessant prayers and supplications of devout people, for the assuaging of so dangerous a sickness.

About the beginning of the year it also began in very strange manner, as appeared by divers admirable effects ; yet not as it had done in the east countries, where lord or lady, being touched therewith, manifest signs of inevitable death followed thereon, by bleeding at the nose. But here it began with young children, male and female, either under the armpits or in the groin, by certain swellings, in some to the bigness of an apple, in others like an egg, and so in divers greater or lesser, which in their vulgar language they termed to be a botch or boil. In very short time after, those two infected parts were grown mortiferous, and would disperse abroad indifferently to all parts of the body ; whereupon, it was the quality of the disease to show itself by black or blue spot, which would appear on the arms of many, others on their thighs, and every part else of the body—in some, great and few ; in others, small and thick.

Now, as the boil at the beginning was an assured sign of near approaching death, so proved the spots likewise to such as had them : for the curing of which sickness it seemed that the physician's counsel, virtue of medicines, or any application else, could not yield any remedy, but rather it plainly appeared, that either the nature of the disease would not endure it, or ignorance in the physicians could not comprehend from whence the cause proceeded, and so by consequence no resolution was to be determined. Moreover, beside the number of such as were skilful in art, many more, both women and men, without ever having any knowledge in physic, became physicians ; so that not only few were healed, but well-near all died within three days after the said signs were seen, some sooner, and others later—commonly without either fever or any other accident.

And this pestilence was yet of far greater power or violence. For not only healthful persons speaking to the sick, coming to see them, or airing clothes in kindness to comfort them, was an occasion of ensuing death ; but touching their garments or any food whereon the sick person fed, or anything else used in his service, seemed to transfer the disease from the sick to the sound, in very rare and miraculous manner. Among which matter of marvel, let me tell you one thing, which if the eyes of many, as well as mine own, had not seen, hardly could I be persuaded to write it, much less to believe it, albeit a man of good credit should report it. I say that the quality of this contagious pestilence was not only of such efficacy in taking and catching it one of another, either men or women, but it extended further, even in the apparent view of many, that the clothes, or anything else wherein one died of that disease, being touched or lain on by any beast, far from the kind or quality of man, they did not only contaminate and infect the said beast, were it dog, cat, or any other, but also it died very soon after.

Mine own eyes, as formerly I have said, among divers other, one day had evident experience hereof ; for some poor ragged clothes of linen and woollen, torn from a wretched body dead of that disease, and hurled in the open street, two swine going by, and, according to their natural inclination, seeking for food on every dunghill, tossed and tumbled the clothes with their snouts, rubbing their heads likewise upon them, and immediately, each turning twice or thrice about, they both fell down dead on the said clothes, as being fully infected with the contagion of them ; which accident, and other the like, if not far greater, begat divers fears and imaginations in them that beheld them, all tending to a most inhuman and uncharitable end—namely, to fly thence from the sick, and from touching anything of theirs, by which means they thought their health should be safely warranted.

Some there were who considered with themselves that, living soberly, with abstinence from all superfluity, would be a sufficient resistance against all hurtful accidents ; so combining themselves in a sociable manner, they lived as separatists from all other company, being shut up in such houses where no sick body should be near them. And there, for their more security, they used delicate viands and excellent wines, avoiding luxury and refusing speech to one another, not looking forth at the windows to hear any cries of dying people, or see any corpses carried to burial ; but, having musical instruments, lived there in all possible pleasure. Others were of a contrary opinion, who avouched that there was no other physic more certain, for a disease so desperate, than to drink hard, be merry among themselves—singing continually, walking everywhere, and satisfying their appetites with whatsoever they desired, laughing and mocking at every mournful accident ; and so they vowed to spend day and night, for now they would go to one tavern, then to another, living without any rule or measure, which they might very easily do, because every one of them—as if he were to live no longer in this world—had even forsaken all things that he had. By means whereof the most part of the houses were become common, and all strangers might do the like, if they pleased to adventure it, even as boldly as the lord or owner, without any let or contradiction.

Yet in all this their beastly behaviour they were wise enough to shun, so much as they might, the weak and sickly. In misery and affliction of our city, the venerable authority of the laws, as well divine as human, was even destroyed, as it were, through want of the lawful ministers of them. For they were all dead, or lying sick with the rest, or else lived so solitary, in such great necessity of servants and attendants, as they could not execute any office; whereby it was lawful for every one to do as he listed.

Between these two rehearsed extremities of life there were other of more moderate temper, not being so daintily dieted as the first, nor drinking so dissolutely as the second; but used all things sufficient for their appetites, and without shutting up themselves, walked abroad—some carrying sweet nosegays of flowers in their hands, others odoriferous herbs, and other divers kinds of spiceries, holding them to their noses, and thinking them most comfortable for the brain, because the air seemed to be much infected by the noisome smell of dead carcases and other hurtful savours. Some other there were also of more inhuman mind (howbeit peradventure it might be the surest), saying that there was no better physic against the pestilence, nor yet so good, as to fly away from it; which argument mainly moving them, and caring for nobody but themselves, very many, both men and women, forsook the city, their own house, their parents, kindred, friends, and goods, flying to other men's dwellings elsewhere. As if the wrath of God, in punishing the sins of men with this plague, would fall heavily upon none but such as were enclosed within the city walls, or else persuading themselves that not any should there be left alive, but that the final ending of all things was come.

Now albeit these persons, in their diversity of opinions, died not all, so undoubtedly they did not all escape; but many among them becoming sick, and making a general example of their flight and folly among them that could not stir out of their beds, they languished more perplexedly than the other did. Let it stand, that one citizen fled after another, and one neighbour had not any care of another; parents or kindred never visiting them, but utterly they were forsaken on all sides. This tribulation pierced into the hearts of men, and with such a dreadful terror, that one brother forsook another, the uncle the nephew, the sister the brother, and the wife her husband. Nay, a matter much greater, and almost incredible, fathers and mothers fled away from their own children, even as if they had no way appertained to them; in regard whereof it could be no otherwise but that a countless multitude of men and women fell sick, finding no charity among their friends, except a very few, and subject to the avarice of servants, who attended them constrainedly, for great and unreasonable wages. Yet few of those attendants to be found anywhere too, and they were men or women but of base condition, as also of grosser understanding, who never before had served in any such necessities, nor indeed were any way else to be employed, but to give the sick person such things as he called for, or to await the hour of his death, in the performance of which service, oftentimes for gain, they lost their own lives.

In this extreme calamity, the sick being thus forsaken of neighbours, kindred, and friends, standing also in such need of servants, a custom came up among them, never heard before, that there was not any woman, how noble, young, or fair soever she was, but, falling sick, she must of necessity have a man to attend her, were he young or otherwise ; whereon ensued afterward, that upon the party's healing and recovery, it was occasion of further dishonesty, while many, being more modestly curious of, refused such disgraceful attending, choosing rather to die than by such help to be healed. In regard whereof, as well through the want of convenient remedies (which the sick by no means could attain unto), as also the violence of the contagion, the multitude of them that died night and day was so great, that it was a dreadful sight to behold, and as much to hear spoken of. So that mere necessity (among them that remained living) begat new behaviours, quite contrary to all which had been in former times, and frequently used among the city inhabitants.

The custom of the present days (as now again it is) was, that women, kindred, neighbours, and friends would meet together at the deceased party's house, and there, with them that were of nearest alliance, express their hearts' sorrow for their friend's loss. If not thus, they would assemble before the door, with many of the citizens and kindred, and, according to the quality of the deceased, the clergy met there likewise, and the dead body was carried in comely manner on men's shoulders, with funeral pomp of torchlight and singing, to the church appointed by the deceased. But these seemly orders, after the fury of the pestilence began to increase, they in like manner altogether ceased, and other new customs came in their place, because not only people died without having any women about them, but multitudes also passed out of this life not having any witness how, when, or in what manner they departed. So that few or none there were to deliver outward show of sorrow and grieving ; but instead thereof, divers declared idle joy and rejoicing, a use soon learned of immodest women who had put off all feminine compassion, yea, or regard of their own welfare.

Very few also would accompany the body to the grave, and they not any of the neighbours, although it had been an honourable citizen, but only the meanest kind of people, such as were grave-makers, coffin-bearers, or the like, that did these services only for money ; and the bier being mounted on their shoulders, in all haste they would run away with it, not perhaps to the church appointed by the dead, but to the nearest at hand, having four or six poor priests following, with lights or no lights, and those of the simplest; short service being said at the burial and the body irreverently thrown in the first open grave they found. Such was the pitiful mercy of poor people, and divers who were of better condition, as it was most lamentable to behold, because the greater number of them, under hope of healing, or compelled by poverty, kept still within their house, weak and faint, thousands falling sick daily, and having no help or being succoured in any way with food or physic, all of them died, few or none escaping.

Great store there were that died in the streets, by day or night, and many more besides, although they died in their houses ; yet first they made it known to their neighbours that their lives perished rather by the noisome smell of the dead and putrefied bodies, than by any violence of the disease in themselves. So that of these and the rest, dying in this manner everywhere, the neighbours observed one course of behaviour (moved thereto no less by fear that the smell and corruption of dead bodies should harm them, than charitable respect of the dead), that themselves when they could, or being assisted by some bearers of corpses, when they were able to procure them, would hale the bodies, already dead, out of their houses, laying them before their doors, where such as passed by, especially in the mornings, might see them lying in no mean numbers. Afterward, biers were brought thither, and such as might not have the help of biers were glad to lay them on tables ; and biers have been observed not only to be charged with two or three dead bodies at once, but many times it was seen also that the wife with the husband, two or three brethren together, yea, the father and mother, have thus been carried along to the grave upon one bier.

Moreover, oftentimes it hath been seen that when two priests went with one cross to fetch the body, there would follow behind three or four bearers with their biers, and when the priest intended the burial but of one body, six or eight more have made up the advantage, and yet none of them being attended by any seemly company, lights, tears, or the very least decency ; but it plainly appeared that the very like account was then made of men or women as if they had been dogs or swine. Wherein might manifestly be noted, that what the natural course of things could not show to the wise with few and small losses—to wit, the patient support of miseries and misfortunes, even in their greatest height— not only the wise might now learn, but also the very simplest people, and in such sort that they should always be prepared against all infelicities whatsoever.

Hallowed ground could not now suffice for the great multitude of dead bodies which were daily brought to every church in the city, and every hour in the day. Neither could the bodies have proper places of burial, according to our ancient custom ; wherefore after that the churches and churchyards were filled, they were constrained to make use of great deep ditches, wherein they were buried by hundreds at once, ranking dead bodies along in graves, as merchandises are laid along in ships, covering each after other with a small quantity of earth ; and so they filled up at last the whole ditch to the brim.

Now, because I would wander no further in every particularity concerning the miseries happening in our city, I tell you that, extremities running on in such manner as you have heard, little less was suffered in the villages round about, wherein, setting aside enclosed castles, which were now filled like to small cities, poor labourers and husbandmen, with their whole families, died most miserably in outhouses, yea and in the open fields also, without any assistance of physic or help of servants; and likewise in the highways or their ploughed lands, by day or night indifferently—yet not as men, but like brute beasts.

By means whereof they became lazy and slothful in their daily endeavours, even like to our citizens, not minding nor meddling with their wonted affairs, but, as awaiting for death every hour, employed all their pains, not in caring any way for themselves, their cattle, or gathering the fruits of the earth, or any of their accustomed labours, but rather wasted and consumed even such as were for their instant sustenance. Whereupon it fell so out that their oxen, asses, sheep, and goats, their swine, pullen, yea their very dogs, the truest and faithfullest servants to men, being beaten and banished from their houses, went wildly wandering abroad in the fields, where the corn grew still on the ground without gathering, or being so much as reaped or cut. Many of the foresaid beasts, as endued with reason, after they had pastured themselves in the daytime, would return, full fed, at night, home to their houses, without any government of herdsmen or any other.

How many fair palaces, how many goodly houses, how many noble habitations, filled before with families of lords and ladies, were then to be seen empty, without any one there dwelling, except some simple servant? How many kindreds worthy of memory, how many great inheritances, and what plenty of riches, were left without any true successors? How many good men, how many worthy women, how many valiant and comely young men, whom none but Galen, Hippocrates, and Æsculapius, if they were living, could have reputed any way unhealthful, were seen to dine at morning with their parents, friends, and familiar confederates, and went to sup in another world with their predecessors?

It is a growing grief to me to make repetition of so many miseries; wherefore, being willing to part with them as easily as I may, I say that our city, being in this case void of inhabitant, it came to pass, as afterward I understood by some of good credit, that in the venerable church of Santa Maria Novella, on a Tuesday morning, there being then no other person, after the hearing of divine service, in mourning habits as the season required, returned thence seven discreet young gentlewomen, all allied together either by friendship, neighbourhood, or parentage. She among them that was most entered into years exceeded not twenty-eight, and the youngest was no less than eighteen, being of noble descent, fair form, adorned with exquisite behaviour and gracious modesty.

Their names I could report, if just occasion did not forbid it, in regard of the occasions following, by them related, and because times hereafter shall not tax them with reproof; the laws of pleasure being more straitened nowadays (for the matters before revealed) than at that time they were—not only to their years but to many much riper. Neither will I likewise minister matter to rash heads, over-ready in censuring commendable life, any way to impair the honesty of ladies by their idle, detracting speeches. And therefore, to the end that what each of them saith may be comprehended without confusion, I purpose to style them by names wholly agreeing, or in part conformable, to their qualities. The first and most aged we will name Pampinea, the second Fiametta, the third Filomena, the fourth Emilia, the fifth Lauretta, the sixth Neifile, and the last we term (not without occasion) Elisa. All of them being assembled at a corner of the church, not by any deliberation formerly appointed, but merely by accident, and sitting as it were in a round ring, after divers sighs severally delivered, they conferred on sundry matters answerable to the sad quality of the time, and within a while after Pampinea began in this manner :

" Fair ladies, you may, no doubt, as well as I, have heard that no injury is offered to any one by such as make use but of their own right. It is a thing natural for every one who is born in this world to aid, conserve, and defend her life as long as she can ; and this right hath been so powerfully permitted, that although it hath sometimes happened that, to defend themselves, men have been slain without any offence, yet laws have allowed it to be so, in whose solicitude lieth the best living of all mortals. How much more honest and just is it then for us, and for every other well-disposed person, to seek for, without wronging any, and to practise, all remedies that we can for the preservation of our lives ? When I well consider what we have here done this morning and many other already past—remembering withal what likewise is proper and convenient for us—I conceive, as all you may do the like, that every one of us hath a due respect of herself ; and then I marvel not, but rather am much amazed—knowing none of us to be deprived of a woman's best judgment—that we seek not after some remedies for ourselves against that which every one among us ought in reason to fear.

" Here we meet and remain, as it seemeth to me, in no other manner than as if we would or should be witnesses to all the dead bodies at rest in their graves, or else to listen when the religious sisters here dwelling—whose numbers now are well-near come to be none at all—sing service at such hours as they ought to do ; or else to acquaint all comers hither, by our mourning habits, with the quality and quantity of our hearts' miseries. And when we part hence we meet with none but dead bodies or sick persons transported from one place to another ; or else we see, running through the city, in most offensive fury, such as by authority of public laws were banished hence only for their bad and brutish behaviour in contempt of those laws, because now they know that the executors of them are dead and sick. And if not these, more lamentable spectacles present themselves to us by the base rascality of the city, who, being fatted with our blood, term themselves grave-makers, and in mere contemptible mockeries of us are mounted on horseback, galloping everywhere, reproaching us for our losses and misfortunes with lewd and dishonest songs, so that we can hear nothing else but such and such are dead, and such and such lie a-dying—here hands wringing, and everywhere most pitiful complaining.

"If we return home to our houses—I know not whether your case be answerable to mine—when I can find none of all my family but only my poor waiting chambermaid. So great are my fears that the very hair of my head declareth my amazement, and wheresoever I go or sit down methinks I see the ghosts and shadows of deceased friends, not with such lovely looks as I was wont to behold them, but with most horrid and dreadful regards, newly stolen upon them I know not how; in these respects, both here, elsewhere, and at home in my house, methinks I am always ill and much more, in mine own opinion, than any other body not having means or place of retirement, as all we have, and none to remain here but only we.

"If it be so, as manifestly it maketh show of itself, what do we here? what stay we for? and whereon do we dream? Why are we more respectless of our health than all the rest of the citizens? Repute we ourselves less precious than all the other? Or do we believe that life is linked to our bodies with stronger chains than to others, and that therefore we should not fear anything that hath power to offend us? We err therein, and are deceived. What brutishness were it in us if we should urge any such belief? So often as we call to mind what and how many gallant young men and women have been devoured by this cruel pestilence, we may evidently observe a contrary argument.

"Wherefore, to the end that by being over-scrupulous and careless, we fall not into such danger, whence when we would perhaps we cannot recover ourselves by any means, I think it meet, if your judgment therein shall jump with mine, that all of us, as we are— at least if we will do as divers before us have done, and yet daily endeavour to do—shunning death by the honest example of others, make our retreat to our country houses, wherewith all of us are sufficiently furnished, and thereto delight ourselves as best we may, yet without transgressing in any act the limits of reason. There shall we hear the pretty birds sweetly singing, see the hills and plains verdantly flowering, the corn waving in the field like the billows of the sea, infinite store of goodly trees, and the heavens more fairly open to us than here we can behold them. And although they are justly displeased, yet will they not there deny us better beauties to gaze on than the walls in our city, emptied of inhabitants, can afford us.

"Moreover, the air is much more fresh and clear, and generally there is far greater abundance of all things whatsoever needful at this time for preservation of our health, and less offence or molestation than we find here.

"And although country people die, as well as here our citizens do, the grief notwithstanding is so much the less, as the houses and dwellers there are rare in comparison of them in our city. And beside, if we will observe it, here we forsake no particular person, but rather we may term ourselves forsaken, in regard that our husbands, kindred, and friends, either dying or flying from the dead, have left us alone in this great affliction, even as if we were no way belonging unto them. And therefore, by following this counsel, we cannot fall into any reprehension; whereas, if we neglect and refuse it, danger, distress, and death perhaps, may ensue thereon.

"Wherefore, if you think good, I would allow it for well done to take our waiting-women, with all such things as are needful for us, and, as this day, betake ourselves to one place, to-morrow to another, taking there such pleasure and recreation as so sweet a season liberally bestowed on us. In which manner we may remain, till we see (if death otherwise prevent us not) what end the gracious heavens have reserved for us. I would have you also to consider that it is no less seemly for us to part hence honestly, than for a great number of other women to remain here immodestly."

The other ladies and gentlewomen having heard Pampinea, not only commended her counsel, but, desiring also to put it in execution, had already particularly consulted with themselves by what means they might instantly depart from thence. Nevertheless, Filomena, who was very wise, spake thus :

"Albeit, fair ladies, the case propounded by Pampinea hath been very well delivered, yet for all that it is against reason for us to rush on, as we are over-ready to do. Remember that we are all women, and no one among us so childish but may consider that when we shall be so assembled together, without providence or conduct of some man, we can hardly govern ourselves. We are frail, offensive, suspicious, weak-spirited, and fearful, in regard of which imperfections I greatly doubt, if we have no better direction than our own, this society will sooner dissolve itself, and perchance with less honour to us, than if we never had begun it. And therefore it shall be expedient for us to provide before we proceed any further."

Elisa hereon thus replied : "Most true it is that men are the chief or head of women, and without their order seldom times do any matters of ours sort to recommendable end. But what means shall we make for men ? We all know well enough that the most part of our friends are dead, and such as are living, some be dispersed here, others there, into divers places and companies, where we have no knowledge of their being, and to accept of strangers would seem very inconvenient ; wherefore, as we have such care of our health, so should we be as respective withal, in ordering our intention, that wheresoever we aim at our pleasure and contentment, reproof and scandal may by no means pursue us."

While this discourse was thus held among the ladies, three young gentlemen came forth of the church (yet not so young but the youngest had attained to five-and-twenty years), in whom neither malice of the time, loss of friends or kindred, nor any conceit of fear in themselves, had the power to quench affection, or even to

cool it.   One of them called himself Pamfilo, the second Filostrato,
and the last Dioneo.   Each of them was very affable and well-conditioned, and walked abroad, for their greater comfort in such a time
of tribulation, to try if they could meet with their fair friends who
haply might all three be among these seven, and the rest kin unto
them in one degree or other.   No sooner were these ladies espied by
them, but they met with them also in the same advantage, whereupon
Pampinea, amiably smiling, said :

"See how graciously fortune is favourable to our beginning, by
presenting our eyes with three so wise and worthy young gentlemen,
who will gladly be our guides and servants, if we do not disdain,
them the office."

Neifile began immediately to blush because one of them had a
love in the company, and said : "Good Pampinea, take heed what
you say, because of mine own knowledge nothing can be spoken but
good of them all, and I think them all to be absolutely sufficient to
a far greater employment than is here intended, as being well worthy
to keep company, not only with us, but them of more fair and precious
esteem than we are.   But because it appeareth plainly enough that
they bear affection to some here amongst us, I fear, if we should make
the motion, that some dishonour or reproof may ensue thereby, and
yet without blame either in us or them."

"That is nothing at all," answered Filomena ; "let me live
honestly, and my conscience not check me with any crime ;
speak then who can to the contrary ; God and truth shall enter
arms for me.   I wish that they were as willing to come as all
we are to bid them welcome ; for truly, as Pampinea said, we
may very well hope that Fortune will be furtherous to our proposed
journey."

The other ladies, hearing them speak in such manner, not
only were silent to themselves, but all with one accord and consent said, that "it were well done to call them, and to acquaint
them, with their intention, entreating their company in so pleasant a voyage."   Whereupon, without any more words, Pampinea, rising to her feet, because one of the three was her
kinsman, went towards them as they stood respectfully observing
them, and, with a pleasing countenance, giving them a gracious
salutation, declared to them their deliberation, desiring, on behalf of
all the rest, that with a brotherly and modest mind they would
vouchsafe to bear them company.

The gentlemen imagined at the first apprehension that this was
spoken in mockery, but when they better perceived that her words
tended to solemn earnest, they made answer that "they were all
heartily ready to do them any service."   And without any further
delaying, before they departed thence, took order for their aptest
furnishing with all convenient necessaries, and sent word to the
place of their first appointment.   On the morrow, being Wednesday,
about break of day, the ladies, with certain of their attending
gentlewomen, and the three gentlemen, having three servants to
wait on them, left the city to begin their journey, and having

travelled about a league's distance, arrived at the place of their first purpose of stay, which was seated on a little hill, distant on all sides from any highway, plentifully stored with fair spreading trees, affording no mean delight to the eye. On the top of all stood a stately palace, having a large and spacious court in the midst, round engirt with galleries, halls, and chambers, every one separate alone by themselves, and beautified with pictures of admirable cunning. Nor was there any want of gardens, meadows, and other most pleasant walks, with wells and springs of fair running waters, all encompassed with branching vines, fitter for curious and quaffing bibbers than women sober and singularly modest. This palace the company found fully fitted and prepared, the beds in the chambers made and daintily ordered, thickly strewed with variety of flowers, which could not but give them the greater contentment.

Dioneo, who above the others was a pleasant young gallant, and full of infinite witty conceits, said : " Your wit, fair ladies, hath better guided us hither than our providence. I know not how you have determined to dispose of your ears ; as for mine own, I left them at the city gate when I came thence with . you ; and therefore let your resolution be to spend the time here in smiles and singing (I mean, as may fittest agree with your dignity), or else give me leave to go seek my sorrows again, and so to remain discontented in our desolate city."

Pampinea having in like manner shaken off her sorrows, delivering a modest and bashful smile, replied in this manner : "Dioneo, well have you spoken. It is fit to live merrily, and no other occasion made us forsake the sick and sad city. But because such things as are without mean or measure are subject to no long continuance, I, who began the motion whereby this society is thus assembled, and aim at the long lasting thereof, do hold it very convenient that we should all agree to have one chief commander among us, in whom the care and providence should consist, for direction of our merriment, performing honour and obedience to the party, as to our patron and sole governor. And because every one may feel the burthen of solicitude, as also the pleasure of commanding, and consequently have a sensible taste of both, whereby no envy may arise on any side, I could wish that each one of us, for a day only, should feel both the burthen and honour, and the person so to be advanced shall receive it from the election of us all. As for such as are to succeed after him or her that hath had the days of dominion, the party thought fit for succession must be named so soon as night approacheth. And being in this eminency, according as he or she shall please, he may order and dispose how long the time of his rule shall last, as also of the place and manner where best we may continue our delight."

These words were highly pleasing to them all, and by general voice Pampinea was chosen queen for the first day. Whereupon Filomena ran presently to a bay-tree, because she had often heard what honour belonged to those branches, and how worthy of honour they were that rightfully were crowned with them. Plucking off divers branches, she made of them an apparent and honourable chaplet, placing it by general consent upon her head; and this, so long as their company continued, manifested to all the rest the signal of dominion and royal greatness.

After that Pampinea was thus made queen, she commanded public silence, and causing the gentlemen's three servants, and the waiting-women also, being four in number, to be brought before her, thus she began : " Because I am to give the first example to you all whereby, proceeding on from good to better, our company may live in order and pleasure, acceptable to all and without shame to any, I create Parmeno, servant to Dioneo, master of the household; he taking the care and charge of all our train, and for whatsoever appertaineth to our hall service. I appoint also that Sirisco, servant to Pamfilo, shall be our dispenser and treasurer, performing that which Parmeno shall command him. Likewise that Tindaro serve as groom of the chamber to Filostrato his master, and the other two, when his fellows, impeached by their offices, cannot be present. Misia, my chambermaid, and Licisca, belonging to Filomena, shall serve continually in the kitchen, and diligently make ready such viands as shall be delivered them by Parmeno. Chimera, waiting-woman to Lauretta, and Stratilia, appertaining to Fiammetta, shall have the charge and government of the ladies' chambers, and preparing all places where we shall be present. Moreover, we will and command every one of them, as they desire to deserve our grace, that wheresoever they go or come, or whatsoever they hear or see, they bring none but cheerful tidings from outside." After she had summarily delivered them these orders, very much commended of every one, she arose fairly, saying : " Here we have gardens, orchards, meadows, and other places of sufficient pleasure, where every one may sport and recreate themselves ; but so soon as the ninth hour striketh, then all to meet here again, to dine in the cool shade."

This jocund company having received licence from their Queen to disport themselves, the gentlemen walked with the ladies into a goodly garden, making chaplets and nosegays of divers flowers, and singing silently to themselves. When they had spent the time limited by the Queen, they returned into the house, where they found that Parmeno had effectually executed his office; for when they entered into the hall they saw the tables covered with delicate white napery, and the glasses looking like silver, they were so transparently clear ; all the room, beside, strewed with flowers of juniper. When the Queen and all the rest had washed, according as Parmeno gave order, so every one was seated at the table. The viands, delicately dressed, were served in, and excellent wines plentifully delivered, none attending but the three servants, and little or no loud table-talk passing among them.

Dinner being ended, and the table withdrawn, all the ladies, and the gentlemen likewise, being skilful both in singing and dancing, and playing on instruments artificially, the Queen commanded that divers instruments should be brought, and, as she gave charge, Dioneo took a lute, and Fiammetta a *viol de gamba* and began to play an excellent dance. Whereupon the Queen, with the rest of the ladies and the other two young gentlemen, having sent their attending servants to dinner, paced forth a dance very majestically. And when the dance was ended, they sung sundry excellent canzonets ; outwearing so the time until the Queen commanded them all to rest, because the hour did necessarily require it. The gentlemen, having their chambers severed from the ladies, curiously strewed with flowers, and their beds adorned in exquisite manner—as those of the ladies were not a jot inferior to them—the silence of the night bestowed sweet rest on them all. In the morning, the Queen and all the rest being risen, accounting over-much sleep to be very hurtful, they walked abroad into a goodly meadow, where the grass grew verdantly, and the beams of the sun heated not over-violently, because the shades of fair spreading trees gave a temperate calmness, cool and gentle winds fanning their sweet breath pleasingly among them. All of them being there, sat down in a round ring, and the Queen in the midst, as being in the place of this eminency, she spake in this manner :

" You see, fair company, that the sun is highly mounted, the heat elsewhere too extreme for us, and therefore here is our fittest refuge, the air being so cool, delicate, and acceptable, and our folly well worthy reprehension if we should walk farther and speed worse. Here are tables, cards and chess, as your dispositions may be addicted ; but if my advice might pass for current, I would admit none of those exercises, because they are too troublesome both to them that play and such as look on. I could rather wish that some quaint discourse might pass among us—a tale or fable related by some one, to urge the attention of all the rest. And so, wearing out the warmth of the day, one pretty novel will draw on another, until the sun be lower declined, and the heat's extremity more diminished, to solace ourselves in some other place, as to our minds shall seem convenient. If therefore what I have said be acceptable to you, I proposing to follow in the same course of pleasure, let it appear by your immediate answer ; for till the evening I think we can devise no exercise more pleasant for us."

The ladies and gentlemen allowed of the motion, to spend the time in telling tales ; whereupon the Queen said : " Seeing you have approved mine advice, I grant free permission for this day, that every one shall relate what to him or her is best pleasing." And turning herself to Pamfilo, who was seated on her right hand, gave him favour with one of his own novels to begin the recreation, which he not daring to deny, and perceiving general attention prepared for him, thus he began.

———

THE FIRST NOVEL.

Master Chappelet deceives a holy friar with a false confession, and then dies ; and having been one of the worst of men when living, when dead is reputed a saint, and called Saint Chappelet.

IT is a matter most convenient, dear ladies, that a man ought to begin whatsoever he doth in the great and glorious name of Him who was the Creator of all things. Wherefore, seeing that I am the man appointed to begin this your invention of discoursing novelties, I intend to begin also with one of his wonderful works ; to the end, that this being heard, our hope may remain on Him, as the thing only permanent, and His name for ever to be praised by us. Now, as there is nothing more certain but that even as temporal things are mortal and transitory, so are they, both in and out of themselves, full of sorrow, pain, anguish, and subject to infinite danger ; so in the same manner we live mingled among them, seeming as part of them, and cannot, without some error, continue or defend ourselves, if God by His special grace and favour give us not strength and good understanding, which power we may not believe, that either it descended to us, or liveth in us, by any merits of our own, but of His only most gracious benignity. Moved, nevertheless, and entreated by the intercessions of them who were, as we are, mortals, and having diligently observed His commandments, are now with Him in eternal blessedness—to whom, as to advocates and to procurators, informed by the experience of our frailty, we are not to present our prayers in the presence of so great a Judge, but only to Himself, for the obtaining of all such things as His wisdom knoweth to be most expedient for us. And well may we credit that His goodness is more fully inclined towards us, in His continual bounty and liberality, than the subtilty of mortal eye can reach into the secret of so divine a thought ; and sometimes, therefore, we may be beguiled in opinion by electing such and such as our intercessors before His Majesty, who perhaps are far off from Him, or driven into perpetual exile as unworthy to appear in so glorious a presence. For He from whom nothing can be hidden, more regardeth the sincerity of him that prayeth, than ignorant devotion committed to the trust of a heedless intercessor, and such prayers have always gracious acceptation in His sight, as manifestly will appear by the novel which I intend to relate : manifestly, I say, not as in the judgment of God, but according to the apprehension of men. There was one named Musciatto Francesi, who, from being a most rich and great merchant in France, was become a knight, and preparing to go into Tuscany with Messer Charles Without Land, brother to the King of France, who was desired and incited to come thither by Pope Boniface, found his affairs greatly intricated here and there, as oftentimes the matters of merchants fall out to be, and that very hardly he should suddenly disentangle them, without referring the charge to divers persons. And for all he took indifferent good order, only he remained doubtful whom he might sufficiently leave to recover his debts among many Burgundians ; and his care was the more herein, because he knew the Burgundians to be people of bad nature and without any faithfulness, so that he could not bethink himself of any man in whom he might repose trust to prevent their lewdness. Having a long while examined his thoughts upon this point, at last he remembered one Master Ciapperello da Prato, who oftentimes had resorted to his house in Paris ; and because he was a man of little stature, yet handsome enough, the French, not knowing what this word Ciapperello might mean, esteeming he should be called rather, in their tongue, Chappel, imagined that, in regard of his small stature, they termed him Chappelet, and not Chappel; and so by the name of Chappelet he was everywhere known, and by few or none acknowledged for Chappel.

This Master Chappelet was of so good and commendable life, that, being a notary, he held it in high disdain that any of his contracts, although he made but few, should be found without falsehood. He took the only pleasure in the world to bear false witness, if he were thereto entreated, and oftentimes when he was not requested at all. Likewise, because in those times great trust and belief was given to an oath, he made no care or conscience to be perjured ; greatly advantaged himself by lawsuits, in regard that many matters relied upon his oath, and delivering the truth according to his knowledge.

He delighted beyond measure, and addicted his best studies to cause enmities and scandals betwixt kindred and friends, or any other persons agreeing well together ; and the more mischief he could procure in this kind, so much the more pleasure and delight took he therein. If he were called to kill any one, or to do any other villanous deed, he never would make denial, but go to it very willingly ; and divers times it was well known that many were cruelly beaten, yea slain, by his hands. He was a most horrible blasphemer of God and His saints upon the very least occasion, as being more addicted to choler than any other man could be. Never would he frequent the church, but basely contemned it, with the sacraments and religious rites therein administered, accounting them for vile and unprofitable things ; but very voluntarily would visit taverns and other places of dishonest resort, which were continually pleasing unto him, to satisfy his lust and inordinate pleasure. He would steal both in public and private, even with such a conscience as if it were given to him by Nature so to do. He was a great glutton and a drunkard, even till he was not able to take any more ; being also a continual gamester, and carrier of false dice, to cheat with them the very best friends he had.

In fine, there never was a worse man born ; and yet his wickedness was for long time supported by the favour, power, and authority of Monsieur Musciatto, for whose sake many wrongs and injuries were patiently endured, as well by private persons, whom he would abuse notoriously, as others of the Court, between whom he made no difference at all in his vile dealing. This Master Chappelet, being thus remembered by Musciatto, who very well knew his life and behaviour, he perfectly persuaded himself that this was a man apt in all respects to meet the treachery of the Burgundians; whereupon, having sent for him, thus he began :

"Chappelet, thou knowest how I am wholly to retire myself from hence, and having some affairs among the Burgundians, men full of wickedness and deceit, I can bethink myself of no fitter a man than yourself to recover such debts as are due to me among them. And because it falleth out so well that thou art not now hindered by any other business, if thou wilt undergo this office for me, I will procure thee favourable letters from the Court, and give thee a reasonable proportion in all thou recoverest." Master Chappelet, seeing himself idle, and greedy after worldly goods, considering that Messer Musciatto, who had been always his best buckler, was now to depart from thence, without any dreaming on the matter, constrained thereto as it were by necessity, fixed his resolution, and answered that he would gladly do it.

Having made their agreement together, and received from Musciatto his express procuration, and also the King's gracious letters, after that Musciatto was gone on his journey, Master Chappelet went into Burgundy, where he was unknown, well-near, of any. And there (quite from his natural disposition) began benignly and graciously in recovering the debts due ; which course he took the rather because they should have a further feeling of him in the end. Being lodged in the house of two Florentine brethren, that lived on the interest of their moneys, and, for Messer Musciatto's sake, using him with honour and respect, it fortuned that he fell sick, and the two brethren sent for physicians to attend him, ordering their servants to be diligent about him, not sparing anything which gave any likelihood of restoring his health. But all their pains proved to no purpose, because he being now grown aged, and having lived all his lifetime very disorderly, fell day by day, according to the physician's judgment, from bad to worse, till no other way appeared but death, whereat the brethren greatly grieved.

Upon a day, near the chamber where the sick man lay, they entered into this communication : "What shall we do," saith the one to the other, "with this man ? We are much hindered by him ; for to send him away, sick as he is, we shall be greatly blamed, and it will be a manifest note of our weak wisdom, the people knowing that first of all we gave him entertainment, and have allowed him physical attendance ; and he, not having any way injured or offended us, to let him be suddenly expelled our house, sick to death as he is, it can be no way for our credit.

"On the other side, we are to consider also that he hath been so bad a man as he would not now make any confession thereof, neither receive the blessed sacrament of the Church ; and dying so, without confession, there is no church that will accept his body, but it must be buried in profane ground like a dog. And yet if he would confess himself, his sins are so many and monstrous as the like case also may happen, because there is not any priest or religious person that can or will absolve him. And being not absolved, he must be cast into some ditch or pit ; and then the people of the town, as well in regard of the trade we drive here, which to them is so little pleasing that we are daily pursued with their worst words, as also coveting our spoil and overthrow, upon this will cry out and mutiny against us : ' Behold these Lombard dogs, which are not to be received into the Church, why should we suffer them to live here amongst us ? ' In furious madness will they come upon us and our house, where peradventure, not contented with robbing us of our goods, our lives will remain in their mercy and danger ; so that, in what sort soever it happen, this man dying here must needs be hurtful to us."

Master Chappelet, who, as we have formerly said, was lodged near the place where they thus conferred, having a subtle attention, as oftentimes we see sick persons to bear, heard all these speeches spoken of him, and causing them to be called unto him, thus he spake :

" I would not have you to be any way doubtful of me, neither that you should receive the least damage by me. I have heard what you have said, and am certain that it will happen according to your words, if matters should fall out as you conceit ; but I am minded to deal otherwise. I have committed so many offences against our Lord God in the whole current of my life, that now I intend one action, at the hour of my death, which I trust will make amends for all. Procure therefore, I pray you, that the most holy and religious man that is to be found, if there be any one at all, may come unto me ; and refer the case then to me, for I will deal in such sort for you and myself that all shall be well, and you no way discontented."

The two brethren, although they had no great hope in his speeches, went to a monastery of Grey Friars, and requested that some one holy and learned man might come to hear the confession of a Lombard that lay very weak and sick in their house. And one was granted unto them, being an aged and religious friar, a person skilled in the sacred Scripture, a very venerable man, who, being of good and sanctified life, all the citizens held him in great respect and esteem, and on he went with them to their house. When he was come up into the chamber where Master Chappelet lay, being there seated down by him, he began first to comfort him very lovingly, demanding also of him how many times he had been at confession ? Whereto Master Chappelet, who never had been shrived in all his lifetime, thus replied :

" Holy father, I always used, as a common custom, to be confessed once at the least every week, albeit sometimes much more often ; but true it is that, being fallen into this sickness now eight days since, I have not been confessed, so violent hath been the extremity of my weakness." " My son," answered the good old man, " thou hast done well, and so keep thee hereafter in that mind ; but

I plainly perceive, seeing thou hast so often confessed thyself, that I shall take the less labour in urging questions to thee."

Master Chappelet replied : " Say not so, good father, for albeit I have been so oftentimes confessed, yet am I willing now to make a general confession, even to all sins that I can bring to my remembrance from the very day of my birth until this instant hour of my shrift. And therefore I entreat you, holy father, to have no respect to my sickness, for I had rather be offensive to mine own flesh than by favouring or allowing it ease to hazard the perdition of my soul which my Redeemer bought with so precious a price."

These words were highly pleasing to the holy friar, and seemed to him an argument of a good conscience ; wherefore, after he had commended this forwardness in him, he began to demand of him how far he had been guilty of Gluttony? When, breathing forth a great sigh, he answered : " Too much and too often, good father, for, over and besides the fasts of our Lent season, which every year ought to be duly observed by devout people, I brought myself to such a customary use that I could fast three days in every week with bread and water. But indeed, holy father, I confess I have drunk water with such a pleasing appetite and delight, especially in praying or walking on pilgrimage, even as greedy drunkards do in drinking good wine. And many times I have desired salads of such herbs as women gather abroad in the open fields, and feeding only upon them, without desiring any other sustenance, hath seemed much more pleasing to me than I thought to agree with the nature of fasting."

" Son, son," replied the confessor, " these sins are natural and very light, and therefore I would not have thee to charge thy conscience with them more than is needful. It happeneth to every man, how holy soever he be, that after he hath fasted overlong, feeding will be welcome to him and drinking good drink after his travel." " O sir," said Master Chappelet, "never tell me this to comfort me, for well you know, and I am not ignorant therein, that such things as are done for the service of God ought all to be performed purely and without any blemish of the mind ; what otherwise is done savoureth of sin." The friar being well contented with these words, said : " It is not amiss that thou understandest it in this manner, and thy conscience, thus purely cleared, is no little comfort to me. But tell me now concerning Avarice, hast thou sinned therein by desiring more than was reasonable, or withholding from others such things as thou oughtest not to detain ?" Wherein Master Chappelet answered : " Good father, I would not have you to imagine, because you see me lodged here in the house of two usurers, that therefore I am of any such disposition. No truly, sir, I came hither to no other end but only to chastise and admonish them in friendly manner, to cleanse their minds from such abominable profit ; and assuredly I should have prevailed therein had not this violent sickness hindered mine intention. But understand, holy father, that my parents left me a rich man, and immediately after my father's death the greater part of his goods I gave away for God's sake ; and then to sustain mine own life and to help the poor members of Jesus Christ, I betook myself to a mean estate of merchandise, desiring none other than honest gain thereby, and evermore whatsoever benefit came to me I imparted half thereof to the poor, converting mine own small portion about my necessary affairs, which that other part would scarcely serve to supply. Yet always God gave thereto such a merciful blessing that my business daily thrived more and more."

"Well hast thou done therein, good son," said the confessor ; "but how oftentimes hast thou been Angry ?" "Oh, sir," said Master Chappelet, "therein I assure ye I have often transgressed ; and what man is able to forbear it, beholding the daily actions of men to be dishonest—no care of keeping God's commandments, nor any fear of His dreadful judgments ? Many times in a day I have rather wished myself dead than living, beholding youth pursuing idle vanities, to swear and forswear themselves, tippling in taverns, and never haunting churches, but rather affecting the world's follies than any such duties as they owe to God." "Alas ! son," quoth the friar, "this is a good and holy anger, and I can impose no penance on thee for it. But tell me, hath not rage or fury at any time so overruled thee as to commit murder or manslaughter, or to speak evil of any man, or to do any such kind of injury ?" "Oh, father," answered Master Chappelet, "you that seem to be a man of God, how dare you use any such vile words ? If I had had the very least thought to do any such act as you speak, do you think that God would have suffered me to live? These are deeds of darkness fit for villains and wicked livers, of which hellish crew, when at any time I have happened to meet with some one of them, I have said, ' Go : God convert thee.'"

"Worthy and charitable words," replied the friar. "But tell me, son, didst thou ever bear false witness against any man, or hast spoken falsely, or taken aught from any one contrary to the will of the owner?" "Yes, indeed, father," said Master Chappelet, "I have spoken ill of another, because I have sometime seen one of my neighbours, who, with no mean shame of the world, would do nothing else but beat his wife ; and of him once I complained to the poor man's parents, saying, he never did it but when he was overcome of drink." "Those were no ill words," quoth the friar ; "but I remember you said that you were a merchant : did you ever deceive any, as some merchants use to do ?" "Truly, father," answered Master Chappelet, "I think not any, except one man, who one day brought me money which he owed me for a certain piece of cloth I sold him, and I put it into a purse without accounting it. About a month afterwards I found that there were four small pence more than was due to me ; and never happening to meet with the man again, after I had kept them the space of a whole year, I then gave them away unto four poor people for God's sake."

"A small matter," said the friar, "and truly paid back again to the owner in bestowing them on the poor." Many other questions he demanded of him, whereto still he answered in the same

manner; but before he proceeded to absolution, Master Chappelet
spake thus : " I have yet one sin more, which I have not revealed
to you." When, being urged by the friar to confess it, he said : " I
remember that I should afford one day in the week to cleanse the
house of my soul for better entertainment to my Lord and Saviour,
and yet I have done no such reverence to the Sunday, or Sabbath,
as I ought to have done." "A small fault, son," replied the friar.
" Oh, no," quoth Master Chappelet, " do not term it a small fault,
because Sunday, being a holy day, is highly to be reverenced, for on
that day our blessed Lord arose from death to life." " But," quoth
the confessor, " hast thou done nothing else on that day ? " " Yes,"
said he, " being forgetful of myself, once I did spit in God's church."
The friar, smiling, said : " Alas ! son, that is a matter of no moment,
for we that are religious persons do use to spit there every day."
" The more is your shame," answered Master Chappelet ; " for no
place ought to be kept more pure and clean than the sacred temple
wherein our daily sacrifices are offered up to God."

In this manner he held on an hour or more uttering the like
transgressions as these ; and at last he began to sigh very passion-
ately and to shed a few tears, as one that was skilful enough in such
dissembling pranks. Whereat the confessor, being much moved,
said : " Alas ! son, what ailest thou ? " " O father," quoth Chappelet,
" there remaineth yet one sin more upon my conscience whereof I
never at any time made confession, so shameful it appeareth to me
to disclose it ; and I am partly persuaded that God will never pardon me for that sin." " How now, son ? " said the friar. " Never
say so, for if all the sins that ever were committed by men, or shall
be committed so long as the world endureth, were only in one man,
and he, repenting them, and being so contrite for them as I see thou
art, the grace and mercy of God is so great that upon penitent confession he will freely pardon him, and therefore spare not to speak
it boldly." " Alas, father," said Chappelet, still weeping, " this sin
of mine is so great that I can hardly believe, if your earnest
prayers do not assist me, that ever I shall obtain remission for it."
" Speak it, son ; " said the friar, " and fear not, I promise that I will
pray to God for thee."

Master Chappelet still wept and sighed, and continued silent,
notwithstanding all the confessor's comfortable persuasions ; but
after he had held him a long while in suspense, breathing forth a
sigh, even as if his very heart would have broken, he said : " Holy
father, seeing you promise to pray to God for me, I will reveal it to
you. Know, then, that when I was a little boy I did once curse my
mother," which he had no sooner spoken but he wrung his hands
and grieved extraordinarily. " Oh, good son," said the friar, " doth
that seem so great a sin to thee ? Why, men do daily blaspheme
our Lord God, and yet nevertheless, upon their hearty repentance,
He is always ready to forgive them ; and wilt not thou believe to
obtain remission for a sin so ignorantly committed ? Weep no
more, dear son, but comfort thyself, and rest resolved that if thou
wert one of them who nailed our blessed Saviour to His cross, yet

being so truly repentant as I see thou art He would freely forgive thee." " Say you so, father?" quoth Chappelet. " What, my own dear mother, that did bear me in her womb nine months, day and night, and afterwards fed me with her breasts a thousand times, can I be pardoned for cursing her? Oh no; it is too heinous a sin, and except you pray to God very instantly for me, He will not forgive me, for I fear it comes near to be a sin unpardonable."

When the religious man perceived that nothing more was to be confessed by Master Chappelet, he gave him absolution, and his own benediction beside, reputing him to be a most holy man, as verily believing all that he had said. And who would not have done the like, hearing a man to speak in this manner, and being upon the very point of death? Afterward he said unto him : " Master Chappelet, by God's grace you may be soon restored to health, but if it so come to pass that God do take your blessed and well-disposed soul to His mercy, will it please you to have your body buried in our convent?" Whereto Master Chappelet answered : " I thank you, father, for your good motion, and sorry should I be if my friends did bury me anywhere else, because you have promised to pray to God for me ; and beside, I have always carried a religious devotion to your Order. Wherefore I beseech you, so soon as you are come home to your convent, prevail so much by your good means, that the holy Eucharist, consecrated this morning on your high altar, may be brought unto me; for although I confess my self utterly unworthy, yet I purpose, by your reverend permission, to receive it, as also your holy and latest unction, to this end, that having lived a grievous sinner, I may yet, at the last, die a Christian. These words pleased the good old man, and he caused everything to be performed according as Master Chappelet had requested.

The two brethren, who much doubted the dissembling of Chappelet, being both in a small partition which parted the sick man's chamber from theirs, heard all that passed between him and the ghostly father, being many times scarce able to refrain from laughter at his feigned confession. Notwithstanding, seeing he had so ordered the matter that he had burial freely allowed him, they cared for no more.

After that Chappelet had received the communion and the other ceremonies appointed for him, weakness increasing upon him more and more, the very same day of his goodly confession he died, towards the evening. Whereupon the two brethren took order that all needful things should be in a readiness to have him buried honourably ; sending to acquaint the fathers of the convent therewith, that they might come to say their vigils, according to custom, and then on the morrow to fetch the body. The honest friar that had confessed him, hearing he was dead, went to the prior of the convent, and by sound of the house bell caused all the brethren to assemble together, giving them credibly to understand that Master Chappelet was a very honest man, as appeared by all the parts of his confession, and made no doubt but that many miracles would be wrought by his sanctified body, persuading them to fetch it thither with all devout solemnity and reverence; whereto the prior and all the credulous brethren presently condescended very gladly.

When night was come they went to visit the dead body of Master Chappelet, where they used an especial and solemn vigil, and on the morrow, appareled in their richest coats and vestments, with books in their hands and the cross borne before them, singing in the form of a very devout procession, they brought the body pompously into their church, accompanied with all the people of the town, both men and women. The father confessor, ascending up into the pulpit, preached wonderful things of him, and the rare holiness of his life, his fasts, his virginity, simplicity, innocency; recounting also, among other especial observations, what Chappelet had confessed, as this most great and grievous sin, and how hardly he could be persuaded that God would grant him pardon for it. Whereby he took occasion to reprove the people then present, saying: "And you, accursed of God, for the least trifling matter happening, will not spare to blaspheme God, his blessed Mother, and the whole court of heavenly paradise. Oh, take example by this singular man, this saint-like man—nay, a very saint indeed."

Many additions more he made concerning his faithfulness, truth, and integrity; so that by the vehement asseveration of his words, whereto all the people there present gave credible belief, he provoked them unto such zeal and earnest devotion, that the sermon was no sooner ended, but, in mighty crowds and throngs, they pressed about the bier, kissing his hands and feet; and all the garments about him were torn in pieces, as precious relics of so holy a person, and happy they thought themselves that could get the smallest piece or shred of anything that came near to his body. And thus they continued all the day, the body lying still open, to be visited in this manner.

When night was come they buried him in a goodly marble tomb, erected in a fair chapel purposely, and for many days after it was most strange to see how the people of the country came thither in heaps, with holy candles and other offerings, with images of wax fastened to the tomb, in sign of sacred and solemn vows to this new-created saint. And so far was spread the fame and renown of his sanctity, devotion, and integrity of life, maintained constantly by the fathers of the convent, that if any one fell sick, in need, distress, or adversity, they would make their vows to no other saint but him, naming him, as yet to this day they do, St. Chappelet; affirming upon their oaths that infinite miracles were there daily performed by him, and especially on such as came in devotion to visit his shrine.

In this manner lived and died Master Ciapperello da Prato, who before he became a saint was as you have heard; and I will not deny it to be impossible but that he may be at rest among other blessed bodies; for although he lived lewdly and wickedly, yet such might be his contrition in the latest extremity that question-less he might find mercy.

THE SECOND NOVEL.

Abraham, a Jew, being admonished or advised by a friend of his named Jehannot de Chevigny, travelled from Paris unto Rome, and beholding there the wicked behaviour of men in the Church, returned back to Paris again, where yet, nevertheless, he became a Christian.

THE novel recited by Pamfilo was highly pleasing to the company, and much commended by the ladies, and after it had been diligently observed among them, the Queen commanded Neifile, who was seated nearest to Pamfilo, that in relating another of hers she should follow on in the pastime thus begun. She being no less gracious in countenance than merrily disposed, made answer that she would obey her charge, and began in this manner :

Pamfilo hath declared to us by his tale how the goodness of God regardeth not our errors when they proceed from things which we cannot discern ; and I intend to approve by mine what argument of infallible truth the same benignity delivereth of itself by enduring patiently the faults of them that both in word and work should declare unfeigned testimony of such gracious goodness, and not to live so dissolutely as they do ; to the end that others illuminated by their light of life may believe with the stronger constancy of mind.

As I have heretofore heard, gracious ladies, there lived a wealthy merchant in Paris, being a mercer or seller of silks, named Jehannot de Chevigny, a man of faithful, honest, and upright dealing, who held great affection and friendship with a very rich Jew named Abraham, that was a merchant also, and a man of very direct conversation. Jehannot, well noting the honesty and loyal dealing of this Jew, began to have a religious kind of compassion in his soul, much pitying that a man so good in behaviour, so wise and discreet in all his actions, should be in danger of perdition through want of faith. In which regard lovingly he began to entreat him that he would leave the errors of his Jewish belief, and follow the truth of Christianity, which he evidently saw, as being good and holy, daily to prosper and enlarge itself ; whereas, on the contrary, his profession decreased and grew to nothing.

The Jew made answer, that he believed nothing to be so good and holy as the Jewish religion, and having been born therein, therein also he proposed to live and die, no matter whatsoever being able to remove him from that resolution. For all this stiff denial, Jehannot would not give him over, but pursued him still day by day, reiterating continually his former speeches to him ; delivering infinite excellent and pregnant reasons, that merchants themselves were not ignorant how far the Christian faith excelled the Jewish falsehoods. And albeit the Jew was a very learned man in his own law, yet, notwithstanding,

the entire amity he bore to Jehannot, or perhaps his words, forti-
fied by the Blessed Spirit, grew so prevalent with him, that the Jew
felt a pleasing apprehension in them, though as yet his obstinacy
stood far off from conversion.   But as he thus continued strong in
opinion, so Jehannot left not hourly to labour him ; insomuch that
the Jew, being conquered by such earnest and continual importunity,
one day spake to Jehannot, saying :

" My worthy friend Jehannot, thou art extremely desirous that I
should convert to Christianity, and I am well contented to do it ;
only upon this condition : that first I will journey to Rome, to see
him who.thou sayest is God's general Vicar here on earth, and to
consider on the course of his life and manners, and likewise of his
College of Cardinals.   If he and they do appear such men to me as
thy speeches affirm them to be, and thereby I may comprehend that
thy faith and religion is better than mine, as with no mean pains
thou endeavourest to persuade me, I will become a Christian as
thou art ; but if I find it otherwise, I will continue as I am—a Jew."

Jehannot hearing these words, became exceedingly sorrowful,
and said within himself : " I have lost all the pains which I did
think to be well employed, as hoping to have this man converted
here.   For, if he go to the Court of Rome, and behold there the
wickedness of the priests' lives, farewell all hope in me of ever
seeing him to become a Christian.   But rather, were he already a
Christian, without all question he would turn a Jew."   And so, going
nearer to Abraham, he said : " Alas, my loving friend, why shouldst
thou undertake such a tedious travel and so great a charge as thy
journey from hence to Rome will cost thee ?   Consider, that to a
rich man (as thou art) travel by land or sea is full of dangers.
Dost thou not think that here are religious men enough, who will
gladly bestow baptism upon thee ?   To me therefore it plainly
appeareth that such a voyage is to no purpose.   If thou standest
upon any doubt or scruple concerning the faith whereto I wish
thee, where canst thou desire conference with greater doctors,
or men more learned in all respects, than this famous city doth
afford thee, to resolve thee in any questionable case ?   Thou must
think that the prelates are such there as here thou seest them to
be ; and yet they must needs be in much better condition at Rome,
because they are near to the principal pastor.   And therefore, if
thou wilt credit my counsel, reserve this journey to some time more
convenient, when the jubilee of general pardon happeneth, and
then, perchance, I will bear thee company, and go along with thee
as in vowed pilgrimage."

Whereto the Jew replied : " I believe, Jehannot, that all which
thou hast said may be so.   But, to make short with thee, I am
fully determined, if thou wouldst have me a Christian, as thou instantly urgest me to be, to go thither, for otherwise I will continue
as I am."   Jehannot, perceiving his settled purpose, said : " Go,
then, in God's name ;" but persuaded himself that he would never
become a Christian after he had seen the Court of Rome.   Nevertheless, he counted his labour not altogether lost, in regard he

B

bestowed it to a good end, and honest intentions are to be commended.

The Jew mounted on horseback, and made no lingering in his
journey to Rome, where, being arrived, he was very honourably
entertained by other Jews dwelling in Rome. And during the time
of his abiding there (without revealing to any one the reason of
his coming thither) very heedfully he observed the manner of the
Pope's life, of the cardinals, prelates, and all the courtiers. And
being a man very discreet and judicious, he apparently perceived,
both by his own eye and further information of friends, that from
the highest to the lowest, without any restraint, remorse of conscience, shame, or fear of punishment, all sinned in abominable
luxury. Moreover, drunkards, belly-gods, and servants of the paunch,
more than of anything else, even like brutish beasts after their luxury,
were everywhere to be met withal. And upon further observation,
he saw all men so covetous and greedy of coin, that everything was
bought and sold for ready money ; not only the blood of men, but,
in plain terms, the faith of Christians ; yea, and matters of divinest
qualities, how or to whomsoever appertaining, were it for sacrifices
or benefices, whereof was made no mean merchandise. And more
brokers were there to be found than in Paris, attending upon all
trades of manifest simony, under the nice name of negotiation, and
for gluttony, not sustentation ; even as if God had not known the
signification of vocables nor the intentions of wicked hearts, but
would suffer Himself to be deceived by the outward names of
things, as wretched men use to do.

These things, and many more, fitter for silence than for publication, were so deeply displeasing to the Jew, being a most sober and
modest man, that he had soon seen enough, resolved on his return
to Paris, which very speedily he performed. And when Jehannot
heard of his arrival, crediting much rather other news from him
than ever to see him a converted Christian, he went to welcome him,
and kindly they feasted one another. After some few days of
resting, Jehannot demanded of him what he thought of our holy
father the Pope and his cardinals, and generally of all the other
courtiers ? Whereto the Jew answered : " It is strange, Jehannot,
that God should give them so much as He doth ; for I will truly
tell thee, that if I had been able to consider those things which
there I have both heard and seen, I could then have resolved
myself never to have found in any priest either sanctity, devotion,
good work, or example of honest life. But if a man desire to see
luxury, avarice, gluttony, and such wicked things—yea, worse,
if worse may be—and held in general estimation of all men, let him
but go to Rome, which I think rather to be the forge of damnable
actions than any way leaning to grace or goodness. And, for aught
I could perceive, methinks your chief pastor, and consequently all
the rest of his dependants, do strive so much as they may, with all
their engine, art, and endeavour, to bring to nothing, or to banish
quite out of the world, Christian religion, whereof they should
be the support and foundation.

" But because I perceive that their wicked intent will never come to pass, but, contrariwise, that your faith enlargeth itself, shining every day much more clear and splendent, I gather thereby evidently that the blessed Spirit is the true ground and defence thereof, as being more true and holy than any other. In which respect, whereas I stood stiff and obstinate against the good ad-monitions, and never minded to become a Christian, now I freely open my heart unto thee, that nothing in the world can or shall hinder me but I will be a Christian as thou art. Let us therefore presently go to the church, and there, according to the true custom of your holy faith, help me to be baptized."

Jehannot, who expected a far contrary conclusion than this, hearing him speaking with such constancy, was the very gladdest man in the world, and went with him to the Church of Notre Dame in Paris, where he requested the priests there abiding to bestow baptism on Abraham, which they joyfully did, hearing him earnestly to desire it. Jehannot was his godfather, and named him John, and afterward by learned divines he was more fully instructed in the grounds of our faith, wherein he grew of great understanding, and led a very virtuous life.

THE THIRD NOVEL.

Melchisedech, a Jew, by recounting a tale of three rings to the great Soldan, named Saladin, prevented a great danger which was prepared for him.

NEIFILE having ended her discourse, which was well allowed of by all the company, it pleased the Queen that Filomena should next succeed in order, who thus began :

The tale delivered by Neifile maketh me remember a doubtful case which sometime happened to another Jew. And because that God and the truth of His holy faith hath been already very well dis-coursed on, it shall not seem unfitting, in my poor opinion, to descend now into the accidents of men. Wherefore, I will dilate a matter unto you, which, being attentively heard and considered, may make you much more circumspect in answering to divers questions and demands than perhaps otherwise you would be. Consider, then, most worthy assembly, that like as folly and dullness many times hath overthrown some men from place of eminency into most great and grievous miseries, even so discreet sense and good understanding hath delivered many out of irksome perils and seated them in safest security. And to prove it true that folly hath made many fall from high authority into poor and despised calamity, may be avouched by infinite examples which now were needless to remember; but that good sense and able understanding may prove to be the occasion of great desolation, without happy prevention, I will declare unto you in very few words, and make it good according to my promise.

Saladin was a man so powerful and valiant as not only his valour made him Soldan of Babylon, but also gave him many signal victories over kings of the Saracens and of Christians likewise. Having in divers wars and other magnificent employments of his own wasted all his treasure, and, by reason of some sudden accident happening to him, standing in need to use some great sum of money, yet not readily knowing where or how to procure it, he remembered a rich Jew named Melchisedech, that lent out money to use or interest in the city of Alexandria. This man he imagined best able to furnish him, if he could be won to do it willingly, but he was known to be so gripple and miserable, that hardly any means would draw him to it. In the end, constrained by necessity, and labouring his wits for some apt device whereby he might have it, he concluded, though he might not compel him to do it, yet by a practice shadowed with good reason to ensnare him; and having sent for him, entertained him very familiarly in his Court, and sitting down by him, thus began :

" Honest man, I have often heard it reported by many that thou art very skilful, and in cases concerning God thou goest beyond all other of these times; wherefore I would gladly be informed by thee, which of these three laws or religions thou takest to be truest, that of the Jew, the other of the Saracen, or that of the Christian ?" The Jew, being a very wise man, plainly perceived that Saladin sought to entrap him in his answer, and so to raise some quarrel against him; for if he commended any one of these laws above the other, he knew that Saladin had what he aimed it. Wherefore, bethinking himself to shape such an answer as might no way trouble or entangle him, summoning all his senses together, and considering that dallying with the Soldan might redound to his no mean danger, thus he replied :

" My lord, the question propounded by you is fair and worthy, and to answer my opinion truly thereof doth necessarily require some time of consideration, if it might stand with your liking to allow it; but if not, let me first make entrance to my reply with a pretty tale, and well worth the hearing. I have oftentimes heard it reported that, long since, there was a very wealthy man who, among other precious jewels of his own, had a goodly ring of great value, the beauty and estimation whereof made him earnestly desirous to leave it as a perpetual memory and honour to his successors. Whereupon he willed and ordained that he, among his male children, with whom this ring, being left by the father, should be found in custody after his death, he and none other was to be reputed his heir, and to be honoured and reverenced by all the rest as being the prime and worthiest person. That son to whom this ring was left by him kept the same course to his posterity, dealing in all respects as his predecessors had done, so that in short time the ring from hand to hand had many owners by legacy.

" At length it came to the hand of one who had three sons, all of them goodly and virtuous persons, and very obedient to their father, in which regard he affected them all equally, without any difference or partial respect. The custom of this ring being known to them, each one of them, coveting to bear esteem above the other, desired, as he could best make his means, his father, that in regard he was now grown very old, he would leave that ring to him, whereby he should be acknowledged for his heir. The good man, who loved no one of them more than the other, knew not how to make his choice, nor to which of them he should leave the ring ; yet having passed his promise to them severally, he studied by what means to satisfy them all three. Wherefore, secretly having conferred with a curious and excellent goldsmith, he caused two other rings to be made so really resembling the first made ring that himself, when he had them in his hand, could not distinguish which was the right one.

Lying upon his deathbed, and his sons then plying him by their best opportunities, he gave to each of them a ring. And they, after his death, presuming severally upon their right to the inheritance and honour, grew to great contradiction and square ; each man producing then his ring ; but they were so truly all alike in resemblance as no one could know the right ring from the other, and therefore suit in law to distinguish the true heir to his father continued long time, and so it doth yet to this very day. In like manner, my good lord, concerning those three laws given by God the Father to three such people as you have propounded ; all of them do imagine that they have the heritage of God and his true law, and also that they duly perform his commandments ; but which of them do so indeed, the question, as of the three rings, is yet remaining.

Saladin well perceiving that the Jew was too cunning to be caught in his snare, and had answered so well that to do him further violence would redound unto his perpetual dishonour, resolved to reveal his need and extremity, and try if he would therein friendly stead him. Having disclosed the matter, and how he proposed to have dealt with him if he had not returned so wise an answer, the Jew lent him so great a sum of money as he demanded, and Saladin repaid it again to him justly, giving him other gifts beside, respecting him as his special friend, and maintaining him in very honourable condition near unto his own person.

THE FOURTH NOVEL.

A monk having committed an offence deserving to be very grievously punished, freed himself from the pain to be inflicted on him by wittily reprehending his abbot with the very same fault.

So ceased Madam Filomena after the conclusion of her tale, when Dioneo, sitting next unto her, without tarrying for any other command from the Queen, knowing by the order formerly begun that he was to follow in the same course, spake in this manner :

[OMITTED.]

THE FIFTH NOVEL.

The Lady Marquess of Montserrat, with a banquet of hens, and divers other gracious speeches beside, repressed the fond love of the King of France.

THE tale reported by Dioneo at the first hearing of the ladies began to relish of some immodesty, as the bashful blood mounting up into their faces delivered by apparent testimony. And behold-ing one another with scarce pleasing looks during all the time it was in discoursing, no sooner had he concluded but, with a few mild and gentle speeches, they gave him a modest reprehension, meaning to let him know that such tales ought not to be told among women. Afterwards the Queen commanded Fiametta, sitting on a bank of flowers before her, to take her turn as next in order; and she, smiling with such a virgin blush as very beautifully became her, began in this manner.

[OMITTED.]

THE SIXTH NOVEL.

An honest, plain-meaning man simply and consciably reprehended the malignity, hypocrisy, and misdemeanour of many religious persons.

EMILIA, sitting next to the gentle Lady Fiametta, perceiving that the modest chastisement which the virtuous Lady Marquess had given to the King of France was generally graced by the whole assembly, began (the Queen thereto appointing her) in these words. Nor will I conceal the deserved reprehension which an honest simple layman gave to a covetous holy father in very few words, yet more to be commended than derided:

Not long since, worthy ladies, there dwelt in our own native city a Friar Minor, an inquisitor after matters of faith, who, although he laboured greatly to seem a sanctified man and an earnest affecter of Christian, religion as all of them appear to be in outward show, yet he was a much better inquisitor after them that had their purses plenteously stored with money than of such as were slenderly grounded in faith. By which diligent continued care in him he found out a man more rich in purse than understanding, and yet not so defective in matters of faith as misguided by his own simple speaking, and perhaps, when his brain was well warmed with wine, words fell more foolishly from him than in better judgment they could have done.

Being on a day in company very little differing in quality from himself, he chanced to say that he had been at such good wine as God himself did never drink better. Which words (by some syco-phant then in presence) being carried to this curious inquisitor, and he well knowing that the man's faculties were great, and his bags swollen up full with no mean abundance, *cum gladiis et fustibus*, with book, bell, and candle, he raised a host of execrations against him, and the summoner cited him with a solemn process to appear before him, understanding sufficiently that this course would sooner get money from him than amend any misbelief in the man ; for no further reformation did he seek after.

The man coming before him, he demanded if the accusation intimated against him was true or no ? Whereto the honest man answered that he could not deny the speaking of these words, and declared in what manner they were uttered. Presently the inquisitor, most devoutly addicted to St. John with the golden beard, said : "What ? Dost thou make our Lord a drinker, a glutton, a belly-god or a tavern-haunter, as thou and other drunkards are? Being a hypocrite as thou art, thou thinkest this to be but a slight matter, because it may seem so in thy own opinion; but I tell thee plainly that it deserveth fire and faggot, if I should proceed in justice to inflict it on thee." With these and other such like threatening words, as also a very stern and angry countenance, he made the man believe himself to be an Epicure, and that he denied the eternity of the soul, whereby he fell into such a trembling fear, as doubting indeed lest he should be burned, that to be more mercifully dealt withal, he rounded him in the ear, and by secret means so anointed his hands with St. John's golden grease, a very singular remedy against the disease pestilential in covetous priests, especially Minorite Friars that dare touch no money, as the case became very quickly altered.

This sovereign unction was of such virtue, though Galen speaks not a word thereof among all his chiefest medicines, and so far prevailed, that the terrible threatening words of fire and faggot became merely frozen up, and gracious language blew a more gentle and calmer air; the inquisitor, delivering him an hallowed crucifix, created him a soldier of the cross, because he had paid crosses good store for it, and even as if he were to travel under that standard to the Holy Land, so did he appoint him a home-paying penance—namely, to visit him thrice every week in his chamber, and to anoint his hands with the selfsame yellow ungent, and afterward to hear mass of the holy cross, visiting him also at dinnertime; which being ended, to do nothing all the rest of the day but according as he directed him.

"The simple man, yet not so simple but seeing that this weekly greasing the inquisitor's hands would in time grasp away all his gold, grew weary of this anointing, and began to consider with himself how to stay the course of this chargeable penance. And coming one morning, according to his injunction, to hear mass, in the Gospel he observed these words : "You shall receive an hundred for one, and so possess eternal life ;" which saying he kept perfectly in his memory. And as he was commanded, at dinnertime he came to the inquisitor, finding him among his fellows seated at the table. The inquisitor presently demanded of him whether he had heard mass that morning or no. "Yes, sir," replied the man very readily. "Hast thou heard anything therein," quoth the inquisitor, "whereof thou art doubtful or desirest to be further informed?" "Surely, sir," answered the plain-meaning man, "I make no doubt of anything I have heard, but do believe all constantly; only one thing troubleth me much and maketh me very compassionate of you, and of all these holy fathers your brethren, perceiving in what woeful and wretched estate you will be when you shall come into another world." "What words are these?" quoth the inquisitor; "and why art thou moved to such compassion of us?" "O good sir," said the man, "do you remember the words in the Gospel this morning, 'you shall receive an hundred for one?'" "That's very true," replied the inquisitor; "but what moveth thee to urge those words?"

"I will tell you, sir," answered the plain fellow, "so it might please you not to be offended. Since the time of my resorting hither, I have daily seen many poor people at your door, and out of your abundance, when you and your brethren have fed sufficiently, every one hath had a great kettleful or two of pot liquor. Now, sir, if for every kettleful given you are sure to receive an hundred again, you will be merely drowned in pot liquor." Although the rest, sitting at the table with the inquisitor, laughed heartily at the jest, yet he found himself touched in another nature, having hypocritically received for one poor offence above three hundred pieces of gold, and not a mite to be restored again. But fearing to be further disclosed, yet threatening him with another process in law for abusing the words of the Gospel, he was content to dismiss him for altogether, without any more golden greasing in the hand.

THE SEVENTH NOVEL.

Bergamino, by telling a tale of a skilful man named Primasso. and of an abbot of Cligni, honestly checked a new kind of covetousness in Messer Can de la Scala.

THE courteous demeanour of Emilia. and the quaintness of her discourse, caused the Queen and the rest of the company to commend the invention of carrying the cross and the golden ointment appointed for penance. Afterward Filostrato, who was in order to speak next, began in this manner:

It is a commendable thing, fair ladies, to hit a butt that never stirreth out of his place, but it is a matter much more admirable to see a thing, suddenly appearing and seldom or never frequented before, to be as suddenly hit by an ordinary archer. The vicious and polluted lives of priests yieldeth matter of itself in many things deserving speech and reprehension, as a true butt of wickedness, and well worthy to be sharply shot at. And therefore, though that honest-meaning man did wisely in touching Master Inquisitor to the quick with the hypocritical charity of monks and friars in giving such things to the poor as were more meet for swine, or to

be worse thrown away; yet I hold him more to be commended
who by occasion of a former tale, and which I purpose to relate,
pleasantly reproved Messer Can de la Scala, a magnifico and
mighty lord, for a sudden and unaccustomed covetousness appearing in him, figuring by other men that which he intended to say of
him in manner following :

Messer Cane de la Scala, as fame ran abroad of him in all
places, was, beyond the infinite favours of fortune towards him, one
of the most notable and magnificent lords that ever lived in Italy
since the days of Frederick, the second emperor.   He determined
to procure a very solemn assembly at Verona, and many people
being met there from divers places, especially gentlewomen of all
degrees, suddenly, upon what occasion I know not, his mind
altered, and he would not go forward with his intention.   Most of
them he partly recompensed which were come thither, and they
were dismissed to depart at their pleasure ; one man only remained
unrespected, or in any kind sort sent away, whose name was
Bergamino, a man very pleasantly disposed, and so wittily ready
in speaking and answering as none could easily credit it but such
as heard him, and although his recompense seemed over-long
delayed, yet he made no doubt of a beneficial ending.

By some enemies of his, Messer Can de la Scala was incensed
that whatsoever he gave or bestowed on him was as ill-employed
and utterly lost as if it were thrown into the fire, and therefore he
neither did nor spake anything to him.   Some few days being passed
over, and Bergamino perceiving that he was neither called nor any
account made of, notwithstanding many manly good parts in him,
observing beside that he found a shrewd consumption in his purse,
his inn, horses, and servants being chargeable to him, he began to
grow extremely melancholy, and yet he attended in expectation
day by day as thinking it far unfitting for him to depart before he
was bidden farewell.

Having brought with him thither three goodly rich garments,
which had been given him by sundry lords for his more sightly
appearance at this great meeting, the importunate host being
greedy of payment, first he delivered him one of them, and yet not
half the score being wiped off, the second must needs follow ; and
beside except he meant to leave his lodging, he must live upon the
third so long as it would last, till he saw what end his hopes would
sort to.   It fortuned during the time of living thus upon the last
refuge that he met with Messer Can one day at dinner, where he presented himself before him with a discontented countenance, which
Messer Can well observing, more to distaste him than take delight
in anything that could come from him, he said : "Bergamino,
how cheerest thou ?   Thou art very melancholy ; I pray thee tell
us why?" Bergamino suddenly, without any premeditation, yet
seeming as if he had long considered thereon, reported this tale :

"Sir, I have heard of a certain man, named Primasso, one skil-
fully learned in the grammar, and, beyond all other, a very witty
and ready versifier, in regard whereof he was so much admired and

far renowned that such as never saw him but only heard of him could easily say : ' This is Primasso.' It came to pass that being once at Paris in poor estate—as commonly he could light on no better fortune, because virtue is slenderly rewarded by such as have the greatest possessions—he heard much fame of the Abbot of Cligni—a man reputed, next to the Pope, to be the richest prelate of the Church. Of him he heard wonderful and magnificent matters, that he always kept an open and hospitable court, and never made refusal of any, from whencesoever he came or went ; but they did eat and drink freely there, provided that they came when the abbot was set at the table. Primasso hearing this, and being an earnest desirer to see magnificent and virtuous men, he resolved to go see the rare bounty of the abbot, demanding how far he dwelt from Paris. Being answered about some three leagues thence, Primasso made account that if he went on betimes in the morning he should easily reach thither before the hour for dinner.

" Being instructed in the way, and not finding any to walk along with him, fearing, if he went without some furnishment, and should stay long there for his dinner, he might perhaps complain of hunger, he therefore carried three loaves of bread with him, knowing that he could meet with water everywhere, albeit he used to drink but little. Having aptly conveyed his bread about him, he went on his journey, and arrived at the Lord Abbot's court an indifferent while before dinner-time. Wherefore, entering into the great hall, and so from place to place, beholding the great multitude of tables, bountiful preparation in the kitchen, and what admirable provision there was for dinner, he said to himself : ' Truly this man is more magnificent than Fame hath made him, because she speaks too sparingly of him.'

" While thus he went about considering on all these things very respectively, he saw the master of the abbot's household—because then it was the hour of dinner—command water to be brought for washing of hands. So every one sitting down at the table, it fell to the lot of Primasso to sit directly against the door whereat the abbot must enter into the hall. The custom in this court was such that no manner of food should be served to any of the table until such time as the Lord Abbot was himself set. Whereupon, everything being fit and ready, the master of the household went to tell his lord that nothing now wanted but his only presence.

" The abbot coming from his chamber to enter the hall, looking about him as he was wont to do, the first man he saw was Primasso, who being but in homely habit, and he having not seen him before to his remembrance, a present bad conceit possessed his brain, that he never saw an unworthier person, saying within himself, ' See how I give my goods away to be devoured.' So, returning back to his chamber again, commanded the door to be made fast, demanding of every man near about him if they knew the base knave that sat before his entrance into the hall ? and all his servants answered no. Primasso being extremely hungry with travelling on foot so far, and never used to fast so long, expecting still when meat should be served in, and that the abbot came not at all, drew out one of his loaves which he brought with him, and very heartily fell a-feeding.

"My Lord Abbot, after he had stayed within an indifferent while, sent forth one of his men to see if the poor fellow was gone or no. The servant told him that he stayed there and fed upon dry bread, which it seemed he had brought thither with him. 'Let him feed on his own,' replied the abbot, 'for he shall taste of none of mine this day.' Gladly would the abbot that Primasso should have gone thence of himself, and yet held it scarcely honest in his lordship to dismiss him by his own command. Primasso having eaten one of his loaves and yet the abbot was not come, began to feed upon the second, the abbot still sending to expect his absence, and answered as he was before. At length, the abbot not coming, and Primasso having eaten up his second loaf, hunger compelled him to begin with the third.

"When this news was carried to the abbot, suddenly he brake forth and said : ' What new kind of needy trick hath my brain begot this day? Why do I grow disdainful against any man whatsoever? I have long time allowed my meat to be eaten by all comers that did please to visit me, without exception against any person— gentleman, yeoman, poor or rich, merchant and minstrel, honest man or knave ; never restraining my presence in the hall by basely contemning one poor man. Believe me, covetousness of one man's meat doth ill agree with mine estate and calling. What though he appeareth a wretched fellow to me? He may be of greater merit than I can imagine, and deserve more honour than I am able to give him.

" Having thus discoursed with himself, he would needs understand of whence and what he was, and finding him to be Primasso, come only to see the magnificence which he heard reported of him ; knowing also by the general fame noised everywhere of him that he was reputed to be a learned, honest, and ingenious man, he grew greatly ashamed of his own folly, and being desirous to make him an amends, strove many ways how to do him honour. When dinner was ended, the abbot bestowed honourable garments on him, such as beseemed his degree and merit, and putting good store of money in his purse, as also giving him a good horse to ride on, left it at his own free election whether he would stay there still with him or depart at his pleasure. Wherewith Primasso, being highly contented, yielding him the heartiest thanks he could devise to do, returned to Paris on horseback ; albeit he came poorly thither on foot."

Messer Can de la Scala, who was a man of good understanding, perceived immediately what Bergamino meant by this moral, and, smiling on him, said : " Bergamino, thou hast honestly expressed thy virtue and necessities and justly reproved mine avarice, niggard-ness, and base folly ; and trust me, Bergamino, I never felt such a fit of covetousness come upon me as this which I have declared unto thee, and I will banish from me with the same correction as thou hast taught me." So, having paid the host all his charges, redeeming also his robes or garments, mounting him on a good gelding, and putting plenty of crowns in his purse, he referred it to his own choice to depart or dwell there still with him.

THE EIGHTH NOVEL.

Guillaume Boursier, with a few quaint and familiar words, checked the miserable covetousness of Signor Ermino de' Grimaldi.

LAURETTA, sitting next to Filostrato, when she had he ard the witty conceit of Bergamino, knowing that she was to say somewhat, without injunction or command pleasantly thus began :

This last discourse, fair and virtuous company, induceth me to tell you how an honest courtier reprehended in like manner—and nothing unprofitably—base covetousness in a merchant of extraordinary wealth ; which tale, although in effect it may seem to resemble the former, yet perhaps it will prove no less pleasing to you in regard it sorted to as good an end.

It is no long time since that there lived in Genoa a gentleman named Signor Ermino de' Grimaldi, who, as every one well knew, was more rich in inheritances and ready sums of current money than any other known citizen in Italy; and as he surpassed other men in wealth, so did he likewise excel them in wretched avarice, being so miserably greedy and covetous as no man in the world could be more wicked that way, because not only he kept his purse locked up from pleasuring any, but denied needful thing to himself, enduring many miseries only to avoid expenses, contrary to the Genoese general custom, who always delighted to be decently clothed and to have their diet of the best; by reason of which most miserable baseness they took away from him the surname of Grimaldi, whereof he was in right descended, and called him " Messer Ermino Avarizia," a nickname very notably agreeing with his gripple nature.

It came to pass, that in this time of his spending nothing, but multiplying daily by infinite means, that a civil honest gentleman, a courtier of ready wit and discoursive in languages, came to Genoa, being named Gulielmo Borsiere; a man very far differing from divers courtiers in these days, who for soothing shameful and graceless manners in such as allow them maintenance, are called and reputed to be gentlemen, yea special favourites ; whereas much more worthily they should be accounted as knaves and villains, being born and bred in all filthiness, and skilful in every kind of basest behaviour, not fit to come in princes' courts. For whereas in past times they spent their days and pains in making peace, when gentlemen were at war or dissension, or treating of honest marriages between friends and familiars, and with loving speeches would recreate disturbed minds, desiring none but commendable exercises in court, and sharply reproving disordered life or ill actions in any, albeit with little recompense ; these upstarts nowadays employ all their pains in detractions, sowing questions and quarrels between one another, making no spare of lies and falsehoods. Nay, which is worse, they will do this in the presence of any man, upbraiding him with injuries, shames, and scandals, true or not true, upon the very least occasion. And by false and deceitful flatteries and villanies of their own inventing, they make gentlemen to become as vile as themselves. For which detestable qualities they are better beloved and respected of their misdemeanoured lords, and recompensed in more bountiful manner, than men of virtuous carriage and desert ; which is an argument sufficient that goodness is gone up to heaven, and hath quite forsaken these loathed lower regions, where men are drowned in the mud of all abominable vices.

But returning where I left (being led out of my way by a just and religious anger against such deformity), this gentleman, Messer Guglielmo Borsiere, was willingly seen and gladly welcomed by all the best men in Genoa. Having remained some few days in the city, and amongst other matters heard much talk of the miserable covetousness of Master Ermino, he grew very desirous to have a sight of him. Ermino had already understood that this gentleman, Messer Guglielmo Borsiere, was virtuously disposed, and having in him some sparks of notable nature, gave him very good words and gracious entertainment, discoursing with him on divers occasions. In company with other Genoese he brought him to a new-erected house of his, a building of great beauty, where, after he had shown him all the valuable rarities, he began thus : " Mr. Guglielmo, no doubt but you have heard and seen many things, and you can instruct me in some quaint conceit or device, to be fairly figured in painting, at the entrance into the hall of my house." Mr. Guglielmo, hearing him speak so simply, returned this answer : " Sir, I cannot advise you in anything so rare or unseen as you speak of, but how to sneeze, after a new manner, upon a full and overcloyed stomach, to avoid base humours that stupefy the brain, or other matters of the like quality. But if you would be taught a good one indeed, and had a disposition to see it fairly effected, I could instruct you in an excellent emblem wherewith as yet you never came acquainted."

Master Ermino hearing him say so, and expecting no such answer as he had, said : " Good Master Guglielmo, tell me what it is, and on my faith I will have it fairly painted." Whereto Master Guglielmo suddenly replied : " Do nothing but this, sir : paint over the portal of your hall's entrance the lively picture of Liberality, to bid all your friends better welcome than hitherto they have been." When Master Ermino heard these words, he became possessed with such a sudden shame that his complexion changed from the former paleness, and answered thus : " Master Guglielmo, I will have your advice so truly figured over my gate, and she shall give such good welcome to all my guests, that both you and all these gentlemen shall say, I have both seen her and am become reasonably acquainted with her." From that time forward the words of Guglielmo were so effectual with Messer Ermino, that he became the most bountiful and best housekeeper that lived in his time in Genoa, no man more honouring and friendly welcoming both strangers and citizens than he continually used to do.

-- -- -- -

THE NINTH NOVEL.

The King of Cyprus was wittily reprehended by the words of a gentlewoman of Gascony, and became virtuously altered from his vicious disposition.

THE last command of the Queen remained upon Elisa, who without any delaying, thus began:

Young ladies, it hath often been seen that much pain hath been bestowed, and many reprehensions spent in vain, till a word happening at adventure, and perhaps not purposely determined, hath effectually done the deed, as appeareth by the tale of Lauretta, and another of my own, wherewith I intend briefly to acquaint you, approving that when good words are discreetly observed they are of sovereign power and virtue.

In the days of the first King of Cyprus, after the conquest made in the Holy Land by Godfrey of Bulloin, it fortuned that a gentlewoman of Gascony, travelling in pilgrimage to visit the Sacred Sepulchre in Jerusalem, returning home again, arrived at Cyprus, where she was villanously abused by certain base wretches. Complaining thereof, without any comfort or redress, she intended to make her moan to the king of the country; whereupon it was told her that she should but lose her labour, because he was womanish and faint-hearted; that not only he refused to punish with justice the offences of others, but also suffered shameful injuries done to himself. And therefore, such as were displeased by his negligence might easily discharge their spleen against him, and do him what dishonour they would.

When the gentlewoman heard this, despairing of any consolation or revenge for her wrongs, she resolved to check the king's denial of justice, and coming before him, weeping, spake in this manner: "Sir, I presume not into your presence as hoping to have redress by you for divers dishonourable injuries done unto me; but, as full satisfaction for them, do but teach me how you suffer such vile abuses as daily are offered to yourself, to the end that, being therein instructed by you, I may the more patiently bear mine own, which, as God knoweth, I would bestow on you very gladly, because you know so well how to endure them."

The king (who till then had been very bad, dull, and slothful, even as sleeping out his time of government) began to revenge the wrongs done to this gentlewoman very severely, and thenceforward became a most sharp justice for the least offence offered against the honour of his crown or to any of his subjects besides.

THE TENTH NOVEL.

Master Albert of Bologna honestly made a lady to blush, that thought to have done as much to him, because she perceived him to be amorously affected towards her.

AFTER that Elisa sat silent. The last charge and labour of like employment remained to the Queen herself, whereupon she began thus to speak : Honest and virtuous young ladies, like as the stars, while the air is fair and clear, are the adorning and beauty of heaven ; and flowers, while the spring-time lasteth, do graciously embellish the meadows ; even so sweet speeches and pleasing conferences, to pass the time with commendable discourses, are the best habit of the mind, and an outward beauty to the body. Which ornaments of words, when they appear to be short and sweet, are much more seemly in women than in men, because long and tedious talking, when it may be done in lesser time, is a greater blemish in women than in men.

Among us women this day, I think few or none have therein offended, but as readily have understood short and pithy speeches as they have been quick and quaintly delivered. But when answering suiteth not with understanding, it is generally a shame in us, and all such as live, because our modern times have converted that virtue which was within them who lived before us, into garments of the body, and she whose habits were noted to be most gaudy, fullest of embroideries and fantastic fashions, she was reputed to have most matter in her, and therefore to be most honoured and esteemed. Never considering that whosoever loadeth the back of an ass, or puts upon him the richest bravery, he becometh not thereby a jot the wiser, or meriteth any more honour than an ass should have. I am ashamed to speak it, because in detecting others I may perhaps as justly tax myself.

Such embroidered bodies, tricked and trimmed in such boasting bravery, are they anything else but as marble statues, dumb, dull, and utterly insensible ? Or if perchance they make an answer when some question is demanded of them, it were much better for them to be silent. For defence of honest device and conference among men and women, they would have the world to think that it proceedeth but from simplicity and precise opinion, covering their own folly with the name of honesty, as if there were no other honest woman but she that confers only with her chambermaid, laundress, or kitchen-woman ; as if nature had allowed them, in their own idle conceit, no other kind of talking.

Most true it is that as there is a respect to be used in the action of other things, so time and place are necessarily to be considered, and also whom we converse withal ; because sometimes it happeneth that a man or woman, intending by a word of jest and merriment to make another body blush or be ashamed, not know-

ing what strength of wit remaineth in the opposite, do convert the
same disgrace upon themselves.   Therefore, that we may the more
advisedly stand upon our own guard, and to prevent the common
proverb, that women in all things make choice of the worst, I desire
that this day's last tale, which is to come from myself, may make us
all wise ; to the end that, as in gentleness of mind we confer with
others, so by excellency in good manners we may show ourselves
not inferior to them.

[OMITTED.]

The sun was now somewhat far declined, and the heat's extremity
well worn away, when the tales of the seven ladies and three gentlemen were thus finished ; whereupon their Queen pleasantly said :
For this day, fair company, there remaineth nothing more to be
done under my regiment, but only to bestow a new Queen upon you,
who, according to her judgment, must take her turn, and dispose
what next is to be done for continuing our time in honest pleasure.
And although the day should endure till dark night, in regard that
when some time is taken before, the better preparation may be made
for occasions to follow; to the end also, that whatsover the new
Queen shall please to appoint may be the better fitted for to-
morrow, I am of opinion that at the same hour as we now cease
the following days shall severally begin. And therefore, in reference
to Him that giveth life to all things, and in hope of comfort by our
second day, Filomena, a most wise young lady, shall govern as
Queen of this our kingdom."

So soon as she had thus spoken, arising from her seat of dignity
and taking the laurel crown from off her own head, she reverently
placed it upon Filomena's, the first of all humbly saluting her,
and then all the rest openly confessing her to be their Queen,
made gracious offer to obey what she commanded. Filomena,
her cheeks delivering a scarlet tincture to see herself thus
honoured as their Queen, and well remembering the words so
lately uttered by Pampinea, that dullness or neglect might not
be noted in her, took cheerful courage to her ; and first of all she
confirmed the officers which Pampinea had appointed the day
before, then she ordained the morrow's provisions, as also for the
supper so near approaching, before they departed away from
thence, and then thus began :

" Lovely companions, although that Pampinea, more in her
own courtesy than any matter of merit remaining in me, hath
made me your Queen, I am not determined to alter the form of
our intended life, nor to be guided by mine own judgment, but to
associate the same with your assistance. And because you may
know what I intend to do, and so consequently add or diminish at
your pleasure, in very few words you shall plainly understand
my meaning. If you have well considered on the course which
this day hath been kept by Pampinea, methinks it hath been
very pleasing and commendable, in which regard, until by over-
tedious continuation or other occasions of irksome offence, it shall

seem injurious, I am of the mind not to alter it. Holding on the order, then, we have begun to do, we will depart from hence to recreate ourselves a while, and when the sun groweth towards setting we will sup in the fresh and open air ; afterward, with canzonets and other pastimes we will outwear the hours till bed-time. To-morrow morning, in the fresh and gentle breath thereof, we will rise and walk to such places as every one shall find fittest for them, even as already this day we have done, until due time shall summon us hither again to continue our discoursive tales, wherein methinks consisteth both pleasure and profit, especially by discreet observation.

"Very true it is, that some things which Pampinea could not accomplish by reason of her small time of authority, I will begin to undertake, to wit, in restraining some matters whereon we are to speak, that better premeditation may pass upon them. For when respite and a little leisure goeth before them, each discourse will savour of the more formality, and if it might so please you, thus would I direct the order. As since the beginning of the world all men have been guided by Fortune through divers accidents and occasions, so beyond all hope and expectation the issue and success hath been good and successful, and accordingly should every one of our arguments be chosen."

The ladies, and young gentlemen, likewise, commended her advice, and promised to imitate it, only Dioneo excepted, who, when every one was silent, spake thus : " Madam, I say, as all the rest have done, that the order by you appointed is most pleasing and worthy to be allowed. But I entreat one special favour for myself, and to have it confirmed to me so long as our company continueth ; namely, that I may not be constrained to this law of direction, but to tell my tale at liberty after my own mind, and according to the freedom first instituted. And because no one shall imagine that I urge this grace of you, as being unfurnished of discourses in this kind, I am well contented to be the last in every day's exercise."

The Queen, knowing him to be a man full of mirth and matter, began to consider very advisedly that he would not have moved this request but only to the end that if the company grew wearied by any of the tales recounted, he would shut up the day's disport with some mirthful accident ; wherefore willingly, and with consent of all the rest, he had his suit granted. So arising all, they walked to a crystal river, descending down a little hill into a valley graciously shaded with goodly trees, where, washing both their hands and feet, much pretty pleasure passed among them till supper-time drawing near, made them return home to the palace. When supper was ended, books and instruments being laid before them, the Queen commanded a dance, and that Emilia, assisted by Lauretta and Dioneo, should sing a sweet ditty ; at which command Lauretta undertook the dance and led it, Emilia singing this song ensuing :—

THE SONG.

So much delight my beauty yields to me
    That any other love,
    To wish or prove,
Can never suit itself with my desire.

Therein I see upon good observation,
    What sweet content due understanding lends ;
Old or new thoughts cannot in any fashion
    Rob me of that which mine own soul commends.
        What object then,
        'Mongst infinites of men,
        Can I ever find
        To possess my mind,
And plant therein another new desire?
        So much delight, &c.

But were it so, the bliss that I would choose
    Is by continual sight to comfort me ;
So rare a presence never to refuse,
    Which mortal tongue or thought, whate'er it be
        Must still conceal—
        Not able to reveal
        Such a sacred sweet—
        For none other meet
But hearts inflaméd with the same desire.
        So much delight, &c.

The song being ended, the chorus whereof was answered by them all, it passed with general applause, and after a few other dances, the night being well run on, the Queen gave ending to this first day's recreation. So lights being brought, they departed to their several lodgings, to take their rest till the next morning.

THE SECOND DAY.

Wherein all the discourses are under the government of Filomena; concerning such men or women as, in divers accidents, have been much molested by Fortune, and yet afterward, contrary to their hope and expectation, have had a happy and successful deliverance.

ALREADY had the bright sun renewed the day everywhere with his splendent beams, and the birds sat merrily singing on the blooming branches, yielding testimony thereof to the ears of all hearers, when the seven ladies and the three gentlemen, after they had risen, entered the gardens, and there spent some time in walking, as also making of nosegays and chaplets of flowers. And even as they had done the day before, so did they now follow the same course; for after they had dined in a cool and pleasant air, they fell to dancing, and then went to sleep awhile, from which being awaked, they took their places, according as it pleased the Queen to appoint, in the same fair meadow about her. And she being a goodly creature and highly pleasing to behold, having put on her crown of laurel, and giving a gracious countenance to the whole company, commanded Neifile that her tale should begin this day's delight; whereupon she, without returning any excuse or denial, began in this manner.

THE FIRST NOVEL.

Martellino, counterfeiting to be lame of his members, caused himself to be set on the body of Saint Arrigo, where he made show of his sudden recovery; but when his dissimulation was discovered, he was well beaten, being afterward taken prisoner, and in great danger of being hanged and strangled by the neck, and yet he escaped in the end.

FAIR ladies, it hath happened many times that he who striveth to scorn and flout other men, and especially in occasions deserving to be respected, proveth to mock himself with the selfsame matter, yea, and to his no mean danger beside; as you shall perceive by a tale which I intend to tell you, obeying therein the command of our Queen, and according to the subject by her enjoined; in which discourse you may first observe what great mischance happened to one of our citizens, and yet afterward how, beyond all hope, he happily escaped.

Not long since there lived in the city of Treves an Almain or German, named Arrigo, who, being a poor man, served as a porter or burden-bearer for money, when any man pleased to employ him; and yet, notwithstanding his poor and mean condition, he was generally reputed to be of good and sanctified life. In which regard, whether it were true or no, I know not, it happened that when he died, at least as the men of Treves themselves affirmed, in the very instant hour of his departure, all the bells in the great church of Treves, not being pulled by the help of any man, began to ring; which being accounted for a miracle, every one said that this Arrigo had been and was a saint. And presently all the people of the city ran to the house where the dead body lay, and carried it, as a sanctified body, in the great church, where people, halt, lame, and blind, or troubled with any other diseases, were brought about it, even as if every one should forthwith be holpen only by their touching the body.

It came to pass that in so great a concourse of people as resorted thither from all parts, three of our citizens went to Treves, one of them being named Stecchi, the second Martellino, and the third Marchese, all being men of such condition as frequented princes' courts, to give them delight by pleasant and counterfeited qualities. None of these men having ever been at Treves before, seeing how the people crowded through the streets, wondered greatly thereat; but when they knew the reason why the throngs ran in heaps in such sort together, they grew as desirous to see the shrine as any of the rest. Having ordered all affairs at their lodging, Marchese said: "It is fit for us to see this saint, but I know not how we shall attain thereto, because, as I have heard, the place is guarded by Germain soldiers and other warlike men, commanded thither by the governor of this city, lest any outrage should be there committed; and beside, the church is so full of people as we shall never compass to get near." Martellino being also as forward in desire to see it, presently replied: "All this difficulty cannot dismay me, but I will to the very body of the saint itself." "But how?" quoth Marchese. "I will tell thee," answered Martellino. "I purpose to go in the disguise of an impotent lame person, supported on the one side by thyself, and on the other by Stecchi, as if I were not able to walk of myself. And you two, thus fastening me, desiring to come near the saint to cure me, every one will make way, and freely give you leave to go on."

This device was very pleasing to Marquiso and Stecchi, so that, without any further delaying, they all three left their lodging, and resorting into a secret corner aside, Martellino so writhed and mis-shaped his hands, fingers, and arms, his legs, mouth, eyes, and whole countenance, that it was a dreadful sight to look upon him, and whosoever beheld him would verily have imagined that he was utterly lame of his limbs and greatly deformed in his body. Marchese and Stecchi, seeing all sorted so well as they could wish, took and led him towards the church, making very piteous moan, and humble desiring, for God's sake, of every one that they met, to grant them free passage, whereto they charitably con-descended.

Thus leading him on, crying "Beware there before, and give way, for God's sake!" they arrived at the body of Saint Arrigo,

that by his help he might be healed. And while all eyes were
diligently observing what miracle would be wrought on Martellino.
He having sitten a small space upon the saint's body, and being
sufficiently skilful in counterfeiting, began first to extend forth the
one of his fingers, next his hand, then his arm, and so by degrees
the rest of his body. Which when the people saw, they made such a
wonderful great noise in praise and commendation of Saint Arrigo,
even as if it had thundered in the church.

Now it chanced by ill fortune that there stood near to the body
a Florentine who knew Martellino very perfectly, but appearing so
monstrously misshapen when he was brought into the church he
could take no knowledge of him. But when he saw him stand up and
walk, he knew him then to be the man indeed ; whereupon he said :
" How cometh it to pass that this fellow should be so miraculously
cured that never truly was any way impotent ?"   Certain men
of the city hearing these words, entered into further questioning,
demanding how he knew that the man had no such imperfection ?
" Well enough," answered the Florentine ; " I knew him to be as
straight in his limbs and body as you, I, or any of us all are; but indeed he knows better how to dissemble counterfeit tricks than any
man else that ever I saw in all the days of my life."

When they heard this they discoursed no further with the
Florentine, but pressed on mainly to the place where Martellino
stood, crying out aloud : " Lay hold on this traitor, a mocker of God
and his saints, that had no lameness in his limbs ; but, to make a
mock of our saint and us, came hither in false and counterfeit manner." So laying hands upon him, they threw him against the
ground, and plucking him by the hair of his head and tearing the
garments from his back, spurning him with their feet, and beating
him with their fists, that many were much ashamed to see it.

Poor Martellino was in pitiful case, crying out for mercy, but no
man would hear him ; for the more he cried the more still they did
beat him, as meaning to leave no life in him; which Stecchi and Marchese seeing, considered with themselves that they were likewise in
a desperate case, and therefore, fearing to be as much misused,
they cried out amongst the rest, " Kill the counterfeiting knave !
lay on, load, and spare him not !"   Nevertheless, they took care
how to get him out of the people's hands, as doubting lest they
would kill him indeed by their extreme violences.

Suddenly Marchese bethought him how to do it, and proceeded
thus : All the sergeants for justice standing at the church door, he
ran with all possible speed he could to the Podesta's Lieutenant,
and said unto him : " Good my Lord Justice, help me in a hard case.
Yonder is a villain that hath cut my purse. I desire that he may
be brought before you, that I may have my money again."   He
hearing this, sent for a dozen of the sergeants, who went to appre-
hend unhappy Martellino, and recover him from the people's fury,
leading him on with them to the palace, no mean crowds thronging
after him when they heard that he was accused to be a cutpurse.
Now durst they meddle no more with Martellino, but assisted the

officers, some of them charging him in like manner that he had cut their purses also.

Upon these clamours and complaints, the Podesta's Lieutenant, being a man of rude quality, took him suddenly aside, and examined him of the crimes wherewith he was charged. But Martellino, as making no account of these accusations, laughed, and returned scoffing answers. Whereat the Judge, waxing much displeased, delivered him over to the strappado, and stood by himself, to have him confess the crimes imposed on him, and then to hang him afterwards. Being let down to the ground, the Judge still demanded of him whether the accusations against him were true or no, affirming that it nothing availed him to deny it. Whereupon he thus spake to the Judge : " My lord, I am here ready before you to confess the truth. But I pray you demand of all them that accuse me when and where I did cut their purses? and then I will tell you that which as yet I have not done ; otherwise, I purpose to make you no more answer."

" Well," quoth the Judge, " thou requirest but reason." And calling divers of the accusers, one of them said that he lost his purse eight days before, another said six, another four, and some said the very same day. Which Martellino hearing, replied : " My lord, they all lie in their throats, as I will plainly prove before you. I would God I had never set foot within this city, as it is not many hours since my first entrance. And presently after my arrival I went, in an evil hour I may say for me, to see the saint's body, where I was thus beaten, as you may behold. That all this is true which I say unto you, the Seigneury officer that keeps your Book of Presentations will testify for me, as also the host where I am lodged. Wherefore, good my lord, if you find all no otherwise than I have said, I humbly entreat you that upon these bad men's reports and false informations I may not be thus tormented and put in peril of my life."

While matters proceeded in this manner, Marchese and Stecchi, understanding how roughly the Podesta's Lieutenant dealt with Martellino, and that he had already given him the strappado, were in heavy perplexity, saying to themselves : " We have carried this business very badly, redeeming him out of the frying-pan and flinging him into the fire." Whereupon, trudging about from place to place, and meeting at length with their host, they told him truly how all had happened, whereat he could not refrain from laughing. Afterward he went with them to one Master Alexander Agolanti, who dwelt in Treves, and was in great credit with the city's chief magistrate, to whom he related the whole discourse, all three earnestly entreating him to commiserate the case of poor Martellino.

Master Alexander, after he had laughed heartily at this hot piece of service, went with him to the Lord of Treves, prevailing so well with him that he sent to have Martellino brought before him. The messengers that went for him found him standing in his shirt before the judge, very shrewdly shaken with the strappado, trembling and quaking pitifully ; for the judge would not hear anything in his excuse, hating him, perhaps, because he was a Florentine, flatly determined to have him hanged by the neck, and would not deliver him to the Lord until in mere despite he was compelled to do it.

The Lord of Treves, when Martellino came before him, and had acquainted him truly with every particular, Master Alexander requested that he might be despatched thence for Florence, because he thought the halter to be about his neck, and that there was no other help but hanging. The lord, smiling a long while at the accident, and causing Martellino to be handsomely apparelled, delivering them also his pass, they escaped out of further danger, and tarried nowhere till they came unto Florence.

THE SECOND NOVEL.

Rinaldo d'Asti, after he was robbed by thieves, arrived at Castel Guglielmo, where he was friendly lodged by a fair widow, and recompensed likewise for all his losses, returning after, safe and well, home unto his own house.

MUCH merriment was among the ladies hearing this tale of Martellino's misfortune, so familiarly reported by Neifile, and of the men it was best respected by Filostrato, who, sitting nearest unto Neifile, the Queen commanded his tale to be the next, when presently he began to speak thus.

[OMITTED.]

THE THIRD NOVEL.

Three young gentlemen, being brethren, and having spent all their lands and possessions vainly, became poor. A nephew of theirs, falling almost into as desperate a condition, became acquainted with an abbot, whom he afterward found to be the King of England's daughter, and made him her husband in marriage, recompensing all his uncles' losses, and seating them again in good estate.

THE fortunes of Rinaldo d'Asti, being heard by the ladies and gentlemen, they admired his happiness, and commended his devotion to St. Julian, who, in such extreme necessity, sent him so good succour. Pampinea, sitting next to Filostrato, considering that her discourse must follow in order, and thinking on what she was to say, the Queen had no sooner sent out her command, but she, being no less fair than forward, began in this manner.

[OMITTED.]

THE FOURTH NOVEL.

Landolfo Ruffolo, falling into poverty, became a pirate on the seas, and being taken by the Genoese, hardly escaped drowning, which yet, nevertheless, he did upon a little chest or coffer full of very rich jewels, being carried thereon to Corsica, where he was well entertained by a good woman, and afterward returned richly home to his own house.

LAURETTA sat next to Pampinea, and seeing how triumphantly she had finished her discourse without attending anything else, spoke thus : Gracious ladies, we shall never behold, in mine opinion, a greater act of fortune than to see a man so suddenly exalted, even from the lowest depth of poverty, to a royal estate of dignity, as the discourse of Pampinea hath made good by the happy advancement of Alessandro. And because it appeareth necessary that whosoever discourseth on the subject proposed should no way vary from the very same terms, I shall not shame to tell a tale which, though it contain far greater mishaps than the former, may sort to as happy an issue, albeit not so noble and magnificent. In which respect it may perhaps merit the less attention, but howsoever that fault shall be found in me, I mean to discharge my own duty.

Opinion hath made it famous for a long time that the sea-coast of Rheggio to Gaeta is the only delectable part of all Italy, wherein, somewhat near to Salerno, is a shore looking upon the sea which the inhabitants there dwelling do call the coast of Amalfi, full of small towns, gardens, springs, and wealthy men, trading in as many kinds of merchandises as any other people that I know; among which town there is one named Ravello, wherein as yet to this day there are rich people. There was, not long since, a very wealthy man named Landolfo Ruffolo, who, being not contented with his riches, but coveting to multiply them double and treble, fell in danger to lose both himself and wealth together.

This man, as other merchants are wont to do, after he had considered on his affairs, bought him a very goodly ship, lading it with divers sorts of merchandises, all belonging to himself only, and made his voyage to the isle of Cyprus, where he found, over and beside the merchandises he had brought thither, many ships more there arrived, and all of them laden with the same commodities, in regard whereof it was needful for him not only to make a good mart of his goods, but also he was further constrained, if he meant to vend his commodities, to sell them away almost for nothing, endangering his utter destruction and overthrow. Whereupon, grieving exceedingly at so great a loss, not knowing what to do, and feeling that from very abundant wealth he was like to fall into as low poverty, he resolved to die, or to recompense his losses upon others, because he would not return home poor, having departed thence so rich.

Meeting with a merchant who bought his great ship of him, with the money made thereof, and also his other merchandises, he purchased another, being a lighter vessel, apt and proper for the use of a pirate, arming and furnishing it in ample manner for roving and robbing upon the seas. Thus he began to make other men's goods his own; especially from the Turks he took much wealth, fortune being always so favourable to him that he could never compass the like by trading. So that within the space of one year he had robbed and taken so many galleys from the Turk, that he found himself well recovered, not only of all his losses by merchandise, but likewise his wealth was wholly redoubled. Finding his losses to be very liberally requited, and having now sufficient, it were folly to hazard a second fall; wherefore, conferring with his own thoughts, and finding that he had enough, and needed not to covet after more, he fully concluded now to return home to his own house again, and live upon his goods thus gotten.

Continuing still in fear of the loss he had sustained by traffic, and minding never more to employ his money that way, but to keep this light vessel which had helped him to all his wealth, he commanded his men to put forth their oars and shape their course for his own dwelling. Being aloft in the higher seas, dark night overtaking them, and a mighty wind suddenly coming upon them, it not only was contrary to their course, but held on with such impetuous violence, that the small vessel being unable to endure it, made to landward speedily, and in expectation of a more friendly wind entered a little port of the sea directing up into a small island, and there safely sheltered itself. Into the same port which Landolfo had thus taken for his refuge, entered, soon after, two great carracks of the Genoese, lately come from Constantinople. When the men in them had espied the small bark, and locked up her passage from getting forth, understanding the owner's name, and that report had famed him to be very rich, they determined, as men evermore addicted naturally to covet after money and spoil, to make it their own as a prize at sea.

Landing some store of their men, well armed with crossbows and other weapons, they took possession of such a place where none durst issue forth of the small bark but endangered his life with their darts and arrows. Entering aboard the bark, and making it their own by full possession, all the men they threw overboard, without sparing any but Landolfo himself, whom they mounted into one of the carracks, leaving him nothing but a poor shirt of mail on his back, and having rifled the bark of all her riches, sunk it into the bottom of the sea. The day following, the rough winds being calmed, the carracks set sail again, having a prosperous passage all the day long; but upon the entrance of dark night the winds blew more tempestuously than before, and swelled the sea in such rude storms that the two carracks were sundered each from other, and by violence of the tempest it came to pass that the carrack wherein lay poor miserable Landolfo, beneath the isle of Cephalonia, ran against a rock, and, even as a glass against a wall, so split the carrack in pieces, the goods and merchandises floating on the sea, chests, coffers, beds, and such like other things, as often happeneth in such lamentable accidents.

Now, notwithstanding the night's obscurity and impetuous violence of the billows, such as could swim made shift to save their lives by swimming; others caught hold on such things as by fortune's favour floated nearest to them, among whom distressed Landolfo, desirous to save his life, if possible it might be, espied a chest or coffer before him, ordained no doubt to be the means of his safety from drowning.

Now, although the day before he had wished for death infinite times, rather than to return home in such wretched poverty, yet seeing how other men strove for safety of their lives by any help, were it never so little, he took advantage of this favour offered him, and the rather in a necessity so urgent. Keeping fast upon the coffer so well as he could, and being driven by the winds and waves, one while this way, and anon quite contrary, he made shift for himself till day appeared, when, looking every way about him, he saw nothing but clouds, the seas, and the coffer, which one while shrunk from under him, and another while supported him, according as the winds and billows carried it. All that day and night thus he floated up and down, drinking more than willingly he would, but almost hunger-starved through want of food. The next morning, either by the appointment of heaven or power of the winds, Landolfo who was well-near become a sponge, holding his arms strongly about the chest as we have seen some do who, dreading drowning, take hold on any the very smallest help, drew near unto the shore of the island Corfu, where, by good fortune, a poor woman was scouring dishes with the salt water and sand to make them, housewife-like, neat and clean.

When she saw the chest drawing near her, and not discerning the shape of any man, she grew fearful, and retiring from it, cried out aloud. He had no power of speaking to her, neither did his sight do him the smallest service; but even as the waves and winds pleased, the chest was driven still nearer to the land, and then the woman perceived that it had the form of a coffer, and looking more advisedly, beheld two arms extended over it, and afterward she espied the face of a man, not being able to judge whether he were alive or no. Moved by charitable and womanly compassion, she stepped in among the billows, and getting fast hold on the hair of his head, drew both the chest and him to the land; and calling forth her daughter to help her, with much ado she unfolded his arms from the chest, setting it upon her daughter's head, and then between them Landolfo was led into the town, and there conveyed into a warm stove, where quickly he recovered, by her pains, his strength, benumbed with extreme cold.

Good wines and comfortable broths she cherished him withal, that his senses, being indifferently restored, he knew the place where he was, but not in what manner he was brought thither, till the good woman had showed him the coffer that had kept him floating upon the waves, and, next under God, had saved his life.

The chest seemed of such slender weight that nothing of any value could be expected in it, either to recompense the womn's great pains and kindness bestowed on him, or any matter of his own benefit.   Nevertheless, the woman being absent, he opened the chest, and found innumerable precious stones therein, some costly and curious set in gold, and others not fixed in any metal.   Having knowledge of their great worth and value—being a merchant and skilled in such matters—he became much comforted, praising God for his good success, and such an admirable means of deliverance from danger.

Then considering with himself that in a short time he had been twice well buffeted and beaten by fortune, lest a third mishap might follow in like manner, he consulted with his thoughts how he might safely order the business, and bring so rich a booty without peril to his own home.   Wherefore, wrapping up the jewels in very unsightly colours, that no suspicion at all should be conceived of them, he said to the good woman that the chest would not do him any further service ; but if she pleased to lend him a small sack or bag, she might keep the coffer, for in her house it would divers ways stead her.   The woman gladly did as he desired, and Landolfo, returning her infinite thanks for the loving-kindness she had offered him, throwing the sack on his neck, passed by a bark to Brundusium, and from thence to Tranium, where merchants in the city bestowed good garments on him, he acquainting them with his disastrous fortunes, but not a word concerning his last good success.

Being come home in safety to Ravello, he fell on his knees and thanked God for all his mercies towards him.   Then, opening the sack and viewing the jewels at more leisure than formerly he had done, he found them to be of so great estimation, that, selling them but at ordinary and reasonable rates, he was three times richer than when he departed first from his house.   And having vended them all, he sent a great sum of money to the good woman at Corfu, that had rescued him out of the sea and saved his life in a danger so dreadful ; the like he did at Tranium to the merchants that newly clothed him, living richly upon the remainder, and never adventuring more to the sea, but ending his days in wealth and honour.

THE FIFTH NOVEL.

Andreuccio di Pietro, travelling from Perugia to Naples to buy horses, was in the space of one night surprised by three admirable accidents out of all of which he fortunately escaped, and with a rich ring returned home to his own house.

THE precious stones and jewels found by Landolfo maketh me to remember, said Fiametta, who was next to deliver her discourse, a tale containing no less perils than that reported by Lauretta, but somewhat different from it, because the one happened in sundry years, and this other had no longer time than the compass of one poor night, as instantly I will relate unto you.

[OMITTED.]

THE SIXTH NOVEL.

Beritola Caracciola was found in an island with two goats, having lost her two sons, and thence travelled into Lunigiana, where one of her sons became servant to the lord thereof, who caused him to be imprisoned. Afterward, when the country of Sicily rebelled against King Charles, the aforesaid son chanced to be known by his mother, and was married to his master's daughter. And his brother being found likewise, they both returned to great estate and credit.

THE ladies and gentlemen also having smiled sufficiently at the several accidents which did befall the poor traveller Andreuccio, reported at large by Fiametta, the Lady Emilia, seeing her tale to be fully concluded, began by commandment of the Queen to speak in this manner :—

The diversity of changes and alterations in Fortune, as they are great, so must they needs be grievous, and as often as we take occasion to talk of them, so often do they, awake and quicken our understandings, avouching that it is no easy matter to depend upon her flatteries. And I am of opinion that to hear them recounted ought not any way to offend us, be it of men wretched or fortunate, because as they instruct the one with good advice, so they animate the other with comfort ; and therefore, although great occasions have been already related, yet I purpose to tell a tale, no less true than lamentable, which albeit it sorted to a successful ending, yet notwithstanding such and so many were the bitter thwartings as hardly can I believe that ever any sorrow was more joyfully sweetened.

You must understand then, most gracious ladies, that after the death of Frederick, the second Emperor, one named Manfredi was crowned King of Sicily, about whom lived in great account and authority a Neapolitan gentleman called Arrighetto Capece, who had to wife a bountiful gentlewoman and a Neapolitan also, named Beritola Caracciola. This Arrighetto held the government of the kingdom of Sicily ; and understanding that King Charles the First had won the battle at Benevento and slain King Manfredi, the whole kingdom revolting also to his devotion, and little trust to be reposed in the Sicilians, or he willing to subject himself to his lord's enemy, provided for his secret flight from thence. But this being discovered to the Sicilians, he and many more who had been loyal servants to King Manfredi were suddenly taken and imprisoned by King Charles, and the sole possession of the island confirmed to him.

Madame Beritola not knowing, in so sudden and strange an alteration of State affairs, what was become of her husband, fearing also greatly before those inconveniences which afterward followed, being overcome with many passionate considerations, having left and forsaken all her goods, going aboard a small barque with a son of hers, aged about some eight years, named Geoffrey, and grown great with child with another, she fled thence to Lipari, where she was brought to bed of another son, whom she named—answerable both to his and her hard fortune—"The Poor Expelled" (*lo Scacciato*).

Having provided herself of a nurse, they all together went aboard again, setting sail for Naples to visit her parents; but it chanced quite contrary to her expectation, because by stormy winds and weather, the vessel, being bound for Naples, was hurried to the Isle of Ponzo, where, entering into a small port of the sea, they concluded to make their abode till a time more furtherous should further their voyage.

As the rest, so did Beritola go on shore in the island, where, having found a separate and solitary place, fit for her silent and sad meditations, secretly by herself she sorrowed for the absence of her husband. Resorting daily to this her sad exercise, and continuing there her complaints, unseen by any of the mariners or whosoever else, there arrived suddenly a galley of pirates, who seizing on the small bark, carried it and all the rest in it away with them. When Beritola had finished her woful complaints, as daily she was accustomed to do, she returned back to her children again; but finding no person there remaining—whereat she wondered not a little, immediately suspecting what had happened indeed—she lent her looks on the sea, and saw the galley, which as yet had not gone far, drawing the smaller vessel after her. Hereby she plainly perceived that now she had lost her children as formerly she had lost her husband; being left there poor, forsaken, and miserable, not knowing when, where, or how to find any of them again; and calling for her husband and children, she fell down in a swoon upon the shore.

Now was not anybody near with cold water or any other remedy to help the recovery of her lost powers, wherefore her spirits might the more freely wander at their own pleasure; but after they were returned back again, and had won their wonted offices in her body, drowned in tears and wringing her hands, she did nothing but call for her children and husband, straying all about in hope to find them, seeking in caves, dens, and everywhere else that presented the very least glimpse of comfort. But when she saw all her pains sought to no purpose, and dark night drawing swiftly on, hope and dismay raising infinite perturbations, made her yet to be somewhat respective of herself; and therefore, departing from the sea-shore, she returned to the solitary place where she used to sigh and mourn alone by herself.

The night being overpast, with infinite fears and affrights, and bright day saluting the world again, with the expense of nine hours and more, she fell to her former fruitless travels. Being somewhat sharply bitten with hunger, because the former day and night she had not tasted any food; she made therefore a benefit of necessity, and fed on the green herbs so well as she could, not without many piercing afflictions what should become of her in this extraordinary misery. As she walked in these pensive meditations she saw a goat enter into a cave, and within a while after come forth again, wandering along through the woods. Whereupon she stayed, and entered where she saw the beast issue forth, where she found two young kids, yeaned, as it seemed, the selfsame day; which sight was very pleasing to her, and nothing in that distress could more content her.

As yet she had milk freshly running in both her breasts, by reason of her so late delivery in child-bed; wherefore she lay down unto the two young kids, and taking them tenderly in her arms, suffered each of them to suck a teat, whereof they made not any refusal, but took them as lovingly as their dam's, and from that time forward they made no distinguishing between their dam and her.

Thus this unfortunate lady, having found some company in this solitary desert, fed on herbs and roots, drinking fair running water, and weeping silently to herself, so often as she remembered her husband, children, and former days, passed in much better manner. Here she resolved now to live and die, being at last deprived both of the dam and younger kid also, by their wandering further into the near adjoining woods, according to their natural inclinations, whereby the poor distressed lady became more savage and wild in her daily conditions than otherwise she would have been.

After many months were over-passed, at the very same place where she took landing, by chance there arrived another small vessel of certain Pisans, which remained there divers days. In this bark was a gentleman named Currado de' Marchesi Malespini, with his holy and virtuous wife, were returned back from a pilgrimage, having visited all the sanctified places that then were in the kingdom of Apulia, and now were bound homeward to their own abiding. This gentleman, for the expelling of melancholy perturbations, one especial day amongst other, with his wife, servants, and waiting hounds, wandered up into the island, not far from the place of Beritola's desert solitary dwelling. The hounds questing after game, at last happening on the two kids where they were feeding, and by this time had attained indifferent growth, and finding themselves thus pursued by the hounds, fled to no other part of the wood than to the cave where Beritola remained, and seeming as if they thought to be rescued only by her, she suddenly caught up a staff and forced the hounds thence to flight.

By this time Currado and his wife, who had followed closely after the hounds, was come thither, and seeing what had happened, looking on the lady, who was become black, swarthy, meagre, and hairy, they wondered not a little at her, and she a great deal more at them. When upon her request Currado had checked back his hounds, they prevailed so much by earnest entreaties to know what she was, and the reason of her living there, that she entirely related her quality, and strange determination for living there. Which when the gentleman had heard, who very well knew her husband, compassion forced tears from his eyes, and earnestly he laboured by kind persuasions to alter so cruel a deliberation, making an honourable offer for conducting her home to his own dwelling, where she should remain with him in noble respect, as if she were his own sister, without parting from him till fortune should smile as fairly on her as ever she had done before.

When these gentle offers could not prevail with her, the gentleman left his wife in her company with her, saying that he would go fetch some food for her; and because her garments were rent and torn, he would bring her other of his wife's, not doubting but to win her thence with them. His wife abode there with Beritola, very much bemoaning her great disasters; and when both viands and garments were brought, by extremity of intercession, they caused her to put them on, and also to feed with them, albeit she protested that she would not depart thence into any place where any knowledge should be taken of her. In the end, they persuaded her to go with them into Lunigiana, carrying also with her the the two young goats and their dam, which were then in the cave altogether, prettily playing before Beritola, to the great admiration of Currado and his wife, as also the servants attending on them.

When the winds and weather grew favourable for them, Beritola went abroad with Currado and his wife, being followed by the two young goats and their dam; and because her name should be known to none but Currado and his wife only, she would be styled no otherwise but Cavrivuola (the Goatherdess). Merrily yet gently blew the gale which brought them to enter the river of Magra, where, going on shore, and into their own castle, Beritola kept company with the wife of Currado, but in a mourning habit; and a waiting gentlewoman of theirs, honest, humble, and very dutiful, the goats always familiarly keeping them company.

Return we now to the pirates, which at Ponzo seized on the small bark wherein Madam Beritola was brought thither, and carried thence away without any sight or knowledge of her. With such other spoils as they had taken, they shaped their course for Genoa, and there, by consent of the patrons of the galley, made a division of their booties. It came to pass that, among other things, the nurse that attended on Beritola, and the two children with her, fell to the share of one Messer Guasparrin d'Oria, who sent them together to his own house, there to be employed in service as servants. The nurse weeping beyond measure for the loss of her lady, bemoans her own miserable fortune, whereinto she was now fallen with the two young lads; and after long lamenting, which she found utterly fruitless and to none effect, though she was used as a servant with them, and being but a poor woman, yet was she wise and discreetly advised. Wherefore comforting both herself and them so well as she could, and considering the depth of their disaster, she conceited thus, that if the children should be known, it might redound to their greater danger, and she be no way advantaged thereby.

Hereupon, hoping that fortune, early or late, would alter her stern malice, and that they might, if they lived, regain once more their

former condition, she would not disclose them to any one whatsoever till she should see the time aptly disposed for it. Being thus
determined, to all such as questioned her concerning them, she
answered, that they were her own children, naming the eldest not
Geoffrey, but Giannotto di Procida. As for the youngest she cared
not greatly for changing his name, and therefore wisely informed
Geoffrey upon what reason she had altered his name, and what
danger he might fall into if he should otherwise be discovered ;
being not satisfied with thus telling him once, but remembering him
thereof very often, which the gentle youth, being so well instructed
by the wise and careful nurse, did very warily observe.

The two young lads, very poorly garmented, but much worse hosed
and shod, continued thus in the house of Guasparrin, where both
they and the nurse were long time employed about very base and
drudging offices, which yet they endured with admirable patience.
But Giannotto, aged already about sixteen years, having a loftier
spirit than belonging to a slavish servant, despising the baseness of
his servile condition, departed from the drudgery of Messer
Guasparrin, and going aboard the galleys, which were bound for
Alexandria, fortuned into many places, yet none of them affording
him any advancement.   In the end, about three or four years after
his departure from Guasparrin, being now a brave young man and
of very goodly form, he understood that his father, whom he supposed
to be dead, was as yet living, but in captivity, and prisoner to King
Charles.   Wherefore, despairing of any successful fortune, he wan-·
dered here and there, till he came to Lunigiana, and there, by
strange accident, he became servant to Messer Currado Malespini,
where the service proved well liking to them both.

Very seldom times he had a sight of his mother, because she
always kept company with Currado's wife, and yet when they came
in view of each other, she knew not him, nor he her, so much years
had altered them both from what they were wont to be, and when
they saw each other last.   Giannotto being thus in the service of
Messer Currado, it fortuned that a daughter of his named Spina,
being the widow of one Messer Nicolò da Grignano, returned home
to her father's house.   Very beautiful and amiable she was, young
likewise, aged but little above sixteen, growing wonderful amorous
of Giannotto, and he of her.

Upon a day, he and she walking to a goodly wood plentifully
furnished with spreading trees, having outgone the rest of their
company, they made choice of a pleasant place, very daintily shaded
and beautified with all sorts of flowers.   There they spent some time
in amorous talking, which, though it seemed over-short to them, yet
was so unadvisedly prolonged, that they were on a sudden suprised,
first by the mother, and next by the Messer Currado himself, who
grieving beyond measure to be thus treacherously dealt withal,
caused them to be apprehended by three of his servants, and, without telling them any reason why, led bound to another castle of his,
and fretting with extremity of rage, concluded in his mind that they
should both shamefully be put to death.

The mother of this regardless daughter having heard the angry words of her husband, and how he would be revenged on the faulty, could not endure that he should be so severe ; wherefore, although she was likewise much afflicted in mind, and reputed her daughter worthy, for so great an offence, of all cruel punishment, yet she hasted to her displeased husband, and began to entreat that he would not run on in such a furious spleen, now in his aged years to be the murderer of his own child, and soil his ha..ds in the blood of his servant. Rather, he might find out some mild course for the satisfaction of his anger, by committing them to close imprisonment, there to remain and mourn for their folly committed. The virtuous and religious lady alleged so many commendable examples, and used such plenty of moving persuasions, that she quite altered his mind from putting them to death, and he commanded only that they should separately be imprisoned, with little store of food, and lodging of the uneasiest, until he should otherwise determine of them ; and so it was done. What their life now was in captivity and continual tears, with stricter abstinence than was needful for them, all this I must commit to your consideration.

Giannotto and Spina remaining in this comfortless condition, and a whole year being now outworn, yet Currado keeping them thus still imprisoned, it came to pass that Don Pedro, King of Arragon, by the means of Messer John of Procida, caused the Isle of Sicily to revolt, and took it away from King Charles, whereat Currado, he being of the Ghibbeline faction, not a little rejoiced. Giannotto having intelligence thereof, by some of them that had him in custody, breathing forth a vehement sigh, spake in this manner : " Alas, poor miserable wretch as I am, that have already gone begging through the world above fourteen years, in expectation of nothing else but this opportunity ; and now it is come, must I be in prison to the end that I should never more hope for any future happiness ? And how can I get forth of this prison except it be by death only ?" " How now ?" replied the officer of the guard ; " what doth this business of great kings concern thee ? What affairs hast thou in Sicily ! "

Once more Giannotto sighed extremely, and returned him this answer : " Methinks my heart," quoth he, " doth cleave in sunder when I call to mind the charge which my father had there ; for although I was but a little boy when I fled thence, yet I can well remember that I saw him governor there at such time as King Manfredi lived." The guard, pursuing on still his purpose, demanded of him what and who his father was. " My father ?" replied Giannotto. " I may now securely speak of him, being out of the peril which nearly concerned me if I had been discovered. He was then named, and so still if he be living, Arrighetto Capece, and my name is Geoffrey and not Giannotto ; and I make no doubt but, if I were freed from hence and might be returned home to Sicily, I should, for his sake, be placed in some authority."

The honest man of the guard, without seeking after any further information, so soon as he could compass any leisure, reported all to

C

Messer Currado, who having heard this news, albeit he made no show thereof to the revealer, went to Madonna Beritola, graciously demanding of her if she had any son by her husband who was called Geoffrey. The lady replied in tears, that if her eldest son were yet living he was so named, and aged about twenty-two years. Currado hearing this, imagined this same to be the man; considering further withal that, if it fell out to prove so, he might have the better means of mercy, and closely concealing his daughter's shame, joyfully join them in marriage together.

Hereupon he secretly called Giannotto before him, examining him particularly of all his past life; and finding, by most manifest arguments, that his name was truly Geoffrey, and the eldest son of Arrighetto Capece, he spake thus to him: " Giannotto, thou knowest how great the injuries are that thou hast done me and my dear daughter, gently entreating thee, as became an honest servant, that thou shouldst always have been respective of mine honour and all that appertain unto me. There are many noble gentlemen who, sustaining the wrong that thou hast offered me, they would have procured thy shameful death, which pity and compassion will not suffer in me. Wherefore seeing, as thou informest me, that thou art honourably derived both by father and mother, I will give end to all thy anguishes, even when thyself art so pleased, releasing thee from that captivity wherein I have so long kept thee, and in one instant reduce thine honour and mine into complete perfection. As thou knowest, my daughter Spina is a widow, and her marriage is both great and good; what her manners and conditions are thou indifferently knowest, and art not ignorant of her father and mother. Concerning thine own estate, as now I purpose not to speak anything. Therefore, when thou wilt, I am determined that she shall become thy wife, and, accepting thee as my son, to remain with me so long as you both please."

Imprisonment had somewhat misshapen Giannotto in his outward form, but not impaired a jot of his noble spirit, much less the true love which he bore his friend; and although most earnestly he desired that which now Currado had so frankly offered him, and was in his power only to bestow on him, yet could he not cloud any part of his greatness, but with a resolved judgment thus replied: " My lord, affectation of rule, desire of wealthy possessions, or any other matter whatsoever, could never make me a traitor to you or yours, but that I have loved, do love, and for ever shall love your beauteous daughter. If that be treason I do freely confess it, and will die a thousand deaths before you or any else shall enforce me to deny it, for I hold her highly worthy of my love. What you make offer of so willingly I have always desired; and if I had thought it would have been granted, long since I had most humbly requested it, and so much the more acceptable would it have been to me by how much the farther off it stood from my hopes. But if you be so forward as your words do witness, then feed me not with any further fruitless expectation, but rather send me back to prison, and lay as many afflictions on me as you please. For my

endeared love to your daughter Spina maketh me to love you the
more for her sake, how hardly soever you entreat me, and bindeth
me in the greater reverence to you as being the father of my fairest
friend."

Messer Currado hearing these words, stood as confounded with
admiration, reputing him to be a man of lofty spirit, and his affection most fervent to his daughter, which was not a little to his
liking. Wherefore, embracing him and kissing his cheek, without
any longer dallying, he sent in like manner for his daughter. Her
restraint in prison had made her looks meagre, pale, and wan, and
very weak was she also of her person, far differing from the woman
she was wont to be before her affection to Giannotto. There in
presence of her father, and with free consent of either, they were
contracted as man and wife, and the espousals agreed on according
to custom. Some few days after, without any one's knowledge of
that which was done, having furnished them with all things fit for
the purpose, and time aptly serving, that the mothers should be
partakers in this joy, he called his wife and Beritola, to whom first
he spake in this manner :

"What will you say, Madam, if I cause you to see your eldest
son, not long since married to one of my daughters?" Whereunto
Beritola thus replied : "My lord, I can say nothing else unto you
but that I shall be much more obliged to you than already I am;
and the rather because you will let me see the thing which is
dearer than mine own life ; and rendering it unto me in such
manner as you speak of, you will recall back some part of my
former lost hopes ;" and with these words the tears streamed
abundantly from her eyes. Then turning to his wife, he said :
"And you, dear love, if I show you such a son-in-law, what will
you think of it ?" " Sir," quoth she, " what pleaseth you must and
shall satisfy me, be he gentleman or beggar." "Well said, Madam,"
answered Messer Currado; "I hope shortly to make you both
joyful." So when the amorous couple had recovered their former
feature, and honourable garments prepared for them, privately thus
he said to Geoffrey : "Beyond the joy which already thou art
enriched withal, how would it please thee to meet with thine own
mother here ?" " I cannot believe, sir," replied Geoffrey, " that her
grievous misfortunes have suffered her to live so long ; and yet, if
heaven hath been so merciful to her, my joys were incomparable,
for by her gracious counsel I might well hope to recover no mean
happiness in Sicily." Soon after both the mothers were sent for,
who were transported with unspeakable joy when they beheld the
so-lately-married couple, being much amazed what inspiration had
guided Messer Currado to this extraordinary benignity in joining
Giannotto in marriage with Spina.

Hereupon Beritola, remembering the speeches between her and
Messer Currado, began to observe him very advisedly, and by a
hidden virtue which long had silently slept in her, and now with
joy of spirit awaked, calling to mind the lineaments of her son's
infancy, without awaiting for any other demonstration, she folded

him in her arms with earnest affection. Motherly joy and pity now contended so violently together that she was not able to utter one word, the sensitive virtues being so closely combined that, even as dead, she fell down in the arms of her son; and he, wondering greatly thereat, making a better recollection of his thoughts, remembered that he had before seen her in the castle without any other knowledge of her. Nevertheless, by mere instinct of nature, whose power in such actions declares itself to be highly predominate, his very soul assured him that she was his mother, and, blaming his understanding that he had not before been better advised, he threw his arms about her and wept exceedingly.

Afterward, by the loving pains of Currado's wife, as also her daughter Spina, Beritola, being recovered from her passionate trance, and her vital spirits executing their offices again, fell once more to the embracing of her son; kissing him infinite times, with tears and speeches of motherly kindness, he likewise expressing the same dutiful humanity to her. Which ceremonious courtesies being passed over and over, to no little joy in all the beholders, beside repetition of their several misfortunes, Messer Conrado made all known to his friends, who were very glad of this new alliance made by him, which was honoured with many solemn feastings ; which being all concluded, Geoffrey having found out fit place and opportunity for conference with his new-created father, without any sinister opposition, began as followeth :

" Honourable father, you have raised my contentment to the highest degree, and have heaped also many gracious favours on my noble mother, but now in the final conclusion, that nothing may remain uneffected which consisteth in your power to perform, I would humbly entreat you to honour my mother with your company at a feast of my making, where I would gladly also have my brother present. Messer Guasparrin d'Oria, as I have heretofore told you, questing as a common pirate on the seas, took us and sent us home to his house as slaves, where as yet he detaineth him. I would likewise send into Sicily one who, informing himself more amply in the state of the country, may understand what is become of Arrighetto my father, and whether he be living or no. If he be alive, then to know in what condition he is ; and being secretly instructed in all things, then to return back again to you."

This motion made by Geoffrey was so pleasing to Currado, that without any reference or further leisure, he dispatched thence two discreet persons, the one to Genoa and the other to Sicily ; he which went for Genoa, having met with Guasparrin, earnestly entreated him, on behalf of Currado, to send him the poor expelled, and his nurse ; recounting everything in order which Currado had told him concerning Geoffrey and his mother. When Guasparrin had heard the whole discourse, he marvelled greatly thereat, and said : " True it is that I will do anything for Messer Currado which may be to his love and liking, provided that it lie in my power to perform ; and, about some fourteen years since, I brought such a lad as you seek for, with his mother, home to my house, whom I will gladly send unto him. But you may tell him from me, that I advise him from over-rash crediting the fables of Giannotto, that now terms himself by the name of Geoffrey, because he is a more wicked boy than he taketh him to be, and so did I find him."

Having this spoken, and given kind welcome to the messenger, secretly he called the nurse unto him, whom he heedfully examined concerning this case. She having heard the rebellion in the kingdom of Sicily, and understanding withal that Arrighetto was yet living, joyfully threw off all her former fear, relating everything to him orderly, and the reasons moving her to conceal the whole business in such manner as she had done. Guasparrin well perceiving that the report of the nurse, and the message received from Currado, varied not in any one circumstance, began the better to credit her words. And being a man most ingenious, making further inquisition into the business by all the possible means that he could devise, and finding everything to yield undoubted assurance, ashamed of the vile and base usage wherein he had so long time kept the lad, and desiring by his best means to make him amends, he had a beautiful daughter, aged about thirteen years, and knowing what manner of man he was, his father Arrighetto also yet living, he gave her to him in marriage, with a bountiful and honourable dowry.

The jovial days of feasting being past, he went aboard a galley with the poor expelled, his daughter, the ambassador, and the nurse, departing thence to Lerici, where they were nobly welcomed by Messer Currado, and his castle being not far from thence, with an honourable train they were conducted thither and entertained with all possible kindness. Now concerning the comfort of the mother, meeting so happily with both her sons, the joy of the brethren and mother together; having also found the faithful nurse, Guasperrin and his daughter, in company now with Currado and his wife, friends, families, and all generally in a jubilee of rejoicing; it exceedeth capacity in me to express it, and therefore I refer it to your more able imagination.

In the time of this mutual contentment, to the end that nothing might be wanting to complete and perfect this universal joy, our lord, a most abundant bestower where he beginneth, added long-wished tidings concerning the life and good estate of Arrighetto Capece. For even as they were feasting, and the concourse great of worthy guests, both lords and ladies, the first service was scarcely set on the tables, but the ambassador who was sent to Sicily, arrived there before them. Among many other important matters, he spoke of Arrighetto, who being so long a time detained in prison by King Charles, when the commotion arose in the city against the king, the people, grudging at Arrighetto's long imprisonment, slew the guard, and set him at liberty. Then as capital enemy to King Charles, he was created Captain General, following the chase, and killing the French.

Now by this means he grew great in the grace of King Pedro,

who replanted him in all the goods and honours which he had before, with very high and eminent authority. Hereunto the ambassador added that he was entertained with extraordinary grace, and delivery of public joy and exaltation when his wife and son were known to be living, of whom no tidings had at any time been heard since the hour of his surprisal. Moreover, that a swift-winged bark was now sent thither, upon the happy hearing of this news, well furnished with noble gentlemen, to attend till their returning back. We need to make no doubt concerning the tidings brought by this ambassador, nor of the gentlemen's welcome, thus lent to Beritola and Geoffrey, who, before they would sit down at the table, saluted Messer Currado and his kind lady on the behalf of Arrighetto for all the great graces extended to her and her son, with promise of anything lying in the power of Henriet, to rest continually at their command. The like they did to Signor Guasparrin, whose liberal favours came unlooked for, with certain assurance that when Arrighetto should understand what he had done for his others on, the poor expelled, there would be no want of reciprocal courtesies.

As the longest joys have no perpetuity of lasting, so all these graceful ceremonies had their conclusion, with as many sighs and tears at parting as joys abounded at their first encountering. Imagine then that you see such aboard as were to have no longer abiding, Beritola, Geoffrey, with the rest, as the poor expelled, the so late married wives, and the faithful nurse bearing them company. With prosperous winds they arrived in Sicily, where the wife, sons, and daughters were joyfully met by Arrighetto at Palermo, and with such honourable pomp as a case so important equally deserved. The histories make further mention that there they lived, a long while after, in such felicity, with thankful hearts no doubt to heaven, in acknowledgment of so many great mercies received.

THE SEVENTH NOVEL.

The Soldan of Babylon sent one of his daughters to be joined in marriage with the King of Garbo, who by divers accidents, in the space of four years, happened into the custody of nine men, and in sundry places. At length, being restored back to her father, she went to the said King of Garbo, as at first she was intended to be his wife.

PERADVENTURE the novel related by Emilia did not extend itself so far in length as it moved compassion in the ladies' minds, hearing the hard fortune of Beritola and her children, which had incited them to weeping, but that it pleased the Queen, upon the tale's conclusion, to command Pamfilo to follow next in order with his discourse, and he being thereto very obedient, began in this manner :

It is a matter of no mean difficulty, virtuous ladies, for us to take entire knowledge of everything we do, because, as oftentimes hath been observed, many men imagine if they were rich, they should live securely and without any care. And therefore, not only have their prayers and intercessions aimed at that end, but also their studies and daily endeavours, without refusal of any pains or perils, have not meanly expressed their hourly solicitude. And although it hath happened accordingly to them and their covetous desires fully accomplished, yet at length they have met with such kind of people, who likewise thirsting after their wealthy possessions, have bereft them of life, being their kind and intimate friends, before they attained to such riches. Some other being of low and base condition, by adventuring in many skirmishes and having fought ten battles, trampling in the blood of their brethren and friends, have been mounted to the sovereign dignity of kingdoms, believing that therein consisted the truest happiness, but bought with the dearest price of their lives. For, beside their infinite cares and fears wherewith such greatness is continually attended, at their royal tables they have drunk poison in a golden pot. Many other in like manner, with most earnest appetite, have coveted beauty and bodily strength, not foreseeing with any judgment that these wishes were not without peril; when being endued with them, they either have been the occasion of their death, or such lingering lamentable estate of life, as death were a thousand times more welcome to them.

But because I would not speak particularly of all our frail and human affections, I dare assure you that there is not any one of these desires to be elected among us mortals, with entire foresight or providence, warrantable against their ominous issue. Wherefore, if we would walk directly, we should dispose our wills and affections to be guided only by Him who best knoweth what is needful for us, and will bestow them at His good pleasure. Nor let me lay this blameful imputation upon me only for offending in many things through our lavish desire, because you yourselves, gracious ladies, sin highly in one—namely, in coveting to be beautiful. So that it is not sufficient for you to enjoy those beauties bestowed on you by Nature, but you practise to increase them by the rarities of art. Wherefore let it not offend you that I tell you the hard fortune of a fair Saracen, to whom it happened by strange adventures that, within the compass of four years, nine several times she was married, and only for her beauty.

[OMITTED.]

THE EIGHTH NOVEL.

The Count of Anguersa being falsely accused, was banished out of France, and left his two children in England in divers places. Returning afterward, unknown, through Scotland he found them advanced unto great dignity. Then repairing in the habit of a servitor into the King of France's army, and his innocency made publicly known, he was reseated in his honourable degree.

THE ladies sighed very often, hearing the variety of woful miseries happening to Alatiel ; but who knoweth what occasion moved them to those sighs ?   Perhaps there were some among them who rather sighed they could not be so often married as she was, rather than for any other compassion they had of her disasters. But leaving that to their own construction, they smiled merrily at the last speeches of Pamfilo.   And the Queen, perceiving the novel to be ended, she fixed her eye on Elisa, as signifying thereby that she was the next to succeed in order, which she, joyfully embracing, spake as followeth :

The field is large wherein all this day we have walked, and there is not any one here so wearied with running the former races but nimbly would adventure on as many more, so copious are the alterations of fortune, in sad repetition of her wonderful changes, and among the infinity of her various courses, I must make addition of another, which I trust will no way discontent you.

[OMITTED.]

THE NINTH NOVEL.

Bernabò, a merchant of Genoa, being deceived by another merchant named Ambruogivolo, lost a great part of his goods.   And commanding his innocent wife to be murdered, she escaped, and, in the habit of a man, became servant to the Soldan.   The deceiver being found at last, she compassed such means that her husband Bernabò came into Alexandria, and there after due punishment inflicted on the false deceiver, she resumed the garments again of a woman, and returned home with her husband to Genoa.

ELISA having ended her compassionate discourse, which indeed had moved all the rest to sighing, the Queen, who was fair, comely of stature, and carrying a very majestical countenance, smiling more familiarly than the other, spake to them thus : " It is very necessary that the promise made to Dioneo should carefully be kept ; and because now there remaineth none to report any more novels but only he and myself, I must deliver mine, and he who takes it for an honour to be the last in relating his own last, let him be for his own deliverance."   Then, pausing a little while, thus she began again :

"Many times among vulgar people it hath passed as a common proverb, that the deceiver is often trampled on by such as he hath deceived; and this cannot show itself by any reason to be true, except such accidents as await on treachery do really make a just discovery thereof. And therefore, according to the course of this day observed, I am the woman that must make good what I have said for the approbation of that proverb; no way, I hope, distasteful to you in the hearing, but advantageable to preserve you from any such beguiling: There was a fair and goodly inn in Paris much frequented by many great Italian merchants, according to such variety of occasions and business as urged their often resorting thither. One night, among many other, having had a merry supper together, they began to discourse on divers matters, and falling from one relation to another, they communed in very friendly manner concerning their wives, left at home in their houses. Quoth the first: "I cannot well imagine what my wife is now doing, but I am able to say for myself that if a pretty female should fall into my company, I could easily forget my love to my wife."

A second replied: "And trust me I should do no less, because I am persuaded that if my wife be willing to wander, the law is in her own hand, and I am far enough from home; dumb walls blab no tales, and offences unknown are seldom or ever called in question." A third man was apt to censure with his former fellows of the jury; and it plainly appeared that all the rest were of the same opinion, condemning their wives over-rashly.

Only one man among them all, named Bernabò Lomellin, and dwelling in Genoa, maintained the contrary, boldly avouching that, by the special favour of fortune, he had a wife so perfectly complete in all graces and virtues as any lady in the world possibly could be, and that Italy scarcely contained her equal. She was goodly of person, and yet very young, quick, quaint, mild, and courteous, and not wanting anything appertaining to the office of a wife, either for domestic affairs, or any other employment whatsoever, but in womanhood she went beyond all other. No lord, knight, esquire, or gentleman, could be better served at his table than himself daily was, with more wisdom, modesty, and discretion. After all this he praised her for riding, hawking, hunting, fishing, fowling, reading, writing, inditing, and most absolute keeping his books of accounts, that neither himself nor any other merchant could therein excel her. After infinite other commendations, he came to the former point of their argument, maintaining with a solemn oath that no woman possibly could be more honest than she; in which respect he was verily persuaded that if he stayed from her ten years' space, yea all his lifetime, out of his house, yet never would she falsify her faith to him.

Amongst these merchants thus communing together there was a young proper man, named Ambruogivolo, of Piacenza, who began to laugh at the last praises which Bernabò had used of his wife, and seeming to make a mockery thereto, demanded if the Emperor had given him this privilege above all other married men? Bernabò being somewhat offended answered: "No emperor hath done it, but the especial blessing of heaven, exceeding all the emperors on the

earth in grace, and thereby I have received this favour." Whereto
Ambruogivolo presently thus replied : " Bernabò, without all question to the contrary, I believe that what thou hast said is true ; but
for aught I can perceive ,thou hast slender judgment in the nature
of things, because if thou didst observe them well, thou couldst not
be of so gross understanding. For, by comprehending matters in
their kind and nature, thou wouldst speak of them more correctly
than thou dost ; and to the end thou mayest not imagine that we
who have spoken of our wives do think any otherwise of them than
as well and honestly as thou canst of thine, nor that anything else
did urge these speeches of them, or falling into this kind of discourse, but only by a natural instinct and admonition, I will proceed
familiarly a little further with thee upon the matter already propounded.

"I have evermore understood that man was the most noble
creature formed by God to live in this world, and woman in the
next degree to him ; but man, as generally is believed, and as is
discerned by apparent effects, is the most perfect of both. Having
then the most perfection in him, without all doubt he must be so
much the more firm and constant. So in like manner, it hath
been, and is universally granted, that women are more various and
mutable, and the reason thereof may be approved by many natural
circumstances, which were needless now to make any mention of.
If a man then be possessed of the greater stability, and yet cannot
contain himself from condescending, I say not to one that entreats
him, but to desire any other that may please him ; and beside, to
covet the enjoying of his own pleasing contentment (a thing not
chancing to him once in a month, but infinite times in a day's
space) ; what can you then conceive of a frail woman, subject by
nature to entreaties, flatteries, gifts, persuasions, and a thousand
other enticing means which a man that is affected to her can use ?
For I am sure thou believest, and must needs confess it, that thy
wife is a woman made of flesh and blood, as other women are ; if
it be so, she cannot be without the same desires, and the weakness
or strength, as other women have, to resist natural appetites as her
own are. In regard whereof it is merely impossible, although she
be most honest, but she must needs do that which other women do ;
for there is nothing else possible, either to be denied or affirmed to
the contrary, as thou most unadvisedly hast done."

Bernabò answered in this manner : " I am a merchant, and no
philosopher, and like a merchant I mean to answer thee. I am not
to learn that these accidents by thee related may happen to fools,
who are void of understanding or shame, but such as are wise, and
endued with virtue, have always such a precious esteem of their
honour that they will contain those principles of constancy which
men are merely careless of, and I justify my wife to be one of them."
Believe me, Bernabò," replied Ambruogivolo, "that what women
may accomplish in secret they will rarely fail to do ; or if they
abstain, it is through fear and folly. Yea, and let me tell thee more,
Bernabò, were I in private company with thy wife, howsoever thou

presumest to think her to be, I should account it a matter of no impossibility to find in her the self-same frailty.

Bernabò's blood now began to boil, and patience being a little put down by choler, thus he replied : "A combat of words requires over-long continuance, for I maintain the matter which thou deniest, and all this sorts to nothing in the end. But seeing thou presumest that all women are so apt and tractable, and thyself so confident of thine own power, I willingly yield, for the better assurance of my wife's constant loyalty, to have my head smitten off if thou canst win her to any such dishonest act by any means whatsoever thou canst use unto her, which if thou canst not do, thou shalt only lose a thousand ducats of gold." Now began Ambruogivolo to be heated with these words, answering thus Bernabò : "If I had won the wager, I know not what I should do with thy head, but if thou be willing to stand npon the proof, pawn down five thousand ducats of gold—a matter of much less value than thy head—against a thousand ducats of mine, granting me a lawful limited time, which I require to be no more than the space of three months after the day of my departing hence. I will stand bound to go for Genoa, and there win such kind consent of thy wife as shall be to mine own content. In witness whereof I will bring back with me such private and especial tokens as thou thyself shalt confess I have not failed; provided that thou do first promise upon thy faith to absent thyself from thence during my limited time, and be no hindrance to me by thy letters concerning the attempt by me undertaken."

Bernabò said : " Be it a bargain. I am the man that will make good my five thousand ducats." And albeit the other merchants then present earnestly laboured to break the wager, knowing great harm must needs ensue thereon, yet both the parties were so hot and fiery as all the other men spake to no effect; but writings were made, sealed, and delivered under either of their hands, Bernabò remaining at Paris and Ambruogivolo departing for Genoa. There he remained some few days to learn the street's name where Bernabò dwelt, as also the conditions and qualities of his wife, which scarcely pleased him when he heard them, because they were far beyond her husband's relation, and she reputed to be the only wonder of women, whereby he plainly perceived that he had undertaken a very idle enterprise, yet would he not give it over so, but proceeded therein a little further.

He wrought such means that he came acquainted with a poor woman who often frequented Bernabò's house, and was greatly in favour with his wife, upon whose poverty he so prevailed by earnest persuasions, but much more by large gifts of money, that he won her to further him in this manner following. A fair and artificial chest he caused to be purposely made wherein himself might be aptly contained, and so conveyed into the house of Bernabò's wife under the colour of a formal excuse, that the poor woman should be absent from the city two or three days, and she must keep it safe till she return. The gentlewoman, suspecting no guile but that the chest was the receptacle of all the woman's wealth, would trust it in no other room than her own bed-chamber, which was the place where Ambruogivolo most desired to be.

Being thus conveyed into the chamber, the night going on apace, and the gentlewoman fast asleep in her bed, a lighted taper stood burning on the table by her as in her husband's absence she ever used to have ; Ambruogivolo softly opened the chest according as cunningly he had contrived it, and stepping forth in his socks made of cloth, observed the situation of the chamber, the paintings, pictures, and beautiful hangings, with all things else that were remarkable, which perfectly he committed to his memory ; going near to the bed, he saw her lie there sweetly sleeping, and her young daughter in like manner by her, she seeming then as complete and pleasing a creature as when she was attired in her best bravery. No especial note or mark could he descry whereof he might make credible report, but only a small wart upon her left pap, with some few hairs growing thereon, appearing to be as yellow as gold.

Sufficient had he seen and durst presume no further ; but taking one of the rings which lay upon the table, a purse of hers, hanging on the wall by a light wearing robe of silk, and her girdle, all which he put into the chest, and being in himself, closed it fast as it was before, so continuing there in the chamber two several nights, the gentlewoman neither mistrusting or missing anything. The third day being come, the poor woman, according as formerly was con. cluded, came to have home her chest again, and brought it safely into her own house, where Ambruogivolo coming forth of it, satisfied the poor woman to her own liking, returning, with all the forenamed things, as fast as conveniently he could to Paris.

Being arrived there long before his limited time, he called the merchants together who were present at the passed words and wagers, avouching before Bernabò that he had won his five thousand ducats, and performed the task he undertook. To make good his protestation, first he described the form of the chamber, the curious pictures hanging about it, in what manner the bed stood, and every circumstance else beside. Next he showed the several things which he brought away thence with him, affirming that he had received them of herself. Bernabò confessed that his description of the chamber was true, and acknowledged, moreover, that these other things did belong to his wife ; "but," quoth he, "this may be gotten by corrupting some servant of mine, both for intelligence of the chamber, as also of the ring, purse, and what else is beside, all which suffice not to win the wager without some more apparent and pregnant token." "In troth," answered Ambruogivolo, "methinks these should serve for sufficient proofs, but seeing thou art so desirous to know more, I plainly tell thee that fair Ginevra, thy wife, hath a small round wart upon her left pap, and some few little golden hairs growing thereon."

When Bernabò heard these words they were as so many stabs to his heart, yea, beyond all compass of patient sufferance, and by the changing his colour it was noted manifestly, being unable to utter one word, that Ambruogivolo had spoken nothing but the truth. Within a while after he said : " Gentlemen, that which Ambruogivolo hath said is very true, wherefore let him come when he will and he shall be paid ;" which accordingly he performed on the very next day, even to the utmost penny ; departing then from Paris towards Genoa with a most malicious intention to his wife. Being come near to the city, he would not enter it, but rode to a country house of his, standing about ten miles distant thence. Being there arrived, he called a servant in whom he reposed especial trust, sending him to Genoa with two horses, writing to his wife that he was returned, and she should come thither to see him ; but secretly he charged his servant that so soon as he had brought her to a convenient place, he should there kill her without any pity or compassion, and then return to him again.

When the servant was come to Genoa, and had delivered his letter and message, Ginevra gave him most joyful welcome, and on the morrow morning, mounted on horseback with the servant, rode merrily toward the country house. Divers things she discoursed on by the way, till they descended into a deep solitary valley, very thickly beset with high and huge spreading trees, which the servant supposed to be a meet place for the execution of his master's command. Suddenly drawing forth his sword, and holding Ginevra fast by the arm, he said : " Mistress, quickly commend your soul to God, for you must die before you may forward pass any further." Ginevra seeing the naked sword, and hearing the words so peremptorily delivered, fearfully answered : " Alas, dear friend, mercy for God's sake ; and before thou kill me, tell me wherein I have offended thee, and why you must kill me ?" " Alas, good mistress, you have not offended me, but in what occasion you have displeased your husband it is utterly unknown to me, for he hath strictly commanded me, without respect of pity or compassion, to kill you by the way as I bring you, and if I do it not, he hath sworn to hang me by the neck. You know, good mistress, how much I stand obliged to him, and how impossible it is for me to contradict anything that he commandeth. God is my witness that I am truly compassionate of you, and yet by no means may I let you live."

Ginevra kneeling before him weeping, wringing her hands, thus replied : " Wilt thou turn monster, and be a murderer of her that never wronged thee, to please another man, and on a bare command ? God, who truly knoweth all things, is my faithful witness that I never committed any offence whereby to incur the dislike of my husband, much less so harsh a recompense as this is. But flying from mine own justification, and appealing to thy manly mercy, thou mayest, wert thou but so well pleased, in a moment satisfy both thy master and me in such manner as I will make plain and apparent to thee. Take thou my garments, spare me only thy doublet and such a bonnet as is fitting for a man ; so return with my habit to thy master, assuring him that the deed is done. And here I swear to thee, by that life which I enjoy but by thy mercy, I will so strangely disguise myself, and wander so far off from these countries, as neither he nor thou, nor any person belonging to these parts, shall ever hear any tidings of me."

The servant, who had no great good will to kill her, very easily grew pitiful, took off her upper garments, and gave her a poor ragged doublet, a rustic hat, and such small store of money as he had, desiring her to forsake that country, and so left her to walk on foot out of the valley. When he came to his master, and had delivered him her garments, he assured him that he had not only accomplished his command, but also was most secure from any discovery, because he had no sooner done the deed, but four or five very ravenous wolves came presently running to the dead body and gave it burial in their bellies. Bernabò soon after returning to Genoa, was much blamed for such unkind cruelty to his wife, but his constant avouching of her treason to him, according then to the country's custom, did clear him from all pursuit of law.

Poor Ginevra was left thus alone and disconsolate, and night stealing fast upon her, she went to a silly village near adjoining, where, by the means of a good old woman, she got such provision as the place afforded, making the doublet fit to her body, and converted her petticoat to a pair of breeches, according to the mariner's fashion; then cutting her hair, and quaintly disguised like unto a sailor, she went to the sea-coast. By good fortune, she met there with a gentleman of Catalonia, whose name was Señor Encararh, who came on land from his ship, which lay hulling there about Alba, to refresh himself at a pleasant spring. Encararh, taking her to be a man, as she appeared no otherwise by her habit, upon some conference passing between them, she was entertained into his service, and being brought aboard the ship, she went under the name of Sicuran da Finale. There she had better apparel bestowed on her by the gentleman, and her service proved so pleasing and acceptable to him that he liked her care and diligence beyond all comparison.

It came to pass within a short while after, that this gentleman of Catalonia sailed, with some charge of his, into Alexandria, carrying thither certain falcons, which he presented to the Sultan, who oftentimes welcomed this gentleman to his table, where he observed the behaviour of Sicuran, attending on his master's trencher, and therewith was so highly pleased that he requested to have him from the gentleman, who, for his more advancement, willingly parted with his so lately entertained servant. Sicuran was so ready and discreet in his daily services, that he grew in as great grace with the Sultan as before he had done with Encararh.

At a certain season in the year, as customary order there observed, had formerly been in the city of Acre, which was under the Sultan's subjection, there yearly met a great assembly of merchants—as Christians, Moors, Jews, Saracens, and many other nations besides—as at a common mart or fair. And to the end that the merchants, for the better sale of their goods, might be there in the safer assurance, the Sultan used to send thither some of his ordinary officers, and a strong guard of soldiers beside, to defend them from all injuries and molestation, because he reaped thereby no small benefit. And who should be now sent about this business but his new elected favourite Sicuran, because she was skilful and perfect in the languages.

Sicuran being come to Acre, as lord and captain of the guard for the merchants and for the safety of their merchandise, she discharged her office most commendably, walking with her train through every part of the fair, where she observed a worthy company of merchants—Sicilians, Pisans, Genoese, Venetians, and other Italians—whom the more willingly she noted in remembrance of her native country. At one especial time, among others, chancing into a shop or booth belonging to the Venetians, she espied, hanging up with other costly wares, a purse and a girdle, which suddenly she remembered to be sometime her own, whereat she was not a little abashed in her mind. But without making any such outward show, courteously she requested to know whose they were, and whether they should be sold or no.

Ambruogivolo of Piacenza was likewise come thither, and great store of merchandise he had brought with him, in a carrack appertaining to the Venetians; and he, hearing the captain of the guard demand whose they were, stepped forth before him, and smiling answered that they were his, but not to be sold; yet if he liked them, gladly he would bestow them on him. Sicuran, seeing him smile, suspected lest himself had, by some unfitting behaviour, been the occasion thereof, and therefore, with a more settled countenance, he said : "Perhaps thou smilest because I, that am a man possessing arms, should question after such womanish toys." Ambruogivolo replied : "My lord, pardon me ; I smile not at you or at your demand, but at the manner how I came by these things."

Sicuran, upon this answer, was ten times more desirous than before, and said : "If fortune favoured thee in friendly manner by the obtaining of these things, if it may be spoken, tell me how thou hadst them." "My lord," answered Ambruogivolo, "these things, with many more besides, were given me by a gentlewoman in Genoa, named Ginevra, the wife to one Bernabò Lomellin, in a recompense of one night's lodging with her, and she desired me to keep them for her sake. Now, the main reason of my smiling was the remembrance of her husband's folly, in waging five thousand ducats of gold against one thousand of mine, that I should not obtain my will of his wife, which I did, and thereby won the wager. But he, who better deserved to be punished for his folly than she, who was but sick of all women's disease, returning from Paris to Genoa, caused her to be slain, as was reported by himself."

When Sicuran heard this horrible lie, immediately she conceived that this was the occasion of her husband's hatred to her and all the hardships which she had since suffered; whereupon she reputed it for more than a mortal sin if such a villain should pass without due punishment. Sicuran seemed to like well this report, and grew into such familiarity with Ambruogivolo, that by her persuasions, when the fair was ended, she took him higher with her into Alexandria, and all his wares along with him, furnishing him with a fit and convenient shop, where he made great benefit of his merchandise, trusting all his money in the captain's custody, because it was the safest course for him, and so he continued there with no mean contentment.

Much did she pity her husband's perplexity, devising by what good and warrantable means she might make known her innocency to him ; wherein her place and authority did greatly stead her, and she wrought with divers gallant merchants of Genoa that then remained in Alexandria, and by virtue of the Sultan's friendly letters besides, to bring him thither upon an especial occasion. Come he did, albeit in poor and mean order, which soon was better altered by her appointment, and he very honourably, though in private, entertained by divers of her worthy friends till time did favour what she further intended.

In the expectation of Bernabò's arrival, she had so prevailed with Ambruogivolo, that the same tale which he formerly told to her he delivered again in presence of the Sultan, who seemed to be well pleased with it. But after she had once seen her husband, she thought upon her more serious business, providing herself of an apt opportunity, when she entreated such favour of the Sultan that both the men might be brought before him, where, if Ambruogivolo would not confess without constraint that which he had made his vaunt of concerning Bernabò's wife, he might be compelled thereto perforce.

Sicuran's word was a law with the Sultan, so that, Ambruogivolo and Bernabò being brought face to face, the Sultan, with a stern and angry countenance, in the presence of a most princely assembly, commanded Ambruogivolo to declare the truth, upon the peril of his life, by what means he won the wager of the five thousand golden ducats he received of Bernabò. Ambruogivolo, seeing Sicurano there present, upon whose favour he wholly relied, yet perceiving her look likewise to be as dreadful as the Sultan's, and hearing her threatening him most grievous torments except he revealed the truth indeed, you may easily guess in what condition he stood at that instant.

Frowns and fury he beheld on either side, and Bernabò standing before him, with a world of witnesses, to hear his lie confounded by his own confession, and his tongue to deny what it had before so constantly avouched. Yet dreaming on no other pain or penalty but restoring back the five thousand ducats of gold and the other things by him purloined, truly he revealed the whole form of his falsehood. Then Sicuran, according as the Sultan formerly had commanded him, turning to Bernabò, said : "And thou, upon the suggestion of this foul lie, what didst thou do to thy wife?" "Being," quoth Bernabò, "overcome with rage for the loss of my money, and the dishonour I supposed to receive by my wife, I caused a servant of mine to kill her, and, as he credibly avouched, her body was devoured by ravenous wolves in a moment after."

These things being spoken and heard in the presence of the Sultan, and no reason as yet made known why the case was so seriously urged, and to what end it would succeed, Sicuran spoke in this manner to the Sultan : " My gracious lord, you may plainly perceive in what degree that poor gentlewoman might make her vaunt, being so well provided both of a loving friend and a husband. Such was the friend's love, that in an instant, and by a wicked lie, he robbed her both of renown and honour, and bereft her also of her husband. And her husband, rather crediting falsehood than the invincible truth, whereof he had faithful knowledge by long and very honourable experience, caused her to be slain and made food for devouring wolves. Beside all this, such was the goodwill and affection borne to that woman both by friend and husband, that the longest continuer of them in their company makes them alike in knowledge of her. But because your great wisdom knoweth perfectly what each of them hath worthily deserved, if you please, in your ever-known gracious benignity, to permit the punishment of the deceiver and pardon the party so deceived, I will procure such means that she shall appear here in your presence and theirs."

The Sultan, being desirous to give Sicuran all manner of satisfaction, having followed the course so industriously, bade him to produce the woman, and he was well contented. Whereat Bernabò stood much amazed, because he verily believed that she was dead. And Ambruogivolo, foreseeing already a preparation for punishment, feared that the repayment of the money would not now serve his turn, not knowing also what he should further hope or suspect if the woman herself did personally appear, which he imagined would be a miracle. Sicuran, having thus obtained the Sultan's permission, in tears, humbling herself at his feet, in a moment she lost her manly voice and demeanour, as knowing that she was now no longer tò use them, but must truly witness what she was indeed, and therefore thus spake :

"Great Sultan, I am the miserable and unfortunate Ginevra, that for the space of six whole years have wandered through the world in the habit of a man, falsely and most maliciously slandered by the villanous traitor Ambruogivolo, and by this unkind cruel husband, betrayed to his servant to be slain, and left to be devoured by savage beasts. Afterwards desiring such garments as better befitted her, and showing her breasts, she made it apparent before the Sultan and his assistants that she was the same woman indeed. Then turning herself to Ambruogivolo, with more than manly courage she demanded of him when and where it was that he lay with her, as, villanously, he was not ashamed to make his vaunt? But he having already acknowledged the contrary, being stricken dumb with shameful disgrace, was not able to utter one word.

The Sultan who had always reputed Sicuran to be a man, having heard and seen so admirable an incident, was so amazed in his mind that many times he was very doubtful whether this was a dream or an absolute relation of truth. But after he had more seriously considered thereon, and found it to be real and infallible, with extraordinary gracious praises, he recommended the life, constancy, condition and virtues of Ginevra, whom till that time he had always called Sicuran. So committing her to the company of honourable ladies to be changed from her manly habits, he pardoned Bernabò her husband, according to her request formerly made, although he had more justly deserved ; which likewise himself confessed, and falling at the feet of Ginevra, desired her, in tears, to forgive his rash transgression, which most lovingly she did, kissing and embracing him a thousand times.

Then the Sultan strictly commanded that on some high and eminent place of the city, Ambruogivolo should be bound and impaled on a stake, having his naked body anointed all over with honey, and never to be taken off, until of itself it fell in pieces, which according to the sentence was presently performed. Next he gave express charge that all his money and goods should be given to Ginevra, which was valued above ten thousand double ducats. Forthwith a solemn feast was prepared wherein much honour was done to Bernabò, being the husband of Ginevra : and to her, as to a most worthy woman and matchless wife, he gave in costly jewels, as also vessels of gold and silver plate, so much as did amount to above ten thousand double ducats more.

When the feasting was finished he caused a ship to be furnished for them, granting them licence to depart for Genoa when they pleased ; whither they returned most richly and joyfully, being welcomed home with great honour, especially Ginevra, whom every one supposed to be dead ; and always after, so long as she lived, she was most famous for her manifold virtues. But as for Ambruogivolo, the very same day that he was impaled on a stake, anointed with honey, and fixed in the place appointed to his no mean torment, he not only died, but likewise was devoured to the bare bones by flies, wasps, and hornets, whereof the country notoriously aboundeth. And his bones, in full form and fashion, remained strangely black for a long time after, knit together by the sinews, as a witness to many thousands of people, which afterwards beheld the carcase, of his wickedness against so good and virtuous a woman, that had not a thought of evil towards him. And thus was the proverb truly verified, that shame succeedeth after ugly sin, and the deceiver is trampled and trod by such as himself hath deceived.

THE TENTH NOVEL.

Paganino da Monaco, a roving pirate on the seas, carried away the fair wife of Signor Ricciardo di Chinzica, who, understanding where she was, went thither, and falling into friendship with Paganino, demanded his wife of him, whereto he yielded—provided that she would willingly go away with him. She denied to part thence with her husband, and Signor Ricciardo dying, she became the wife of Paganino.

EVERY ONE in this honest and gracious assembly most highly commended the novel recounted by the Queen, but especially Dioneo, who remained to finish that day's pleasure with his own discourse, and after many praises of the former tale were past thus he began : Fair ladies, part of the Queen's novel hath made an alteration of my mind from that which I intended to proceed next withal, and therefore I will report another.

[OMITTED.]

This tale was so merrily entertained among the whole company, that each one, smiling upon another, with one consent commended Dioneo, maintaining that he spake nothing but the truth, and condemning Bernabò for his cruelty. Upon a general silence commanded, the Queen, perceiving that the time was now very far spent, and every one had delivered their several novels, which likewise gave a period to her royalty, she gave the crown to Neifile, pleasantly speaking to her in this order : "Hereafter the government of this poor people is committed to your trust and care, for with the day concludeth my dominion." Madam Neifile, blushing at the honour that was done unto her, her cheeks appeared of a vermilion tincture, her eyes glittering with graceful desires and sparkling like the morning star. And after the modest murmur of the assistants was ceased, and her courage in cheerful manner settled, seating herself higher than she did before, thus she spake :

"Seeing it is so that you have elected me your Queen, to vary somewhat from the course observed by them that went before me, whose government you have all so much commended, by approbation of your counsel I am desirous to speak my mind concerning what I would have to be next followed. It is not unknown to you all that to-morrow shall be Friday, and Saturday the next day following, which are days somewhat molestous to the most part of men, for preparation of their weekly food and sustenance. Moreover, Friday ought to be reverently respected, in remembrance of Him who died to give us life, and endured His bitter passion as on that day, which makes me hold it fit and expedient that we should mind more weighty matters, and rather attend our prayers and devotions than the repetition of tales or novels. Now, concerning Saturday, it hath been a custom observed among women to bathe and wash themselves from such immundicities as the former week's toil hath imposed on them. Beside, it is a day of fasting in honour of the ensuing Sabbath, whereon no labour may be done but the observation of holy exercises.

" By that which hath been said, you may easily perceive that the course which we have hitherto continued cannot be prosecuted in one and the same manner. Wherefore, I would advise, and do hold it an action well performed by us, to cease for these few days from recounting any other novels. And because we have remained here four days already, except we would allow the enlarging of our company with some other friends that may resort unto us, I think it necessary to remove from hence and take our pleasure in another place, which is already by me determined. When we shall be there assembled, and have slept on the discourses formerly delivered, let our next argument be still the mutabilities of Fortune, but especially to concern such persons as by their wit and ingenuity industriously have attained to some matter earnestly desired, or else recovered again after the loss. Hereon let us severally study and premeditate, that the hearers may receive benefit thereby, with the comfortable maintenance of our harmless recreations, the privilege of Dioneo always reserved to himself.'

Every one commended the Queen's deliberation, concluding that it should be accordingly prosecuted, and thereupon the master of the household was called, to give him order for that evening's table service, and what else concerned the time of the Queen's royalty, wherein he was sufficiently instructed ; which being done, the company arose, licensing every one to do what they listed. The ladies and gentlemen walked to the garden, and having sported there a while, when the hour of supper came they sat down and fared very daintily. Being risen from table, according to the Queen's command, Emilia led the dance, and the ditty following was sung by Pampinea, being answered by all the rest as a chorus :

THE SONG.

And if not I, what lady else can sing
Of those delights which kind contentment bring?
Come, come, sweet love, the cause of my chief good,
   Of all my hopes, the firm and full effect ;
Sing we together, but in no sad mood
   Of sighs or tears, which joy doth countercheck :
Stolen pleasures are delightful in the taste,
   But yet love's fire is oftentimes too fierce,
Consuming comfort with o'er-speedy haste,
   Which into gentle hearts too far doth pierce.
      And if not I, &c.

The first day that I felt this fiery heat,
   So sweet a passion did possess my soul,
That though I found the torment sharp and great,
   Yet still methought 'twas but a sweet control,
Nor could I count it rude or rigorous
   Taking my wound from such a piercing eye,
As made the pain most pleasing, gracious,
   That I desire in such assaults to die.
      And if not I, &c.

Grant then, great God of Love, that I may still
  Enjoy the benefit of my desire ;
And honour her with all my deepest skill,
  That first inflamed my heart with holy fire.
To her my bondage is free liberty ;
  My sickness, health ; my torture, sweet repose ;
Say she the word in full felicity,   .
  All my extremes join in a happy close.
        Then if not I, what lover else can sing
        Of those delights which kind contentment bring ?

After this song was ended they sung divers other besides, and,
having great variety of instruments, they played to them as many
pleasing dances. But the Queen considering that the meet hour
for rest was not yet come, with their lighted torches before them,
they all repaired to their chambers, sparing the other days next
succeeding for those reasons by the Queen alleged, and spending
the Sunday in solemn devotion.

THE THIRD DAY.

Upon which day all matters to be discoursed on do pass under the regimen of Nefile, concerning such persons as, by their wit and industry, have attained to their long-wished desires, or recovered something supposed to be lost.

INDUCTION.

THE vermillion glow of the morning was changed already to orange by the sun's approach, when the Queen and all the fair company were come abroad forth of their chambers ; the seneschal or great master of the household having long before sent all things necessary to the place of their next intended meeting, and the people who prepared there every needful matter suddenly, when they saw the Queen was setting forward, charged all the rest of their followers, as if it had been preparation for a camp, to make haste away with the carriages ; the rest of the family remaining behind, to attend upon the ladies and gentlemen.

With a mild, majestic, and gentle pace the Queen rode on, being followed by the other ladies and the three young gentlemen, taking the way towards the west, conducted by the musical notes of sweet singing nightingales and infinite other pretty birds beside, riding in a tract not much frequented but richly abounding with fair herbs and flowers ; which by reason of the sun's high mounting, began to open their bosom and fill the fresh air with their odoriferous perfumes. Before they had travelled two small miles distance, all of them pleasantly conversing together, they arrived at another goodly palace, which, being somewhat mounted above the plain, was seated on the side of a little rising hill.

When they were entered thereinto, and had seen the great hall, the parlours, and beautiful chambers, every one so stupendously furnished, with all convenient commodities to them belonging, and nothing wanting that could be desired, they highly commended it, reputing the lord thereof for a most worthy man that had adorned it in such princely manner. Afterward, being descended lower, and noting the most spacious and pleasant court, the cellars stored with the choicest wines, and delicate springs of water everywhere running, their praises exceeded more and more. And being weary with beholding such variety of pleasures, they sat down in a fair gallery, which took the view of the whole court, it being round engirt with trees and flowers, whereof the season then yielded great plenty ; and then came the discreet master of the household, with divers servants attending on him, presenting them with comfits and other banqueting, as also very singular wines, to serve instead of breakfast.

Having thus reposed themselves awhile, a gate was set open to them of a garden, coasting on one side the palace and round enclosed with high mounted walls. Whereinto, when they were entered, they found it to be a most beautiful garden, stored with all varieties that possibly could be devised ; and therefore they observed it the more respectively.. The walks and alleys were good and spacious, yet directly straight as an arrow, environed with spreading vines, whereon the grapes hung in copious clusters, which, being come to their full ripeness, gave so rare a smell throughout the garden, with other sweet savours intermixed among, that they seemed to be among all the spices that had ever been brought from the East.

By the sides of the paths grew red and white roses and sweet jasmine, that let the morning light pass through, but gave just overhead an odorous shade from the noon sun. In the midst of this garden was a square plot, after the resemblance of a meadow, flourishing with high grass, herbs, and plants, besides a thousand diversities of flowers. Round was it, encircled with very verdant orange and cedar trees, their branches plenteously stored with fruit both old and new, as also the flowers growing among them, yielding not only a rare aspect to the eye, but also a delicate flavour to the smell.

In the midst of this meadow stood a fountain of white marble, whereon was engraven most admirable workmanship, and within it—I know not whether it were by a natural vein or artificial— flowing from a figure standing on a column in the midst of the fountain, such abundance of water, and so mounting up toward the skies, that it was a wonder to behold ; for after the high ascent, it fell down again into the bosom of the fountain with such a noise and pleasing murmur as the stream that glideth from a mill. When the receptacle of the fountain did overflow the bounds it streamed along the meadow by secret passages and channels, very fair and artificially made, returning again into every part of the meadow, by the like ways of cunning conveyance, which allowed it a full course into the garden, running swiftly thence down towards the plain ; but before it came thither the very swift current of the stream did drive two goodly mills, which brought in great benefit to the lord of the soil.

The sight of this garden, the goodly grafts, plants, trees, herbs, fruitages, and flowers, the springs, fountains, and pretty rivulets streaming from it, so highly pleased the ladies and gentlemen that, among other infinite commendations, they spared not to say, if any paradise remained on the earth to be seen, it could not possibly be in any other place, but only was contained within the compass of this garden. With no mean pleasure and delight they walked round about it, making chaplets of flowers and other fair branches of the trees, continually hearing the birds in melodious notes, echoing and warbling one to another, even as if they envied each other's felicities.

But yet another beauty, which before had not presented itself to them; on a sudden they perceived divers creatures in many parts of the garden. In one place conies tripping about, in another place hares, in a third part goats browsing on the herbs, and little young hinds feeding everywhere, yet without strife or warring together, but rather living in such a domestic and pleasing kind of company even as if they were appointed to instruct the most noble of all creatures to imitate their sociable conversation.

When their senses had sufficiently banqueted on those several beauties, the tables were suddenly prepared about the fountain, where first they sung six canzonets ; and having paced two or three dances they sat down to dinner, according as the Queen ordained, being served in very sumptuous manner with all kind of costly and delicate viands, yet not any babbling noise among them. The tables being withdrawn, they played again upon their instruments, singing and dancing gracefully together, till, in regard of the extreme heat, the Queen commanded to give over, and permitted such as were so pleased to take their ease and rest. But some, as not satisfied with the place's pleasures, gave themselves to walking, others fell to reading the lives of the Romans, some to chess, and the rest to other recreations.

But after the day's warmth was more mildly qualified, and every one had made benefit of the best content, they went, by order sent from the Queen, into the meadow where the fountain stood, and being set about it as they used to do in telling their tales—the argument appointed by the Queen being propounded—the first that had the charge imposed was Filostrato, who began in this manner :—

THE FIRST NOVEL.

Masetto da Lamporecchio, by counterfeiting himself to be dumb, became a gardener in a monastery of nuns.

[OMITTED.]

THE SECOND NOVEL.

An cquerry of the stable belonging to Agilulf, King of the Lombards, found the means of access to the queen without any knowledge or consent in her. This being secretly discovered by the king, and the party known, he gave him a mark by shearing the hair off his head. Whereupon he that was so shorn, sheared likewise all his fellows in the lodging, and so escaped the punishment intended towards him.

WHEN the novel of Filostrato was concluded, which made some of the ladies blush and the rest to smile, it pleased the Queen that Pampinea should follow next, to second the other gone before; when she, smiling on the whole assembly, began thus : There are some men so shallow of capacity that they will, nevertheless, make show of knowledge and understanding such things, as neither they are able to do, nor appertain to them ; whereby they will sometimes reprehend other new errors, and such faults as they have unwillingly committed, thinking thereby to hide their own shames, when they make it much more apparent and manifest. For proof whereof, fair company, in a contrary kind, I will show you the subtle cunning of one, who perhaps might be reputed of less reckoning than Masetto, and yet he went beyond a king that thought himself to be a much wiser man.

[OMITTED.]

THE THIRD NOVEL.

Under colour of confession and a most pure conscience, a fair young gentlewoman induced a devout and solemn religious friar, without his suspicion or perceiving, to assist her designs on a young gentleman.

WHEN Pampinea sat silent, and the equerry's boldness equalled with his crafty cunning, and great wisdom in the king, had passed amongst them with a general applause, the Queen, turning herself to Filomena, appointed her to follow next in order, as the rest had done before her, whereupon Filomena began after this manner.

[OMITTED.]

THE FOURTH NOVEL.

A young scholar named Felice instructed Puccio di Rinieri how to become rich in a very short time. While Puccio made experience of the instructions taught him, Felice obtained the favour of his daughter.

AFTER that Filomena had finished her tale, she sat still, and Dioneo, with fair and pleasing language, commended the gentlewoman's quaint cunning, but smiling at the confessor's witless simplicity.   Then the Queen, turning with cheerful looks towards Pamfilo, commanded him to continue their delight, who gladly yielded, and thus began : Madam, many men there are who, while they strive to climb from a good estate to a seeming better, do become in much worse condition than they were before. As happened to a neighbour of ours, and no long time since, as the accident will better acquaint you withal.

[OMITTED.

[The Fifth Novel, by Elisa, of Zima and Messer Francesco, and the Sixth, by Fiammetta, of Ricciardo Minutolo, are also omitted.]

THE SEVENTH NOVEL.

Tedaldo degli Elisei having received an unkind repulse by his beloved, departed from Florence, and returning thither, a long while after, in the habit of a pilgrim, he spake with her, and made his wrongs known to her. He delivered her father from the danger of death, because it was proved that he had slain Tedaldo. He made peace with his brethren, and, in the end, wisely enjoyed his heart's desire.

So ceased Fiammetta her discourse, being generally commended, when the Queen, to prevent the loss of time, commanded Emilia to follow next, who thus began : It liketh me best, gracious ladies, to return home again to our own city, which it pleased the former two discoursers to depart from ; and there I will show you how a citizen of ours recovered the kindness of his love after he had lost it.

Sometime there dwelt in Florence a young gentleman, named Tedaldo degli Elisei, descended of a noble house, who became earnestly enamoured of a widow called Hermelina, the daughter to Aldobrandino Palermini, well deserving for his virtues and commendable qualities. Secretly they were espoused together, but Fortune, the enemy to lovers' felicities, opposed her malice against them, in depriving Tedaldo of those dear delights which sometime he held in free possession, and making him a stranger to her gracious favours. Now grew she contemptibly to despise him, not only denying to hear any message sent from him, but scorning also to vouchsafe so much as a sight of him, causing in him extreme grief and melancholy, yet concealing all her unkindness to himself, as no one could understand the reason of his sadness.

After he had laboured by all hopeful courses, to obtain that favour of her which he had formerly lost, without any offence in him, as his innocent soul truly witnessed with him, and saw that all his further endeavours were fruitless and in vain, he concluded to retreat himself from the world, and not to be any longer irksome in her eye that was the only occasion of his unhappiness. Hereupon, storing himself with such sums of money as suddenly he could collect together, secretly he departed from Florence, without speaking any word to his friends or kindred, except one kind companion of his, whom he acquainted with most of his secrets, and so travelled to Ancona, where he termed himself by the name of Sanlodeccio. Repairing to a wealthy merchant there, he placed himself as his servant, and went in a ship of his with him to Cyprus; his actions and behaviour proved so pleasing to the merchant, as not only he allowed him very sufficient wages, but also grew into such association with him as he gave the most of his affairs into his hands, which he guided with such honest and discreet care, that himself, in a few years' compass, proved to be a rich merchant, and of famous report.

While matters went on in this successful manner, although he could not choose but still he remembered his cruel mistress and was very desperately transported for her love, as coveting, above all things else, to see her once more, yet was he of such powerful constancy as seven whole years together he vanquished all those fierce conflicts. But on a day it chanced he heard a song sung in Cyprus, which he himself had formerly made in honour of the love he bare to his mistress, and what delight he conceived by being daily in her presence ; whereby he gathered that it was impossible for him to forget her, and proceeded on so desirously as he could not live except he had a sight of her once more, and therefore determined on his return to Florence. Having set all his affairs in due order, taking one of his servants, he passed to Ancona, where when he was arrived he sent his merchandise to Florence, in name of the merchant of Ancona, who was his especial friend and partner; travelling himself alone with his servant in the habit of a pilgrim, as if he had been newly returned from Jerusalem.

Being come to Florence, he went to an inn kept by two of his brothers, near neighbours to the dwelling of his mistress, and the first thing he did was, passing by her door, to get a sight of her, if he were so happy. But he found the windows, doors, and all the parts of the house fast shut up, whereby he suspected her to be dead, or else to be changed from her dwelling : wherefore, much perplexed in mind, he went on to the inn, finding four of his brothers standing at the gate attired in mourning, whereat he marvelled not a little. Knowing himself to be so transfigured both in body and habit, far from the manner or common use of his parting thence, as it was a difficult matter to know him, he stepped boldly to a shoemaker's shop near adjoining, and demanded the reason of their wearing mourning. The shoemaker made answer thus : " Sir, those men are clad in mourning because a brother of theirs, being named Tedaldo, who hath been absent hence a long while, about some fifteen days since was slain. And since they had heard by proof made in the Court of Justice that one Aldobrandino Palermini, who is kept close prisoner, was the murderer of him, as he came in a disguised habit to his daughter, of whom he was most affectionately enamoured, they cannot choose but let the world know by their outward habits the inward affliction of their hearts for a deed so dishonourably committed."

Tedaldo wondered greatly hereat, imagining that some man by like resembling him in shape might be slain in this manner, and by Aldobrandino, for whose misfortune he grieved marvellously. As concerning his mistress, he understood that she was living and in good health ; and night drawing on apace, he went to his lodging with an infinite number of molestations in his mind, where after supper he was lodged in a corn-loft with his man. Now, by reason of many disturbing imaginations which incessantly wheeled about his brain, his bed also being none of the best, and his supper, perhaps, somewhat of the coarsest ; a great part of the night was spent, yet could he not close his eyes together ; but lying still broad awake about the dead time of the night, he heard the treading of divers persons over his head, who descended down a pair of stairs by his chamber into the lower parts of the house, carrying a light with them, which he discerned by the chinks and crannies in the wall. Stepping softly out of his bed to see what the meaning hereof might be, he espied a fair young woman, who carried a light in her hand, and three men in her company, descending down the stairs together, one of them speaking thus to the young woman : " Now we may boldly warrant our safety, because we have heard it assuredly that the death of Tedaldo Elisei hath been sufficiently proved by the brethren against Aldobrandin Palermini, and he hath confessed the fact ; whereupon the sentence is already set down in writing. But yet it behoveth us, notwithstanding, to conceal it very secretly, because if ever hereafter it should be known that we are they who murdered him, we should be in the same danger as now Aldobrandino is."

When Tedaldo had heard these words he began to consider with himself how many and great the dangers are wherewith men's minds may daily be molested. First he thought on his own brethren in their sorrow, who buried a stranger instead of him, accusing afterward, by false opinion and upon the testimony of as false witnesses, a man most innocent, making him ready for the stroke of death. Next he made a strict observation in his soul concerning the blinded severity of law, and the ministers thereto belonging, who pretending a diligent and careful inquisition for truth, do oftentimes, by their tortures and torments, hear lies vouched only for ease of pain, in the place of a true confession, yet thinking themselves, by doing so to be the ministers of God's justice whereas indeed they are the devil's executioners of his wickedness. Lastly, converting his thoughts to Aldobrandino, the imagined murderer of a man yet living, infinite cares beleaguered his soul in devising what might best be done for his deliverance.

So soon as he was risen in the morning, leaving his servant behind him at his lodging, he went, when he thought it fit time, all alone toward the house of his mistress, where finding by good fortune the gate open, he entered into a small parlour beneath, and where he saw his mistress sitting on the ground wringing her hands and woefully weeping, which, in mere compassion, moved him to weep likewise ; and going somewhat near her, he said, " Madam, torment yourself no more for your peace is not far off from you." The gentlewoman hearing him say so, lifted up her head, and in tears spake thus : " Good man, thou seemest to me to be a pilgrim stranger ; what dost thou know either concerning my peace or mine affliction ? " " Madam," replied the pilgrim, " I am of Constantinople, and doubtless am conducted hither by the hand of Heaven to convert your tears into rejoicing and to deliver your father from death." " How is this ? " answered she, " if you be of Constantinople, and art but now arrived here, dost thou know who we are, either I or my father ? "

The pilgrim discovered to her even, from one end to the other, the history of her husband's sad disasters, telling her how many years since she was espoused to him, and many other important matters, which well she knew, and was greatly amazed thereat, thinking him verily to be a prophet, and kneeling at his feet entreated him very earnestly, that if he were come to deliver her father Aldobrandino from death, to do it speedily, because the time was very short. The pilgrim appearing to be a man of great holiness, said : "Rise up, madam ; refrain from weeping, and observe attentively what I shall say, yet with this caution, that you never reveal it to any person whatsoever. This tribulation whereinto you have fallen, as by revelation I am faithfully informed, is for a grievous sin by you heretofore committed, whereof divine mercy is willing to purge you and to make a perfect amends by a sensible feeling of this affliction ; as seeking your sound and absolutely recovery lest you fall into far greater danger than before." "Good man," quoth she, "I am burthened with many sins, and do not know for which any amends should be made by me any sooner than other : wherefore, if you have intelligence thereof, for charity's sake tell it me, and I will do so much as lieth in me to make a full satisfaction for it." "Madam," answered the pilgrim, "I know well enough what it is, and will demand it no more of you, to win any further knowledge thereof than I have already, but because in revealing it yourself it may touch you with the more true compunction of soul, let us go to the point indeed, and tell me, do you remember that at any time you were married to an husband, or no ?"

At the hearing of these words she breathed forth a very vehement sigh, and was stricken with admiration at this question, believing that not any one had knowledge thereof. Howbeit, since the day of the supposed Tedaldo's burial, such rumour ran abroad by means of such speeches rashly dispersed by a friend of Tedaldo's, who indeed knew it ; whereupon she returned this answer : "It appeareth to me, good man, that divine ordination hath revealed unto you all the secrets of men ; and therefore I am determined not to conceal any of mine from you. True it is that in my younger years, being left a widow, I entirely affected a young gentleman, who in secret was my husband, and whose death is imposed on my father. The death of him I have the more bemoaned, because, in reason, it did nearly concern me by showing myself so savage and rigorous to him before his departure ; nevertheless, let me assure you, sir, that neither his parting, long absence from me, or his untimely death, never had the power to bereave my heart of his remembrance."

"Madam," said the pilgrim, "the unfortunate young gentleman that is slain did never love you, but sure I am that Tedaldo Elisei loved you dearly. But tell me, what was the occasion whereby you conceived such hatred against him ? Did he at any time offend you ?" "No truly sir," quoth she, "but the reason of my anger towards him was by the words and threatenings of a religious friar, to whom once I revealed, under confession, how faithfully I affected him ; when instantly he used such dreadful threatenings to me, and which, even yet, do afflict my soul, that if I did not abstain and utterly refuse him, the devil would fetch me quick to hell, and cast me into the bottom of his quenchless and everlasting fire.

" These menaces were so prevailing with me, as I refused all further conversation with Tedaldo, in which regard I would receive neither letters nor messages from him. Howbeit, I am persuaded that if he had continued here still, and not departed hence in such desperate manner as he did, seeing him melt and consume daily away, even as snow by the power of the sunbeams, my austere deliberation had been long ago quite altered, because not at any time, since then, life hath allowed me one merry day, neither did I or ever can love any man like unto him."

At these words the pilgrim sighed, and then proceeded on again thus : " Surely, madam, this one only sin may justly torment you, because I know for a certainty that Tedaldo never offered you any injury since the day he first became enamoured of you ; and what grace or favour you afforded him was your own voluntary gift, and, as he took it, no more than modesty might well become you, for he loving you first, you had been most cruel and unkind if you should not have requited him with the like affection. If then he continued so just and loyal to you as, of mine own knowledge, I am able to say he did, what should move you to repulse him so rudely ? Such matters ought well to be considered on beforehand ; for if you did imagine that you should repent it as an action ill done, yet you could not do it, because as he became yours, so were you likewise only his ; and he being yours, you may dispose of him at your pleasure, as being truly obliged to none but you. How could you then withdraw yourself from him, being only his, and not commit most manifest theft, a far unfitting thing for you to do, except you had gone with his consent.

" Now, madam, let me further give you to understand that I am a religious person, and a pilgrim, and therefore am well acquainted with all the courses of their dealing ; if therefore I speak somewhat more amply of them, and for your good, it cannot be so unseeming for me to do it as it would appear ugly in another. In which respect I will speak the more freely to you, to the end, that you may take better knowledge of them than, as it seemeth, hitherto you have done. In former passed times, such as professed religion, were learned and most holy persons ; but our religious professors nowadays, and such as covet to be so esteemed, have no matter at all of religion in them, but only the outward show and habit. Which yet is no true badge of religion neither, because it was ordained by religious institutions, that their garments should be made of narrow, plain, and coarsest spun cloth, to make a public manifestation to the world that, in mere devotion and religious disposition, by wrapping their bodies in such base clothing, they condemned and despised all temporal occasions. But nowadays they make them large, deep, glistering, and of the finest cloth or stuffs to be gotten, reducing those habits to so proud and pontifical a form, that they walk peacock-like, rustling and strutting with them in the churches, yea, and in open public places, as if they were ordinary secular persons, to have their pride more notoriously observed. And as the angler bestowed his best cunning with one line and bait to catch many fishes at one strike, even so do these counterfeit habit-mongers, by their dissembling and crafty dealing, beguile many credulous widows, simple women, yea, and men of weak capacity, to credit whatsoever they shall either do or say, and herein they do most of all exercise themselves.

"And to the end that my speeches may not favour of any untruth against them, these men which I speak of have not any habit at all of religious men, but only the colour of their garments ; and whereas they in times past desired nothing more than the salvation of men's souls, these fresher-witted fellows covet after women and wealth, and employ all their pains, by their whispering confessions and figures of painted fearful examples, to affright and terrify unsettled and weak consciences by horrible and blasphemous speeches, yet adding persuasion withal, that their sins may be purged by alms-deeds and masses. To the end that such as credit them in these their daily courses, being guided more by appearance of devotion than any true compunction of heart, to escape severe penances by them enjoined, may some of them bring bread and wine, and others coin, all of them matter of commodity, benefit, and simply say, these gifts are for the souls of their good friends deceased.

"I make no doubt but alms-deeds and prayers are very mighty and prevailing means to appease Heaven's anger for some sins committed ; but if such as bestow them did either see or know to whom they gave them, they would more warily keep them, or else cast them before swine, in regard they are altogether so unworthy of them. But come we now to the case of your ghostly father, crying out in your ear that secret marriage was a most grievous sin. Is not the breach thereof far greater? Familiar conversation between man and woman is a concession merely natural ; but to rob, kill, or banish any one, proceedeth from the mind's malignity. That you did rob Tedaldo, yourself hath already sufficiently witnessed, by taking that from him which with free consent in marriage you gave him. Next, I must say, that by all the power remaining in you, you killed him, because you would not permit him to remain with you, declaring yourself in the very height of cruelty, that he might destroy his life by his own hands. In which case the law requireth that whosoever is the occasion of an ill act committed, he or she is as deep in the fault as the party that did it. Now concerning his banishment and wandering seven years in exile through the world, you cannot deny but that you were the only occasion thereof. In all which three several actions far more capitally have you offended than by contracting of marriage in such manner.

"But let us see whether Tedaldo deserved all these several castigations or not. In truth he did not, yourself have confessed, beside that which I know, that he loved you more dearly than himself, and nothing could be more honoured, magnified and exalted, than daily you were by him, above all other women whatsoever. When he came in any place, where honestly and without suspicion he might speak to you, all his honour and all his liberty lay wholly committed to your power. Was he not a noble young gentleman ? Was he, among all those parts that most adorn a man, and appertain to the very choicest respect, inferior to any one of best merit in your city ? I know that you cannot make denial o any of these demands. How could you then, by the persuasion of a beast, a fool, a villain, yea, a vagabond, envying both his happiness and yours, enter into so cruel a mind against him ? I know not what error misguideth women in scorning and despising their husbands ; but if they entered into a better consideration, understanding truly what they are, and what nobility of nature God hath endued man withal, far above all other creatures, it would be their highest title of glory, when they are so preciously esteemed of them, so dearly affected by them, and so gladly embraced in all their best abilities.

"This is so great a sin as the divine Justice, which in an equal balance bringeth all operations to their full effect, did not purpose to leave unpunished ; but as you enforced, against all reason, to take away Tedaldo from yourself, even so your father Aldo- brandino, without occasion given by Tedaldo, is in peril of his life, and you a partaker of his tribulation. Out of which, if you de- sire to be delivered, it is very convenient that you promise one thing which I shall tell you, and may much better be by you performed ; namely, that if Tedaldo do return from his long banishment, you shall restore him to your love, grace, and good acceptation, ac- counting him in the self-same degree of favour and private enter- tainment as he was at the first, before your wicked ghostly father so hellishly incensed you against him."

When the pilgrim had finished his speeches, the gentlewoman, who had listened to them very attentively, because all the alleged reasons appeared to be plainly true, became verily persuaded that all these afflictions had fallen on her and her father for the un- grateful offence by her committed, and therefore thus replied : "Worthy man and the friend to goodness, I know undoubtedly that the words which you have spoken are true, and also I understand by your demonstration what manner of people some of these re- ligious persons are, whom heretofore I have reputed to be saints, but find them now to be far otherwise ; and, to speak truly, I per- ceive the fault to be great and grievous wherein I have offended against Tedaldo, and would, if I could, willingly make amends, even in such manner as you advised. But how is it possible to be done ? Tedaldo being dead, can be no more recalled to this life ; and therefore I know not what promise I should make in a matter which is not to be performed."

Whereto the pilgrim, without any longer pausing, thus answered : "Madam, by such relations as have been shown to me, I know for a certainty that Tedaldo is not dead, but living, in health and in good estate, if he had the fruition of your grace and favour." "Take heed what you say, sir," quoth the gentlewoman, "for I saw him lie slain before my door, his body having received many

wounds, which I folded in mine arms, and washed his face with
my brinish tears; whereby perhaps that scandal arose that flew
abroad to my disgrace." "Believe me, madam," replied the pilgrim, "say what you will, I dare assure you that Tedaldo is
living, and if you dare make promise concerning what hath been
formerly requested, and keep it inviolably, I make no doubt but
you yourself shall shortly see him." "I promise it," said she, "and
bind myself thereto by a sacred oath to keep it faithfully : for never
could anything happen to yield me the like contentment as to see
my father free from danger and Tedaldo living."

At this instant Tedaldo thought it to be a very apt and convenient time to disclose himself and to comfort the lady with an
assured signal of hope for the deliverance of her father, wherefore
he said : "Lady, to the end that I may comfort you infallibly in
this dangerous peril of your father's life, I am to make known an
especial secret to you, which you are to keep carefully, as you
tender your own life, from ever being revealed to the world." They
were then in a place of sufficient privacy, and by themselves, because she reposed great confidence in the pilgrim's sanctity of life,
as thinking him none other than he seemed to be. Tedaldo
took out of his purse a ring, which she gave him the last night of
their conversing together, and he had kept with no mean care;
and showing it to her, said : "Do you know this ring, ma.'am?"
So soon as she saw it, immediately she knew it, and answered : "Yes,
sir. I know the ring, and confess that I gave it to Tedaldo."

Hereupon the pilgrim stood up, and suddenly putting off his poor
linen frock and the hood from his head, using the Florentine
tongue, he said : "Tell me, madam, do you know me?" When she
had advisedly beheld him, and knew him indeed to be Tedaldo,
she was stricken into a wonderful astonishment, being as fearful of
him as she was of the dead body which she saw lying in the street.
And I dare assure you that she durst not go near him, to respect
him as Tedaldo lately come from Cyprus, but, in terror, fled away
from him, as if Tedaldo had been newly risen out of his grave,
and came thither purposely to affright her; wherefore he said :
"Be not afraid, madam, I am your Tedaldo, in health, alive, and
never as yet died, neither have I received any wounds to kill me, as
you and my brethren had formerly imagined."

Some better assurance getting possession of her, as knowing him
perfectly by his voice, and looking more steadfastly on his face, which
constantly avouched him to be Tedaldo, the tears trickling amain
down her fair cheeks, she ran to embrace him, casting her arms
about his neck, and kissing him a thousand times, saying : "Tedaldo, my faithful husband, nothing in the world can be so welcome
to me." Tedaldo having most kindly kissed and embraced her,
said : "Sweet wife, time will not now allow us those ceremonious
courtesies which indeed so long a separation do justly challenge,
for I must about a more weighty business—to have your father
safely delivered, which I hope to do before to-morrow night, when
you shall hear tidings to your better contentment. And, question-

D

less, if I speed no worse than my good hope persuadeth me, I will
see you again to-night, and acquaint you at better leisure in such
things as I cannot now at this present."

So, putting on his pilgrim's habit again, kissing her once more,
and comforting her with future good success, he departed from her,
going to the prison where Aldobrandino lay, whom he found more
pensive, as being in hourly expectation of death, than any hope he
had to be freed from it. Being brought nearer to him by the
prisoner's favour, as seeming to be a man come only to comfort
him, sitting down by him, thus he began : "Aldobrandino, I am a
friend of thine, whom Heaven hath sent to do thee good in mere
pity and compassion of thy innocence ; and therefore, if thou wilt
grant me one small request, which I am to crave at thy hands, thou
shalt hear without any failing, before to-morrow at night, the sentence of thy free absolution, whereas now thou expectest nothing
but death." Whereunto Aldobrandino thus answered : " Friendly
man, seeing thou art so careful of my safety, although I know thee
not, neither do remember that ever I saw thee till now, thou must
needs be some especial kind friend of mine. And, to tell you the
truth, I never committed the sinful deed for which I am condemned
to death. True it is I have other heinous and grievous sins, which
undoubtedly have thrown this heavy judgment on me, and therefore
I am the more willing to undergo it. Nevertheless, let me thus far
assure thee that I would gladly not only promise something which
might be to the glory of God, if He were pleased in this case to have
mercy on me, but also would as willingly perform and accomplish
it. Wherefore demand whatsoever thou pleasest, for unfeignedly,
if I escape with life, I will truly keep promise with thee."

" Sir," replied the pilgrim, " I desire nor demand anything of you
but that you would pardon the three brethren of Tedaldo, that
brought you to this hard extremity, as thinking you to be guilty of
their brother's death, and that you would also accept them as your
brethren and friends, upon their craving pardon for what they have
done." " Sir," answered Aldobrandino, " no man knoweth how
sweet revenge is, nor with what heat it is to be desired, but only the
man who hath been wronged. Notwithstanding, not to hinder any
hope which only aimeth at Heaven, I freely forgive them, and
henceforth pardon them for ever, intending, moreover, that if mercy
give me life and clear me from this bloody imputation, to love and
respect them so long as I shall live." This answer was most
pleasing to the pilgrim, and without any further multiplication of
speeches, he entreated him to be of good comfort, for he feared not
but before the time prefixed he should hear certain tidings of his
deliverance.

At his departing from him he went directly to the signora, and prevailed so far that he spake privately with a knight, who was then one
of the State's chiefest lords, to whom he said : " Sir, a man ought to
bestow his best pains and diligence, that the truth of things should
be apparently known, especially such men as hold the place and
office you do, to the end that those persons which have committed

no foul offence should not be punished, but only the guilty and heinous transgressors. And because it will be no mean honour to you to lay the blame where it worthily deserveth, I am come hither purposely to inform you in a case of most weighty importance. It is not unknown to you with what rigour the State hath proceeded against Aldobrandino Palermini, and you think verily he is the man that hath slain Tedaldo Elisei, whereupon your law hath condemned him to die. I dare assure you, sir, that a very unjust course hath been taken in this case, because Aldobrandino is falsely accused, as you yourself shall confess before midnight, when they are delivered into your power that were the murderers of the man."

The honest knight, who was very sorrowful for Aldobrandino, gladly gave attention to the pilgrim, and having conferred on many matters appertaining to the fact committed, the two brethren, who were Tedaldo's hosts, and their chambermaid, upon good advice given, were apprehended in their first sleep, without any resistance made in their defence. But when the tortures were sent for, to understand truly how the case went, they would not endure any pain at all, but each aside by himself, and then all together, confessed openly that they did the deed, yet not knowing him to be Tedaldo Elisei. And when it was demanded of them upon what occasion they did so foul an act, they answered that they were so hateful against the man's life, because he would have abused one of their wives when they both were absent from home.

When the pilgrim had heard their voluntary confession he took his leave of the knight, returning secretly to the house of Ermelina, and there, because all her people were in their beds, she carefully awaited his return to hear some glad tidings of her father, and to make a further reconciliation between her and Tedaldo, when, sitting down by her, he said: "Dear love, be of good cheer, for, upon my word, to-morrow you shall have your father home safe, well, and delivered from all further danger;" and to confirm her the more confidently in his words, he declared at large the whole carriage of the business. Ermelina being wondrously joyful for two such sudden successful · accidents, to enjoy her husband alive and in health, and also to have her father freed from so great a danger, kissed and embraced him most affectionately, welcoming him lovingly.

No sooner did bright day appear but Tedaldo arose, having acquainted her with such matters as were to be done, and once more earnestly desiring her to conceal, as yet, these occurrences to herself. So, in his pilgrim's habit, he departed from her house, to await convenient opportunity for attending on the business belonging to Aldobrandino. At the usual hour appointed, the lords were all set in the signoria, and had received full information concerning the offence imputed to Aldobrandino, setting him at liberty by a public consent, and sentencing the other malefactors with death, who, within a few days after, were beheaded in the place where the murder was committed,

Thus, Aldobrandino being released, to his exceeding comfort and no small joy of his daughter, kindred, and friends, all knowing perfectly that this had happened by the pilgrim's means, they conducted him home to Aldobrandino's house, where they desired him to continue so long as himself pleased, using him with most honourable and gracious respect, but especially Ermelina, who knew better than the rest on whom she bestowed her liberal favours, yet concealing all closely to herself.

After two or three days were overpast in these complimentary intercoursings of kindness, Tedaldo began to consider that it was high time for reconciliation to be solemnly passed between his brethren and Aldobrandino; for they were not a little amazed at his strange deliverance, and went likewise continually armed, as standing in fear of Aldobrandino and his friends, which made him the more earnest for accomplishment of the promise formerly made unto him. Aldobrandino lovingly replied that he was ready to make good his word; whereupon the pilgrim provided a goodly banquet, whereat he purposed to have present Aldobrandino, his daughter, kindred, and their wives. But first himself went in person to invite them in peace to his banquet, using many pregnant and forcible reasons to them, such as are requisite in the like discordant cases. In the end, they were so wise and prevailing with them, that they willingly condescended, and thought it no disparagement unto them, for the recovery of Aldobrandino's kindness again, to crave pardon for their great error committed.

On the morrow following, about dinner-time, the three brethren of Tedaldo, attired in their mourning garments, with their wives and friends, came first to the house of Aldobrandino, who purposely stayed for them; and having laid down their weapons on the ground, in the presence of all such as Aldobrandino had invited as his witnesses, they offered themselves to his mercy, and humbly required pardon of him for the matter therein they had offended him. Aldobrandino, shedding tears, most lovingly embraced them, and, to be brief, pardoned whatsoever injuries he had received. After this the sisters and wives, all clad in mourning, courteously submitted themselves, and were graciously welcomed by Ermelina, as also divers other gentlewomen there present with her. Being all seated at the tables, which were furnished with all such rarities as could be wished for, all things else deserved their due commendation, but only sad silence, occasioned by the fresh remembrance of sorrow, appearing in the habits of Tedaldo's friends and kindred, which the pilgrim himself perceived to be the only disgrace to him and his feast. Wherefore, as before he had resolved, when time served, to purge away this melancholy, he arose from the table when some as yet had scarce begun to eat, and thus spake:

"Gracious company, there is no defect in this banquet, that debars it of the honour it might else have, but only the presence of Tedaldo, who, having been continually in your company, it seems you are not willing to take knowledge of him, and therefore I mean myself to show him." So, uncasing himself out of his pilgrim's clothes, and standing in his hose and doublet, to their no little admiration, they all knew him, yet doubted whether it were he or no. Which he perceiving, he repeated his brethren and absent kindred's name, and what occurrences happened between them from time to time, beside the relation of his own past fortunes, inciting tears in the eyes of his brethren and all else there present, every one hugging and embracing him, yea, many beside, who were no kin at all to him, Ermelina only excepted; which when Aldobrandino saw, he said unto her. "How now, Ermelina? Why dost thou not welcome home Tedaldo, so kindly as the rest have done?"

She making a modest curtsey to her father, and answering so loud as every one might hear her, said: "There is not any in this assembly that more willingly would give him all expression of a joyful welcome home and thankful gratitude for such especial favours received than in my heart I could afford to do, but only in regard of those infamous speeches noised out against me on the day when we wept for him who was supposed to be Tedaldo, which slander was to my great discredit." "Go on boldly," replied Aldobrandino; "dost thou think that I regard any such praters? In the procuring of my deliverance he hath approved them to be manifest liars, albeit myself did never credit them. Go then, I command thee, and let me see thee both kiss and embrace him." She, who desired nothing more, showed herself not slothful in obeying her father to do but her duty to her husband. Wherefore being risen, as all the rest had done, but yet in a far more effectual manner, she declared her unfeigned love to Tedaldo. These bountiful favours of Aldobrandino were joyfully accepted by Tedaldo's brethren, as also to every one there present; so that all former rancour and hatred which had caused heavy variances between them was now converted to mutual kindness and solemn friendship on every side.

When the feasting days were finished the garments of sad mourning were quite laid aside, and those becoming so general a joy put on, to make their hearts and habits suitable. Now, concerning the man slain and supposed to be Tedaldo, he was one that in all the parts of his body and trueness of complexion so nearly resembled him as Tedaldo's own brethren could not distinguish the one from the other; but he was of Lunigiana, named Fatinulo, and not Tedaldo, whom the two brethren innkeepers maliced about some idle suspicion conceived, and having slain him, laid his body at the door of Aldobrandino, where, by reason of Tedaldo's absence, it was generally reputed to be he, and Aldobrandino charged to do the deed, by vehement persuasion of the brethren, knowing what love had passed between him and his daughter Ermelina. But happy was the pilgrim's return, first to hear those words in the inn, the means to bring the murder to light, and then the discreet carriage of the pilgrim until he plainly approved himself to be truly Tedaldo.

THE EIGHTH NOVEL.

Ferondo, by drinking a certain kind of powder, was buried for dead, and by the abbot, who was enamoured of his wife, was taken out of his grave and put into a dark prison, where they made him believe that he was in purgatory.

WHEN the long discourse of Emilia was ended, not displeasing to any in regard of the length, but rather held too short, because no exceptions could be taken against it, comparing the rarity of the accidents and changes together, the Queen turned to Lauretta, giving her such a manifest sign as she knew that it was her turn to follow next, and therefore she took occasion to begin thus :

Fair ladies, I intend to tell you a tale of truth, which perhaps in your opinions will seem to sound like a lie ; and yet I heard by the very last relation that a dead man was wept and mourned for, instead of another, being then alive at the present time. In which respect I am now to let you know how a living man was buried for dead, and being raised again, yet not as living, himself and divers more beside did believe that he came forth of his grave, and adored him as a saint who was the occasion thereof, and who, as a bad man, deserved justly to be condemned.

[OMITTED.]

THE NINTH NOVEL.

Giletta of Narbonne cured the King of France of a dangerous fistula, in recompense whereof she requested to enjoy as her husband in marriage Bertram, Count of Roussillon. He having married against his will, as utterly despising her, went to Florence, where he made love to a young gentlewoman. Giletta, by a quaint and cunning policy, compassed the means to be accepted into his favour again, and loved as his loyal and honourable wife.

NOW there remained no more to preserve the privilege granted to Dioneo uninfringed, but the Queen only to declare her novel. Wherefore, when the discourse of Lauretta was ended, without attending any motion to be made for her next succeeding, with a gracious and pleasing disposition, she began to speak :

Who shall tell my tale hereafter, to carry any hope or expectation of a liking, having heard the witty discourse of Lauretta ? Believe me, it was very advantageous to us all that she was not this day's beginner, because few or none would have any courage to follow after her, and therefore the rest yet remaining are the more to be feared and suspected.

There lived some time in the kingdom of France a gentleman named Isnarde, being the Count of Roussillon, who, because he was continually weak and crazy, kept a physician daily in his house, who was called Master Gerard, of Narbonne. Count Isnarde had one only son, very young in years, fair and comely, named Bertram, with whom many other children of his age had their education, and among them a daughter of the fore-named physician, called Giletta, who in these tender years fixed her affection upon young Bertram with such an earnest resolution as was most admirable in so young a maiden. Old Count Isnarde dying, young Bertram fell a ward to the King, and being sent to Paris, remained there under his royal protection, to the no little discomfort of young Giletta, who became afflicted in mind, because she had lost the company of Bertram.

Within some few years after, the physician her father also died, and then her desires grew wholly addicted to visit Paris herself in person, only because she would see the young Count, awaiting but time and opportunity to fit her stolen journey thither. But her friends to whose care she was committed, in regard of her rich dowry and being left as a fatherless orphan, were so circumspect of her walks and behaviour as she could not by any means escape. Her years made her almost fit for marriage, which so much more increased her love to the Count, making refusal of many worthy husbands, and laboured by the motions of her friends, yet all denied, they not knowing any reasons for her refusals. By this time the Count was become a gallant gentleman, and able to make election of his wife, whereby her affections were the more violently inflamed, as fearing lest some other should be preferred before her, and so her hopes be utterly disappointed.

It was noised abroad by common report that the King of France was in a very dangerous condition, by reason of a strange swelling on his stomach, which, failing of apt and convenient curing, became a fistula, afflicting him daily with extraordinary pain, no chirurgeon or physician being found that could minister any hope of healing, but rather increased the grief, compelling the King, as despairing of all help, to give over any further advice. Hereof fair Giletta was very joyful, as hoping this accident could be the means not only of her journey to Paris, but if the disease were no more than she imagined, she could easily cure it, and thereby compass Bertram to be her husband. Hereupon, quickening up her wits with remembrance of those rules of art which, by long practice and experience, she had learned of her skilful father, she compounded certain herbs together such as she knew fitting for that kind of infirmity, and, having reduced her compound into powder, away she rode forthwith to Paris.

Being there arrived, all other serious matters set aside, first she must needs have a sight of Count Bertram, as being the only saint that caused her pilgrimage. Next, she made means for her access to the King, humbly entreating his majesty to vouchsafe her the sight of his fistula. When the King saw her, her modest looks did plainly deliver that she was a fair, comely, and discreet young gentlewoman, wherefore he could no longer hide it, but laid it open

to her view. When she had seen and felt it, presently she put the
King in comfort, affirming that she knew herself able to cure
his fistula, saying : " Sir, if your highness will refer the matter to
me, without any peril of life, or any the least pain to your person,
I hope, by the help of Heaven, to make you whole and sound within
eight days' space." The King, hearing her words, began merrily to
smile at her, saying: " How is it possible for thee, being a young
maiden, to do that which the best physicians in Europe are not
able to perform ? I commend thy kindness, and will not remain
unthankful for thy forward willingness ; but I am fully determined
to use no more counsel or to make any further trial of physic or
chirurgery." Whereto fair Giletta thus replied : " Great King, let
not my skill and experience be despised because I am young and a
maiden, for my profession is not physic, neither do I undertake the
administering thereof, as depending on my own knowledge ; but
by the gracious assistance of Heaven, and some rules of skilful
observation which I learned of reverend Gerard of Narbonne, who
was my worthy father and a physician of no mean fame all the while
he lived."

At the hearing of these words, the King began somewhat to
admire of her gracious carriage, and said within himself : " What
know I whether this virgin is sent to me by the direction of Heaven
or no ? Why should I disdain to make proof of her skill ? Her
promise is to cure me in a small time's compass, and without any
pain or affliction to me. She shall not come so far to return
again with the loss of her labour. I am resolved to try her cunning." And thereon said : " Fair virgin, if you cause me to break
my settled determination and fail of curing me, what can you expect to follow thereon ? " " Whatsoever, great King," quoth she,
" shall please you. Let me be strongly guarded, yet not hindered,
when I am to prosecute the business. And then, if I do not perfectly heal you within eight days, let a good fire be made, and therein
consume my body unto ashes. But if I accomplish the cure, and
set your highness free from all further grievance, what recompense
then shall remain to me ? "

Much did the King commend the confident persuasion which
she had of her own power, and presently replied : " Fair beauty,"
quoth he, " in regard that thou art a maid and unmarried, if thou
keep promise, and I find myself fully cured, I will match thee with
some such gentleman in marriage as shall be of honourable and
worthy reputation, with a sufficient dowry beside." " My gracious
Sovereign," said she, " willing am I, and most heartily thankful
withal, that your highness shall bestow me in marriage ; but I
desire, then, to have such a husband as I shall desire or demand,
by your gracious favour, without presuming to crave any of your
sons, kindred, or alliance, or appertaining unto your royal blood."
Whereto the King gladly granted. Young Giletta began to minister
her physic, and within fewer days than her limited time, the King
was sound and perfectly cured, which when he perceived, he
said unto her : " Trust me, gracious maid, most worthily hast

thou won a husband; name him, and thou shalt have him."
"Royal King," quoth she, "then have I won the Count Bertram
of Roussillon, whom I have most entirely loved from my infancy,
and cannot, in my soul, affect any other." Very loth was the King
to grant the young Count; but in regard of his solemn passed
promise, and his royal word engaged, which he would not by any
means break, he commanded that the Count should be sent for,
and spake thus to him:

"Noble Count, it is not unknown to us that you are a gentleman
of great honour, and it is our royal pleasure to discharge your
wardship, that you may repair home to your own house, there to
settle your affairs in such order as you may be the readier to enjoy
a wife, which we intend to bestow upon you." The Count returned
his Highness most humble thanks, desiring to know of whence and
what she was? "It is the gentlewoman," answered the King, "who,
by the help of Heaven, hath been the means to save my life." Well
did the Count know her, as having very often before seen her; and
although she was very fair and amiable, yet in regard of her mean
birth, which he held as a disparagement to his nobility of blood, he
made a scorn of her, and spake thus to the King: "Would your
Highness give me a quacksalver to my wife, one that deals in drugs
and physicary? I hope I am able to bestow myself much better
than so." "Why," quoth the King, "wouldst thou have us break
our faith, which for the recovery of our health, we have given to this
virtuous virgin? and she will have no other reward, but only Count
Bertram to be her husband." "Sir," replied the Count, "you may
dispossess me of all that is mine, because I am your ward and
subject, and anywhere else you may bestow me, but pardon me to
tell you that this marriage cannot be made with any liking or allowance of mine, neither will I ever give consent thereto."

"Sir," said the King, "it is our will that it should be so. Virtuous
she is, fair and wise; she loveth thee most affectionately; and with
her mayest thou lead a more noble life than with the greatest lady
in our kingdom." Silent and discontented stood the Count, but the
King commanded preparation for the marriage; and when the
appointed time was come, the Count, albeit against his will, received
his wife at the King's hand, she loving him dearly as her life.
When all was done, the Count requested of the King that what else
remained for further solemnization of the marriage it might be performed in his own country, reserving to himself what else he intended. Being mounted on horseback, and humbly taking leave of
the King, the Count would not ride home to his own dwelling, but
into Tuscany, where he heard of a war between the Florentines and
the Siennese, purposing to take part with the Florentines, to whom
he was willingly and honourably welcomed, being created captain of
a worthy company, and continuing there a long while in service.

The poor forsaken new-married Countess could scarcely be pleased
with such dishonourable unkindness, yet governing her impatience
with no mean discretion, and hoping by her virtuous carriage to
compass the means of his recall, home she rode to Roussillon,

where all the people received her very lovingly. Now by reason of the Count's so long absence, all things were far out of order; mutinies, quarrels, and civil dissensions, having procured many dissolute irruptions to the expense of much blood in many places. But she, like a jolly stirring lady, very wise and provident in such disturbances, reduced all occasions to such civility again, that the people admired her rare behaviour, and condemned the Count for his unkindness towards her.

After that the whole county of Roussillon, by the policy and wisdom of this worthy lady, was fully re-established in their ancient liberties, she made choice of two secret knights, whom she sent to the Count her husband, to let him understand that if in displeasure to her, he was thus become a stranger to his own country, upon the return of his answer, to give him contentment, she would depart thence, and by no means disturb him. Roughly and churlishly he replied : " Let her do as she list, for I have no determination to dwell with her or near where she is. Tell her from me, when she shall have this ring which you behold here on my finger and a son in her arms begotten by me, then will I come live with her and be her love." The ring he made most precious and dear account of, and never took it off from his finger, in regard of a special virtue and property which he well knew to be remaining in it. And these two knights, hearing the impossibility of the two strict conditions, with no favour else to be derived from him, sorrowfully returned back to their lady, and acquainted her with his unkind answer, as also his unalterable determination, which well you may conceive must needs be very unwelcome unto her.

After she had an indifferent while considered with herself, her resolution became so undauntable that she would adventure to practise such means whereby to compass those two apparent impossibilities, and so to enjoy the love of her husband. Having absolutely concluded what was to be done, she assembled all the chiefest men of the country, revealing unto them in mournful manner what an attempt she had made already in hope of recovering her husband's favour, and what a rude answer was thereon returned. In the end she told them that it did not suit with her unworthiness to make the Count live as an exile from his own inheritance, upon no other inducement but only in regard of her, wherefore she had determined between heaven and her soul to spend the remainder of her days in pilgrimages and prayers for preservation of the Count's soul and her own ; earnestly desiring them to undertake the charge and government of the country, and signifying to the Count how she had forsaken his house, and purposed to wander as far thence that never would she visit Roussillon any more. In the delivery of these words the lords and gentlemen wept and sighed extraordinarily, using many earnest deprecations to alter this resolve in her, but all was in vain.

Having taken her sad and sorrowful farewell of them all, accompanied only with her maid and one of her kinsmen, away she went, attired in a pilgrim's habit, yet well furnished with money and precious jewels, to avoid all wants which might befall her in travel, not acquainting any one whither she went. In no place staid she until she was arrived at Florence, where happening into a poor widow's house, like a poor pilgrim, she seemed content therewith. And desiring to hear some tidings of the Count, the next day she saw him pass by the house on horseback with his company. Now albeit she knew him well enough, yet she demanded of the good old widow what gentleman he was? She made answer that he was a stranger there, yet a nobleman, called Count Bertram of Roussillon, a vir-tuous knight, beloved and much respected in the city. Moreover, that he was far in love with a neighbour of hers, a young gentle-woman, but very poor and mean in substance, yet of honest life, virtuous, and never taxed with any evil report, only her poverty was the main embarment of her marriage, dwelling in house with her mother, who was a wise, honest, and worthy lady.

The Countess having well observed her words, and considering thereon from point to point, debated soberly with her own thoughts in such a doubtful case what was best to be done. When she had understood which was the house, the ancient lady's name, and like-wise her daughter's, to whom her husband was so affectionately devoted, she made choice of a fit and convenient time when, in her pilgrim's habit, secretly she went to the house. There she found the mother and daughter in poor condition, and with as poor a family, whom after she had ceremoniously saluted, she told the old lady that she requested but a little conference with her. The lady arose, and giving her kind entertainment, they went together into a withdrawing chamber, where being both set down, the Countess began in this manner :—

" Madam, in my poor opinion, you are not free from the frowns of Fortune, no more than I myself am ; but if you were so well pleased, there is no one that can comfort both our calamities in such manner as you are able to do." "And believe me," answered the lady, "there is nothing in the world that can be so welcome to me as honest comfort." The Countess proceeding on in her former speeches said : " I have now need, good madam, both of your trust and fidelity, whereon if I should rely, and you fail me, it will be your own undoing as well as mine." "Speak then boldly," replied the old lady, " and remain constantly assured that you shall no way be deceived by me." Hereupon the Countess declared the whole course of her love, from the very original to the instant, revealing also what she was, and the occasion of her coming thither ; relating everything so perfectly that the lady verily believed her, by some reports, which she had formerly heard, and which moved her the more to compassion. Now, when all circumstances were at full discovered, thus spake the Countess :

"Among my other miseries and misfortunes, which have half broken my heart in the mere repetition, beside the sad and afflicting sufferance, two things there are, which if I cannot compass to have, all hope is quite frustrate for ever of gaining the grace of my lord and husband. Yet these two things may I obtain by your help, if all be true which I have heard, and you can therein best resolve me. Since my coming to this city, it hath credibly been told me that the Count, my husband, is deeply in love with your daughter.' " If the Count," quoth the lady, " love my daughter, and have a wife of his own, he must think, and so shall surely find it, that his greatness is no privilege for him whereby to work dishonour upon her poverty.   But indeed, some appearances there are, and such a matter as you speak of may be presumed, yet so far from a very thought of entertaining in her or me, as whatsoever I am able to do, to yield you any comfort and content, you shall find me therein both willing and ready ; for I prize my daughter's spotless poverty at as high a rate as he can do the pride of his honour."

" Madam," quoth the Countess, " most heartily I thank you. But before I presume any further on your kindness, let me first tell you what faithfully I intended to do for you, if I can bring my purpose to effect.   I see that your daughter is beautiful, and of sufficient years for marriage, and is debarred thereof, as I have heard, only by lack of a competent dowry. Wherefore, Madam, in recompense of the favour I expect from you, I will enrich her with so much ready money as you shall think sufficient to match her in the degree of honour."   Poverty made the poor lady very well to like of such a bountiful offer, and, having a noble heart, she said : " Great Countess, say wherein am I able to do you any service, as can deserve such a gracious offer? If the action be honest, without blame or scandal to my poor yet undetected reputation, gladly I would know it, and it being accomplished, let the requital rest in your own noble nature."

" Observe me then, Madam," replied the Countess, " it is most convenient for my purpose, that by some trusty and faithful messenger you should advertise the Count my husband, that your daughter is, and shall be at his command ; but that she may remain absolutely assured, that his love is constant to her, and above all other, she must entreat him to send her, as a testimony thereof, the ring which he weareth upon his little finger, albeit she hath heard that he loveth it dearly.   If he send the ring, you shall give it me, and afterward send him word, that for the more safety and secresy, he must repair hither to your house, where I being, instead of your daughter, fair fortune may so favour me that, unknown to him, I may conceive with child.   Upon which good success, when time shall serve, having the ring on my finger and a child in my arms begotten by him, his love and liking may be recovered, and, by your means, I continue with my husband, as every virtuous wife ought to do."

The good old lady imagined that this was a matter somewhat difficult, and might lay a blameful imputation on her daughter. Nevertheless, considering what an honest office it was in her, to be the means whereby so worthy a Countess should recover an unkind husband, she knew the intent to be honest, the Countess virtuous, and her promise religious, and therefore undertook to effect it. Within a few days after, very ingeniously, and according to the instructed order, the ring was obtained, albeit much against the Count's will, and the Countess conceived of two goodly sons, and her deliverance agreed correspondently with the just time.

Thus the old lady, not at this time only, but at many other meetings besides, gave the Countess free possession of her husband, yet always in such dark and concealed secresy as it was never suspected nor known to any but themselves, the Count being with his own wife, and disappointed of her whom he so dearly loved. Always at his uprising in the mornings, which usually was before the break of day, for preventing the least scruple of suspicion, many familiar conferences passed between them, with the gifts of divers fair and costly jewels, all which the Countess carefully kept, and perceiving assuredly that she was conceived with child, she would no longer be troublesome to the good old lady, but calling her aside, spake thus to her : " Madam, I must needs give thanks to heaven and you, beeause my desires are amply accomplished, and both time and your deserts do justly challenge that I should accordingly quit you before my departure. It remaineth now in your own power to make what demand you please of me, which yet I will not give you by way of reward, because that would seem to be base and mercenary ; but only whatsoever you shall receive of me is in honourable recompense of fair and virtuous deservings, such as any honest and well-minded lady in the like distress may with good credit allow, and yet no prejudice to her reputation."

Althought poverty might well have tutored the lady's tongue, to demand a liberal recompense for her pains, yet she requested but an hundred pounds as a friendly help towards her daughter's marriage, and that with a bashful blushing was uttered too ; yet the Countess gave her five hundred pounds, besides so many rich and costly jewels as amounted to a far greater sum. So she returned to her wonted lodging at the aged widow's house, where first she was entertained at her coming to Florence ; and the good old lady, to avoid the Count's repairing to her house any more, departed thence suddenly with her daughter, to divers friends of hers that dwelt in the country, whereat the Count was much discontented ; albeit afterward he did never hear any more tidings of her or her daughter, who was worthily married, to her mother's great comfort.

Not long after, Count Bertram was recalled home by his people, and he having heard of his wife's absence, went to Roussillon so much the more willingly. And the Countess knowing her husband's departure from Florence, as also his safe arrival at his own dwelling, remained still in Florence until the time of her deliverance, which was of two goodly sons, lively resembling the looks of their father, and all the perfect lineaments of his body. Persuade yourselves she was not a little careful of their nursing, and when she saw the time answerable to her determination she took her journey, unknown to any, and arrived with them at Montpellier, where she rested for divers days, after so long and wearisome a journey.

Upon the day of All Saints the Count kept a solemn festival, for the assembly of his lords, knights, ladies, and gentlewomen : upon which jovial day of general rejoicing, the Countess, attired in her wonted pilgrim's weeds, repaired thither, entering into the great hall where the tables were readily covered for dinner. Pressing through the throng of people, with her two children in her arms, she presumed to the place where the Count sat, and falling on her knees before him, the tears trickling abundantly down her cheeks, thus she spake :

"Worthy Lord, I am thy poor, despised, and unfortunate wife, who, that thou mightest return home, and not be an exile from thine own abiding, have thus long gone begging through the world. Yet now at length, I hope thou wilt be so honourably minded as to perform thine own two strict imposed conditions, made to the two knights which I sent unto thee, and which, by thy command, I was enjoined to do. Behold here in my arms, not only one son by thee begotten, but two twins, and thy ring beside. High time is it now, if men of honour respect their promises, and after so long and tedious travel, I should at last be welcomed as thy true wife."

The Count hearing this, stood as confounded with admiration for full well he knew the ring ; and both the children were so perfectly like him, as he was confirmed to be their father by general general judgment. Upon his urging by what possible means this could be brought to pass, the Countess, in presence of the whole assembly, and unto her eternal commendation, related the whole history, even in such manner as you have formerly heard it. More-over, she reported the private speeches in bed, uttered between himself and her, being witnessed more apparently by the costly jewels there openly shown. All which infallible proofs, proclaiming his shame and her most noble carriage to her husband, he con-fessed that she had told nothing but the truth in every point which she had reported.

Commending her admirable constancy, excellency of wit, and sprightly courage, in making such a bold adventure, he kissed the two sweet boys, and to keep his promise, whereto he was earnestly importuned, by all his best esteemed friends there present, especially the honourable ladies, who would have no denial, but by forgetting his former harsh and uncivil carriage towards her, to accept her for ever as his lawful wife ; folding her in his arms, and sweetly kissing her divers times together, he bade her welcome to him as his virtuous, loyal, and most loving wife, and so, for ever after, he would acknowledge her. Well knew he that she had store of better beseeming garments in the house, and therefore requested the ladies to walk with her to her chamber, to uncase her of those pilgrim's weeds, and clothe her in her own more sumptuous garments, even those which she wore on her wedding day, because that was not the day of his contentment, but only this ; for now he confessed her to be his wife indeed, and now he would give the King thanks for her, and now was Count Bertram truly married to the fair Giletta of Narbonne.

THE TENTH NOVEL.

Alibech, a young convert to Christianity, goes into the desert of the Thebaid, where Rustico, a pious hermit, teaches him how to put the devil in hell.

[OMITTED.]

THE Queen perceiving that as the tale was ended, so her dignity must now be expired, she took the crown of laurel from off her head, and and graciously placed it on the head of Filostrato, saying : " The discourse of Dioneo causeth me, at the resignation of mine authority, to make choice of him as our next commander who is best able to order and instruct us all ; and so I yield both my place and honour to Filostrato, I hope with the good liking of all our assistants, as plainly appeareth by their instant carriage towards him, with all their heartiest love and suffrages."

Whereupon Filostrato, beginning to consider on the charge committed to his care, called the master of the household, to know in what estate all matters were, because where any defect appeared, everything might be the sooner remedied for the better satisfaction of the company during the time of his authority. Then returning back to the assembly, thus he began : " Lovely ladies, I would have you to know that since the time of ability in me to distinguish between good and evil, I have always been subject, perhaps by the means of some beauty here amongst us, to the proud and imperious dominion of love, with expression of all duty, humility, and most intimate desire to please ; yet all hath proved to no purpose, but still I have been rejected for some other, whereby my condition hath fallen from ill to worse, and so still it is likely even to the hour of my death. In which respect it best pleaseth me that our conferences to-morrow shall extend to no other argument, but only such cases as are most comfortable to my calamity, namely, of such whose love hath had unhappy ending, because I await no other issue of mine ; nor willingly would I be called by any other name, but ' The miserable and unfortunate lover.' "

Having thus spoken, he rose again, granting leave to the rest, to recreate themselves till supper-time. The garden was very fair and spacious, affording large limits for their several walks ; the sun being already so low descended that it could not be offensive to any one, the conies, kids, and young hinds skipping everywhere about them, to their no mean pleasure and contentment. Dioneo and Fiametta sat singing together of Messer Guiglielmo and the lady of Vergiu. Filomena and Pamfilo were playing at the chess, all sporting themselves as best they pleased. But the hour of supper being come, and the tables covered about the fair fountain, they sat down and supped in most loving manner. Then Filostrato, not to swerve from the course which had been observed by the Queens before him, so soon as the tables were taken away, gave command

hat Lauretta should begin the dance, and likewise sing
' My gracious lord," quoth she, " I can skill of no other s‹
‹nly a piece of mine own, which I have already learned by h
nay well beseem this assembly : if you please to allow o:
.m ready to perform it with all obedience." "Lady," re|
‹ing, " you yourself being so fair and lovely, so needs must
‹oever cometh from you ; therefore let us hear such as y‹
.auretta gave instruction to the chorus prepared, and t
his manner.

THE SONG.

No soul so comfortless
   Hath more cause to express
   Its woe and heaviness
     Than I, poor amorous maid.

He that did form the heavens and every star
   Made me as best Him pleased,
Gracious and fair, no element at jar,
Seeking in gentle breasts to move no war,
   But to have strifes appeased
Where Beauty's eye should make the deepest fear.
   And yet, when all things are confessed,
   Never was any soul distrest,
   Like me, poor amorous maid.
     No soul so comfortless, &c.

There was a time when once I was held dear—
   Blest were those happy days—
Numberless love-suits whispered in my ear,
All of fair hope, but none of desperate fear ;
   And all sung Beauty's praise.
Why should black clouds obscure so bright a clear?
   And why should others swim in joy,
   And no heart be drowned in annoy,
   Like mine, poor amorous maid ?
     · No soul so comfortless, &c.

Well may I curse that sad and dismal day
   When, in unkind exchange,
Another beauty did my hopes betray,
And stole my dearest love from me away ;
   Theft I thought passing strange,
Considering vows were past, and what else may
   Assure a loyal maiden's trust.
   Never was lover so unjust,
   As mine, poor amorous maid !
     No soul so comfortless, &c.

Come, then, kind Death, and finish all my woes,
   Thy help is now the best.
Come, lovely Nymphs, lend hands mine eyes to close,
And let him wander wheresoe'r he goes,
   Vaunting of mine unrest,
Beguiling others by his treacherous shows.

Grave on my monument,
No true love was worse spent
Than mine, poor amorous maid,
No soul so comfortless,
Hath more cause to express
Its woes and heaviness
Than I, poor amorous maid.

So did Lauretta finish her song, which being well observed of them all, was understood by some in divers kinds, some alluding it one way, and others according to their own apprehensions, but all consenting that it was an excellent ditty, well devised and most sweetly sung. Afterward, lighted torches being brought, because the stars had already richly spangled all the heavens, and the fit hour of rest approaching, the King commanded them all to their chambers.

THE FOURTH DAY.

Wherein all the several discourses are under the government of honourable Filostrato, and concerning such persons whose loves have had successless ending.

INDUCTION.

MOST worthy ladies, I have always heard, as by the sayings of the judicious, so also by mine own observation and reading, that the impetuous and violent winds of envy do seldom blow turbulently but on the highest towers and tops of the trees most eminently advanced. Yet in my opinion I have found myself much deceived, because, by striving with my very utmost endeavour to shun the outrage of those implacable winds, I have laboured to go, not only by plain and even paths, but likewise through the deepest valleys. As very easily may be seen and observed in the reading of these few small novels, which I have written, not only in our vulgar Florentine prose, without any ambitious title, but also in a most humble style, so low and gentle as possibly I could. And although I have been rudely shaken, yea almost half unrooted, by the extreme agitation of those blustering winds, and torn in pieces by the base backbiter Envy: yet have I not for all that discontinued or broken any part of mine intended enterprise. Wherefore I can sufficiently witness by mine own comprehension the saying so much observed by the wise to be most true, that nothing is without envy in the world but misery only.

Among variety of opinions, fair ladies, some, seeing these novelties, spared not to say that I have been over-pleasing to you, and wandered too far from mine own respect, imbasing my credit and repute by delighting myself too curiously for the fitting of your humours, and have extolled your worth too much with addition of worse speeches than I mean to utter. Others, seeming to express more maturity of judgment, have likewise said that it was very unsuitable for my years to meddle with women's wanton pleasures, or contend to delight you by the very least of my labours. Many more, making show of affecting my good name and esteem, say I had done much more wisely to have kept me with the Muses at Parnassus than to confound my studies with such effeminate follies. Some others beside, speaking more despitefully than discreetly, said I had declared more humanity in seeking means for mine own maintenance, and therewith to support my continual necessities, than to glut the world with gulleries, and feed my hopes with nothing but wind ; and others, to calumniate my travels, would make you believe that such matters as I have spoken of are merely disguised by me and figured in a contrary nature, quite from the course as they are related. Whereby you may perceive, virtuous ladies, how, while I labour in your service, I am agitated and molested with these blusterings, and bitten even to the bare bones by the sharp and venomous teeth of envy; all which, as heaven best knoweth, I gladly endure, and with good courage.

Now, albeit it belongeth only to you to defend me in this desperate extremity, yet, notwithstanding all their utmost malice, I will make no spare of my best abilities, and without any answering them any otherwise than is fitting, will quietly keep their slanders from mine ears, with some slight reply, yet not deserving to be dreamed on. For I apparently perceive that, having not already attained to the third part of my pains, they are grown to so great a number and presume so very far upon my patience, that they may increase, except they be repulsed in the beginning, to such an infinity before I can reach to the end, as with their very least painstaking they will sink me to the bottomless depth, if your sacred forces, which are great indeed, may not serve for me in their resistance. But before I come to answer any one of them, I will relate a tale in mine own favour, yet not a whole tale, because it shall not appear that I purpose to mingle mine among those which are to proceed from a company so commendable. Only I will report a parcel thereof, to the end that what remaineth untold may sufficiently express it is not to be numbered among the rest to come.

By way then of familiar discourse, and speaking to my malicious detractors, I say that a long time since there lived in our city a citizen who was named Philippo Balducci, a man but of mean condition, yet very wealthy, well qualified, and expert in many things appertaining to his calling. He had a wife whom he loved most entirely, as she did him, leading together a sweet and peaceable life, studying on nothing more than how to please each other mutually. It came to pass that, as all flesh must, the good woman left this wretched life for a better, leaving one only son to her husband, about the age of two years. The husband remained so disconsolate for the loss of his kind wife as no man possible could be more sorrowful, because he had lost the only jewel of his joy; and being thus divided from the company which he most esteemed, he determined also to separate himself from the world, addicting all his endeavours to the service of God, and applying his young son likewise to the same holy exercises. Having given away all his goods for God's sake, he departed to the mountain Asinaio, where he made him a small cell, and lived there with his little son only upon charitable alms, with abstinence and prayer, forbearing to speak of any worldly occasions or letting the lad see any vain sight, but conferred with him continually on the glories of eternal life, of God and his saints, and taught him nothing else but devout prayers, leading this kind of life for many years together, not permitting him ever to go forth out of his cell, or showing him any other but himself.

The good old man used divers times to go to Florence, where having received, according to his opportunities, the alms of divers well-disposed people, he returned back again to his hermitage. It fortuned that the boy, being now about eighteen years old, and his father grown very aged, he demanded of him one day whither he went? wherein the old man truly resolved him. Whereupon the youth thus spake unto him: "Father, you are now grown very aged, and hardly can endure such painful travel; why do you not let me go to Florence, that by making me known to your well-disposed friends, such as are devoutly addicted both to God and you, I who am young and better able to endure travel than you are, may go thither to supply our necessities, and you take your ease in the meanwhile?" The aged man perceiving the growth of his son, and thinking him to be so well instructed in God's service as no worldly vanities could easily allure him from it, did not dislike the lad's honest motion, but when he went next to Florence, took him thither along with him.

When he was there, and had seen the goodly palaces, houses, and churches, with all other sights to be seen in so pompous a city, he began greatly to wonder at them, as one that had never seen them before, at least within the compass of his remembrance, demanding many things of his father, both what they were and how they were named; wherein the old man still resolved him. The answers seemed to content him highly, and caused him to proceed on in further questions, according still as they found fresh occasions, till at the last they met with a troop of very beautiful women, going on in seemly manner together, as returning back from a wedding. No sooner did the youth behold them, but he demanded of his father what things they were; whereto the old man replied thus: "Son, cast down thy looks unto the ground, and do not seem to see them at all, because they are bad things to behold." "Bad things, father," answered the lad. "How do you call them?" The good old man, not to quicken any desire to aught but goodness, would not term them by their proper name of women, but told him that they were called young goslings.

Here grew a matter of no mean marvel—that he who had never seen any women before now, appeared not to respect the fair churches, palaces, goodly horses, gold, silver, or anything else which he had seen; but as fixing his affection only upon this sight, suddenly said to the old man: "Good father, do so much for me as let me have one of these goslings." "Alas, son," replied the father, "hold thy peace, I pray thee, and do not desire any such naughty thing." Then by way of demand he thus proceeded, saying: "Father, are these naughty things made of themselves?" "Yes, son," answered the old man. "I know not, father," quoth the lad, "what you mean by naughtiness, nor why these goodly things should be so badly termed, but in my judgment I have not seen anything so fair and pleasing in mine eye as these are, who excel those painted angels which here in the churches you have shown me. And therefore, father, if ever you love me, or have any care of me, let me have one

of these goslings home to your cell, where we can make means sufficient for their feeding." "I will not," said the father, "be so much
thine enemy, because neither thou nor I can rightly skill of their
feeding." Perceiving presently that Nature had far greater power
than his son's capacity and understanding, this made him repent
that he had fondly brought his son to Florence.

Having gone so far in this fragment of a tale, I am content to
pause here, and will return again to them of whom I spake before—
I mean my envious depravers ; such as have said, fair ladies, that
I am double blameworthy in seeking to please you, and that you
are also over-pleasing to me, who freely confess before all the
world that you are singularly pleasing to me, and I have striven
how to please you effectually. I would demand of them, if they
seem so much amazed hereat, considering I never knew what belonged to true love kisses so often received from your graces, but
only that I have yet seen, and do daily behold your commendable
conditions, admired beauties, noble adornments by Nature, and,
above all the rest, your womanly and honest conversation. If be
that was nourished, bred, and educated on a savage solitary mountain, within the confines of a poor small cell, having no other company than his father—if such a one, I say, upon the very first sight
of your sex, could so constantly confess that women are only worthy
of affection, and the object which, above all things else, he most
desired—why should these contumelious spirits so murmur against
me, tear my credit with their teeth, and wound my reputation to the
death, because your virtues are pleasing to me, and I endeavour
likewise to please you with my utmost pains? Never had the
auspicious Heavens allowed me life but only to love you ; and
from my very infancy mine intentions have always been that way
bent ; feeling what virtue flowed from your fair eyes, understanding the mellifluous accents of your speech, whereto the enkindled
flames of your sighs gave no mean grace. But remembering
especially that nothing could so please a hermit as your divine
perfections, an unnurtured lad, without understanding, and little
differing from a mere brutish beast—undoubtedly, whosoever loveth
not women, and desireth to be affected of them again, may well be
ranked among women-haters, speaking out of cankered spleen, and
utterly ignorant of the secret power, as also the virtue, of natural
affection, whereof they seem so careless ; as careless am I of their
depraving.

Concerning them that touch me with mine age : Do not they
know that, although leeks have white heads yet the blades of them
are always green? But referring them to their flouts and taunts, I
answer that I shall never hold it any disparagement to me, so long
as my life endureth, to delight myself with those exercises which
Guido Cavalcanti and Dante Alighieri, already aged, as also Messer
Cino da Pistoia, older than either of them both, held it to be their
chiefest honour. And were it not wandering too far from our
present argument, I would allege histories to approve my words,
full of very ancient and famous men who in the ripest maturity of

all their time were carefully studious for the contenting of women, albeit these cockbrains neither know the way how to do it, nor are so wise as to learn it.

Now for my dwelling at Parnassus with the Muses, I confess their counsel to be very good; but we cannot always continue with them, nor they with us. And yet, nevertheless, when any man departeth from them, they, delighting themselves to see such things as may be thought like them (for like will to like), do not therein deserve to be blamed. We find it recorded that the Muses were women, and albeit women cannot equal the performance of the Muses, yet in their very prime aspect they have a lively resemblance with the Muses; so that, if women were pleasing for nothing else, yet they ought to be generally pleasing in that respect. Besides all this, women have been the occasion of my composing a thousand verses; whereas the Muses never caused me to make so much as one. True it is, that they gave me good assistance, and directed me in writing of these Novels. And how basely soever they judge of my studies, yet have the Muses never scorned to dwell with me, perhaps for the respective service and honourable resemblance of those ladies with themselves, whose virtues I have not spared to commend by them. Wherefore, in the composing of these varieties, I have not strayed so far from Parnassus nor the Muses as in their silly conjectures they imagine.

But what shall I say to them who take so great compassion on my poverty, as they advise me to get something whereon to make my living? Assuredly I know not what to say in this case except by due consideration made with myself, how they could answer me, if necessity should drive me to crave kindness of them. Questionless then would they say: "Go seek comfort among thy fables and follies." Yet would I have them know that poor poets have found more among their fables and fictions than many rich men ever could do by ransacking all their bags of treasure. Besides, many others might be spoken of who made their age and times to flourish merely by their inventions and fables. Whereas, on the contrary, a great number of other busier brains, seeking to gain more than would serve them to live on, have utterly run upon their own ruin and overthrown themselves for ever. What shall I say more? To such men as are either suspicious of their own charity, or of my necessity, whensoever it shall happen, I can answer, I thank my God for it, with the Apostle: "I know how to abound and how to abate, yea, how to endure both prosperity and want, and therefore let no man be more careful of me than I of myself."

For them that are so inquisitive into my discourses to have a further construction of them than agrees with my meaning or their own good manners, taxing me with writing one thing but intending another, I could wish that their wisdom would extend so far as to compare them with their originals to find them a jot discordant from my writing; and then I would freely confess that they had some reason to reprehend me, and I would endeavour to make them amends. But until they can touch me with anything else but words only, I must let them wander in their own giddy opinions, and follow the course projected to myself, saying of them as they do of me.

Thus holding them all sufficiently answered for this time, I say, most worthy ladies, that by Heaven's assistance and yours, whereunto I only lean, I will proceed on, armed with patience, and turning my back against these impetuous winds, let them breathe till they burst, because I see nothing can happen to harm me but only the venting of their malice. For the roughest blast doth but raise the smallest dust from off the ground, driving it from one place to another, or carrying it up to the air. Many times it falleth down again on men's heads, yea, upon the crowns of emperors and kings, and sometimes on the highest palaces and tops of towers, from whence, if it chance to descend again by contrary blasts, it cannot light any lower than from whence it came at the first. And therefore, if ever I strove to please you with my uttermost abilities in anything, surely I must now contend to express it more than ever. For I know right well that no man can say with reason, except some such as myself, who love and honour you, that we do anything otherwise than as Nature hath ordained us. And to resist her laws requires a greater and more powerful strength than ours, and the contenders against her supreme privileges have either laboured merely in vain or else incurred their own bane. Which strength I freely confess myself not to have, neither covet to be possessed of in this case ; but if I had it I would rather lend it to some other than any way use it on mine own behalf. Wherefore I would advise them that thus check and control me to give over and be silent ; and if their cold humours cannot learn to love, let them live still in their frosty complexion, delighting themselves in their corrupted appetites, suffering me to enjoy mine own for the little while I have to live ; and this is all the kindness I require of them.

But now it is time, bright beauties, to return whence we parted, and to follow our former order begun, because it may seem we have wandered too far. By this time the sun had chased the star-light from the heavens and shady moisture from the ground, when Filostrato the king being risen, all the company arose likewise; when, being come into the goodly garden, they spent the time in variety of sports, dining where they had supped the night before. And after the sun was at his highest, and they had refreshed their spirits with a little slumbering, they sat down, according to custom, about the fair fountain ; and then the King commanded Fiammetta that she would give beginning to the day's Novels, when she, without any longer delaying, began in this manner.

THE FIRST NOVEL.

Tancredi, Prince of Salerno, caused the amorous friend of his daughter to be slain, and sent her his heart in a cup of gold, which afterwards she steeped in an impoisoned water, and then drinking it so died.

OUR King, most noble and virtuous ladies, hath this day g.ven us a subject very rough and stern to discourse on, and so much the rather if we consider that we are come hither to be merry and pleasant, where sad tragical reports are no way suitable, especially by reviving the tears of others to bedew our own cheeks withal. Nor can any such argument be spoken of without moving compassion both in the reporters and hearers. But, perhaps, it was his highness's pleasure to moderate the delights which we have already had ; or whatsoever else hath provoked him thereto, seeing it is not lawful for me to alter or contradict his appointment, I will recount an accident very pitiful, or rather most unfortunate, and well worthy to be graced with our tears.

Tancredi, Prince of Salerno (which city, before the Consuls of Rome held dominion in that part of Italy stood free, and thence perchance took the modern title of a principality), was a very humane lord and of ingenious nature, if in his elder years he had not soiled his hands in the blood of lovers, especially one of them, being both near and dear unto him. So it fortuned that during the whole lifetime of this prince he had but one only daughter (albeit it had been much better if he had had none at all), whom he so choicely loved and esteemed as never was any child more dearly affected of a father, and so far extended his over-curious respect of her as he would seldom admit her to be forth of his sight ; neither would he suffer her to marry, although she had outstepped by divers years the age meet for marriage. Nevertheless, at length he matched her with the son to the Duke of Capua, who lived no long while with her, but left her in a widowed estate, and then she returned home to her father again.

This lady had all the most absolute perfections, both of favour and feature, that could be wished in any woman—young, quaintly disposed, and of admirable understanding—more, perhaps, than was requisite in so weak a body. Continuing thus in Court with the King her father, who loved her beyond all his future hopes, like a lady of great and glorious magnificence, she lived in all delights and pleasure. She, well perceiving that her father thus exceeding in his affection to her, had no mind at all of remarrying her, and holding it most immodest in her to solicit him with any such suit, concluded in her mind's consultations to make choice of some one special friend or favourite, if fortune would prove so furtherous to her, whom she might acquaint secretly with her sober, honest, and familiar purpose. Her father's Court, being much frequented with plentiful access of brave gentlemen and others of inferior quality,

as commonly the courts of kings and princes are, whose carriage
and demeanour she very heedfully observed. There was a young
gentleman among all the rest, a servant to her father and named
Guiscardo—a man not derived from any great descent by blood,
yet much more noble by virtue and commendable behaviour than
appeared or was to be observed and found in any of the other—
none pleased her opinion like as he did.

The young gentleman, though poor, being neither block nor
dullard, perceiving what he made no outward show of, and understood himself so sufficiently that, holding it no mean happiness to
be affected by her, he thought it very base and cowardly in him if
he should not express the like to her again. So loving mutually,
yet secretly, in this manner, and she coveting nothing more than to
have private conference with him, yet not daring to trust any one
with so important a matter, at length she devised a new stratagem
to compass her longing desire, and acquaint him with her private
purpose, which proved to be in this manner. She wrote a letter
concerning what was the next day to be done for their secret
meeting together, and, conveying it within the joint of a hollow
cane, in jesting manner threw it to Guiscardo, saying : " Let your
man use this for a pair of bellows when he meaneth to make a fire
in your chamber." Guiscardo, taking up the cane, and considering
within himself that neither was it given or the words thus spoken
but doubtless on some important occasion, went unto his lodging
with the cane, where, viewing it respectively, he found it to be
cleft, and, opening it with his knife, found there the written letter
enclosed.

After he had read it, and well considered on the service therein
concerned, he was the most joyful man of the world, and began to
contrive the aptest means for meeting with his gracious mistress,
and according as she had given him direction. In a corner of the
King's palace, it being seated on a rising hill, a cave had long been
made in the body of the same hill, which received no light into it
but by a small spiracle or vent-loop made out ingeniously on the
hill's side ; and because it had not been a long time frequented by
the access of anybody, that vent-light was overgrown with briars
and bushes, which almost engirt it round about. No one could
descend into this cave or vault but only by a secret pair of stairs,
answering to a lower chamber of the palace, and very near to the
Princess's lodging, as being altogether at her command, by reason
of a strong and barred defensible door whereby to mount or descend
at her pleasure. And both the cave itself, as also the steps conducting down into it, were now so quite worn out of memory, in
regard it had not been visited by any one in long time before, as no
man remembered that there was any such thing.

But love, from whose bright discerning eyes nothing can so
closely be concealed but at the length it cometh to light, had made
this amorous lady mindful thereof, and because she would not be
discovered in her intention, many days together her soul became
perplexed by what means that strong door might best be opened

before she could compass to perform it. But after that she had found out the way, and gone down herself alone into the cave, observing the loop-light, and had made it commodious for her purpose, she gave knowledge thereof to Guiscardo to have him devise an apt course for his descent, acquainting him truly with the height, and how far it was distant from the ground within. After he had found the souspiral in the hill's side, and given it a large entrance for his safer passage, he provided a ladder of cords, with steps sufficient for his descending and ascending, as also a wearing suit made of leather to keep his skin unscratched of the thorns, and to avoid all suspicion of his resorting thither. In this manner went he to the said loop-hole the night following, and having fastened one end of his corded ladder to the strong stump of a tree being close by it, by means of the said ladder he descended down into the cave, and there attended the coming of his lady.

She, on the morrow morning, pretended to her waiting woman that she was scarcely well, and therefore would not be disturbed the most part of that day, commanded them to leave her alone in her chamber, and not return until she called for them, locking the door herself for the better security. Then opened she the door of the cave, and going down the stairs found there her amorous friend Guiscardo, whom she saluted with a chaste and modest kiss; causing him to ascend up the stairs with her into her chamber. This long desired and now obtained meeting, caused the two dearly affected lovers in kind discourse of amorous argument, without uncivil or rude demeanour, to spend there the most part of that day to their hearts' joy and mutual contentment. And having concluded on their often meeting there in this concealed sort, Guiscardo went down into the cave again, the Princess making the door fast after him, and then went forth among her women. And so, in the night season, Guiscardo ascended up again by his ladder of cords, and covering the loop-hole with brambles and bushes, returned, unseen of any, to his own lodging : the cave being afterward guilty of their often meeting there in this manner.

But Fortune, who hath always been a fatal enemy to lovers' stolen felicities, became envious of their thus secret meeting, and overthrew, in an instant, all their poor happiness by an accident most spiteful and malicious. The King had used divers days before dinner-time, to resort all alone to his daughter's chamber, there conversing with her in most loving manner. One unhappy day among the rest, when the Princess, being named Ghismonda, was sporting in her private garden among her ladies, the King, at his wonted time, went to his daughter's chamber, being neither seen nor heard by any. Nor would he have his daughter called from her pleasure ; but finding the windows fast shut, and the curtains close drawn about the bed, he sat down in a chair behind it, and leaning his head upon the bed, his body being covered with the curtain, as if he hid himself purposely ; he mused on so many matters till at last he fell asleep.

It hath been observed as an ancient adage, that when disasters are ordained to any one, commonly they prove to be inevitable, as poor Ghismonda could witness too well. For while the King thus slept, she having, unluckily, appointed another meeting with her friendly lover Guiscardo, left her gentlewomen in the garden, and stealing softly into her chamber, having made all fast and sure for being descried by any person, opened the door to Guiscardo, who stood there ready on the stair-head awaiting his entrance ; and they sitting down, as they were wont to do, began their usual kind of con- ference again, with sighs and loving kisses mingled among them. It chanced the King awaked, and both hearing and seeing this fami- liarity of Guiscardo with his daughter, he became greatly confounded with grief thereat.   Once he intended to cry out for help, to have them both there apprehended: but he held it a part of greater wisdom to sit silent still, and, if he could, to keep himself so closely concealed : to the end that he might more secretly, and with far less disgrace to himself, perform what he had rashly intended to do.

The poor discovered lovers having ended their amorous inter- parlance without suspicion of the King's being so near in person, or any else to betray their over-confident trust, Guiscardo descended again into the cave, and she, leaving the chamber, returned to her women in the garden ; all which Tancredi well observed, and in a rapture of fury departed, unseen, into his own lodging.   The same night, about the hour of men's first sleep, and according as he had given order, Guiscardo was apprehended even as he was coming forth of the loop-hole, and in his homely leather habit.   Very closely was he brought before the King, whose heart was swollen so great with grief, as hardly was he able to speak.   Notwithstanding at the last he began thus : "Guiscardo, the love and respect I have used towards thee have not deserved the shameful wrong which thou hast requited me withal, and as I have seen with mine own eyes this day."   Whereunto Guiscardo could answer nothing else but only this : "Alas, my lord !   Love is able to do much more than either you or I."   Whereupon Tancredi commanded that he should be secretly well guarded in a near adjoining chamber.   And on the next day, Ghismonda having, as yet, heard nothing thereof, the King's brain being infinitely busied and troubled, after dinner, and as he often had used to do, he went to his daughter's chamber, where calling for her and shutting the doors closely to them, the tears trickling down his aged white beard, thus he spake to her :

"Ghismonda, I was once grounded in a settled persuasion that I truly knew thy virtue and honest integrity of life ; and this belief could never have been altered in me by any sinister reports whatso- ever, had not mine eyes seen and mine ears heard the contrary. Nor did I so much as conceive a thought either of thine affection, or private conversing with any man, but only he that was to be thy husband.   But now I myself being able to avouch thy folly, imagine what a heart-break this will be to me, so long as life remaineth in this poor, weak, and aged body.   Yet, if needs thou must have yielded to this wanton weakness, I would thou hadst made choice of a man answerable to thy birth and nobility: whereas, on the contrary, among so many worthy spirits as resort to my Court, thou likest best to converse with that silly young man Guiscardo, one of very mean and base descent, and by me, even for God's sake, from his very youngest years brought up to this instant in my Court; wherein thou hast given me such affliction of mind and so overthrown my senses, as I cannot well imagine how I should deal with thee. For him, whom I have this night caused to be surprised, even as he came forth of your close contrived conveyance, and detained as my prisoner, I have resolved how to proceed with him , but concerning thyself, mine oppressions are so many and violent as I know not what to say of thee. One way thou hast merely murdered the unfeigned affection I bare thee as never any father could express more to his child, and then again, thou hast kindled a most just indignation in me, by thy immodest and wilful folly, and whereas Nature pleadeth pardon for the one, yet justice standeth up against the other and urgeth cruel severity against thee; nevertheless, before I will determine upon any resolution, I come purposely first to hear thee speak, and what thou canst say for thyself in a base case so desperate and dangerous."

Having thus spoken he hung down the head in his bosom, weeping as abundantly as if he had been a child severely disciplined. On the other side, Ghismonda hearing the speeches of her father, and perceived withal, that not only her secret love was discovered, but also that Guiscardo was in close prison, the matter which most of all did torment her; she fell into a very strange kind of ecstasy, scorning tears and entreating terms, such as feminine frailty are always aptest unto; but rather with height of courage, controlling fear or servile baseness, and declaring invincible fortitude in her very look, she concluded with herself, rather than to urge any humble persuasions she would lay her life down at the stake. For plainly she perceived that Guiscardo already was a dead man in law, and death was likewise welcome to her, rather than the deprivation of her love; and therefore, not like a weeping woman, or as checked by the offence committed, but careless of any harm happening to her, stoutly and courageously, not a tear appearing in her eye, or her soul any way to be perturbed, thus she spake to her father :

"Tancredi, to deny what I have done, or to entreat any favour from you, is now no part of my disposition, for as the one can little avail me, so shall not the other anyway advantage me. Moreover, I covet not that you should extend any clemency or kindness to me, but by my voluntary confession of truth, do intend, first of all, to defend mine honour with reasons sound, good and substantial, and then virtuously pursue, to the full effect, the greatness of my mind and constant resolution. True it is that I have loved, and still do, honourable Guiscardo, purposing the like so long as I shall live, which will be but a small while: but if it be possible to continue the same affection after death, it is for ever vowed to him only, nor did mine own womanly weakness so much thereto induce me, as the

matchless virtue shining clearly in Guiscardo, and the little respect
you had of marrying me again.   Why, royal father, you cannot be
ignorant that you, being composed of flesh and blood, have a
daughter of the self-same composition, and not made of stone or iron.
Moreover, you ought to remember, although you are far stepped in
years, what the laws of youth are, and with what difficulty they are
to be contradicted, considering withal, that albeit, during the vigour ·
of your best time, you evermore were exercised in arms, yet you
should likewise understand that negligence and idle delights have
mighty power, not only in young people, but also in them of greatest
years.

"I then being made of flesh and blood, and so derived, from
yourself, having had also so little benefit of life, that I am yet in the
spring and blooming time of my blood; by either of these reasons
I must needs be subject to natural desires; yet did I strive, even
with all my utmost might, and best virtuous faculties abiding in me,
no way to disgrace either you or myself, as in equal censure, yet
have I not done.   But Nature is above all human power, and love
commanded by Nature hath prevailed; for love, joining with
fortune, in mere pity and commiseration of my extreme wrong, I
found them both most benign and gracious, teaching me a way
secret enough, howsoever you became instructed, or perhaps found
it out by accident, so it was, and I deny it not.

"Nor did I make election of Guiscardo by chance, or rashly,
as many women do, but by deliberate counsel in my soul, and most
mature advice, I made choice of him above all other, and having
his honest harmless conversation, mutually we enjoyed our hearts'
contentment.   Now it appeareth that I have not offended but by
love, in imitation of vulgar opinion, rather than truth ; you seek to
reprove me bitterly, alleging no other main argument for your
anger, but only my not choosing a gentleman, or one more worthy.
Wherein it is most evident, that you do not so much check my fault
as the ordination of fortune, who many times advanceth men of
meanest esteem, and abaseth them of greater merit.   But leaving
this discourse, let us look into the original of things, wherein we are
first to observe, that from one mass or lump of flesh both we and
all other received our flesh, and one Creator hath created all things ;
yea, all creatures, equally in their forces and faculties, and equal
likewise in their virtue ; which virtue was the first that made
distinction of birth and equality, in regard, that such as have the
most liberal portion thereof, and performed actions thereunto
answerable, were thereby termed noble : all the rest remaining
unnoble.   Now although contrary use did afterward hide and
conceal this law, yet was it not therefore banished from Nature or
good manners.   In which respect, whosoever did execute all his
actions by virtue, declared himself openly to be noble ; and he that
termed him otherwise, it was an error in the mis·caller, and not in
the person so wrongfully called, as the very same privilege is yet in
full force among us at this day.

"Cast an heedful eye then, good father, upon all your gentlemen,

and advisedly examine their virtues, conditions, and manner of behaviour.   On the other side, observe those parts remaining in
Guiscardo, and then if you will judge truly, and without affection,
you will confess him to be most noble, and that all your gentlemen,
in respect of him, are base grooms and villains.   His virtues and
excelling perfections, I never credited from the report or judgment
of any person; but only by your speeches, and mine own eyes are
true witnesses.   Who did ever more commend Guiscardo, extolling
all those singularities in him, most requisite to be in an honest,
virtuous man, than you yourself have done ?   Nor need you to be
sorry, or ashamed of your good opinion concerning him, for if
mine eyes have not deceived my judgment, you never gave him the
least part of praise, but I have known much more in him than ever
your words were able to express ; wherefore, if I have been any
way deceived, truly the deceit proceeded only from you.   How will
you then maintain that I have thrown my liking on a man of base
condition ?   In troth, sir, you cannot.   Perhaps you will allege that
he is but mean and poor; I confess it, and surely it is your shame
that you have not bestowed place of more preferment on a man so
honest and well deserving, and having been so long a time your
servant.   Nevertheless, poverty impaireth not any part of noble
nature, but wealth hurries it into horrible confusions.   Many kings
and great princes have heretofore been poor, when divers of them
that have delved into the earth, and kept flocks in the field, have
been advanced to riches, and exceeded the other in wealth.

" Now as concerning your last doubt, which most of all afflicteth
you, namely, how you shall deal with me ; boldly rid your brain of
any such disturbance; for if you have resolved now in your
extremity of years, to do that which your younger days evermore
despised—I mean, to become cruel—use your utmost cruelty against
me, for I will never entreat you to the contrary, because I am the
sole occasion of this offence if it do deserve the name of an
offence.   And this I dare assure you, that if you deal with me as
you have done already, or intend to Guiscardo, mine own hands
shall act as much; and therefore give over your tears to women,
and if you purpose to be cruel, let him and me in death drink both
of one cup, at least if you imagine that we have deserved it."

The King knew well enough the high spirit of his daughter, but
yet, nevertheless, he did not believe that her words would prove
actions, or she do as she said. And therefore parting from her, and
without intent of using any cruelty to her, concluded, by quenching
the heat of another, to cool the fiery rage of her distemper, commanded two of his followers, who had the custody of Guiscardo,
that without any rumour or noise at all, they should strangle him
the night ensuing, and taking the heart forth of his body, to bring
it to him ; which they performed according to their charge. On the
next day, the King called for a goodly standing cup of gold, wherein
he put the heart of Guiscardo, sending it by one of his most
familiar servants to his daughter, with command also to use these
words to her : " Thy father hath sent thee this present, to comfort

thee with that thing which most of all thou affectest, even as thou hast comforted him with that thing which he most hated."

Ghismonda, nothing altered from her cruel deliberation, after her father was departed from her, caused certain poisonous roots and herbs to be brought her, which she, by distillation, made a water of, to drink suddenly, whensoever any cross accident should come from her father; whereupon, when the messenger from her father had delivered her the present, and uttered the words as he was commanded, she took the cup, and looking into it with a settled countenance, by sight of the heart, and effect of the message, she knew certainly that was the heart of Guiscardo; then looking sternly on the servant, thus she spake unto him: "My honest friend, it is no more than right and justice, that so worthy a heart as this is, should have any worse grave than gold, wherein my father hath dealt most wisely." So lifting the heart up to her mouth, and sweetly kissing it, she proceeded thus: "In all things, even till this instant, being the utmost period of my life, I have evermore found my father's love most effectual to me; but now it appeareth far greater than at any time heretofore, and therefore from my mouth thou must deliver him the latest thanks that ever I shall give him for sending me such an honourable present."

These words being ended, holding the cup fast in her hand, and looking seriously upon the heart, she began again in this manner: "Thou sweet entertainer of all my dearest delights, accursed be his cruelty that causeth me to see thee with my corporal eyes, it being sufficient enough for me always to behold thee with the sight of my soul. Thou hast run thy race, and as fortune ordained, so are thy days finished; for as all flesh hath an ending, so hast thou concluded, albeit too soon and before thy due time. The travails and miseries of this world have now no more to meddle with thee, and thy veriest heaviest enemy hath bestowed such a grave on thee as thy greatness in virtue worthily deserveth. Now nothing else is wanting, wherewith to beautify thy funeral, but only her sighs and tears that was so dear unto thee in thy lifetime. And because thou mightest the more freely enjoy them, see how my merciless father, on his own mere motion, hath sent thee to me; and truly I will bestow them frankly on thee, though once I had resolved to die with dry eyes, and not shedding one tear, dreadless of their utmost malice towards me.

"And when I have given thee the due oblation of my tears, my soul which sometime thou hast kept most carefully, shall come to make a sweet conjunction with thine; for in what company else can I travel more contentedly, and to those unfrequented silent shades, but only in thine? As yet I am sure it is present here, in this cup sent me by my father, as having a provident respect to the place for possession of our mutual pleasure; because thy soul affecting mine so truly cannot walk alone without his dear companion."

Having thus finished her complaint, even as if her head had been converted into a well-spring of water, so did tears abundantly flow from her fair eyes, kissing the heart of Guiscardo infinite times.

All which while, her women standing by her, neither knew what heart it was, nor to what effect her speeches tended; but being moved to compassionate tears, they often demanded, albeit in vain, the occasion of her sad complaining, comforting her to their utmost power. When she was not able to weep any longer, wiping her eyes and lifting up her head, without any sign of the least dismay, thus she spake to the heart: "Dear heart, all my duty is performed to thee, and nothing now remaineth uneffected, but only breathing my last to let my ghost accompany thine."

Then calling for the glass of water, which she had readily prepared the day before, and pouring it upon the heart lying in the cup, courageously advancing it to her mouth, she drank it up every drop, which being done, she lay down upon her bed, holding her lover's heart fast in her hand, and laying it so near to her own as she could. Now although her women knew not what water it was, yet when they had seen her to quaff it off in that manner, they sent word to the King, who much suspecting what had happened, went in all haste to his daughter's chamber, entering at the very instant when she was laid upon the bed, beholding her in such passionate pangs, with tears streaming down his reverend beard, he used many kind words to comfort her, when boldly thus she spake unto him: "Father," quoth she, "well may you spare these tears, because they are unfitting for you, and not any way desired by me. Who but yourself hath seen any man to mourn for his own wilful offence? Nevertheless, if but the least jot of that love do yet abide in you, whereof you have made such liberal profession to me, let me obtain this my very last request, to wit, that seeing I might not privately enjoy the benefit of Guiscardo's love while he lived, let yet, in death, one public grave contain both our bodies, that death may afford us what you so cruelly in life denied us."

Extremity of grief and sorrow withheld his tongue from returning any answer, and she perceiving her end approaching, held the heart still close to her own bare breast, saying: "Here, Fortune, receive two true hearts' latest oblation; for in this manner are we coming to thee." So closing her eyes, all sense forsook her, life leaving her body breathless. Thus ended the hapless love of Guiscardo and Ghismonda, for whose sad disaster, when the King had mourned sufficiently and repented fruitlessly, he caused both their bodies to be honourably embalmed, and buried in a most royal monument, not without general sorrow of the subjects of Salerno.

THE SECOND NOVEL.

Friar Albert made a young Venetian gentlewoman believe that god Cupid was fallen in love with her.

THE novel recounted by Fiammetta caused tears many times in the eyes of all the company; but it being finished, the King, showing a stern countenance, said: "I should have much commended the kindness of fortune if in the whole course of my life I had tasted the least moiety of that delight which Guiscardo received by conversing with fair Ghismonda. Nor need any of you to wonder thereat, or how can it be otherwise, because hourly I feel a thousand dying torments, without enjoying any hope of ease or pleasure. But referring my fortunes to their own poor condition, it is my will that Pampinea proceed next in the argument of successless love, according as Fiammetta hath already begun, to let fall more dewdrops on the fire of mine afflictions. Pampinea perceiving what a task was imposed on her, knew well, by her own disposition, the inclination of the company, whereof she was more respective than of the King's command; wherefore choosing rather to recreate their spirits than to satisfy the King's melancholy humour, she determined to relate a tale of mirthful matter, and yet to keep within compass of the purposed argument.

[OMITTED.]

THE THIRD NOVEL.

Three young gentlemen affecting three sisters fled into Crete. The eldest of them, through jealousy, becometh the death of her lover; the second, by consenting to the Duke of Crete's request, is the means of saving her life. Afterward her own friend killeth her, and thence flieth away with the eldest sister. The third couple are charged with her death, and being committed prisoners they confess the facts; and fearing death, by corruption of money they prevail with their keepers, escaping from thence to Rhodes, where they died in great poverty.

WHEN the King perceived that Pampinea had ended her discourse, he sat sadly a pretty while without uttering one word, but afterward spake thus : "Little goodness appeared in the beginning of this novel because it ministered mirth; yet the ending proved better, and I could wish that worse afflictions had fallen on the friar." Then turning towards Lauretta, he said : "Lady, do you tell us a better tale, if possibly it may be." She smiling, thus answered the King : "Sir, you are over cruelly bent against poor lovers, in desiring that their amorous processions should have harsh and sinister concludings. Nevertheless, in obedience to your severe command, among three persons amorously perplexed, I will relate an unhappy ending, whereas all might be said to speed as unfortunately, and thus I proceed."

[OMITTED.]

THE FOURTH NOVEL.

Gerbino, contrary to the former plighted faith of his grandfather, King Guiglielmo, fought with a ship at sea, belonging to the King of Tunis, to take away his daughter, who was then in the same ship. She being slain by them that had possession of her, he likewise slew them, and afterwards had his own head smitten off.

LAURETTA having concluded her novel, and the company complaining on lovers' misfortunes, some blaming the angry and jealous fury of Ninetta, and every one delivering their several opinions, the King, as awaking out of a passionate perplexity, exalted his looks, giving a sign to Elisa that she should follow next in order, whereto she obeying, began in this manner : " I have heard, gracious ladies," quoth she, " of many people who are verily persuaded that Love's arrows never wound anybody, but only by the eyes, looks, and gazes, mocking and scorning such as maintain that men may fall in love by hearing only ; wherein, believe me, they are greatly deceived, as will appear by a novel as I shall now relate unto you, and wherein you shall plainly perceive that not only fame or report is as prevailing as sight, but also hath conducted divers to a wretched and miserable ending of their lives."

Guiglielmo the Second, King of Sicily, according as the Sicilian chronicles record, had two children, the one a son named Ruggieri, and the other a daughter called Gostanza. The said Ruggieri died before his daughter, leaving a son behind him named Gerbino, who, with much care and cost, was brought up by his grandfather, proving to be a very goodly prince, and wonderously esteemed for his great valour and humanity. His fame could not contain itself within the bounds or limits of Sicily only, but being published very prodigally in many parts of the world beside, flourished with no mean commendations throughout all Barbary, which in those days was tributary to the King of Sicily. Among other persons deserving most to be respected, the renowned virtues and affability of this gallant Prince Gerbino was understood by the beauteous daughter to the King of Tunis, who by such as had seen her, was reputed to be one of the rarest creatures, the best conditioned, and of the truest noble spirit that ever Nature framed in her very choicest pride of art.

Of famous, virtuous, and worthy men, it was continually her chiefest delight to hear of the admired actions of valiant Gerbino, reported to her by many singular discourses such as could best describe him, with language answerable to his due deservings. These won such honourable entertainment in her understanding soul, that they were most affectionately pleasing to her, and in recapitulating over and over again his manifold and heroical perfections, mere speech made her extremely amorous of him, nor willingly would she lend an ear to any other discourse but that which tended to his honour and advancement.

On the other side, the fame of her incomparable beauty, with addition of her other infinite singularities beside, as the world had given ear to it in numberless places, so Sicily came at length acquainted therewith in such flowing manner as was truly answerable to her merit. Nor seemed this as a bare babbling rumour in the princely bearing of royal Gerbino, but was embraced with such a real apprehension and the entire probation of a true understanding, that he was no less inflamed with noble affection towards her, than she expressed the like in virtuous opinion of him. Wherefore, awaiting such convenient opportunity when he might entreat license of his grandfather for his own going to Tunis, under colour of some honourable occasion, for the earnest desire he had to see her, he gave charge to some of his especial friends whose affairs required their presence in those parts, to let the Princess understand in such secret manner as best they could devise, what noble affection he bare unto her, devoting himself only to her service.

One of his chosen friends thus put in trust being a jeweller, a man of singular discretion, and often resorting to ladies for sight of his jewels, winning like admittance to the Princess, related at large unto her the honourable affection of Gerbino, with full tender of his person to her service, and that she only was to dispose of him. Both the message and the messenger were most graciously welcome to her; and flaming in the self-same affection towards him, as a testimony thereof, one of the very choicest jewels which she bought of him she sent by him to the Prince Gerbino, it being received by him with such joy and contentment, as nothing in the world could be more pleasing to him. So that afterward, by the trusty carriage of his jeweller, many letters and love-tokens passed between them, each being as highly pleased with this poor, yet happy kind of intercourse, as if they had seen and conversed with one another.

Matters proceeding on in this manner, and continuing longer than their love-sick passions easily could permit, yet neither being able to find out any other means of help, it fortuned that the King of Tunis promised his daughter in marriage to the King of Granada, whereat she grew exceedingly sorrowful: perceiving not only she should be sent further off by a large distance of way from her friend, but also be deprived utterly of all hope ever to enjoy him; and if she could have devised any means, either by secret flight from her father, or any way else to further her intention, she would have adventured it for the Prince's sake. Gerbino in like manner hearing of this purposed marriage, lived in a hell of torments, consulting oftentimes with his soul how he might be possessed of her by power, when she should be sent by sea to her husband, or private stealing her away from her father's Court before; with these and infinite other thoughts was he incessantly afflicted, both day and night.

By some unhappy accident or other, the King of Tunis heard of this their secret love, as also of Gerbino's purposed policy to surprise her, and how likely he was to effect it in regard of his manly valour and store of stout friends to assist him. Hereupon, when the time was come that he would convey his daughter thence to her marriage, and fearing to be prevented by Gerbino, he sent to the King of Sicily to let him understand his determination, craving safe conduct from him, without impeachment of Gerbino or any one else, until such time as his intent was accomplished. King Guiglielmo being aged and never acquainted with the affectionate proceedings of Gerbino, nor any doubtful reason to urge this security from him in a case convenient to be granted, yielded the sooner thereto right willingly, and as a signal of his honourable meaning, he sent him his royal glove, with a full confirmation for his safe conduct.

No sooner were these princely assurances received, but a good ship was prepared in the port of Carthagena, well furnished with all things thereto belonging, for the sending his daughter to the King of Granada, waiting for nothing else but best favouring winds. The young Princess, who understood and saw all this, secretly sent a servant of hers to Palermo, giving him special charge on her behalf to salute the Prince Gerbino, and to tell him withal, that within few days she must be transported to Granada. And now opportunity gave fair and free means to let the world know whether he were a man of that magnanimous spirit or no, as a general opinion had formerly conceived of him, and whether he affected her so firmly as by many close messages he had assured her. He who had the charge of this embassy effectually performed it, and then returned back to Tunis.

The Prince Gerbino, having heard this message from his divine mistress, and knowing also that the King, his grandfather, had passed his safe-conduct to the King of Tunis, for peaceable passage through his seas, was at his wits' end in this urgent necessity what might best be done. Notwithstanding, moved by the settled constancy of his plighted love, and the speeches delivered to him by the messenger from the Princess to show himself a man endued with courage, he departed thence into Messina, where he made ready two speedy galleys, and fitting them with men of valiant disposition, set away to Sardinia, as making full account that the ship which carried the Princess must come along that coast. Nor was his expectation therein deceived, for within few days after, the ship, not over swiftly winded, came sailing near to the place where they attended for her arrival, whereof Gerbino had no sooner gotten a sight, but to animate the resolutes which were in his company, thus he spake:

"Gentlemen, if you be those men of valour as heretofore you have been reputed, I am persuaded that there are some among you who either formerly have, or now instantly do, feel the all-commanding power of love, without which, as I think, there is not any mortal man that can have any goodness or virtue dwelling in him. Wherefore, if ever you have been amorously affected, or presently have any apprehension thereof, you shall the more easily judge of what I now aim at. True it is that I do love, and love hath guided me to be comforted and manfully assisted by you, because in yonder ship which you see coming on so gently under sail, even as if she offered herself to be our prize, not only is the jewel which I most esteem, but also mighty and most invaluable treasure, to be won without any difficult labour or hazard of a dangerous fight, you being men of such undaunted courage.   In the honour of which victory I covet not any part or parcel, but only a lady, for whose sake I have undertaken these arms, and freely give you all the rest contained in the ship. Let us set on them, gentlemen, and, my dearest friends, courageously let us assail the ship.   You see how the wind favours us, and, questionless, in so good an action fortune will not fail us."

Gerbino needed not to have spoken so much in persuading them to seize so rich a booty, because the men of Messina were naturally addicted to spoil and rapine, and before the Prince began his oration they had concluded to make the ship their purchase.   Wherefore giving a loud shout, according to their country manner, and, commanding their trumpets to sound cheerfully, they rowed on amain with their oars, and in mere despite set upon the ship; but before the galleys could come near her, they that had the charge and management of her, perceiving with what speed they made towards them, and no likely means of escaping from them, resolvedly they stood upon their best defence, for now it was no time to be slothful.

The Prince being come near to the ship, commanded that the patrons should come to him except they would adventure the fight.   When the Saracens were thereof advertised, and understood also what he demanded, they returned answer that their motion and proceeding in this manner was both against law and plighted faith, which was promised by the King of Sicily, for their safe passage through the sea, by no means to be molested or assailed.   In testimony whereof they showed his glove, avouching, moreover, that neither by force or otherwise they would yield or deliver him anything which they had aboard their ship.   Gerbino, espying his gracious mistress on the ship's deck, and she appearing to be far more beautiful than fame had made relation of her, being much more inflamed and scorched by the heat of love now, than formerly they had been, replied thus when they showed the glove : "We have," quoth he, "no falcon here now to be humbled at the sight of your glove ; and therefore, if you will not deliver the lady prepare yourselves for fight, for we must have her, whether you will or no."   Hereupon they began to let fly on both sides their darts and arrows, with stones sent in violent sort from their slings, thus continuing the fight a long while, to very great harm on either side.   At the length, Gerbino perceiving that small benefit would redound to him if he did not undertake some other kind of course, he took a small pinnace, which purposely he brought with him from Sardinia, and setting it on a flaming fire, conveyed it, by the galley's help, close to the ship.   The Saracens, much amazed thereat, and evidently perceiving that either they must yield or die, brought the King's daughter to the prow of the ship, most grievously weeping and wringing her hands.   Then calling Gerbino to let him behold their resolution, there they slew her before his face, and throwing her body into the sea, said : " Take her ! There we give her to thee, according to our bounden duty, and as thy perjury hath justly deserved."

This sight was not a little grievous to the Prince Gerbino, who, maddened now with this their monstrous cruelty, and not caring what became of his own life, having lost her for whom he only desired to live ; not dreading their darts, arrows, or slinged stones, or what violence else they could use against him, he leapt aboard their ship, in despite of all that durst resist him, behaving himself there like a hungry starved lion when he enters among a herd of beasts, tearing their carcases in pieces both with his teeth and his paws. Such was the extreme fury of this poor Prince, not sparing the life of any one that durst appear in his presence; so that, what with the bloody slaughter, and violence of the fires increasing in the ship, the mariners got such wealth as possibly they could save, and suffering the sea to swallow up the rest, Gerbino returned unto his galleys again, nothing proud of this so ill-gotten victory.

Afterwards, having recovered the Princess's dead body out of the sea, and embalmed it with sighs and tears, he returned back into Sicily, where he caused it to be most honourably buried in a little island named Ustica, face to face confronting Trapani. The King of Tunis, hearing this disastrous news, sent his ambassador, habited in sad mourning, to the aged King of Sicily, complaining of his faith broken with him, and how the accident had fallen out. Age being suddenly incited to anger, and the King extremely offended at this injury, seeing no way whereby to deny him justice, it being urged so instantly by the ambassador, caused Gerbino to be apprehended, and he himself (in regard that none of his lords and barons would therein assist him, but laboured to divert him by their earnest importunity) pronounced the sentence of death on the Prince, and commanded to have him beheaded in his presence, affecting rather to die without an heir than to be thought a king void of justice. So these two unfortunate lovers, never enjoying the very least benefit of their long-wished desires, ended both their lives in violent manner.

THE FIFTH NOVEL.

The three brethren of Isabella slew a gentleman that secretly loved her. His ghost appeared to her in her sleep, and showed her in what place they had buried his body. She, in silent manner, brought away his head, and putting it into a pot of earth, such as flowers, basil, or other sweet herbs are usually set in, she watered it a long while with her tears. Whereof her brother having intelligence, soon after she died with mere conceit of sorrow.

THE novel of Elisa being finished, and somewhat commended by the King in regard of the tragical conclusion, Filomena was enjoined to proceed next with her discourse. She, being overcome with much compassion for the hard fortunes of noble Gerbino and his beautiful Princess, after an extreme and vehement sigh, thus she spake ·

My tale, worthy ladies, extendeth not to persons of so high birth or quality as they were of whom Elisa gave you relation, yet peradventure it may prove no less pitiful. And now I remember myself, Messina, so lately spoken of, is the place where this accident also happened.

In Messina there dwelt three young men, brethren, and merchants by their common profession, who, becoming very rich by the death of their father, lived in very good fame and repute. Their father was of San Gimignano, and that had a sister named Isabella, young, beautiful, and well-conditioned, who upon some occasion as yet remained unmarried. A proper youth, being a gentleman born in Pisa, and named Lorenzo, as a trusty factor or servant, had the managing of the brethren's business and affairs. This Lorenzo, being of comely personage, affable, and excellent in his behaviour, grew so gracious in the eyes of Isabella that she afforded him many respective looks, yea, kindnesses of no common quality. Which Lorenzo taking notice of, and observing by degrees from time to time, gave over all beauties in the city which might allure any affection from him, and only fixed his heart on her, so that their love grew to a mutual embracing, both equally respecting one another and entertaining kindnesses as occasion gave leave.

Long time continued this amorous league of love, yet not so cunningly concealed, but at length the secret meeting of Lorenzo and Isabella, to ease their poor souls of love's oppressions, was discovered by the eldest of the brethren, unknown to them who were thus betrayed. He being a man of great discretion, although this sight was highly displeasing to him, yet notwithstanding he kept it to himself till the next morning, labouring his brain what might best be done in so urgent a case. When day was come, he resorted to his brethren, and told them what he had seen in the time past between their sister and Lorenzo.

Many deliberations passed on in this case, but after all, thus they concluded together, to let it proceed on with patient supportance, that no scandal might ensue to them or their sister, no evil act being as yet committed. And seeming as if they knew not of their love, had a wary eye still upon her secret walks, awaiting for some convenient time when, without their own prejudice, or Isabella's knowledge, they might safely break off this stolen love, which was altogether against their liking. So, showing no worse countenance to Lorenzo than formerly they had done, but employing and conversing with him in kind manner, it fortuned, that riding all three to recreate themselves out of the city, they took Lorenzo in their company, and when they came to a solitary place, such as suited best with their vile purpose, they ran suddenly upon Lorenzo, slew him, and afterward interred his body, where hardly it could be discovered by any one. Then they returned back to Messina, and gave it forth, as a credible report, that they had sent him abroad about their affairs, as formerly they were wont to do; which every one verily believed, because they knew no reason why they should conceit any otherwise.

Isabella, living in expectation of his return, and perceiving his stay to her was so offensive long, made many demands to her brethren, into what parts they had sent him, that his tarrying was so quite from all wonted course. Such was her importunate speech to them, that they taking it very discontentedly, one of them returned her this frowning answer : " What is your meaning, sister, by so many questionings after Lorenzo ? What urgent affairs have you with him, that makes you so impatient upon his absence ? If hereafter you make any more demands for him, we shall shape you such a reply, as will be but little to your liking." At these harsh words Isabella fell into abundance of tears, where among she mingled many sighs and groans, such as were able to overthrow a far greater constitution ; so that being full of fear and dismay, yet no way distrusting her brethren's so wicked and heinous a cruel deed, she durst not question any more after him.

In the silence of dark night, as she lay afflicted in her bed, often-times would she call for Lorenzo, entreating his speedy return to her. And then again, as if he had been present with her, she checked and reproved him for his long absence. One night among the rest, she being grown almost hopeless of ever seeing him again, having a long while wept and grievously lamented, her senses and faculties utterly spent and tired, that she could not utter any more complaints, she fell into a trance or sleep, and dreamed that the ghost of Lorenzo appeared unto her in torn and unbefitting gar-ments, his looks pale, meagre, and starving, and, as she thought, thus spake to her : " My dear love Isabella, thou dost nothing but torment thyself with calling on me, accusing me for over-long tarrying from thee ; I am come therefore to let thee know that thou canst not enjoy my company any more, because the very same day when last thou sawest me, thy brethren most bloodily murdered me." And acquainting her with the place where they had buried his mangled body, he strictly charged her not to call him at any time afterward, and so vanished away.

The young damsel awaking, and giving some credit to her vision, sighed and wept exceedingly ; and after she was risen in the morning, not daring to say anything to her brethren, she resolutely determined to go see the place formerly appointed her, only to make trial, if that which she seemed to see in her sleep should carry any likelihood of truth. Having obtained favour of her brethren to ride a day's journey from the city, in company of her trusty nurse, who long time had attended on her in the house, and knew the secret passages of her love, they rode directly to the designed place, which being covered with some store of dried leaves, and more deeply sunk than any other part of the ground thereabout, they digged not far, but they found the body of the murdered Lorenzo, as yet very little corrupted or impaired, and then per-ceived the truth of her vision.

Wisdom and government so much prevailed with her, as to instruct her soul, that her tears spent there were merely fruitless and in vain, neither did the time require any long tarrying there.

Gladly would she have carried the whole body with her, secretly to bestow honourable interment on it, but yet exceeded the compass of her ability. Wherefore, in regard she could not have all, yet she would be possessed of a part, and having brought a keen razor with her, by the help of the nurse, she divided the head from the body, wrapped it up in a napkin, which the nurse conveyed into her lap, and then laid the body in the ground again. Thus being undiscovered by any, they departed thence, and arrived at home in convenient time, where being alone by themselves in the chamber, she washed the head over and over with her tears, and bestowed infinite kisses thereon.

Not long after, the nurse having brought her a large earthen pot, such as we use to set basil, marjoram flowers, or other sweet herbs in, and shrouding the head in a silken scarf, putting it into the pot, covering it with earth, and planting divers roots of excellent basil therein, which she never watered but either with her tears, rose water, or water distilled from the flowers of oranges. This pot she used continually to sit by, either in her chamber, or anywhere else ; for she carried it always with her, sighing and breathing forth sad complaints thereto, even as if they had been uttered to her Lorenzo, and day by day this was her continual exercise, to the no mean admiration of her brethren, and many other friends that beheld her.

So long she held on in this mourning manner that, what by the continual watering of the basil, and putrefaction of the head so buried in the pot of earth, it grew very flourishing, and most odoriferous to such as scented it, that as no other basil could possibly yield so sweet a savour. The neighbours noting this behaviour in her, observing the long continuance thereof, how much her bright beauty was defaced, and the eyes sunk into her head by incessant weeping, made many kind and friendly motions to understand the reason of her so violent oppressions, but could not by any means prevail with her, or win any discovery by her nurse, so faithful was she in secrecy to her. Her brethren also waxed weary of this carriage in her, and having very often reproved her for it, without any other alteration in her, at length they closely stole away the pot of basil from her, for which she made infinite woful lamentations, earnestly entreating to have it restored again, avouching that she could not live without it.

Perceiving that she could not have the pot again, she fell into an extreme sickness, occasioned only by her ceaseless weeping, and never urged she to have anything but the restoring of the basil pot. Her brethren grew greatly amazed thereat, because she never called for aught else beside ; and thereupon were very desirous to ransack the pot to the very bottom. Having emptied out all the earth, they found the scarf of silk wherein the head of Lorenzo was wrapped, which was, as yet, not so much consumed, but by the locks of hair they knew it to be Lorenzo's head, whereat they became confounded with amazement.

Fearing lest their offence might come to open publication, they buried it very secretly, and before any could take notice thereof, they departed from Messina, and went to dwell at Naples. Isabella crying and calling still for her pot of basil, being unable to give over mourning, died within a few days after.

Thus have you heard the hard fate of poor Lorenzo and Isabella. Within no long while after, when this accident came to be publicly known, an excellent ditty was composed thereof, beginning thus :

> Ah, who was the bad Christian,
> That robbed me of my basil ?

THE SIXTH NOVEL.

A beautiful virgin named Andreavuola became enamoured of a young gentleman called Gabriotto. In conference together, she declared a dream of hers to him, and he another of his to her; whereupon Gabriotto fell down suddenly dead in her arms. She and her chambermaid were apprehended by the officers belonging to the Signory as they were carrying Gabriotto to lay him before his own door. The Podestà offering violence to the virgin, and she resisting him virtuously; it came to the understanding of her father, who approved the innocence of his daughter, and compassed her deliverance. But she afterward, being weary of all worldly felicities, entered into religion, and became a nun.

THE novel which Filomena had so graciously related was highly pleasing unto the other ladies, because they had oftentimes heard the song, without knowing who made it, or upon what occasion it was composed. But when the King saw that the tale was ended, he commanded Pamfilo that he should follow in his due course : whereupon he spake thus :

[OMITTED.]

THE SEVENTH NOVEL.

Fair Simona affecting Pasquino, and walking with him in a pleasant garden, it fortuned that Pasquino rubbed his teeth with a leaf of sage, and immediately fell down dead. Simona being brought before the Bench of Justice, and charged with the death of Pasquino, she rubbed her teeth likewise with one of the leaves of the same sage, as declaring what she saw him do, and thereon she died also in the same manner.

PAMFILO having ended his tale, the King declaring an outward show of passion in regard of Andreavuola's disastrous fortune, fixed his eye on Emilia, and gave her such an apparent sign as expressed his pleasure for her next succeeding in discourse, which being sufficient for her understanding, thus she began :

Fair assembly, the novel so lately delivered by Pamfilo, maketh me willing to report another to you, varying from it, in any kind of resemblance, only this excepted : that as Andreavuola lost her lover in a garden, even so did she of whom I am now to speak. And being brought before the seat of justice according as Andreavuola was, freed herself from the power of the law; yet neither by force, or her own virtue, but by her sudden and inopinate death. And although the nature of love is such, according as we have oftentimes heretofore maintained, to make his abiding in the houses of the noblest persons, yet men and women of poor and far inferior quality do not always sit out of his reach, though enclosed in their meanest cottages, declaring himself sometimes as powerful a commander in those humble places, as he doth in the richest and most imperious palaces, as will plainly appear unto you, either in all, or a great part of my novel, whereto our city pleadeth some title, though by the diversity of our discourses talking of so many several accidents, we have wandered into many other parts of the world to make all answerable to our own liking.

It is not any long time since there lived in our city of Florence, a young and beautiful damsel, yet lowly according to the nature of her condition, because she was the daughter of a poor father, and called by the name of Simona. Now albeit she was not supplied by any better means than to maintain herself by her own painful travail, and earn her bread before she could eat it, by carding and spinning by such as employed her; yet was she not so base or dejected a spirit, but had both courage and sufficient virtue to understand the secret soliciting of love, and to distinguish the part of well deserving, both by private behaviour and outward ceremony. As natural instinct was her tutor thereto, so wanted she not a second main and urging motion; a chip hewed out of the like timber, one no better in birth than herself, a proper young springall named Pasquino, whose generous behaviour and noble carriage, and graceful actions, in bringing her daily wool to spin by reason his master was a clothier, prevailed upon her liking and affection.

Nor was he negligent in the observation of her amorous regards, but the tinder took, and his soul flamed with the self-same fire, making him as desirous of her loving acceptance, as possibly she could be of his, so that the commanding power of love could not easily be distinguished in which of them it had the greater predominance. For every day as he brought her fresh supply of wools, and found her seriously busied at her wheel, her soul would vent forth many deep sighs, and those sighs fetched floods of tears from her eyes, through the singular good opinion she had conceived of him, and earnest desire to enjoy him. Pasquino, on the other side, as leisure gave him leave for the least conversing with her: his disease was every way answerable to hers, for tears stood in his eyes, sighs flew abroad to ease the poor heart's afflicting oppressions; which though he was unable to conceal, yet would he seem to cloud them cleanly by entreating her that his master's work might be neatly performed, and with such speed as time would permit her, intermixing infinite praises of her artificial spinning, and affirming withal, that the quills of yarn received from her were the choicest beauty of the whole piece; so that when other workwomen played, Simona was sure to want no employment.

Hereupon, the one soliciting, and the other taking delight in being solicited, affection grew the better settled in them both by interchangeable vows of constant perseverance, so that death only, but no disaster else, had power to divide them. Their mutual delight continuing on in this manner with more forcible increasing of their love's equal flame, it fortuned that Pasquino, sitting by Simona, told her of a goodly garden wherein he was desirous to bring her, to the end that they might the more safely converse together, without the suspicion of envious eyes. Simona gave answer of her well liking the motion, and acquainting her father therewith, he gave her leave on the Sunday following after dinner to go fetch the pardon of S. Gallo, and afterwards to visit the garden.

A modest young maiden named Lagina, following the same profession, and being an intimate familiar friend, Simona took along in her company, and came to the garden appointed by Pasquino, where she found him readily expecting her coming, and another friend also with him, called Puccino, albeit more usually termed Bandylegs, a secret well-willer to Lagina, whose love became the more furthered by this friendly meeting. Each lover delighting in his heart's chosen mistress, caused them to walk alone by themselves, as the spaciousness of the garden gave them ample liberty; Puccino with his Lagina in one part, and Pasquino with his Simona in another. The walk which they had made choice of was a long and goodly bed of sage, turning and returning by the same bed as their conference ministered occasion, and as they pleased to recreate themselves, affecting rather to continue still there than in any part of the garden.

One while they would sit down by the sage-bed, and afterwards rise to walk again as ease and weariness seemed to invite them. At length Pasquino chanced to crop a leaf of the sage, wherewith he both rubbed his teeth and gums, and champed it between them also, saying, that there is no better thing in the world to cleanse the teeth withal after feeding. Not long after he had champed the sage in his teeth, he returned to his former kind of discoursing, but his countenance began to change very pale, his sight failed, and speech forsook him; so that, in brief, he fell down dead. Which when Simona beheld, wringing her hands she cried out for help to Puccino and Lagina, who immediately came running to her. They finding Pasquino not only dead but his body swollen very much, and strangely overspread with foul black spots, both on his face, hands, and all parts else beside; Bandylegs cried out, saying, "Ah, wicked maid, what, hast thou poisoned him?"

These words and their shrill outcries also were heard by neighbours dwelling near to the garden, who coming in suddenly upon them, and seeing Pasquino lying dead and hugely swollen, Puccino likewise complaining, and accusing Simona to have poisoned him; she making no answer, but standing in a ghastly amazement, all her senses merely confounded at such a strange and uncouth accident, in losing him whom she so dearly loved, knew not how to excuse herself, and therefore every one verily believed that Puccino had not unjustly accused her.   Poor woful maid ! thus was she instantly apprehended ; and, drowned in her tears, they led her along to the Podestà's palace, where her accusation was justified by Puccino, Lagina, and two men more, the one named Atticciato, and the other Malegevole, fellows and companions with Pasquino, who came into the garden upon the outcry.

The judge without any delay at all gave ear to the business, and examined the cause very strictly, but could by no means comprehend that any malice should appear in her towards him, nor that she was guilty of the man's death.   Wherefore, in the presence of Simona he desired to see the dead body, and the place where he fell down dead, because there he intended to have her relate how she saw the accident to happen, that her own speeches might the sooner condemn her, whereas the case yet remained doubtful and far beyond his comprehension.   So, without any further publication, and to avoid the following of the turbulent multitude, they departed from the bench of justice, and came to the place where Pasquino's body was swollen like a tun.   Demanding there questions concerning his behaviour, when they walked in conference together, he not a little wondered at the manner of his death, while he stood advisedly considering thereon.

She going to the bed of sage, reporting the precedent history, even from the original to the ending, the better to make the case understood, without the least colour of ill-carriage towards Pasquino, according as she had seen him do, even so did she pluck another leaf of the sage, rubbing her teeth therewith, and champing it as he formerly did.   Bandylegs and the other intimate friends of Pasquino, having noted in what manner she used the sage, and this appearing as her utmost refuge, either to acquit or condemn her, in presence of the judge they smiled thereat, mocking and deriding whatsoever she said or did, and desiring the more earnestly the sentence of death against her, that her body might be consumed with fire, as a just punishment for her abominable transgression.

Poor Simona, sighing and sorrowing for her dear love's loss, and, perhaps, not meanly terrified with the strict infliction of torments so severely urged and followed by Puccino and the rest, standing dumb still, without answering so much as one word, by tasting of the same sage, fell down dead by the bed, even by the like accident Pasquino formerly did, to the admirable astonishment of all there present.

O poor unfortunate lovers ! whose stars were so auspicious to you as to finish both your mortal lives and fervent love in less limitation than a day's space.   How to censure your deaths, and happiness to ensue thereon, by an accident so strange and inevitable, it is not within the compass of my power, but to hope the best, and so I leave you.   But yet concerning Simona herself, in the common opinion of us that remain living, her true virtue and innocency —though fortune was otherwise most cruel to her—would not suffer her to sink under the testimony of Puccino, Lagina, Atticciato, and

Malegevole, being but carders of wool, or perhaps of meaner condition. A happier course was ordained for her to pass clearly from
the infamous imputation, and follow her Pasquino in the very same
manner of death, and with such a speedy expedition.

The judge stood amazed, and all there present in his company
were silent for a long while together, but upon better recollection
of his spirits thus he spake : "This inconvenience which thus hath
happened, and confounded our senses with no common admiration,
in mine opinion, concerneth the bed of sage, avouching it either to
be venomous or dangerously infected, which nevertheless is seldom
found in sage. But to the end that it may not be offensive to any
more hereafter, I will have it wholly digged up by the roots, and
then to be burnt in the open market-place."

Hereupon the gardener was presently sent for, and before the
judge would depart hence, he saw the bed of sage digged up by the
roots, and found the true occasion whereby these two poor lovers lost
their lives ; for just in the midst of the bed, and at the main root
which directed all the sage in growth, lay a huge mighty toad,
even weltering, as it were, in a hole full of poison, by means
whereof, in conjecture of the judge and all the rest, the whole bed
of sage became envenomed, occasioning every leaf thereof to be
deadly in taste. None being so hardy as to approach near the
toad, they made a pile of wood directly over it, and setting it on a
flame of fire, threw all the sage therein, and so they were consumed
together. So ended all further suit in law concerning the deaths of
Pasquino and Simona, whose bodies, being carried to the Church
of St. Paul, by their sad and sorrowful accusers, Puccino, Lagina,
Atticciato, and Malegevole, were buried together in one goodly
monument, for a future memory of their hard fortune.

THE EIGHTH NOVEL.

Girolamo affecting a young maiden named Salvestra was constrained, by the
earnest importunity of his mother, to take a journey to Paris. At his return
home from thence again, he found his love Salvestra married. By secret
means he got entrance into her house, and died upon the bed lying by her.
Afterward his body being carried to church to receive burial, she likewise
died there instantly upon his corpse.

EMILIA had no sooner concluded her novel, but Neifile, by the
King's command, began to speak in this manner :

[OMITTED.]

THE NINTH NOVEL.

Messer Guiglielmo of Rossiglione having slain Messer Guiglielmo Guardastagno whom he imagined to love his wife, gave her his heart to eat. Which she knowing afterward, threw herself out of a high window to the ground, and being dead, was then buried with her friend.

WHEN the novel of Neifile was ended, which occasioned much passion in the whole assembly, the King would not infringe the privilege granted to Dioneo. No more remaining to speak but they two, began thus :

I call to mind, gentle ladies, a novel which, seeing we are so far entered into the lamentable accidents of successless love, will urge you unto as much commiseration as that so lately reported to you. All so much the rather because the persons of whom we are to speak were of respective quality, which approveth the accident to be more cruel than those whereof we have formerly discoursed.

According as the people of Provence do report, there dwelt some time in that jurisdiction two noble knights, each well possessed with castles and followers : the one being named Messer Guiglielmo Rossiglione, and the other Messer Guiglielmo Guardastagno. Now, in regard that they were both valiant gentlemen, and singularly expert in actions of arms, they loved together the more mutually, and held it as a kind of custom to be seen in all tilts and tournaments, or any other exercises of arms, going commonly alike in their wearing garments ; and although their castles stood above five miles distant each from other, yet were they daily conversant together as loving and intimate friends. The one of them—I mean Messer Guiglielmo Rossiglione—had to wife a very gallant beautiful lady, of whom Messer Guardastagno, forgetting the laws of respect and loyal friendship, became over-fondly enamoured, expressing the same by such outward means that the lady herself took knowledge thereof, and not with any dislike, as it seemed ; yet she grew not so forgetful of her honour as the other did of faith to his friend.

With such indiscretion was this idle love carried that the husband perceived some such manner of behaviour as he could not easily digest nor thought it fitting to endure ; whereupon the league of friendly amity so long continued began to fail in very strange fashion, and became converted into deadly hatred, which yet he very cunningly concealed, bearing an outward show of constant friendship still, but in his heart he had vowed the death of Guardastagno. Nothing wanted but by what means it might best be effected, which fell out to be in this manner. A public joust or tourney was proclaimed by sound of trumpet throughout all France, wherewith immediately Messer Guiglielmo Rossiglione acquainted Messer Guardastagno, entreating him that they might further confer thereon together, and for that purpose to come and visit him, if he intended to have any hand in the business. Guardastagno being exceeding glad of this accident, which gave him liberty to see his mistress, sent answer back by the messenger that, on the morrow at night, he would come and sup with Rossiglione, who, upon this reply, projected to himself in what manner to kill him.

On the morrow, after dinner, arming himself, and two more of his servants with him, such as he had solemnly sworn to secrecy, he mounted on horseback and rode on about a mile from his own castle, where he lay closely ambushed in a wood through which Guardastagno must needs pass. After he had stayed there some two hours' space or more, he espied him come riding with two of his attendants, all of them being unarmed, as no way distrusting any such intended treason. So soon as he was come to the place where he had resolved to do the deed, he rushed forth of the ambush, and, having a sharp lance ready charged in his rest, ran mainly at him, saying, "False villain, thou art dead!" Guardastagno, having nothing wherewith to defend himself, nor his servants able to give him any succour, being pierced quite through the body with the lance, down he fell dead to the ground, and his men, fearing the like misfortune to befall them, galloped mainly back again to their lord's castle, not knowing them who had thus murdered their master, by reason of their armed disguises, which in those martial times were usually worn.

Messer Guiglielmo Rossiglione, alighting from his horse, and having a keen knife ready drawn in his hand, opened therewith the breast of dead Guardastigno, and taking forth his heart with his own hands, wrapped it in a pennon belonging to the lance, commanding one of his men to the charge thereof, and never to disclose the deed; so mounting on horseback again, and dark night drawing on apace, he returned home to his castle. The lady, who had heard before of Guardastagno's intent to sup there that night, and perhaps being earnestly desirous to see him, marvelling at his so long tarrying, said to her husband : "Believe me, sir," quoth she, "methinks it is somewhat strange that Messer Guiglielmo Guardastagno delays his coming so long ; he never used to do so till now." "I received tidings from his wife," said he, "that he cannot be here till to-morrow ;" whereat the lady appearing to be displeased, concealed it to herself, and used no more words.

Rossiglione leaving his lady, went into the kitchen, where, calling for the cook, he delivered him the heart, saying : "Take this heart of a wild boar, which it was my good hap to kill this day, and dress it in the daintiest manner thou canst devise to do; which being so done, when I am set at the table, send it to me in a silver dish, with sauce beseeming so dainty a morsel." The cook took the heart, believing it to be no otherwise than as his lord had said ; and using his utmost art in dressing it, did divide it into artificial small slices, and made it most pleasing to be tasted. When supper-time was come, Rossiglione sat down at the table with his lady, but he had little or no appetite at all to eat, the wicked deed which he had done so perplexed his soul, and made him to sit very strangely musing. At length the cook brought in the dainty dish, which he himself setting before his wife, began to find fault with his own lack of stomach, yet provoking her with many fair speeches to taste the cook's cunning in so rare a dish.

The lady having a good appetite indeed, when she had first tasted it, fed afterwards so heartily thereon that she left very little or none at all remaining. When he perceived that all was eaten, he said unto her: "Tell me, madam, how you do like this delicate kind of meat?" "In good faith, sir," quoth she, "in all my life I was never better pleased." "Now trust me, madam," answered the knight, "I do verily believe you; nor do I greatly wonder thereat, if you like that dead which you loved so dearly being alive." When she heard these words, a long while she sat silent, but afterwards said : "I pray you tell me, sir, what meat was this which you have made me to eat?" "Muse no longer," said he, "for therein I will quickly resolve thee. Thou hast eaten the heart of Messer Guiglielmo Guardastagno, whose love was so dear and precious to thee, thou false, perfidious, and disloyal lady. I plucked it out of his vile body with mine own hands, and made my cook to dress it for thy diet!"

Poor lady, how strangely was her soul afflicted hearing these harsh and unpleasing speeches! Tears flowed abundantly from her fair eyes, and, like tempestuous winds embowelled in the earth, so did vehement sighs break mainly from her heart, and, after a tedious time of silence, she spake in this manner: "My lord and husband, you have done a most disloyal and damnable deed, mis-guided by your own wicked jealous opinion, and not by any just cause given you, or any other favour allowed him but what might well become so honourable a friend. And seeing my body hath been made the receptacle for so precious a kind of food as the heart of so valiant and courteous a knight as was the noble Guardastagno, never shall any other food hereafter have entertain-ment there, or myself live the wife to so bloody a husband."

So starting up from the table, and stepping unto a great gazing window, the casement whereof standing wide open behind her, violently she leaped out thereat, which being a huge height in distance from the ground, the fall did not only kill her, but also shivered her body into many pieces; which Rossiglione perceiving, he stood like a body without a soul, confounded with the killing of so dear a friend, loss of a chaste and honourable wife, and through his own over-credulous conceit.

Upon further conference with his private thoughts, and re-morseful acknowledgment of his heinous offence, which repentance, too late, gave him eyes now to see, though rashness before would not permit him to consider; these two extremities enlarged his dulled understanding. First, he grew fearful of the followers of murdered Guardastagno, as also the whole country of Provence, in regard of the people's general love unto him, which being two main and important motives, both to the detestation of so horrid an act, and immediate severe revenge to succeed thereon; he made such provision as best he could, and as so sudden a warning would give leave, he fled away secretly in the night season.

These unpleasing news were soon spread abroad the next morning, not only of the unfortunate accidents, but also of Rossiglione's flight ; in regard whereof, the dead bodies being found and brought together, as well by the people belonging to Guardastagno, as them that attended on the lady, they were laid in the chapel of Rossiglione's castle where, after so much lamentation for so great a misfortune to befall them, they were honourably interred in one fair tomb, with excellent verses engraven thereon, expressing both their noble degree, and by what unhappy means they chanced to have their burial there.

THE TENTH NOVEL.

A physician's wife laid a lover of her maid's, supposing him to be dead, in a chest, by reason that he had drunk water which usually was given to procure a sleepy entrancing. Two Lombard usurers, stealing the chest in hope of a rich booty, carried it into their own house, where afterward the man awaking was taken for a thief. The chambermaid to the physician's wife, going before the Bench of Justice, accuseth herself for putting the imagined dead body into the chest, by which means he escaped hanging, and the thieves which stole away the chest were condemned to pay a great sum of money.

AFTER that the King had concluded his novel, there remained none now but Dioneo to tell the last, which himself confessing, and the King commanding him to proceed, he began in this manner :

So many miseries of unfortunate love, as all of you have already related, have not only swollen our eyes with weeping, but also made sick our hearts with sighing ; yea, gracious ladies, I myself find my spirits not meanly afflicted thereby. Wherefore, the whole day hath been very irksome to me, and I not a little glad that it is so near ending. Now, for the better shutting it up altogether, I would be very loth to make an addition of any such sad and mournful matter, good for nothing but to feed melancholy humour, and from which, I hope, my fair stars will defend me. Tragical discourse, thou art no fit companion for me ! I will therefore report a novel which may minister a more jovial kind of argument unto those tales that must be told to-morrow, and with the expiration of our present King's reign, to rid us of all heartburning hereafter.

[OMITTED.]

If the former novels had made all the ladies sad and sigh, this last of Dioneo as much delighted them, as restoring them to their former jocund humour, and banishing tragical discourse for ever. The King perceiving that the sun was near setting, and his government as near ended, with many kind and courteous speeches, excused himself to the ladies for being the motive of such an argument as expressed the infelicity of poor lovers. And having finished his excuse, up he rose, taking the crown of laurel from off his own head, the ladies awaiting on whose head he pleased next to · set it, which proved to be the gracious Lady Fiammetta; and thus he spake : "Here I place this crown on her head that knoweth better than any other how to comfort this fair assembly to-morrow for the sorrow which they have this day endured."

Fiammetta, whose locks of hair were curled, long, and like golden wires, hanging somewhat down over her white and delicate shoulders, her visage round, wherein the damask rose and lily contended for priority, the eyes in her head resembling those of the falcon messenger, and also a dainty mouth, her lips looking like two little rubies, with a comfortable smile thus she replied :

"Filostrato, gladly I do accept your gift; and to the end that ye may the better remember yourselves, concerning what you have done hitherto, I will and command that general preparation be made against to-morrow for fair and happy fortunes happening to lovers, after former cruel and unkind accidents;" which proposition was well pleasing to them all.

Then calling for the master of the household, and taking order with him, which was most needful to be done, she gave leave unto the whole company, who were all risen, to go recreate themselves until supper-time. Some of them walked about the garden, the beauty whereof banished the least thoughts of weariness. Others walked by the river to the mill, which was not far off, and the rest fell to exercises fitting their own fancies, until they heard the summons for supper. Hard by the goodly fountain, according to the wonted manner, they supped all together, and were served to their no mean contentment, but being risen from the table, they fell to their delight of singing and dancing. While Filomena led the dance, the Queen spake in this manner :

"Filostrato, I intend not to vary from those courses heretofore observed by my predecessors, but even as they have already done, so it is my authority to command a song. And because I am well assured that you are not unfurnished of songs answerable to the qualities of the past novels, my desire is, in regard we would not be troubled hereafter with any more discourses of unfortunate love, that you shall sing a song agreeing with your own disposition." Filostrato made answer, that he was ready to accomplish her command, and without all further ceremony, thus he began :

THE SONG.

CHORUS.   My tears do plainly prove,
How justly that poor heart hath cause to grieve,
Which, under trust, finds treason in his love.

When first I saw her that now makes me sigh,
Distrust did never come into my thoughts.
So many virtues clearly shined in her
That I esteemed all martyrdom was light
Which Love could lay on me. Nor did I grieve,
Although I found my liberty was lost.
But now mine error I do plainly see,
Not without sorrow thus betrayed to be.
    My tears do, &c.

For being left by basest treachery
Of her in whom I most reposèd trust;
I then could see apparent flattery
In all the fairest shows that she did make.
But when I strove to get forth of the snare,
I found myself the further plungèd in.
For I beheld another in my place,
Myself cast off with manifest disgrace.
     My tears do, &c.

Then felt my heart such hells of heavy woes,
Not utterable. I curst the day and hour
When first I saw her lovely countenance
Enriched with beauty far beyond all other,
Which set my soul on fire, enflamed each part,
Making a martyrdom of my poor heart;
My faith and hope being basely thus betrayed,
I durst not move, to speak I was afraid.
     My tears do, &c.

Thou canst, thou powerful God of Love, perceive
My ceaseless sorrow, void of all comfòrt;
I make my moan to thee, and do not feign,
Desiring that to end my misery
Death may come speedily, and with his dart
With one fierce stroke, quite piercing to my heart,
Cut off all future fell contending strife,
A happy end so made of love and life.
     My tears do, &c.

No other way of comfort doth remain
To ease me of such sharp afflictions,
But only death. Grant then that I may die,
To finish grief and life in one blest hour.
For being bereft of any future joys,
Come, take me quickly from so false a friend :
Yet in my death let thy great power approve
That I died true and constant in my love.
     My tears do, &c.

Happy shall I account this sighing song
If some beside myself do learn to sing it,
And so consider of my miseries,
As may incite them to lament my wrongs,
And to be warnèd by my wretched fate,
Lest, like myself, themselves do sigh too late.
Learn, lovers, learn, what is to be unjust,
And be betrayed where you repose best trust
     My tears do, &c.

The words contained in this song did manifestly declare what torturing afflictions poor Filostrato felt ; and more, perhaps, had been perceived by the looks of the lady whom he spake of, being then present in the dance, if the sudden ensuing darkness had not hid the crimson blush which mounted up into her face. But the song being ended, and divers others beside, lasting till the hour of rest drew on, by command of the Queen they all repaired to their chambers,

THE FIFTH DAY.

Wherein all the discourses do pass under the government of the most noble lady Fiammetta concerning such persons as have been successful in their love after many hard and perilous misfortunes.

INDUCTION.

Now began the sun to dart forth his golden beams, when Fiammetta, incited by the sweet singing birds, which since the break of day sate merrily chanting on the trees, arose from her bed, as all the other ladies likewise did; and the three young gentlemen descended down into the fields, where they walked in a gentle pace on the green grass, until the sun was risen a little higher. On many pleasant matters they conferred together as they walked in several companies, till at length the Queen finding the heat to enlarge itself strongly, returned back to the castle, where, when they were all arrived, she commanded that after this morning's walking their stomachs should be refreshed with wholesome wines, and also divers sorts of banqueting stuff. Afterward they all repaired into the garden, not departing thence until the hour of dinner was come: at which time the master of the household, having prepared everything in decent readiness, after a solemn song was sung, by order of the Queen, they were seated at the table.

When they had dined to their own liking and contentment they began, in continuation of their former order, to exercise divers dances, and afterward voices to their instruments, and many pretty madrigals and roundelays. Upon the finishing of these delights the Queen gave them leave to take their rest, when such as were so minded went to sleep; others solaced themselves in the garden. But after mid-day was past over, they met, according to their wonted manner, and, as the Queen had commanded, at the fair fountain, where she being placed in her seat royal, and casting her eye upon Pamfilo, she bade him begin the day's discourses of happy success in love, after disastrous and troublesome accidents, who yielding thereto with humble reverence, thus began:

Many novels, gracious ladies, do offer themselves to my memory wherewith to begin so pleasant a day as it is her highness's desire that this should be, among which plenty I esteem one above all the rest, because you may comprehend thereby not only the fortunate conclusion wherewith we intend to begin our day, but also how mighty the forces of love are, deserving to be both admired and reverenced. Albeit there are many, who scarcely know what they say, do condemn them with infinite gross imputations, which I purpose to disprove, and, I hope, to your no little pleasing.

THE FIRST NOVEL.

Cymon by falling in love became wise, and by force of arms winning his fair lady Iphigenia on the seas was afterwards imprisoned at Rhodes. Being delivered by one named Lysimachus, with him he recovered his Iphigenia again, and fair Cassandra, even in the midst of their marriage. They fled with them into Crete, where after they had married them, they were called home to their own dwelling.

ACCORDING to the ancient annals of the Cypriots, there sometime lived in Cyprus a noble gentleman, who was commonly called Aristippus, and exceeded all other of the country in the goods of fortune. Divers children he had, but (amongst the rest) a son, in whose birth he was more unfortunate than the rest, and continually grieved in regard that, having all complete perfections of beauty, good form, and many parts, surpassing all other youths of his age or stature, yet he wanted the real ornament of the soul—reason and judgment, being indeed a mere idiot or fool, and no better hope to be expected from him. His true name, according as he received it by baptism, was Galesus, but because whether by the laborious pains of his tutor's indulgence, with great care and fair endeavour of his parents, or by ingenuity of any other, he could not be brought to civility of life, understanding of letters, or common carriage of a reasonable creature, for his gross and deformed kind of speech, for his qualities also savouring rather of brutish feeding than any way derived from manly education; as an epithet of scorn and derision, generally they gave him the name of Cymon, which in their native country language, and divers other beside, signifieth a very sot or fool, and so was he termed by every one.

This lost kind of life in him was no mean burthen of grief unto his noble father. All hope being already spent of any future happy recovery, he gave command, because he would not always have such a sorrow in his sight, that he should live at a farm of his own in a country village, among his peasants and plough-swains. This was not anyway distasteful to Cymon, but well agreed with his own natural disposition; for their rural qualities and gross behaviour pleased him beyond the cities' civility. Cymon living thus at his father's country village, exercising nothing else but rural demeanour, such as then delighted him above all other, it chanced upon a day, about the hour of noon, as he was walking over the fields with a long staff on his neck, which commonly he used to carry, he entered into a small thicket, reputed the goodliest in all those quarters, and by reason it was then the month of May, the trees had their leaves fairly shot forth.

When he had walked through the thicket it came to pass that, even as good fortune guided him, he came into a fair meadow, on every side engirt with trees; and in one corner thereof stood a goodly fountain, whose current was both cool and clear. Hard by

it upon the green grass he espied a very beautiful damsel, seeming
to be fast asleep, attired in such loose garments as hid very little
of her white body ; only from the girdle downward she wore a
kirtle made close unto her of interwoven delicate silk, and at her
feet lay two other damsels sleeping, and a servant in the same
manner. No sooner had Cymon fixed his eye upon her but he
stood leaning on his staff, and viewed her advisedly, without speaking a word and in no mean admiration, as if he had never seen the
form of a woman before. He began then to feel in his rural understanding (whereunto never till now, either by painful instruction or
any good means used to him, any honest civility had power of
impression) a strange kind of humour to awake, which informed
his gross and dull spirit that this damsel was the very fairest which
any living man beheld.

Then he began to distinguish her parts, commending the tresses
of her hair, which he imagined to be of gold, her forehead, nose,
mouth, neck, arms, but, above all, her breasts, appearing as yet but
only to show themselves like two little mountains. So that of a
fielden clownish joat he would needs now become a judge of beauty,
coveting earnestly in his soul to see her eyes, which were veiled
over with sound sleep that kept them fast enclosed together, and
only to look on them he wished a thousand times that she would
awake, for in his judgment she excelled all the women that ever he
had seen, and doubted whether she were some goddess or no : so
strangely was he metamorphosed from folly to a sensible apprehension, more than common. And so far did this sudden knowledge in him extend that he could conceive of divine and celestial
things, and that they were more to be admired and reverenced than
those of human or terrene consideration ; wherefore the more
gladly he contented himself to tarry till she awaked of her own accord.
And although the time of stay seemed tedious to him, yet notwithstanding, he was overcome with such extraordinary contentment as
he had no power to depart thence, but stood as if he had been glued
to the ground.

After some indifferent respite of time, it chanced that the young
damsel, who was named Iphigenia, awaked before any of the other
with her, and lifting up her head with her eyes wide open she saw
Cymon standing before her leaning still on his staff ; whereat marvelling not a little she said unto him, "Cymon, whither wanderest thou,
or what dost thou seek for in this wood ?"   Cymon, who not only by
his countenance but likewise his folly, nobility of birth, and wealthy
possessions of his father, was generally known throughout the
country, made no answer at all to the demand of Iphigenia ; but so
soon as he beheld her eyes open he began to observe them with a
constant regard, and was persuaded in his soul that from them
flowed such an unutterable singularity as he had never felt till then.
Which the young gentlewoman well noting, she began to wax fearful lest these steadfast looks of his should incite his rusticity to some
attempt which might redound to her dishonour ; wherefore awaking
her women and servants, and they all being risen, she said, "Fare-

well, Cymon, I leave thee to thine own good fortune;" whereto he presently replied, saying, " I will go with you." Now although the gentlewoman refused his company as dreading some act of incivility from him, yet could she not devise any way to be rid of him till he had brought her to her own dwelling, where taking leave mannerly of her, he went directly home to his father's house, saying nothing should compel him to live any longer in the muddy country. And albeit his father was much offended hereat, and all the rest of his kindred and friends, yet not knowing how to help it, they suffered him to continue there still, waiting to know the cause of this his so sudden alteration from the course of life which contented him so highly before.

Cymon being now wounded to the heart, where never any civil instruction could before get entrance, with love's piercing dart, by the bright beauty of Iphigenia, falling from one change to another, moved much admiration in his father, kindred, and all else that knew him. For first he requested of his father that he might be habited and respected like to his brethren, whereto right gladly he condescended. And frequenting the company of civil youths, observing also the carriage of gentlemen, especially such as were amorously inclined, he grew to a beginning in a short time, to the wonder of every one, not only to understand the first instruction of letters, but also became most skilful even amongst them that were best exercised in philosophy. And afterward, love to Iphigenia being the sole occasion of this happy alteration, not only did his harsh and clownish voice convert itself more mildly, but also he became a singular musician and could perfectly play on any instrument. Beside he took delight in the riding and managing of great horses, and finding himself of a strong and able body he used all kinds of military disciplines, as well by sea as on the land. And to be brief, because I would not seem tedious in the repetition of all his virtues, scarcely had he attained to the fourth year after he was thus fallen in love, but he became generally known to be the most civil, wise, and worthy gentleman, as well for all virtues enriching the mind as any whatsoever to beautify the body, that very hardly he could be equalled throughout the whole kingdom of Cyprus.

What shall we say then, virtuous ladies, concerning this Cymon? Surely nothing else but that those high and divine virtues infused into his gentle soul, were by envious Fortune bound and shut up in some small angle of his intellect, which being shaken and set at liberty by Love, as having a far more potent power than Fortune in quickening and reviving the dull and drowsy spirits; declaring his mighty and sovereign authority in setting free so many fair and precious virtues unjustly detained, so let the world's eye behold them truly, by manifest testimony from whence he can deliver those spirits subjected to his power, and guide them, afterward, to the highest degrees of honour. And although Cymon by affecting Iphigenia failed in some particular things, yet notwithstanding his father Aristippus, duly considering that love had made him a man, whereas, before, he was no better than a beast, not only endured all patiently, but also advised him therein to take such courses as best liked himself. Nevertheless Cymon, who refused to be called Galesus, which was his natural name indeed, remembering that Iphigenia termed him Cymon, and coveting, under this title, to compass the issue of his honest amorous desire, made many motion, to Cipseus, the father of Iphigenia, that he would be pleased to let him have her in marriage. But Cipseus told him that he had already passed his promise for her to a gentleman of Rhodes, named Pasimunda, which promise he religiously intended to perform.

The time being come which was concluded on for Iphigenia's marriage, in regard that the affianced husband had sent for her; Cymon thus communed with his own thoughts. "Now is the time," quoth he, "to let my divine mistress see how truly and honourably I do affect her, because, by her, I am become a man. But if I could be possessed of her, I should grow more glorious than the common condition of a mortal man, and have her I will, or lose my life in the adventure." Being thus resolved, he prevailed with divers young gentlemen, his friends, making them of his faction, and secretly prepared a ship furnished with all things for a naval fight, setting suddenly forth to sea, and hulling abroad in those parts by which the vessel should pass that must convey Iphigenia to Rhodes to her husband. After many honours done to them who were to transport her thence unto Rhodes, being embarked they set sail upon their voyage.

Cymon, who slept not in a business so earnestly importing him, set on them, the day following, with his ship, and standing aloft on the deck, cried out to them that had the charge of Iphigenia, saying, "Strike your sails, or else determine to be sunk in the sea." The enemies to Cymon, being nothing daunted with his words, prepared to stand upon their own defence; which made Cymon after the former speeches delivered, and no answer returned, to command the grappling irons to be cast forth, which took so fast hold on the Rhodians' ship, that, whether they would or no, both the vessels joined close together. And he showing himself fierce like a lion, not tarrying to be seconded by any, stepped aboard the Rhodians' ship as if he made no respect at all of them, and having his sword ready drawn in his hand, incited by the virtue of unfeigned love, laid about him on all sides very manfully. Which when the men of Rhodes perceived, casting down their weapons, and all of them, as it were, with one voice yielded themselves his prisoners, whereupon he said . "Honest friends, neither desire of booty, nor hatred to you, did occasion my departure from Cyprus, thus to assail you with drawn weapons, but that which hereto hath moved me is a matter highly importing to me, and very easy for you to grant and so enjoy your present peace. I desire to have fair Iphigenia from you, whom I love above all other ladies living, because I could not obtain her of her father to make her my lawful wife in marriage. Love is the ground of my instant conquest, and I must use you as my mortal enemies, if you stand upon any further terms with me, .

and do not deliver her as mine own, for your Pasimunda must not enjoy what is my right, first by virtue of my love, and now by conquest. Deliver her therefore, and depart hence at your pleasure."

The men of Rhodes being rather constrained thereto than of any free disposition in themselves, with tears in their eyes delivered Iphigenia to Cymon, who beholding her in like manner to weep, thus spake unto her : "Noble lady, do not anyway discomfort yourself, for I am your Cymon, who have more right and true title to you, and much better do deserve you, by my long continued affection to you, than Pasimunda can anyway plead, because you belong to him but only by promise." So bringing her aboard his own ship, where the gentlemen his companions gave her kind welcome; without touching anything else belonging to the Rhodians, he gave them free liberty to depart.

Cymon being more joyful by the obtaining of his heart s desire, than any other conquest else in the world could make him, after he had spent some time in comforting Iphigenia, who as yet sate sadly sighing, he consulted with his companions, who joined with him in opinion, that their safest course was by no means to return to Cyprus ; and therefore all, with one accord, resolved to set sail for Crete, where every one made account, but especially Cymon, in regard of ancient and new combined kindred, as also very intimate friends, to find very worthy entertainment, and so to continue there safely with Iphigenia. But fortune, who was so favourable to Cymon in granting him so pleasing a conquest, to show her inconstancy, so suddenly changed the inestimable joy of our jocund lover into as heavy sorrow and disaster. For, four hours were not fully completed since his departure from the Rhodians, but dark night came upon them, and he sitting conversing with his fair mistress in the sweetest solace of his soul, the winds began to blow roughly, the seas swelled angrily, and a tempest rose impetuously, that no man could see what his duty was to do in such a great unexpected distress, nor how to warrant themselves from perishing.

If this accident were displeasing to poor Cymon, I think the question were in vain demanded ; for now it seemeth to him that the gods had granted his chief desire to the end he should die with the greater anguish in losing both his love and life together. His friends likewise felt the self-same afflictions, but especially Iphigenia, who wept and grieved beyond all measure, to see the ship beaten with such stormy billows as threatened her sinking every minute. Impatiently she cursed the love of Cymon, greatly blamed his desperate boldness, and maintaining that so violent a tempest could never happen but only by the gods' displeasure, who would not permit him to have a wife against their will ; and therefore thus punished his proud presumption, not only in his unavoidable death, but also that her life must perish for company.

She continuing in these woful lamentations, and the mariners labouring all in vain because the violence of the tempest increased more and more, so that every moment they expected wrecking, they were carried contrary to their own knowledge, very near to the Isle

of Rhodes, which they being no way able to avoid, and utterly
ignorant of the coast, for safety of their lives they laboured to land
there if possibly they might.　　Wherein fortune was somewhat
furtherous to them, driving them into a small gulf of the sea,
whereinto, but a little while before, the Rhodians, from whom
Cymon had taken Iphigenia, were newly entered with their ship.
Nor had they any knowledge each of other till the break of day,
which made the heavens to look more clearly, and gave them discovery
of being within a flight's shoot together.　Cymon looking forth, and
espying the same ship which he had left the day before, he grew exceeding sorrowful, as fearing that which after followed, and therefore he willed the mariners to get away from her by all their best
endeavour, and let fortune afterwards dispose of them as she
pleased, for into a worse place they could not come, nor fall into
the like danger.

The mariners employed their utmost pains, and all proved but
loss of time, for the wind was so stern, and the waves so turbulent,
that still they drove them the contrary way ; so that striving to get
forth of the gulf, whether they would or no, they were driven on
land, and instantly known to the Rhodians, whereof they were not
a little joyful.　The men of Rhodes being landed, ran presently to
the near neighbouring villages, where dwelt divers worthy gentlemen, to whom they reported the arrival of Cymon, what fortune
befell them at sea, and that Iphigenia might now be recovered again,
with chastisement to Cymon for his bold insolence.　They being very
joyful of this good news, took so many men as they could of
the same village, and ran immediately to the seaside, where Cymon
being newly landed and his people, intending flight into a near adjoining forest for defence of himself and Iphigenia, they were all
taken, led thence into the village, and afterward unto the chief
city of Rhodes.

No sooner were they arrived, but Pasimunda, the intended
husband for Iphigenia, who had already heard the tidings, went and
complained to the senate, who appointed a gentleman of Rhodes,
named Lysimachus, and being that year sovereign magistrate over
the Rhodians, to go well provided for the apprehension of Cymon and
his company, committing them to prison, which accordingly was
done.　In this manner the poor unfortunate lover Cymon lost his
fair Iphigenia, having won her in so short a time before, and scarcely
requited with so much as a kiss.　But as for Iphigenia, she was
royally welcomed by many lords and ladies of Rhodes, who so
kindly comforted her that she soon forgot all her grief and trouble
on the sea, remaining in company of those ladies and gentlemen
until the day determined for her marriage.

At the earnest entreaty of divers Rhodian gentlemen who were
in the ship with Iphigenia, and had their lives courteously saved by
Cymon, both he and his friends had their lives likewise spared,
although Pasimunda laboured importunately to have them all put
to death ; only they were condemned to perpetual imprisonment
which, you must think, was most grievous to them, as being now

hopeless of any deliverance. But in the meantime, while Pasimunda was ordering his nuptial preparation, Fortune seeming to repent the wrongs she had done to Cymon, prepared a new accident whereby to comfort him in his deep distress, and in such manner as I will relate unto you.

Pasimunda had a brother, younger than he in years, but not a jot inferior to him in virtue, whose name was Ormisda, and long time the case had been in question for his taking to wife a fair young gentlewoman of Rhodes, called Cassandra, whom Lysimachus the governor loved very dearly, and hindered her marriage with Ormisda by divers strange accidents. Now Pasimunda perceiving that his own nuptials required much cost and solemnity, he thought it very convenient that one day might serve for both their weddings, which else would launch into more lavish expenses, and therefore concluded that his brother Ormisda should marry Cassandra at the same time as he wedded Iphigenia. Hereupon he consulted with the gentlewomens parents, who liking the motion as well as he, the determination was set down, and one day to effect the duties of both.

When this came to the hearing of Lysimachus, it was greatly displeasing to him, because now he saw himself utterly deprived of all hope to attain the issue of his desire if Ormisda received Cassandra in marriage. Yet being a very wise and worthy man, he dissembled his distaste, and began to consider on some apt means whereby to disappoint the marriage once more, which he thought impossible to be done except it were by stealth; and that did not appear to him any difficult matter in regard of his office and authority, only it would seem dishonest in him by giving such an unfitting example. Nevertheless, after long deliberation, honour gave way to love, and resolutely he concluded to steal her away, whatsoever became of it.

Nothing wanted now but a convenient company to assist him, and the order how to have it done. Then he remembered Cymon and his friends, whom he detained as his prisoners, and persuaded himself that he could not have a more faithful friend in such a business than Cymon was. Hereupon, the night following, he sent for him into his chamber, and being alone by themselves, thus he began : "Cymon," quoth he, "as the gods are very bountiful in bestowing their blessings on men, so do they therein most wisely make proof of their virtues, and such as they find firm and constant in all occurrences which may happen, them they make worthy, as valiant spirits, of the very best and highest merit. Now, they being willing to have more certain experience of thy virtues than those which heretofore thou hast shown within the bounds and limits of your father's possessions, which I know to be super-abounding ; perhaps do intend to present thee other occasions of more important weight and consequence.

"For first of all, as I have heard, by the piercing solicitudes of love, from a senseless creature they made thee to become a man endued with reason. Afterward, by adverse fortune, and now again by wearisome imprisonment, it seemeth that they are desirous to make trial whether thy manly courage be changed or no from that which heretofore it was, when thou hast won a matchless beauty and lost her again in so short a while. Wherefore if thy virtue be such as it hath been, the gods can never give thee any blessing more worthy any acceptance than she whom they are now minded to bestow on thee ; in which respect, to the end that thou mayest re-assume thy wonted heroic spirit, and become more courageous than ever heretofore, I will acquaint thee more at large.

" Understand then, noble Cymon, that Pasimunda, the only glad man of thy misfortune, and diligent suitor after thy death, maketh all haste he can possibly devise to celebrate his marriage with thy fair mistress, because he would plead possession of the prey, which Fortune, when she smiled, did first bestow, and, afterward frowning, took from thee again. Now, that it must needs be very irksome to thee—at least if thy love be such as I am persuaded it is—I partly can collect from myself, being intended to be wronged by his brother Ormisda, even in the self-same manner and on his marriage-day, by taking from me fair Cassandra, the only jewel of my love and life. For the prevention of two such notorious injuries, I see that fortune hath left us no other means but only the virtue of our courages, and the help of our right hands, by preparing ourselves for arms, opening a way to thee by a second seizure or stealth, and to me the first, for absolute possession of our divine mistresses. Wherefore, if thou art desirous to recover thy loss, I will not only pronounce liberty to thee—which I think thou dost little care for without her—but dare also assure thee to have Iphigenia, so thou wilt assist me in mine enterprise, and follow me in my fortune, if the gods do let them fall into our power."

You may well imagine that Cymon's dismayed soul was not a little cheered at these speeches, and therefore, without craving any longer respite of time for answer, thus he replied : " Lord Lysimachus, in such a business as this is, you cannot have a faster friend than myself, at least if such good hap may betide me as you have more than half promised ; and therefore do no more but command what you would have to be effected by me, and make no doubt of my courage in the execution." Whereupon Lysimachus made this answer : " Know then, Cymon," quoth he, " that three days hence these marriages are to be celebrated in the houses of Pasimunda and Ormisda ; upon which day thou, thy friends, and myself, with some others, in whom I repose especial trust by the friendly favour of night, will enter into their houses while they are in the midst of their jovial feasting, and seizing on the two brides, bear them thence to a ship which I will have lie in secret, waiting for our coming, and kill all such as shall presume to impeach us." This direction gave great contentment to Cymon, who remained still in prison without revealing a word to his own friends, until the appointed time was come.

Upon the wedding-day, performed with great and magnificent triumph, there was not a corner in the brethren's houses but it sung joy in the highest key. Lysimachus, after he had ordered all things as they ought to be, and the hour for dispatch approached near, he made a division in three parts, of Cymon, of his followers, and his own friends, being all well armed under their outward habits. Having first used some encouraging speeches for more resolute prosecution of the enterprise, he sent one troop secretly to the port, that they might not be hindered of going aboard the ship when the urgent occasion should require it. Passing with the other two trains to Pasimunda, he left the one at the door, that such as were in the house might not shut them up fast, and so hinder their passage forth. Then with Cymon and the third band of confederates he ascended the stairs up into the hall, where he found the brides with store of ladies and gentlewomen all sitting in comely order at supper. Rushing in roughly among the attendants, down they threw the tables, and each of them laying hold of his mistress, delivered them into the hands of their followers, commanding that they should be carried aboard the ship for avoiding of further inconveniences.

This hurry and amazement being in the house—the brides weeping, the ladies lamenting, and all the servants confusedly wondering— Cymon and Lysimachus, with their friends, having their weapons drawn in their hands, made all opposers to give them way, and so gained the stairs for their own descending. There stood Pasimunda, with a huge long staff in his hand, to hinder their passage down the stairs, but Cymon saluted him so soundly on the head that, it being cleft in twain, he fell dead before his feet. His brother Ormisda came to his rescue, and sped likewise in the self-same manner as he had done ; so did divers others beside, whom the companions to Lysimachus and Cymon either slew outright or wounded.

So they left the house filled with blood, tears, and outcries, going on together without any hindrance, and so brought both the brides aboard the ship, which they rowed away instantly with their oars. For now the shore was full of armed people, who came in rescue of the stolen ladies, but all in vain, because they were launched into the main, and sailed on merrily towards Crete ; where being arrived they were worthily entertained by honourable friends and kinsmen, who pacified all unkindness between them and their mistresses ; and having accepted them in lawful marriage, there they lived in no mean joy and contentment, albeit there was a long and troublesome difference about these captures between Rhodes and Cyprus.

But yet in the end, by the means of noble friends and kindred on either side, labouring to have such discontentment appeased, endangering war between the kingdoms, after a limited time of banishment, Cymon returned joyfully with Iphigenia home to Cyprus, and Lysimachus with his beloved Cassandra unto Rhodes, each living in their several countries with much felicity.

THE SECOND NOVEL.

Fair Constance of Lipari fell in love with Martuccio Gomito, and hearing
that he was dead, desperately she entered into a bark, which being transported by the wind to Susa in Barbary, from thence she went to Tunis,
where she made herself known to him, and he being in great authority as a
Privy Councillor to the King, he married the said Constance, and returned
richly home with her to the island of Lipari.

WHEN the Queen perceived that the novel recited by Pamfilo was
concluded, which she graced with especial commendations, she
commanded Emilia to take her turn as next in order, whereupon
she thus began :

Methinks it is a matter of equity that every one should take
delight in those things whereby the recompense may be noted,
answerable to their own affection. And because I rather desire to
walk along by the paths of pleasure than dwell in any ceremonious
or scrupulous affection, I shall the more gladly obey our Queen to-
day than yesterday I did our melancholy King.

Understand then, noble ladies, that near to Sicily there is a small
island, commonly called Lipari, wherein, not long since, lived a
young damsel, named Constance, born of very sufficient parentage
in the same island. There dwelt also a young man called Martuccio
Gomito, of comely feature, well-conditioned, and not unexpert in
many virtuous qualities, affecting Constance in hearty manner, and
she so answerable to him in the same kind, that to be in his company was her only felicity. Martuccio coveting to have her in
marriage, made his intent known to her father, who, upbraiding
him with poverty, told him plainly that he should not have her.
Martuccio grieving to see himself thus despised because he was
poor, made such good means that he was provided of a small bark ;
and calling such friends as he thought fit to his association, made a
solemn vow that he would never return back to Lipari until he was
rich and in better condition.

In the nature and course of a rover or pirate so he put thence to
sea, coasting all about Barbary, robbing and spoiling such as he
met with who were of no greater strength than himself; wherein
fortune was so favourable to him that he became wealthy in a very
short while. But as felicities are not always permanent, so he and
his followers, not contenting themselves with sufficient riches, by
greedy seeking to get more, happened to be taken by certain ships
of the Saracens, and so were robbed themselves of all that they had
gotten, yet they resisted them stoutly a long while together, though
it proved to the loss of many lives among them. When the Saracens
had sunk his ship in the sea, they took him with them to Tunis,
where he was imprisoned and lived in extreme misery.

News came to Lipari not only by one but many more beside, that
all those that departed thence in the small bark with Martuccio
were drowned in the sea, and not a man escaped. When Constance

heard these unwelcome tidings, who was exceeding full of grief for his so desperate departure, she wept and lamented extraordinarily, desiring now rather to die than live any longer. Yet she had not the heart to lay any violent hands on herself, but rather to end her days by some new kind of necessity. And departing privately from her father's house, she went to the port or haven, where by chance she found a small fisher-boat, lying distant from the other vessels. The owners whereof being all gone on shore, and it well furnished with masts, sails, and oars, she entered into it; and putting forth the oars, being somewhat skilful in sailing, as generally all women of that island are, she so well guided the sails, rudder, and oars, that she was quickly far off from the land, and solely remained at the mercy of the winds. For thus she had resolved with herself, that the boat being uncharged and without a guide, would either be overwhelmed by the winds, or split in pieces against some rocks, by which means she could not escape although she would, but, as it was her desire, must needs be drowned.

In this determination, wrapping a mantle about her head, and lying down weeping in the boat's bottom, she hourly expected her final expiration. But it fell out otherwise, and contrary to her desperate intention, because the wind, turning to the north and blowing very gently, without disturbing the seas a jot, they conducted the small boat in such sort that, after the night of her entering into it, and the morrow's sailing on until the evening, it came within a hundred leagues of Tunis, and to a strand near a town called Susa. The young damsel knew not whether she were on the sea or land, as one who, not for any accident happening, would then lift up her head to look about her, neither intended ever to do so. Now it came to pass, that as the boat was driven to the shore, a poor woman stood at the seaside, washing certain fishermen's nets, and seeing the boat coming towards her under sail, without any person appearing in it, she wondered thereat not a little. It being close to the shore, and she thinking the fishermen to be asleep therein, stepped boldly and looked into the boat, where she saw not anybody, but only the poor distressed damsel, whose sorrows having brought her now into a sound sleep, the woman gave many calls before she could awake her, which at the length she did, and looked very strangely about her.

The poor woman perceiving by her habit that she was a Christian, demanded of her, in speaking Latin, how it was possible for her, being all alone in the boat, to arrive there in this manner? When Constance heard her speak the Latin tongue, she began to doubt lest some contrary wind had turned her back to Lipari again, and starting up suddenly, to look with better advice about her, she saw herself at land, and not knowing the country, demanded of the poor woman where she was? "Daughter," quoth she, "you are here hard by Susa in Barbary." Which Constance hearing, and plainly perceiving that death had denied to end her miseries, fearing lest she should receive some dishonour in such a barbarous unkind country, and not knowing what should now become of her, she sat .down by the boat-side, wringing her hands and weeping bitterly.

The good woman did greatly compassionate her case, and prevailed so well by gentle speeches, that she conducted her into her own poor habitation, where at length she understood by what means she happened thither so strangely. And perceiving her to be fasting, she set such homely bread as she had before her, a few small fishes, and a cruse of water, praying her for to accept of that poor entertainment, which mere necessity compelled her to do, and showed herself very thankful for it.

Constance hearing that she spake the Latin language so well, desired to know what she was. Whereto the old woman thus answered : " Gentlewoman," quoth she, " I am of Trapani, named Carapresa, and am a servant in this country to certain Christian fishermen." The young maiden, albeit she was very full of sorrow, hearing her name to be Carapresa, conceived it as a good augury to herself, and that she had heard the name before, although she knew not what occasion should move her thus to do. Now began her hopes to quicken again, and yet she could not rely upon what ground ; nor was she so desirous of death as before, but made more precious estimation of her life, and without any further declaration of her tell or country, she entreated the good woman, even for charity's sake, to take pity on her youth, and help her with such good advice to prevent all injuries which might happen to her in such a solitary woful condition.

Carapresa, having heard her last request, like a good woman as she was, left Constance in her poor cottage, and went hastily to leave her nets in safety ; which being done, she returned back again, and covering Constance with her mantle, led her on to Susa with her, where being arrived, the good woman began in this manner : " Constance, I will bring thee to the house of a worthy Saracen lady, to whom I have done many honest services, according as she pleased to command me.. She is an ancient woman, full of charity, and to her I will commend thee as best I may, for I am well assured that she will gladly entertain thee, and use thee as if thou wert her own daughter. Now let it be thy part, during thy time of remaining with her, to employ thy utmost diligence in pleasing her, by deserving and gaining her grace, till Heaven shall bless thee with better fortune." And as she promised so she performed.

The Saracen lady being well stepped into years, upon the commendable speeches delivered by Carapresa, did the more seriously fasten her eye on Constance, and, compassion provoking her to tears, she took her by the hand, and in loving manner kissed her forehead. So she led her further into her house, where dwelt divers other women, but not one man, all exercising themselves in several labours—as working all sorts of silk, with embroideries of gold and silver, and sundry other excellent arts besides, which in short time were very familiar to Constance ; and so pleasing grew her behaviour to the old lady, and all the rest beside, that they loved and delighted in her wonderfully, and by little and little she attained

F

to the speaking of their language, although it were very harsh and difficult.

Constance continuing thus in the old lady's service at Susa, and thought to be dead or lost in her own father's house, it fortuned that one reigned then as King of Tunis, who named himself Mariabdela. There was a young lord of great birth, and very powerful, who lived as then in Granada, and pleaded that the kingdom of Tunis belonged to him. In which respect he mustered together a mighty army, and came to assault the King, as hoping to expel him. These news coming to the ear of Martuccio Gomito, who spake the barbarian language perfectly, and hearing it reported that the King of Tunis made no mean preparation for his own defence, he conferred with one of his keepers, who had the custody of him and the rest taken with him, saying : " If," quoth he, " I could have means to speak with the King, and he were pleased to allow of my counsel, I can instruct in such a course as shall assure him to win the honour of the field." The guard reported these speeches to his master, who presently acquainted the King therewith, and Martuccio being sent for, he was commanded to speak his mind. Whereupon he began in this manner :

" My gracious lord, during the time that I have frequented your country, I have heedfully observed that the military discipline used in your battles dependeth more upon archers than upon other men employed in your war. And therefore, if it could be so ordered, that this kind of artillery may fail in your enemies camp, and yours be sufficiently furnished therewith, you need make no doubt of winning the battle." Whereto the King thus replied : " Doubtless, if such an act were possible to be done, it would give great hope of successfully prevailing." " Sir," said Martuccio, " if you please it may be done, and I can quickly resolve you how. Let the strings of your archers' bows be made more soft and gentle than those which heretofore they have used; and, next, let the notches of the arrows be so provided as not to receive any other than those pliant gentle strings. But this must be done so secretly that your enemies may have no knowledge thereof, lest they should provide themselves in the same manner. Now the reason, gracious lord, why thus I counsel you is to this end. When the archers on the enemies' side have shot their arrows at your men, and yours in like manner at them, it followeth that, upon mere constraint, they must gather up your arrows to shoot them back again at you for so long while as the battle endureth, as no doubt but your men will do the like to them. But your enemies will find themselves much deceived, because they can make no use of your people's arrows, in regard that the notches are too narrow to receive their boisterous strings, which will fall out contrary with your followers, for the pliant string belonging to your bows are as apt for their enemies' great notched arrows as their own, and so they shall have free use of both, reserving them in plentiful store, when your adversaries must stand unfurnished of any but them that they cannot any way use."

This counsel pleased the King very highly, and he being a prince of great understanding, gave orders to have it accordingly followed, and thereby valiantly vanquished his enemies. Hereupon Martuccio came to be great in his grace, as also consequently rich, and seated in no mean place of authority. Now, as worthy and commendable actions are soon spread abroad in honour of the man by whom they happened, even so the fame of this rare-got victory was quickly noised throughout the country, and came to the hearing of poor Constance that Martuccio Gomito (whom she supposed so long since to be dead) was living, and in honourable condition. The love which formerly she bare unto him being not altogether extinct in her heart, of a small spark brake forth into a sudden flame, and so increased day by day that her hope, being before almost quite dead, revived again in cheerful manner.

Having imparted all her fortune to the good old lady with whom she dwelt, she told her beside that she had earnest desire to see Tunis, to satisfy her eyes as well as her ears concerning the rumour blazed abroad. The good old lady commended her desire, and, even as she had been her mother, took her with her aboard a bark and so sailed thence to Tunis, where both she and Constance found honourable welcome in the house of a kinsman to the Saracen lady. Carapresa also went with them thither, and her they sent abroad into the city to understand the news of Martuccio Gomito. After they knew for a certainty that he was living and in great authority about the King, according as the former report went of him, then the good old lady, being desirous to let Martuccio know that his fair friend Constance was come thither to see him, went herself to the place of his abiding, and spake unto him in this manner: "Noble Martuccio, there is a servant of thine in my house, which came from Lipari, and requireth to have a little conference with thee; but because I durst not trust any other with the message, myself, at her entreaty, am come to acquaint thee therewith." Martuccio gave her kind and hearty thanks, and then went along with her to the house.

No sooner did Constance behold him but she was ready to die with conceit of joy, and, being unable to contain her passion, suddenly she threw her arms about his neck, and in mere compassion of her many misfortunes, as also the instant solace of her soul (not being able to utter one word), the tears trickled abundantly down her cheeks. Martuccio also seeing his fair friend, was overcome with exceeding admiration, and stood a while as not knowing what to say, till venting forth a vehement sigh, thus he spake: "My dearest love, Constance! Art thou yet living? It is a tedious long while since I heard thou wast lost, and never any tidings of thee in thy father's house." With which words, the tears standing in his eyes, most lovingly he embraced her. Constance recounted to him all her fortunes, and what kindness she had received from the Saracen lady since her first coming to her; and after much other discourse passing between them Martuccio departed from her, and returning to the King his master, told him all the history of his fortunes, and those beside of his dear love Constance, being purposely minded, with his gracious liking, to marry her according to the Christian law.

The King was much amazed at so many strange accidents, and, sending for Constance to come before him, from her own mouth he heard the whole relation of her continued affection to Martuccio, whereupon he said : " Now trust me, fair damsel, thou hast dearly deserved him to be thy husband." Then sending for very costly jewels and rich presents, the one half of them he gave to her and the other to Martuccio, granting them license withal to marry according to their own minds.

Martuccio did many honours, and gave great gifts to the aged Saracen lady with whom Constance had lived so kindly respected, which although she had no need of, neither ever expected any such rewarding, yet, conquered by their urgent importunity, especially Constance, who could not be thankful enough to her, she was enforced to receive them, and, taking her leave of them weeping, sailed back again to Susa.

Within a short while after, the King, licensing their departure thence, they entered into a small bark, and Carapiesa with them, sailing on with prosperous gales of wind until they arrived at Lipari, where they were entertained with general rejoicing ; and because their marriage was not sufficiently performed at Tunis, in regard of divers Christian ceremonies there wanting, their nuptials were again most honourably solemnized, and they lived many years after in health and much happiness.

THE THIRD NOVEL.

Pedro Boccamaza escaping away with a young damsel which he loved, named Agnolella, met with thieves in his journey. The damsel flying fearfully into a forest, by chance arrived at a castle. Pedro being taken by the thieves, happening afterward to escape from them, cometh accidentally to the same castle where Agnolella was ; and marrying her, they then returned home to Rome.

THERE was not any one in the whole company but much commended the novel of Emilia ; and when the Queen perceived it was ended, she turned towards Elisa, commanding her to continue on their delightful exercise, whereto she declaring her willing obedience, began to speak thus :

Courteous ladies, I remember one unfortunate night which happened to two lovers that were not endued with the greatest discretion ; but because they had very many and happy days afterwards, I am the more willing for to let you hear it.

In the city of Rome, which in times past was called the lady and mistress of the world, though now scarcely so good as the waiting-maid, there dwelt some time a young gentleman, named Pedro Boccamaza, descended from one of the most honourable families in Rome, who was much enamoured of a beautiful gentlewoman, called Agnolella, daughter to one named Giglivozzo Saullo, whose fortunes were none of the fairest, yet he was greatly esteemed amongst the Romans. The intercourse of love between these twain had so equally instructed their hearts and souls, that it could hardly be judged which of them was the more fervent in affection ; but he, not being inured to such oppressing passions, and therefore the less able to support them, except he was sure to compass his desire, plainly made the motion that he might have her in honourable marriage, which his parents and friends hearing, went to confer with him, blaming him with over-much baseness, so far to disgrace himself and his stock. Beside, they advised the father to the maid neither to credit what Pedro said in this case, or to live in hope of any such match, because they all did despise it.

Pedro, perceiving that the way was shut up whereby, and none other, he was to mount the ladder of his hopes, began to wax weary of longer living, and, if he could have won her father's consent, he would have married her in the despite of all his friends. Nevertheless, he had a conceit hammering in his head which, if the maid would be as forward as himself, should bring the matter to full effect. Letters and secret intelligences passing still between, at length he understood her ready resolution to adventure with him through all fortunes whatsoever, concluding on their sudden and secret flight from Rome, for which Pedro did so well provide that, very early in a morning, and well mounted on horseback, they took the way leading to Alagna, where Pedro had some honest friends in whom he reposed special trust. Riding on thus through the country. having no leisure to accomplish their marriage because they stood in fear of pursuit, they were ridden above four leagues from Rome, still shortening the way with their amorous dis-coursing.

It fortuned that Pedro, having no certain knowledge of the way, but following a track guiding too far on the left hand, rode quite out of course, and came at last within sight of a small castle, out of which, before they were aware, issued twelve villains, whom Agnolella sooner espied than Pedro could do, which made her cry out to him, saying, " Help, dear love, to save us, or else we shall be assailed." Pedro then turning his horse so expeditiously as he could, and giving him the spurs as need required, mainly he galloped into a near adjoining forest, more minding the following of Agnolella than any direction of his way or them that endeavoured to be his hindrance ; so that, by often winding and turning about as the passage appeared troublesome to him, when he thought himself free and furthest from them, he was round engirt and seized on by them. When they had made him to dismount from his horse, questioning him of whence and what he was, and he resolving therein, they fell into a secret consultation, saying thus among themselves : " This man is a friend to our deadly enemy ; how can we, then, otherwise dispose of him but drain him of all he hath, and in despite of the Orsini (men in nature hateful to us) hang him up here on one of these trees ? "

All of them agreeing in this dismal resolution, they commanded Pedro to put off his garments, which he yielding to do, albeit unwillingly, it so fell out that five-and-twenty other thieves came suddenly rushing in upon them, crying, " Kill, kill, and spare not a man."

They which before had surprised Pedro, desiring now to shift for their own safety, left him standing quaking in his shirt, and so ran away mainly to defend themselves ; which the new crew perceiving, and that their number far exceeded the other, they followed to rob them of what they had gotten, accounting it as a present purchase for them. Which when Pedro perceived, and saw none tarrying to prey upon him, he put on his clothes again, and mounting on his own horse, galloped that way which Agnolella before had taken, yet could he not descry any track or path, or so much as the footing of a horse, but thought himself in sufficient security, being rid of them that first seized on him, and also of the rest which followed in the pursuit of them.

For the loss of his beloved Agnolella he was the most woful man in the world, wandering first one way and then again another, calling for her all about the forest without any answer returning to him ; and not daring to ride back again on he travelled still, not knowing where to make his arrival. And having formerly heard of savage ravenous beasts which commonly lived in such unfrequented forests, he not only was in fear of losing his own life, but also despaired much for his Agnolella, lest some lion or wolf had torn her body in pieces.

Thus rode on poor unfortunate Pedro until the break of day appeared, not finding any means to get forth of the forest, still crying and calling for his fair friend, riding many times backward, whereas he thought he rode forward, until he became so weak and faint, what with extreme fear, loud calling, and continuing so long a while without any sustenance, that the whole day being thus spent in vain, and dark night suddenly come upon him, he was not able to hold out any longer.

Now was he in far worse case than before, not knowing where or how to dispose of himself, or what might best be done in so great a necessity. From his horse he alighted, and tying him by the bridle unto a great tree, up he climbed into the same tree, fearing to be devoured in the night-time by some wild beast, choosing rather to let his horse perish than himself. Within a while after, the moon began to rise, and the sky appeared bright and clear, yet durst he not nod or take a nap, lest he should fall out of the tree ; but sate still grieving, sighing, and mourning, despairing of ever seeing his Agnolella any more, for he could not be comforted by the smallest hopeful persuasion that any good fortune might befall her in such a desolate forest, where nothing but dismal fears were to be expected, and no likelihood that she should escape with life.

Now concerning poor affrighted Agnolella who, as you heard before, knew not any place of refuge to fly unto but even as it pleased the horse to carry her, she entered so far into the forest that she could not devise where to seek her own safety. And therefore, even as it fared with her friend Pedro, in the same manner did it fall out with her, wandering the whole night and all the day following, one while taking one hopeful track and then another, calling, weeping, and wringing her hands, and grievously complaining of her hard fortune. At the length, perceiving that Pedro came not unto her at all, she found a little path which she lighted on by great good fortune, even when dark night was apace drawing on, and followed it so long till it brought her within the sight of a small poor cottage, whereto she rode on so fast as she could, and found therein a very old man, having a wife rather more aged than he, who seeing her to be without company, the old man spake thus unto her :

"Fair daughter," quoth he, "whither wander you at such an unseasonable hour, and all alone in a place so desolate?" The damsel weeping, replied that she had lost her company in the forest, and inquired how near she was to Alagna. "Daughter," answered the old man, "this is not the way to Alagna, for it is above six leagues hence." Then she desired to know how far off she was from such houses where she might have any reasonable lodging. "There is none so near," said the old man, "that daylight will give you leave to reach." "May it please you then, good father," replied Agnolella, "seeing I cannot travel any whither else, for God's sake do let me remain here with you this night." "Daughter," answered the good old man, "we can gladly give you entertainment here for this night in such poor manner as you see ; but let me tell you withal, that up and down these woods, as well by night as day, walk companies of all conditions, and rather enemies than friends, who do many grievous displeasures and harms. Now, if by misfortune, you being here, any such people should come, and seeing you so lovely fair, as indeed you are, offer you any shame or injury; alas, you see, it lies not in our power to lend you any help or succour. I thought it good, therefore, to acquaint you herewith, because if any such mischance do happen, you should not afterward complain of us."

The young maiden, seeing the time to be so far spent, albeit the old man's words did much dismay her, yet she thus replied : "If it be the will of Heaven, both you and I shall be defended from any misfortune ; but if any such mischance do happen, I account the means less deserving grief if I fall into the mercy of men than to be devoured by wild beasts in this forest." So being dismounted from her horse and entered into the homely house, she supped poorly with the old man and his wife, with such mean cates as their provision afforded, and after supper lay down in her garments on the poor pallet where the aged couple took their rest, and was very well contented therewith ; albeit she could not refrain from sighing and weeping to be thus divided from her dear Pedro, of whose life and welfare she greatly despaired.

When it was almost day she heard a great noise of people

travelling by, whereupon she suddenly arose and ran into a garden plot which was at the back of the poor cottage, espying in one of the corners a great stack of hay, wherein she hid herself, to the end that travelling strangers might not readily find her there in the house. Scarcely was she fully there hidden, but a great company of thieves and villains, finding the door open, rushed into the cottage, where looking round about them for some booty, they saw the damsel's horse stand ready saddled, which made them demand to whom it belonged. The good old man, not seeing the maiden present there, answered thus : "Gentlemen, here is nobody here but my wife and myself ; as for this horse, which seemeth to be escaped from the owner, he came hither yester-night, and we gave him house-room here rather than to be devoured by wolves abroad." "Then," said the principal of the thievish crew, "this horse shall be ours, in regard he hath no other master, and let the owner come claim him of us."

When they had searched every corner of the poor cottage and found no such prey as they looked for, some of them went into the back where they had left their javelins and targets wherewith they used commonly to travel. It fortuned that one of them, being more subtilly suspicious than the rest, thrust his javelin into the stack of hay, in the very same place where the damsel lay hidden, missing very little of killing her, for it entered so far that the iron head pierced quite through her garments and touched her left bare breast ; whereupon she was ready to cry out, as fearing she was wounded, but considering the place where she was, she lay still and spake not a word. This disordered company, after they had fed on some young kids and other flesh which they brought with them thither, they went thence about their thieving exercise, taking the damsel's horse along with them.

After they were gone a great distance off, the good old man began thus to question his wife : " What is become," quoth he, " of our young gentlewoman which came so late to us yester-night ? I have not seen her to-day since our arising." The old woman made answer that she knew not where she was, and sought all about to find her Agnolella's fear being well over-blown, and hearing none of the former noise, which made her the better hope of their departure, she came forth of the haystack ; whereof the good old man was not a little joyful, and because she had so well escaped from them. So seeing it was now broad daylight, he said unto her : " Now that the morning is so fairly begun, if you can be so well contented, we will bring you to a castle which stands about two miles and a half hence, where you may be sure to remain in safety. But you must needs travel thither on foot, because the night-walkers that happened hither have taken away your horse with them."

Agnolella, making little or no account of such a loss, entreated them for charity's sake to conduct her to that castle, which accordingly they did, and arrived there between seven or eight of the clock. The castle belonged to one of the Orsini, being called Liello di Campo di Fiore, and by great good fortune his wife was then there, she being a very virtuous and religious lady. No sooner did she look upon Agnolella but she knew her immediately, and entertained her very willingly, requesting to know the reason of her arriving there; which she at large related, and moved the lady, who likewise knew Pedro perfectly well, to much compassion, because he was a kinsman and dear friend to her husband, and understanding how the thieves had surprised him, she feared that he was slain among them, whereupon she spake thus to Agnolella: "Seeing you know not what is become of my kinsman Pedro, you shall remain here with me until such time as, if we hear no other tidings of him, you may with safety be sent back to Rome."

Pedro all this while sitting in the tree, so full of grief as no man could be more, about the hour of midnight, by the bright splendour of the moon, espied about some twenty wolves, who, as soon as they got sight of the horse, ran and engirt him round about. The horse, when he perceived them so near him, drew his head so strongly backward that, breaking the reins of his bridle, he laboured to escape away from them; but being beset on every side, and utterly unable to help himself, he contended with his teeth and feet in his own defence, till they haled him violently to the ground, and tearing his body in pieces, left not a jot of him but the bare bones, and afterwards ran ranging through the forest. At this sight poor Pedro was mightily dismayed, fearing to speed no better than his horse had done, and therefore could not devise what was best to be done, for he saw no likelihood of getting out of the forest with life. But daylight drawing on apace, and he almost dead with cold, having stood quaking so long in the tree, at length by continual looking everywhere about him, to discern the least glimpse of any comfort, he espied a great fire, which seemed to be about half a mile off from him.

By this time it was broad day, when he descended down out of the tree, yet not without much fear, and took his way toward the fire, where being arrived he found a company of shepherds banqueting about it, whom he courteously saluting, they took pity on his distress, and welcomed him kindly. After he had tasted of such cheer as they had, and was indifferently refreshed by the good fire, he discoursed his hard disasters to them, as also how he happened thither, desiring to know if any village or castle were near thereabout, where he might in better manner relieve himself. The shepherds told him that about a mile and a half from thence was the castle of Signior Liello di Campo di Fiore, and that his lady was residing there, which was no mean comfort to poor Pedro, requesting that one of them would accompany him thither, as two of them did in loving manner, to rid him of all further fears.

When he was arrived at the castle, and found there divers of his familiar acquaintances, he laboured to procure some means that the damsel might be sought for in the forest. Then the lady calling for her, and bringing her to him, he ran and caught her in his arms, being ready to swoon with conceit of joy, for

never could any man be more comforted than he was at the sight
of his Agnolella, and questionless her joy was not a jot inferior
to his, such a sympathy of firm love was settled between them.
The lady of the castle, after she had given them very gracious
entertainment, and understood the scope of their bold adventure,
she reproved them both somewhat sharply for presuming so far
without the consent of their parents. But perceiving, notwithstanding all her remonstrances, that they continued still constant
in their resolution, without any inequality of either side, she said
to herself : " Why should this matter be anyway offensive to me?
They love each other loyally ; they are not inferior to one another
in birth, but in fortune ; they are equally loved and allied to my
husband ; and their desire is both honest and honourable. Moreover, what know I, if it be the will of Heaven to have it so? Thieves
intended to hang him in malice to his name and kindred, from which
hard fate he hath now happily escaped. Her life was endangered
by a sharp-pointed javelin, and yet her fairer stars would not suffer
her so to perish. Besides, they have both escaped the fury of
ravenous wild beasts ; and all these are apparent signs that future
comforts should recompense former passed misfortunes. Far be
it, therefore, from me to hinder the appointment of the Heavens."
    Then turning herself to them, thus she proceeded : " If your
desire be to join in honourable marriage I am well contented therewith, and your nuptials shall here be solemnized at my husband's
charges. Afterward, both he and I will endeavour to make peace
between you and your discontented parents." Pedro was not a little
joyful at her kind offer, and Agnolella much more than he. So they
were married together in the castle, and worthily feasted by the lady
as forest entertainment could permit, and there they enjoyed the
first fruits of their love. Within a short while after, the lady and
they, well mounted on horseback, and attended with an honourable
train, returned to Rome, where her lord Liello and she prevailed so
well with Pedro's angry parents, that the variance ended in love
and peace, and afterwards they lived lovingly together, till old age
made them as honourable as the true and mutual affection formerly
had done.

THE FOURTH NOVEL.

Ricciardo Manardi was found by Messer Lizio da Valbona as he sat fast asleep
    at his daughter's chamber window, having his hand fast in hers, and she
    sleeping in the same manner. Whereupon they are joined together in
    marriage, and their long loyal love mutually recompensed.

ELISA having ended her tale, and heard what commendations the
whole company gave thereof, the Queen commanded Filostrato
to tell a novel agreeing with his own mind, who thus replied :
    Fair ladies, I have been so often checked for yesterday's argu-
ment of discoursing, which was very offensive to you, that if I
intended to make you any amends, I should now undertake to tell

such a tale as might put you into a mirthful humour, which I am
determined to do in relating a brief and pleasant novel.

Not long since there lived in Romagna a knight, a very honest
gentleman, and well qualified, whose name was Messer Lizio da
Valbona, to whom it fortuned that, at his entrance into age, by his
lady and wife, called Giacomina, he had a daughter, the very
choicest and goodliest gentlewoman in all those places.   Now
because such a happy blessing, in their old years, was not a little
comfortable to them, they thought themselves the more bound in
duty to be circumspect of her education, by keeping her out of over-
frequent companies, but only such as agreed best with their gravity,
and might give the least ill example to their daughter, who was
named Caterina, as making no doubt but by this their provident
and wary respect to match her in marriage answerable to their
liking.   There was also a young gentleman, in the very flourishing
estate of his youthful time, descended from the family of the
Manardi da Brettinoro, named Ricciardo, who oftentimes frequented the house of Messer Lizio, and was a continual welcome
guest to his table, Messer Lizio and his wife making the like account
of him even as if he had been their own son.

The young gallant, perceiving the maiden to be very beautiful, of
singular behaviour, and of such years as were fit for marriage, became exceeding enamoured of her, yet concealed his affection so
closely as he could, which was not so covertly carried but that she
perceived it, and grew into as good liking of him.   Many times he
had an earnest desire to have conference with her, which yet still he
deferred, as fearing to displease her ; at the length he lighted on an
apt opportunity, and boldly spake unto her in this manner : " Fair
Caterina, I hope thou wilt not let me die for my love."   " Ricciardo," replied she suddenly again, " I hope you will extend the
like mercy to me as you desire that I should show to you."   This
answer was so pleasing to Ricciardo, that presently he said : " Alas !
dear love. I have dedicated all my fairest fortunes only to thy service, so that it remaineth solely in thy power to dispose of me as
best shall please thee, and to appoint such times of private conversation as may yield more comfort to my poor afflicted soul."

Caterina standing musing a while, at last returned him this
answer : " Ricciardo," quoth she, " you see what a restraint is
set on my liberty, how short I am kept from conversing with any
one, that I hold this our interparlance now almost miraculous and
very rare.   But if you could devise any convenient means to admit
us more familiar freedom, without any prejudice to mine honour, or
the least distaste to my parents, do but instruct me, and I will
adventure it."   Ricciardo having considered on many ways and
means, thought one to be the fittest of all, and therefore thus
replied : " Caterina," quoth he, " the only place for our private
talking together, I conceive to be the gallery over your father's
garden.   If you can win your mother to let you lodge there, I will
make means to climb over the wall, and at the goodly gazing
window we may discourse so long as we please."   " Now trust me,

dear love," answered Caterina, "no place can be more convenient for our purpose ; there shall we hear the sweet birds sing, especially the nightingale, which I have heard singing there all the night long ; I will break the matter to my mother, and how I speed you shall hear further from me." So with divers parting kisses they brake off conference till the next meeting.

On the day following, which was towards the ending of the month of May, Caterina began to complain to her mother that the season was over-hot and tedious to be still lodged in her mother's chamber, because it was a hindrance to her sleeping, and wanting rest, it would be an impairing of her health. " Why, daughter," quoth the mother, " the weather as yet is not so hot but, in my mind, you may very well endure it." " Alas ! mother," said she, " aged people, as you and my father are, do not feel the heats of youthful blood, by reason of your far colder complexion, which is not to be measured by younger years." " I know that well, daughter," replied the mother, " but is it in my power to make the weather warm or cool as thou perhaps wouldst have it ? Seasons are to be suffered according to their several qualities ; and though the last night might seem hot, this night ensuing may be cooler, and then thy rest will be the better." " No, mother," quoth Caterina, " that cannot be, for as summer proceedeth on, so the heat increaseth, and no expectation can be of temperate weather until it grow to winter again." " Why, daughter," said the mother, " what wouldst thou have me to do ? " " Mother," quoth she, " if it might stand with my father's good liking and yours, I would be spared to the garden gallery, which is a great deal more cool lodging. There shall I hear the sweet nightingale sing as every night she useth to do, and many other pretty birds beside, which I cannot do, lodging in your chamber."

The mother loving her daughter dearly, as being somewhat over-fond of her, and very willing to give her contentment, promised to impart her mind to her father, not doubting but to compass what she requested. When she had moved the matter to Messer Lizio, whose age made him somewhat froward and testy, he angerly said to his wife : " Why how now, woman, cannot our daughter sleep except she hear the nightingale sing ? Let there be a bed made in the oven, and there let the crickets make her melody." When Caterina heard this answer from her father, and saw her desire to be disappointed, not only could she take no rest the night following, but also complained more of the heat than before, not suffering her mother to take any rest, which made her go angerly to her husband in the morning, saying, " Why, husband, have we but only one daughter, whom you pretend to love right dearly, and yet can you be so careless of her as to deny her a request which is no more than reason ? What matter is it for you or me to let her lodge in the garden gallery ? Is her young blood to be compared with ours ? Can our weak and crazy bodies feel the frolic temper of hers ? Alas ! she is hardly as yet out of her childish years, and children have many desires far differing from ours ; the singing of birds is rare music to them, and chiefly the nightingale, whose sweet notes will provoke them to rest when neither art nor physic can do it."

"Is it even so, wife?" answered Messer Lizio. "Must your will and mine be governed by our daughter? Well, be it so then, let her bed be made in the garden gallery, but I will have the keeping of the key, both to lock her in at night, and set her at liberty every morning. Woman, woman, young wenches are wily, many wanton crotchets are busy in their brains, and to us that are aged, they sing like lapwings, telling us one thing, and intending another; talking of nightingales, when their minds run on cock sparrow. Seeing, wife, she must needs have her mind, let yet your care and mine extend so far to keep her good fame uncorrupted, and our credulity from being abused." Caterina having so prevailed now with her mother, her bed made in the garden gallery, and secret intelligence given to Ricciardo for preparing his means of access to her window, old provident Lizio locks the door to bedward, and gives her liberty to come forth in the morning, for his lodging was near the gallery.

In the dead and silent time of night, when all but lovers take their rest, Ricciardo having provided a ladder of ropes with grappling hooks to take hold above and below, according as he had occasion to use it, by help thereof, first mounted over the garden wall, and then climbed up to the gallery window, before which, as is everywhere in Italy, was a little round engirting terrace only for a man to stand upon, for making clean the window, or otherwise repairing it. Many nights in this manner enjoyed they their meetings as the window gave leave, he sitting in the terrace and departing always before break of day, for fear to be discovered by any.

But, as excess of delight is the nurse to negligence, and begetteth such an over-presuming boldness, as afterward proveth to be sauced with repentance, so came it to pass with our over-fond lovers in being taken tardy through their own folly. After they had many times met in this manner, the nights, according to the season, growing shorter and shorter, and their senses dulled by night watching, it fortuned that they both fell fast asleep, he having his hand closed in hers, and she one arm folded about his body, and thus they slept till broad daylight. Old Messer Lizio, who continually was the morning cock to the whole house, going forth into his garden, saw how his daughter and Ricciardo were seated at the window. In he went again, and going to his wife's chamber, said to her: "Rise quickly, wife, and you shall see what made your daughter so desirous to lodge in the garden gallery. I perceived that she loved the nightingale, for she hath caught one, and holds him fast in her hands." "Is it possible," said the mother, "that our daughter should catch a live nightingale in the dark?" "You shall see that yourself," answered Messer Lizio, "if you will make haste and go with me."

She putting on her garments in great haste, followed her husband, and being come to the gallery door, he opened it very softly, and going to the window showed her how they both sat fast asleep, and in such manner as hath been before declared; whereupon she perceiving how Ricciardo and Caterina had both deceived her, would have made an outcry, but that Messer Lizio spake thus to her: "Wife, as you love me speak not a word, nor make any noise; for, seeing she hath loved Ricciardo without our knowledge, and they have had their private meetings in this manner, yet free from any blameful imputation, he shall have her, and she him. Ricciardo is a gentleman well derived, and of rich possessions, it can be no disparagement to us that Caterina match with him in marriage, which he neither shall, or dare deny to do in regard of our law's severity, for climbing up to my window with his ladder of ropes, whereby his life is forfeited to the law, except our daughter please to spare it, as it remaineth in her power to do by accepting him as her husband, or yielding his life up to the law, which surely she will not suffer, their love agreeing together in such mutual manner, and he adventuring so dangerously for her." Giacomina, perceiving that her husband spake very reasonably, and was no more offended at the matter, stepped aside with him behind the drawn curtains until they should awake of themselves. At the last, Ricciardo awaked, and seeing it was so far in the day, thought himself half dead, and calling to Caterina, said: "Alas, dear love! What shall we do? We have slept too long and shall be taken here." At which words Messer Lizio stepped forth from behind the curtains, saying: "Nay, Signior Ricciardo, seeing you have found such an unbefitting way hither, we will provide you a better way for your back returning." When Ricciardo saw the father and mother both there, he could not devise what to do or say, his senses became so strangely confounded; yet knowing how heinously he had offended, if the strictness of law should be challenged against him, falling on his knees, he said: "Alas! Messer Lizio, I humbly crave your mercy, confessing myself well worthy of death, that knowing the sharp rigour of the law, I would presume so audaciously to break it. But pardon me, worthy sir, my loyal and unfeigned love to your daughter Caterina hath been the only cause of my transgressing.

"Ricciardo," replied Messer Lizio, "the love I bare thee, and the honest confidence I do repose in thee, step up to plead thy excuse, especially in regard of my daughter, whom I blame thee not for loving, but for this unlawful way of presuming to her. Nevertheless, perceiving how the case standeth, and considering withal that youth and affection were the ground of thine offence, to free thee from death and myself from dishonour, before thou depart hence thou shalt espouse my daughter Caterina, to make her thy lawful wife in marriage, and wipe off all scandal to my house and me." All this while was poor Caterina on her knees likewise to her mother, who, notwithstanding this her bold adventure, made earnest suit to her husband to remit all, because Ricciardo right gladly condescended, as it being the main issue of his hope and desire, to accept Caterina in marriage, whereto she was as willing as he. Messer Lizio presently called for the confessor of his house, and borrowing one of his wife's rings, before they went out of the gallery Ricciardo and

Caterina were espoused together, to their no little joy and contentment.

Now had they more leisure for further conference with the parents and kindred of Ricciardo, who being no way discontented with this sudden match, but applauding it in the highest degree; they were publicly married again in the cathedral church, and very honourable triumphs performed at the nuptials, living long after in happy prosperity.

THE FIFTH NOVEL.

Guidotto of Cremona, departing out of this mortal life, left a daughter of his with Giacomin of Pavia. Giannole di Severino and Minghino di Mingole fell both in love with the young maiden, and fought for her; who being afterward known to be the sister to Giannole, she was given in marriage to Minghino.

ALL the ladies laughing heartily at the novel of the Nightingale, so pleasingly delivered by Filostrato, when they saw the same to be fully ended, the Queen thus spake: "Now trust me, Filostrato, though yesterday you did much oppress me with melancholy, yet you have made me such an amends to-day as we have little reason to complain any more of you." So turning to Neifile, the Queen commanded her to succeed, which willingly she yielded to, beginning in this manner: "Seeing it pleased Filostrato to produce his novel out of Romagna, I mean to walk with him in the same jurisdiction concerning what I have to say."

[OMITTED.]

THE SIXTH NOVEL.

Gian di Procida being found familiarly conversing with a young damsel which he loved and had been given formerly to Federigo, King of Sicily, was bound to a stake to be consumed with fire. From which danger nevertheless he escaped, being known by Ruggieri dell' Oria, Lord-Admiral of Sicily, and afterward married the damsel.

THE novel of Neifile being ended, which proved very pleasing to the ladies, the Queen commanded Pampinea that she should prepare to take her turn next, whereto willingly obeying, thus she began: "Many and mighty, gracious ladies, are the prevailing powers of love, conducting amorous souls into infinite travails, with inconveniences no way avoidable and not easily to be foreseen or prevented. As partly already hath been observed by divers of our former novels related, and some, no doubt, to ensue hereafter; for one of them, coming now to my memory, I shall acquaint you withal in so good terms as I can."

[OMITTED.]

THE SEVENTH NOVEL.

Teodoro falling in love with Violante, the daughter to his master named
Amerigo, was condemned to be hanged. As they were leading him to the
gallows, beating and misusing him all the way, he happened to be known of
his own father, whereupon he was released, and afterward had Violante
in marriage.

GREATLY were the ladies' minds perplexed when they heard that
the two poor lovers were in danger to be burned; but hearing
afterwards of their happy deliverance, they were as joyful again.
Upon the concluding of the novel, the Queen looked on Lauretta,
enjoining her to tell the next tale, which willingly she undertook
to do, and thus began.

[OMITTED.]

THE EIGHTH NOVEL.

Anastasio, a gentleman of the family of the Onesti, by loving the daughter
to Paolo Traversario, lavishly wasted a great part of his substance,
without receiving any love of her again. By persuasion of some of his
kindred and friends, he went to a country dwelling of his at Chiassi,
where he saw a knight desperately pursue a young damsel, whom he slew,
and afterward gave her to be devoured by his hounds. Anastasio invited
his friends, and her also whom he so dearly loved, to take part of a dinner
with him, who likewise saw the same damsel so torn in pieces, which his
unkind love perceiving, and fearing lest the like ill fortune should happen
to her, she accepted Anastasio to be her husband.

SO soon as Lauretta held her peace, Pampinea, by the Queen's
command, began, and said: Lovely ladies, as pity is most highly
commended in our sex, even so is cruelty in us as secretly revenged,
oftentimes by divine ordination. Which that you may the better
know, and learn likewise to shun as a deadly evil, I purpose to
make apparent by a novel, no less full of compassion than delectable.
Ravenna being a very ancient city in Romagna, there dwelt
sometime a great number of worthy gentlemen, among whom I
am to speak of one more especially, named Anastasio, descended
from the family of Onesti, who by the death of his father, and an
uncle of his, was left extraordinarily abounding in riches and growing to years fitting for marriage. As young gallants are easily apt
enough to do, he became enamoured of a very beautiful gentlewoman, who was daughter of Messer Paolo Traversario, one of the
most ancient and noble families in all the country. Nor made he
any doubt, by his means and industrious endeavour, to derive
affection from her again, for he carried himself like a brave-minded
gentleman, liberal in his expenses, honest and affable in all his

actions, which commonly are the true notes of a good nature, and highly·to be commended in any man.   But, howsoever, fortune became his enemy ; these laudable parts of manhood did not any way friend him, but rather appeared hurtful to himself, so cruel, unkind, and almost merely savage did she show herself to him, perhaps in pride of her singular beauty or presuming on her nobility by birth, both which are rather blemishes than ornaments in a woman when they be especially abused.   The harsh and uncivil usage in her grew very distasteful to Anastasio, and so insufferable that after a long time of fruitless service, requited still with nothing but coy disdain, desperate resolutions entered into his brain, and often he was minded to kill himself.   But better thoughts supplanting those furious passions, he abstained from such a violent act, and governed by more manly consideration, determined that as she hated him, he would requite her with the like, if he could, wherein he became altogether deceived, because as his hopes grew to a daily decaying, yet his love enlarged itself more and more.

Thus Anastasio persevering still in his bootless affection, and his expenses not limited within any compass, it appeared in the judgment·of his kindred and friends that he was fallen into a mighty consumption, both of his body and means.   In which respects many times they advised him to leave the city of Ravenna, and live in some other place for such a while as might set a more moderate stint upon his spendings, and bridle the indiscreet course of his love, the only fuel which fed his furious fire.

Anastasio held out thus a long time, without lending an ear to such friendly counsel ; but in the end he was so closely followed by them, as being no longer able to deny them, he promised to accomplish their request.   Whereupon making such extraordinary preparation as if he were to set out thence for France or Spain, or else into some further country, he mounted on horseback, and accompanied with some few of his familiar friends, departed from Ravenna, and rode to a country dwelling-house of his own, about three or four miles distant from the city, at a place called Chiassi ; and there upon a very good green erecting divers tents and pavilions, such as great persons make use of in the time of progress, he said to his friends which came with him thither that there he determined to make his abiding, they all returning back unto Ravenna, and coming to visit him again so often as they pleased.

Now it came to pass that about the beginning of May, it being then a very mild and serene season, and he leading there a much more magnificent life than ever he had done before, inviting divers to dine with him this day and as many to-morrow, and not to leave him till after supper, upon a sudden falling into remembrance of his cruel mistress, he commanded all his servants to forbear his company, and suffer him to walk alone by himself a while, because he had occasion of private meditations, wherein he would not by any means be troubled.   It was then about the ninth hour of the day, and he walking on solitary all alone, having gone some half a mile distance from the tents, entered into a grove of pine-trees, never minding dinner-time or anything else, but only the unkind requital of his love.

Suddenly he heard the voice of a woman seeming to make most mournful complaints, which breaking off his silent considerations, made him to lift up his head to know the reason of this noise. When he saw himself so far entered into the grove before he could imagine where he was, he looked amazedly round about him, and out of a little thicket of bushes and briars round engirt with spreading trees, he espied a young damsel come. running towards him, naked from the middle upward, her hair lying on her shoulders, and her fair skin rent and torn with the briars and brambles, so that the blood ran trickling down mainly, she weeping, wringing her hands, and crying out for mercy so loud as she could. Two fierce blood-hounds also followed swiftly after, and where their teeth took hold did most cruelly bite her. Last of all, mounted on a lusty black courser, came galloping a knight, with a very stern and angry countenance, holding a drawn short sword in his hand, giving her very dreadful speeches, and threatening every minute to kill her.

This strange and uncouth sight bred in him no mean admiration, as also kind compassion to the unfortunate woman, out of which compassion sprung an earnest desire to deliver her, if he could, from a death so full of anguish and horror ; but seeing himself to be without arms, he ran and plucked up the plant of a tree, which handling as if it had been a staff, he opposed himself against the dogs and the knight, who seeing him coming, cried out in this manner to him : "Anastasio, put not thyself in any opposition, but refer to my hounds and me to punish this wicked woman as she hath justly deserved." And in speaking these words, the hounds took fast hold on her body, so staying her until the knight was come nearer to her, and alighted from his horse, when Anastasio, after some other angry speeches, spake thus to him: "I cannot tell what or who thou art, albeit thou takest such knowledge of me, yet I must say it is mere cowardice in a knight, being armed as thou art, to offer to kill a naked woman, and make thy dogs thus to seize on her, as if she were a savage beast ; therefore, believe me, I will defend her so far as I am able."

"Anastasio," answered the knight, "I am of the same city as thou art, and do well remember that thou wast a little lad when I, who was then named Guido Anastasio, and thine uncle, became as entirely in love with this woman as now thou art with Paolo Traversario's daughter. But through her coy disdain and cruelty, such was my heavy fate that desperately I slew myself with this short sword which thou beholdest in mine hand; for which rash sinful deed I was and am condemned to eternal punishment. This wicked woman, rejoicing immeasurably in mine unhappy death, remained no long time alive after me, and for her merciless sin of cruelty, and taking pleasure in my oppressing torments, dying unrepentant, and in pride of her scorn, she had the like sentence of condemnation pronounced on her, and was sent to the same place where I was condemned.

" There the three impartial judges imposed this further infliction on us both—namely, that she should fly in this manner before me, and I, who loved her so dearly while I lived, must pursue her as my deadly enemy, not like a woman that had a taste of love in her. And so often as I can overtake her, I am to kill her with this sword, the same weapon wherewith I slew myself. Then am I enjoined therewith to open her accursed body, and tear out her heart, with her other inwards, as now thou seest me do, which I give to my hounds to feed on. Afterward—such is the appointment of the supreme powers—that she re-assumeth life again, even as if she had not been dead at all, and falling to the same kind of flight, I with my hounds am still to follow her, without any respite or intermission. Every Friday, and just at this hour, our course is this way, where she suffereth the just punishment inflicted on her. Nor do we rest any of the other days, but are appointed unto other places, where she cruelly executed her malice against me, who am now, of her dear affectionate friend, ordained to be her endless enemy, and to pursue her in this manner for so many years as she exercised months of cruelty towards me. Hinder me not, then, in being the executioner of Divine justice, for all thy interposition is but in vain in seeking to cross the appointment of supreme powers."

Anastasio having heard all this discourse, his hair stood upright, like porcupines' quills, and his soul was so shaken with the terror, that he stepped back to suffer the knight to do what he was enjoined, looking yet with mild commiseration on the poor woman, who kneeling most humbly before the knight, and sternly seized on by the two bloodhounds, he opened her breast with his weapon, drawing forth her heart and bowels, which instantly he threw to the dogs, and they devoured them very greedily. Soon after the damsel, as if none of this punishment had been inflicted on her, started up suddenly, running amain towards the seashore, and the hounds swiftly following her, as the knight did the like, after he had taken his sword and was mounted on horseback, so that Anastasio had soon lost all sight of them, and could not guess what could become of them.

After he had heard and observed all these things, he stood a while as confounded with fear and pity, like a simple silly man, hoodwinked with his own passions, not knowing the subtle enemy's cunning illusions in offering false suggestions to the sight, to work his own ends thereby, and increase the number of his deceived servants. Forthwith he persuaded himself that he might make good use of this woman's tormenting, so justly imposed on the knight to prosecute, if thus it should continue still every Friday. Wherefore setting a good note or mark upon the place, he returned back to his own people, and at such times as he thought convenient, sent for divers of his kindred and friends from Ravenna, who being present with him, thus he spake to them :

" Dear kinsmen and friends, ye have long while importuned me to discontinue my over-doating love to her whom you all think,

and I find to be my mortal enemy ; as also to give over my lavish
expenses, wherein I confess myself too prodigal ; both which re-
quests of yours I will condescend to, provided that you will perform
one gracious favour for me—namely, that on Friday next, Messer
Paolo Traversario, his wife, daughter, with all other women linked
in lineage to them, and such beside only as you shall please to
appoint, will vouchsafe to accept a dinner here with me. As for the
reason thereto moving me, you shall then more at large be acquainted
withal." This appeared no difficult matter for them to accomplish.
Wherefore being returned to Ravenna, and as they found the time
answerable to their purpose, they invited such as Anastasio had
appointed them. And although they found it somewhat a hard
matter to gain her company whom he had so dearly affected, yet
notwithstanding, the other women won her along with them.

A most magnificent dinner had Anastasio provided, and the
tables were covered under the pine-trees, where he saw the cruel
lady so pursued and slain ; directing the guests so in their seating
that the young gentlewoman, his unkind mistress, sate with her face
opposite unto the place where the dismal spectacle was to be seen.
About the closing up of dinner, they began to hear the noise of the
poor persecuted woman, which drove them all to much admiration,
desiring to know what it was, and no one resolving them they rose
from the tables, and looking directly as the noise came to them,
they espied the woful woman, the dogs eagerly pursuing her ; the
knight galloping after them with his drawn weapon, and came very
near unto the company, who cried out with loud exclaims against
the dogs, and the knights stepped forth in assistance of the injured
woman.

The knight spake unto them as formerly he had done to Anastasio,
which made them draw back possessed with fear and admiration,
while he acted the same cruelty as he did the Friday before, not
differing in the least degree. Most of the gentlewomen there present,
being near allied to the unfortunate woman, and likewise to the
knight, remembering well both his love and death, did shed tears
as plentifully as if it had been to the very persons themselves in
usual performance of the action indeed. Which tragical scene
being passed over, and the woman and knight gone out of their
sight, all that had seen this strange accident fell into diversity of
confused opinions, yet not daring to disclose them, as doubting
some further danger to ensue thereon.

But beyond all the rest, none could compare in fear and astonishment with the cruel young maid affected by Anastasio, who both
saw and observed all with a more inward apprehension, knowing
very well that the moral of this dismal spectacle carried a much
nearer application to her than any other in the company. For now
she could call to mind how unkind and cruel she had shown herself
to Anastasio, even as the other gentlewoman formerly did to her
lover, still flying from him in great contempt and scorn, for which
she thought the bloodhounds also pursued her at the heels
already, and a sword of vengeance to mangle her body. This

fear grew so powerful upon her, that to prevent the like heavy doom from falling on her, she studied, and therein bestowed all the night season, how to change her hatred into kind love, which at the length she fully obtained, and then purposed to procure in this manner: Secretly she sent a faithful chambermaid of her own to greet Anastasio on her behalf, humbly entreating him to come see her, because now she was absolutely determined to give him satisfaction in all which, with honour, he could request of her. Whereto Anastasio answered that he accepted her message thankfully, and desired no other favour at her hand but that which stood with her own offer, namely, to be his wife in honourable marriage. The maid knowing sufficiently that he could not be more desirous of the match than her mistress showed herself to be, made answer in her name that this motion would be most welcome to her.

Hereupon the gentlewoman herself became the solicitor to her father and mother, telling them plainly that she was willing to be the wife of Anastasio ; which news did so highly content them, that upon the Sunday next following the marriage was very worthily solemnized, and they lived and loved together very kindly. Thus the Divine bounty, out of the malignant enemy's secret machinations, can cause good effects to arise and succeed. For from this conceit of fearful imagination in her, not only happened this long-desired conversion of a maid so obstinately scornful and proud, but likewise all the women of Ravenna, being admonished by her example, grew afterward more tractable to men's honest motions than ever they showed themselves before. And let me make some use hereof, fair ladies, to you not to stand over-nicely conceited of your beauty and good parts when men solicit you with their best services. Remember then this disdainful gentlewoman, but more especially her, who being the death of so kind a lover was therefore condemned to perpetual punishment, and he made the minister thereof whom she had cast off with coy disdain, from which I wish your minds to be free, as mine is ready to do you any acceptable service.

THE NINTH NOVEL.

Federigo of the Alberighi family loved a gentlewoman, and was not requited with like love again. But by bountiful expenses and over-liberal invitations he wasted all his lands and goods, having nothing left him but a hawk or falcon. His unkind mistress happeneth to come to visit him, and he not having any other food for her dinner, made a dainty dish of his falcon for her to feed on. Being conquered by this exceeding kind courtesy, she changed her former hatred towards him, accepting him as her husband in marriage, and made him a man of wealthy possessions.

FILOMENA having finished her discourse, the Queen perceiving that her turn was the next, in regard of the privilege granted to Dioneo, with a smiling countenance, thus she spake :

Now or never am I to follow the order which was instituted when we began this commendable exercise, whereto I yield with all humble obedience. And, worthy ladies, I am to acquaint you with a novel, in some sort answerable to the precedent, not only to let you know how powerful your kindnesses do prevail in such as have a free and gentle soul; but also to advise you, in being bountiful, where virtue doth justly challenge it. And evermore let your favours shine on worthy deservers without the directions of chance or fortune, who never bestoweth any gift by discretion, but rashly without consideration, even to the first she blindly meets withal.

You are to understand then, that Coppo di Borghese Domenichi, who was of our own city, and perhaps, as yet, his name remaineth in great and reverend authority, now in these days of ours, as well deserving eternal memory, yet more for his virtues and commendable qualities than any boast of nobility from his predecessors. This man being well entered into years, and drawing towards the finishing of his days, it was his only delight and felicity in conversation among his neighbours to talk of matters concerning antiquity, and some other things within compass of his own knowledge, which he would deliver in such singular order, having an absolute memory, and with the best language as very few or none could do the like. Among the multiplicity of his quaint discourses, I remember he told us that sometime there lived in Florence a young gentleman named Federigo, son to Signior Fillippo Alberighi, who was held and reputed, both for arms and all other actions beseeming a gentleman, hardly to have his equal through all Tuscany.

This Federigo, as it is no rare matter in young gentlemen, became enamoured of a gentlewoman named Monna Giovanna, who was esteemed in her time to be the fairest lady in all Florence ; in which respect, and to reach to the height of his desire, he made many sumptuous feasts and banquets. Jousts, tilts, tournaments, and all other noble actions of arms, beside sending her infinite rich and costly presents, making spare of nothing, but lashing all out in lavish expense. Notwithstanding she being no less honest than fair, made no reckoning of whatsoever he did for her sake, or the least respect of his own person. So that Federigo, spending thus daily more than his means and ability could maintain, and no supplies anyway redounding to him, his faculties, as very easily they might, diminished in such sort, that he became so poor as he had nothing left him but a small farm to live upon, the silly revenues whereof were so mean as scarcely allowed him meat and drink. Yet had he a fair hawk or falcon hardly anywhere to be followed, so expeditious and sure she was of flight. His low ebb and poverty no way quailing his love to the lady, but rather setting a keener edge thereon, he saw the city life could no longer contain him, where most he coveted to abide, and therefore betook himself to his poor country farm, to let his falcon get his dinner and supper, patiently supporting his penurious estate without suit or means making to one for help or relief in any such necessity.

While thus he continued in this extremity, it came to pass that the husband to Giovanna fell sick, and his debility of body being such as little or no hope of life remained, he made his last will and testament, ordaining thereby that his son (already grown to indifferent stature) should be heir to all his lands and riches, wherein he abounded very greatly. Next unto him, if he chanced to die without a lawful heir, he substituted his wife, whom most dearly he affected, and so departed out of this life. Giovanna being thus left a widow, as commonly it is the custom of our city dames during the summer season, she went to a house of her own in the country, which was somewhat near to poor Federigo's farm, and where he lived in such an honest kind of contented poverty.

Hereupon the young gentleman, her son, taking great delight in hounds and hawks, grew into familiarity with poor Federigo, and, having seen many fair flights of his falcon, they pleased him so extraordinarily that he earnestly desired to enjoy her as his own, yet durst not move the motion for her, because he saw how choicely Federigo esteemed her. Within a short while after the young gentleman became very sick, whereat his mother grieved exceedingly, as having no more but he, and never parting from him either night or day, comforting him so kindly as she could, demanding, if he had a desire to anything, willing him to reveal it, and assuring him withal that, if it were within the compass of possibility, he should have it. The youth, hearing how many times she had made him these offers, and with such vehement protestations of performance, at last thus spake :

"Mother," quoth he; "if you can do so much for me as that I may have Federigo's falcon, I am persuaded that my sickness soon will cease." The lady hearing this, sate some short while musing to herself, and began to consider what she might best do to compass her son's desire, for well she knew how long a time Federigo had most lovingly kept it, not suffering it ever to be out of his sight. Moreover, she remembered how earnest in affection he had been to her, never thinking himself happy but only when he was in her company ; wherefore she entered into private advice with her own thoughts : "Shall I send or go myself in person to request the falcon of him, it being the best that ever flew ? It is his only jewel of delight, and, that taken from him, no longer can he wish to live in this world. How far, then, void of understanding shall I show myself to rob a gentleman of his felicity, having no other joy or comfort left him." These and the like considerations wheeled about her troubled brain, only in tender love to her son, persuading herself assuredly that the falcon were her own if she would but request it, yet not knowing whereon it were best to resolve, she returned no answer to her son, but sate still in her silent meditation. At the length, love to the youth so prevailed with her that she concluded on his contentation, and come of it what could, she would not send for it, but go herself in person to request it, and then return home again with it, whereupon thus she spake : " Son, comfort thyself, and let languishing thoughts no longer offend thee ; for here I promise thee that the first thing I do to-morrow morning

shall be my journey for the falcon, and assure thyself that I will
bring it with me." Whereat the youth was so joyed that he imagined
his sickness began instantly a little to leave him, and promised him
a speedy recovery.

Somewhat early the next morning the lady, in care of her sick
son's health, was up and ready betimes, and taking another gentlewoman with her, only as a morning recreation, she walked to
Federigo's poor country farm, knowing that it would not a little
glad him to see her. At the time of his arrival there he was by
chance in a poor garden on the back of the house, because as yet
it was not convenient time for flight; but when he heard that Giovanna was come thither, and desired to have some conference with
him, as one almost confounded with admiration, in all haste he ran
to her and saluted her with most humble reverence. She, in all
modest and gracious manner, requited him with the like salutations,
thus speaking to him : " Signior Federigo, your own best wishes
befriend you. I am now come hither to recompense some part of
your past travails, which heretofore you pretended to suffer for my
sake, when your love was more to me than did well become you to
offer or myself to accept ; and such is the nature of my recompense
that I make myself your guest, and mean this day to dine with
you, as also this gentlewoman, making no doubt of our welcome "
Whereto, with lowly reverence, thus he replied :

" Madam, I do not remember that ever I sustained any loss or
hindrance by you, but rather so much good ; as, if I was worth anything, it proceeded from your deservings, and by the service in
which I did stand engaged to you. But my present happiness can
no way be equalled, derived from your super-abounding gracious
favour and more than common course of kindness, vouchsafing, of
your own liberal nature, to come and visit so poor a servant. Oh,
that I had as much to spend again as heretofore riotously I have
run through ; what a welcome would your poor host bestow on you
for gracing this homely house with your divine presence ! " With
these words he conducted her into his house and then into his
simple garden, where, having no convenient company for her, he
said : " Madam, the poverty of this place is such that it affordeth
none fit for your conversation. This poor woman, wife to an honest
husbandman, will attend on you while that I with some speed shall
make ready dinner."

Poor Federigo, although his necessity was extreme and his grief
great remembering his former inordinate expenses, a moiety
whereof would now have stood him in some stead, yet he had a
heart as free and forward as ever, not a jot dejected in his mind,
though utterly overthrown by fortune. Alas ! how was his good
soul afflicted that he had nothing to honour his lady with ! Up
and down he runs, one while this way, then again another, ex-
claiming on his disastrous fate like a man enraged or bereft of his
senses, for he had not one penny of money, neither pawn nor pledge,
wherewith to procure any. The time hasted on, and he would
gladly, though in mean measure, express his honourable respect to

the lady. To beg of any his nature denied it, and to borrow he could not, because his neighbours were as needy as himself. At last, looking round about, and seeing his falcon standing on her perch, which he felt to be very plump and fat, being void of all other helps in his need, and thinking her to be a fowl fit for so noble a lady to feed on, without any further demurring or delay he plucked off her neck, and caused the poor woman presently to pull her feathers; which being done he put her on the spit, and in a short time she was daintily roasted. Himself covered the table, set bread and salt on, and laid the napkins, whereof he had but a few left him. Going then with cheerful looks into the garden, telling the lady that dinner was ready, and nothing now wanted but her presence. She and the gentlewoman went in, and being seated at the table, not knowing what they fed on, the falcon was all their food, and Federigo not a little joyful that his credit was so well saved. When they were risen from the table, and had spent some small time in familiar conference, the lady thought it fit to acquaint him with the reason of her coming thither, and therefore, in very kind manner, thus began :

"Federigo, if you do yet remember your former carriage towards me, as also my many modest and chaste denials, which, perhaps, you thought to savour of a harsh, cruel, and unwomanly nature, I make no doubt but you will wonder at my present presumption, when you understand the occasion which expressly moved me to come hither ; but if you were possessed of children, or ever had any, whereby you might comprehend what love in nature is due unto them, then I durst assure myself you would partly hold me excused. Now, in regard that you never had any, and myself for my part only but one, I stand not exempted from those laws which are in common to other mothers ; and being compelled to obey the power of those laws, contrary to mine own will and those duties which reason ought to maintain, I am to request such a gift of you, which I am certain that you do make most precious account of, as in manly equity you can do no less. For Fortune hath been extremely adverse to you, that she hath robbed you of many other pleasures, allowing you no comfort or delight but only that poor one, which is your fair falcon, of which bird my son is become so strangely desirous as, if I do not bring it to him at my coming home, I fear so much the extremity of his sickness as nothing can ensue thereon but his loss of life. Wherefore I beseech you, not in regard of the love you have borne me—for thereby you stand no way obliged—but in your own gentle nature (the which hath always declared itself ready in you to do more kind offices generally than any other gentleman that I know), you will be pleased to give her me, or, at the least, let me buy her of you ; which if you do, I shall freely then confess that only by your means my son's life is saved, and we both shall for ever remain engaged to you."

When Federigo had heard the lady's request, which was quite out of his power to grant because it had been her service at dinner, he stood like a man merely dulled in his senses, the tears trickling amain down his cheeks, and he was not able to utter one word ; which she perceiving, began to conjecture immediately that these tears and passions proceeded rather from grief of mind, as being lother to part with his falcon, than any kind of manner, which made her ready to say that she would not have it. Nevertheless, she did not speak, but rather attended his answer, which, after some small respite, he returned in this manner:

" Madam, since the hour when first my affection became solely devoted to your service, Fortune hath been cross and contrary to me in many occasions, as justly and in good reason I may complain of her, yet all seemed light and easy to be endured in comparison of her present malicious contradictions, to my utter overthrow and perpetual molestation. Considering that you are come hither to my poor house which, while I was rich and able, you would not so much as vouchsafe to look on. And now you have requested a small matter of me, wherein she hath also most crookedly thwarted me, because she hath disabled me in bestowing so mean a gift, as yourself will confess when it shall be related to you in few words.

" So soon as I heard that it was your gracious pleasure to dine with me, having regard to your excellency, and what, by merit, is justly due unto you, I thought it a part of my bounden duty to entertain you with such excellent viands as my poor power could any way compass, and far beyond respect or welcome to other common and ordinary persons. Whereupon, remembering my falcon, which now you ask for, and her goodness excelling all other of her kind ; I supposed that she would make a dainty dish for your diet, and having dressed her so well as I could devise to do, you have fed heartily on her, and I am proud that I have so well bestown her. But perceiving now that you would have her for your sick son, it is no mean affliction to me that I am disabled of yield-ing you contentment, which all my lifetime I have desired to do."

To approve his words, the feathers, feet and beak were brought in, which when she saw, she greatly blamed him for killing so rare a falcon to content the appetite of any woman. Yet she com-mended his spirit which poverty had no power to abase. Lastly, her hopes being frustrate for enjoying the falcon, and fearing the health of her son, she thanked Federigo for his kindness, returning home very melancholy. Shortly after her son, either grieving that he could not have the falcon, or by extremity of his disease, chanced to die, leaving his mother a woful lady. After so much time was expired as might agree with mourning, her brethren made motions to her to marry again because she was very rich, and yet but young. Now although she was well contented to remain a widow, yet being continually importuned by them, and remembering the honourable honesty of Federigo, his last poor yet magnificent dinner, in killing his falcon for her sake, said to her brethren : " This kind of life doth like me so well, as willingly I would not leave it, but seeing you are so earnest, let me plainly tell you that I will never accept of any other husband but only Federigo degli Alberighi."

Her brethren in scornful manner reproved her, telling her, he was a beggar, and had nothing left. " I know it well," quoth she, " and am heartily sorry for it. But give me a man that hath need of wealth, rather than wealth that hath need of a man." The brethren hearing how she stood addicted, and knowing Federigo to be a worthy gentleman, though poor, consented thereto, so she bestowed herself and her riches on him. He on the other side having so noble a lady to his wife, and the same whom he had so long dearly loved, submitting all his fairest fortunes unto her, became a better husband, for the world, than before, and they lived and loved in equal joy and happiness.

THE TENTH NOVEL.

Pietro di Vinciolo returns to his wife suddenly from supper at a friend's house in the city.

THE Queen's novel being ended, and all applauding the happy fortune of Federigo, as also the noble nature of Giovanna; Dioneo, expecting no command, delivered his discourse in this manner : "I know not whether I should term it a vice accidental, and ensuing through the badness of complexions in us mortals, or an error in nature, to rejoice rather at evil accidents than at deeds deserving commendation, especially when they no way concern ourselves. Now in regard that all the pains I have hitherto taken, and am also to undergo at this present, aimeth at no other end, but only to purge your minds of melancholy, pardon me, I pray you, fair ladies, if my tale trip in some parts, and savour a little of immodesty, yet in hearing it you may observe the same course as you do in delightful gardens, pluck a sweet rose, and preserve your fingers from pricking."

[OMITTED.]

Dioneo having ended this his tale, for which the ladies returned him no thanks, but rather angrily frowned on him, the Queen, knowing that her government was now concluded, arose, and taking off her crown of laurel, placed it graciously on the head of Elisa, saying, " Now, madam, it is your turn to command." Elisa having received the honour, did in all respects as others formerly had done, and after she had instructed the Master of the Household concerning his charge during the time of her regiment, for contentation of all the company, thus she spake :

" We have long since heard that with witty words, ready answers, and sudden jests or taunts, many have checked and reproved great folly in others, and to their no mean commendations. Now, because it is a pleasing kind of argument, ministering occasion of mirth and wit, my desire is that all our discourse to-morrow shall tend thereto. I mean of such persons, either men or women, who in some witty answer have encountered a scorner in his own intention, and laid the blame where it justly belonged." Every one commended the Queen's appointment, because it savoured of good wit and judgment ; and the Queen being risen, they were all discharged till supper-time, falling to such several exercises as themselves best fancied.

When supper was ended and the instruments laid before them, by the Queen's consent Emilia undertook the dance, and the song was appointed to Dioneo, who began many, but none that proved to any liking, they were so palpably idle, savouring altogether of his own wanton disposition. At length the Queen, looking strangely on him, and commanding him to sing a good one or none at all, thus he began :

THE SONG.

Eyes, can you not refrain your hourly weeping?
　Ears, how are you deprived of sweet attention?
Thoughts, have you lost your quiet silent sleeping?
　Wit, who hath robbed thee of thy rare invention?
In lack of these, being life and motion giving,
Are senseless shapes and no true signs of living.

Eyes, when you gazed upon her angel beauty ;
　Ears, while you heard her sweet delicious strains ;
Thoughts, sleeping then, did yet perform their duty,
　Wit then took sprightly pleasure in his pains.
While she did live, then none of these were scanting ;
But now, being dead, they all are gone and wanting.

After that Dioneo, by proceeding no further, declared the finishing of his song. Many more were sung beside, and that of Dioneo highly commended.* Some part of the night being spent in other delightful exercises, and a fitting hour for rest drawing on, they betook themselves to their chambers, where we will leave them till to-morrow morning.

---

* It is the old translator who gives this song, which is not Dioneo's, although Dioneo's is honest enough.

THE SIXTH DAY.

Governed under the authority of Elisa, and the argument of the discourses or novels there to be recounted do concern such persons who by some witty words, when any have checked and taunted them, have revenged themselves in a sudden, unexpected and discreet answer, thereby preventing loss, danger, scorn, and disgrace, retorting them on the busy-headed questioners.

INDUCTION.

THE moon having passed the heaven, lost her bright splendour by the arising of a more powerful light, and every part of our world began to look clear, when the Queen, being risen, caused all the company to be called. They walked forth afterwards upon the pearled dew, so far as was supposed convenient, in fair and familiar conference together according as severally they were disposed, and repetition of divers the passed novels, especially those which were most pleasing, and seemed so by their present commendations. But the sun being somewhat higher mounted, gave such a sensible warmth to the air as caused their return back to the palace, where the tables were readily covered against their coming, strewed with sweet herbs and odoriferous flowers, seating themselves at the tables, before the heat grew more violent, according as the Queen commanded.

After dinner they sung divers excellent canzonets, and then some went to sleep, others played at the chess and some at the tables, but Dioneo and Lauretta they sung the love conflict between Troilus and Cressida. Now was the hour come of repairing to their consistory or meeting-place, the Queen having thereto generally summoned them, and seating themselves, as they were wont to do, about the fair fountain. As the Queen was commanding to begin the first novel, an accident suddenly happened which never had befallen before—to wit, they heard a great noise and tumult among the household servants in the kitchen. Whereupon the Queen caused the Master of the Household to be called, demanding of him what noise it was and what might be the occasion thereof? He made answer that Licisca and Tindaro were at some words of discontentment, but what was the occasion thereof he knew not. Whereupon the Queen commanded that they should be sent for, their anger and violent speeches still continuing, and, being come into her presence, she demanded the reason of their discord. And Tindaro offering to make answer, Licisca (being somewhat more ancient than he, and of a fiercer fiery spirit, even as if her heart would have leapt out of her mouth) turned herself to him, and with a scornful frowning countenance, said : " See how this bold, unmannerly fellow dare presume to speak in this place before me. Stand by, saucy impudence, and give your betters leave to answer." Then turning to the Queen thus she proceeded.

[OMITTED.]

While Licisca was delivering these speeches, the ladies smiled on one another, not knowing what to say in this cause ; and although the Queen five or six several times commanded her to silence, yet such was the earnestness of her spleen that she gave no attention, but held on still, even until she had uttered all that she pleased. But after she had concluded her complaint, the Queen, with a smiling countenance, turned towards Dioneo, saying : " This matter seemeth most properly to belong to you ; therefore I dare to repose such trust in you, that when our novels for this day shall be ended, you will conclude the case with a definitive sentence." Whereto Dioneo presently thus replied : " Madam, the verdict is already given, within any further expectation, and I affirm that Licisca hath spoken very sensibly, because she is a woman of good apprehension, and Tindaro is but a puny in practice and experience to her."

When Licisca heard this, she fell in a loud laughter, and turning herself to Tindaro, said : " The honour of the day is mine, and thine own quarrel hath overthrown thee in the field. Thou that as yet hast scarcely learned to suck, wouldst thou presume to know so much as I do ? Couldst thou imagine me to be such a truant in the loss of my time that I come hither as an ignorant creature ? " And had not the Queen, looking very frowningly on her, strictly enjoined her to silence, she would have continued still in this triumphing humour ; but fearing further chastisement for disobedience, both she and Tindaro were commanded thence, where was no other allowance all this day, but only silence and attention, to such as should be enjoined speakers.

And then the Queen, somewhat offended at the folly of the former controversy, commanded Filomena that she should give beginning to the day's novels, which in dutiful manner she undertook to do, and seating herself in formal fashion, with modest and very gracious gesture, thus she began.

———

THE FIRST NOVEL.

A knight requested Oretta to ride behind him on horseback, and promised to tell her an excellent tale by the way. But the lady perceiving that his discourse was idle, and much worse delivered, entreated him to let her walk on foot again.

GRACIOUS ladies, like as in our fair, clear, and serene seasons, the stars are bright ornaments to the heavens, and the flowery fields, so long as the spring-time lasteth, wear their goodliest liveries, the trees likewise bragging in their best adornings—even so at friendly meetings, short, sweet, and sententious words are the beauty and ornament of any discourse, savouring of wit and sound judgment, worthily deserving to be commended. And so much the rather, because in few and witty words, aptly suiting with the time and the occasion, more is delivered than was expected, or sooner answered than rashly apprehended, which, as they become men very highly, yet do they show more singular in women.

True it is, what the occasion may be I know not, either by the badness of our wits, or the especial enmity between our complexions and the celestial bodies, there are scarcely any, or very few, women to be found among us that well know how to deliver a word when it should and ought to be spoken ; or, if a question be moved, understand to suit it with an apt answer, such as rightly is required, which is no mean disgrace to us women. But in regard that Pampineo hath already spoken sufficiently of this matter, I mean not to press it any further ; but at this time it shall satisfy me to let you know how wittily a lady made due observation of opportunity in answering of a knight whose talk seemed tedious and offensive to her.

No doubt there are some among you who either do know, or, at the least, have heard, that it is no long time since when there dwelt a gentlewoman in our city, of excellent grace and good discourse, with all other rich endowments of nature remaining in her, as pity it were to conceal her name ; and therefore let me tell you that she was Madonna Oretta, the wife to Messer Geri Spina. She being upon some occasion, as now we are, in the country, and passing from place to place, by way of neighbourly invitations, to visit her loving friends and acquaintance, accompanied with many knights and gentlewomen, who on the day before had dined and supped at her house, as now, belike, the self-same courtesy was intended for her, walking along with her company upon the way, and the place for her welcome being farther off than she expected, a knight chanced to overtake this fair troop, who well knowing Oretta, using a kind and courteous salutation, spake thus unto her :

" Madam, this foot travel may be offensive to you, and were you so well pleased as myself, I would ease your journey behind me on my gelding, even so far as you shall command me ; and beside, will shorten your weariness with a tale worth the hearing." " Courteous sir," replied the lady, " I embrace your kind offer with such acceptation that I pray you to perform it, for therein you shall do me an especial favour." The knight, whose sword, perhaps, was as unsuitable to his side as his wit out of fashion for any ready discourse, having the lady mounted behind him, rode on with a gentle pace, and, according to his promise, began to tell a tale, which indeed of itself deserved attention, because it was a known and commendable history, but yet delivered so abruptly, with idle repetitions of some particulars, three or four several times, mistaking one thing for another, and wandering erroneously from the essential subject, seeming near an end, and then beginning again, that a poor tale could not possibly be more mangled or worse tortured in telling than this was ; for the persons therein concerned were so abusively nick-named, their actions and speeches so monstrously mistaken, that nothing could appear to be more ugly.

Oretta being a lady of unequalled ingenuity, admirable in judgment, and most delicate in her speech, was afflicted in soul beyond all measure, overcome with many cold sweats and passionate heart-aching qualms, to see a fool thus in a pin-fold, and unable to get out, albeit the door stood wide open to him, whereby she became so sick, that converting her distaste to a pleasing kind of acceptation, merrily thus she spake: " Believe me, sir, your horse trots so hard, and travels so uneasy, that I entreat you to set me on my feet again."

The knight being, perchance, a better understander than a discourser, perceived by this saying that his bowl had run a contrary bias, and he as far out of tune as he was from the town. So he tried his hand at another tale, and left unfinished that which he had so ill begun.

THE SECOND NOVEL.

Cisti, a baker, by a witty answer which he gave unto Messer Geri Spina caused him to acknowledge a very indiscreet motion which he had made to the said Cisti.

THE words of Oretta were much commended by the men and women, and the discourse being ended, the Queen gave command to Pampinea that she should follow next in order, which made her to begin in this manner :

Worthy ladies, it exceedeth the power of my capacity to censure in the case whereof I am to speak by saying who sinned most, either Nature, in seating a noble soul in a vile body, or Fortune in bestowing on a body, beautified with a noble soul, a base or wretched condition of life—as we may observe by Cisti, a citizen of our own, and many more beside ; for this Cisti being endued with a singular good spirit, Fortune hath made him no better than a baker. And believe me, ladies, I could in this case lay as much blame on Nature as on Fortune, if I did not know Nature to be most absolutely wise, and that Fortune hath a thousand eyes, albeit fools have figured her to be blind.   But upon more mature and deliberate consideration, I find that they both, being truly wise and judicious, have dealt justly, in imitation of our best advised mortals who being uncertain of such inconveniences as may happen unto them, do bury, for their own benefit, the very best and choicest things of esteem in the most vile and abject places of their houses, as being subject to least suspicion, and where they may be sure to have them at all times for supply of any necessity whatsoever, because so base a conveyance hath better kept them than the very best chamber in the house could have done.   Even so these two great commanders of the world do many times hide their most precious jewels of worth under the clouds of arts or professions of worst estimation, to the end that fetching them thence when need requires, their splendour may appear to be the more glorious.   Nor was any such matter noted in our homely baker Cisti by the best observation of Messer Geri Spina, who was spoken of in the late repeated novel as being the husband to Oretta, whereby this accident came to my remembrance, and which, in a short tale, I will relate unto you.

Let me then tell you that Pope Boniface—with whom the fore-named Messer Geri Spina was in great regard—having sent divers gentlemen of his Court to Florence as ambassadors about very serious and important business, they were lodged in the house of Messer Geri Spina, and he employed with them in the said Pope's negotiation. It chanced that, as being the most convenient way for passage, every morning they walked on foot by the Church of Saint Mario Ughi, where Cisti the baker dwelt, and exercised the trade belonging to him. Now although Fortune had humbled him to so mean a condition, yet she added a blessing of wealth to that contemptible quality, and, as smiling on him continually, no disasters at any time befell him, but still he flourished in riches, lived like a jolly citizen, with all things fitting for honest entertain-ment about him, and plenty of the best wines, both white and claret, that Florence or any part thereabout yielded.

Our frolic baker perceiving that Messer Geri Spina and the other ambassadors used every morning to pass by his door, and afterward to return back the same way, seeing the season to be somewhat hot and sultry, he took it as an action of kindness and courtesy to make them an offer of tasting his white wine. But having respect to his own mean degree and the condition of Messer Geri, he thought it far unfitting for him to be so forward in such presumption, but rather entered into consideration of some such means whereby Messer Geri might be the inviter of himself to taste his wine. And having put on him a truss or thin doublet of very white and fine linen cloth, as also breeches and an apron of the same, and a white cap upon his head, so that he seemed rather to be a miller than a baker, at such times as Messer Geri and the ambassadors should daily pass by, he set before his door a new bucket of fair water, and another small vessel of Bologna earth, as new and sightly as the other, full of his best and choicest white wine, with two small glasses, looking like silver, they were so clear. Down he sate, with all this provision before him, and even as the gentlemen were pass-ing by, he drank one or two rouses of his wine so heartily and with such a pleasing appetite as might have moved a longing almost in a dead man.

Messer Geri well noting his behaviour, and observing the very same course in him two mornings together, on the third day, as he was drinking, he said unto him: "Well done, Cisti; what, is it good, or no?" Cisti starting up, forthwith replied: "Yes, sir, the wine is good indeed, but how can I make you to believe me, except you taste of it?" Messer Geri, either in regard of the times, quality, or by reason of his painstaking, perhaps more than ordinary, or else because he saw Cisti had drunk so sprightly, was very desirous to taste of the wine, and turning unto the ambassadors, in merriment he said : " My lords, methinks it were not much amiss if we took a taste of this honest man's wine ; perhaps it is so good that we shall not need to repent our labour."

Hereupon he went with them to Cisti, who had caused a handsome seat to be fetched forth of his house, whereupon he requested them to sit down, and having commanded his men to wash clean the glasses, he said : " Fellows, now get you gone, and leave me to the performance of this service, for I am no worse a skinker than a baker, and tarry you never so long, you shall not drink a drop." Having thus spoken, himself washed four or five small glasses, fair and new, and causing a vial of his best wine to be brought him, he diligently filled it out to Messer Geri and the ambassadors, to whom it seemed the very best wine that they had drunk of in a long while before. And having given Cisti most hearty thanks for his kindness, and the wine his due commendation, many days afterwards, so long as they continued there, they found the like courteous entertainment, and with the good liking of honest Cisti.

But when the affairs were fully concluded for which they were sent to Florence, and their parting preparation in due readiness, Messer Geri made a very sumptuous feast for them, inviting thereto the most part of the honourable citizens, and Cisti to be one amongst them ; who by no means would be seen in an assembly of such state and pomp, albeit he was thereto, by the said Messer Geri, most earnestly entreated.

In regard of which denial, Messer Geri commanded one of his servants to take a small bottle and request Cisti to fill it with his good wine, and to serve it in such sparing manner to the table that each gentleman might be allowed half a glassful at their down sitting. The serving man, who had heard great report of the wine, and was half offended because he could never taste thereof, took a great flagon bottle, containing four or five gallons at the least, and coming therewith unto Cisti said unto him : " Cisti, because my master cannot have your company among his friends, he prays you to fill this bottle of your best wine." Cisti looking upon the huge flagon, replied thus : " Honest fellow, Messer Geri never sent thee with such a message to me ;" which although the serving man very stoutly maintained, yet getting no other answer, he returned back therewith to his master.

Messer Geri returned the servant back again unto Cisti, saying : " Go and assure Cisti, that I sent thee to him, and if he make thee any more such answers, then demand of him to what place else I should send thee." Being come again to Cisti, he avouched that his master had sent him, but Cisti affirming that he did not, the servant asked to what place else he should send him? " Marry," quoth Cisti, "unto the River of Arno, which runneth by Florence, there thou mayst be sure to fill thy flagon." When the servant had reported this answer to Messer Geri, the eyes of his understanding began to open, and calling to see what bottle he had carried with him, no sooner looked he on the huge flagon, but severely reproving the sauciness of his servant, he said : " Now trust me, Cisti told thee nothing but truth, for neither did I send thee with any such dishonest message, nor had he reason to yield or grant it."

Then he sent him a bottle of more reasonable competency, which as soon as Cisti saw : "Yea marry, my friend," quoth he, "now I am sure that thy master sent thee to me, he shall have his desire with all my heart." So commanding the bottle to be filled, he sent it away by the servant, and presently followed after him. When he came to Messer Geri, he spake unto him after this manner : "Sir, I would not have you to imagine that the huge flagon which first came did any jot dismay me, but rather I conceived that the small vial whereof you tasted every morning, yet filled many mannerly glasses together, was fallen quite out of your remembrance ; in plainer terms, it being no wine for grooms or peasants, as yourself affirmed yesterday. And because I mean to be a skinker no longer, by keeping wine to please any other palate but mine own, I have sent you half my store, and hereafter think of me as you shall please." Messer Geri took both his gift and speeches in most thankful manner, accepting him always after as his intimate friend, because he had so graced him before the ambassadors.

THE THIRD NOVEL.

Monna Nonna de' Pulci, by a sudden answer, did put to silence a Bishop of Florence, and the Lord Marshal.

WHEN Pampinea had ended her discourse, and, by the whole company, the answer and bounty of Cisti had passed with deserved commendation, it pleased the Queen that Lauretta should next succeed ; whereupon very cheerfully thus she began.

[OMITTED.]

THE FOURTH NOVEL.

Chichibio, the cook to Messer Currado Gianfiliazzi, by a sudden pleasant answer which he made to his master, converted his anger into laughter, and thereby escaped the punishment that Messer meant to impose upon him.

LAURETTA sitting silent, and the answer of Lady Nonna having passed with general applause, the Queen commanded Neifile to follow next in order, who instantly thus began :

Although a ready wit, fair ladies, doth many times afford worthy and commendable speeches, according to the accidents happening to the speaker, yet, notwithstanding, fortune (being a ready helper divers ways to the timorous) doth often tip the tongue with such a present reply as the party to speak had not so much leisure as to think on, nor yet to invent, as I purpose to let you perceive by a pretty short novel.

Messer Currado Gianfiliazzi, as most of you have both seen and known, living always in our city in the estate of a noble citizen, being a man bountiful, magnificent, and within the degree of knighthood, continually kept both hawks and hounds, taking no mean delight in such pleasures as they yielded, neglecting for them far more serious employments, wherewith our present subject presumeth not to meddle. Upon a day, having killed with his falcon a crane, near to a village called Peretola, and finding her to be young and fat he sent it to his cook, a Venetian born, named Chichibio, with command to have it prepared for his supper. Chichibio, who resembled no other than (as he was indeed) a plain, simple, honest, merry fellow, having dressed the crane as it ought to be, put it on the spit and laid it to the fire.

When it was well near roasted, and gave forth a very delicate pleasing savour, it fortuned that a young woman dwelling not far off, named Brunetta, and of whom Chichibio was somewhat enamoured, entered into the kitchen, and feeling the excellent smell of the crane to please her beyond all savours that ever she had felt before, she entreated Chichibio very earnestly that he would bestow a leg thereof upon her; whereto Chichibio, like a pleasant companion, and evermore delighting in singing, sung her this answer:

> My Brunetta, fair and feat, no, no.
> Why should you say so? Oh, oh!
> The meat of my master
> Takes you for no taster.
> Go from the kitchen, go.

Many other speeches passed between them in a short while, but in the end Chichibio, because he would not have his mistress Brunetta angry with him, cut off one of the crane's legs from the spit and gave it to her to eat. Afterward, when the fowl was served up to the table before Messer Currado, who had invited certain strangers his friends to sup with him, wondering not a little, he called for Chichibio his cook, demanding what was become of the crane's other leg. Whereto the Venetian, being a liar by nature, suddenly answered: "Sir, cranes have no more but one leg each bird." Messer Currado, growing very angry, replied: "Wilt thou tell me that a crane hath no more but one leg? Did I never see a crane before this?" Chichibio, persisting resolutely in his denial, said: "Believe me, sir, I have told you nothing but the truth; and when you please I will make good my words by such fowls as are living."

Messer Currado, in kind love to the strangers that he had invited to supper, gave over any further contestation; only he said, "Seeing thou assurest me to let me see thy affirmation for truth by other of the same fowls living (a thing which as yet I never saw or heard of), I am content to make proof thereof to-morrow morning—till then I shall rest satisfied; but, upon my word, if I find it otherwise, expect such a sound payment as thy knavery justly deserveth, to make thee remember it all thy lifetime." The contention ceasing for the night season, Messer Currado, who, although he had slept well, remained still discontented in his mind, arose in the morning by break of day, and puffing and blowing angrily, called for his horses, commanding Chichibio to mount on one of them ; so, riding on towards the river, where early every morning he had seen plenty of cranes, he said to his man : "We shall see anon, sirrah, whether thou or I lied yester-night."

Chichibio, perceiving that his master's anger was not as yet assuaged, and now it stood him upon to make good his lie, not knowing how he should do it, rode after his master, fearfully trembling all the way. Gladly he would have made an escape, but he could not by any possible means, and on every side he looked about him, now before and after behind, to espy any cranes standing on both their legs, which would have been an ominous sight to him. But being come near to the river he chanced to see, before any of the rest, upon the bank thereof, about a dozen cranes in number, each standing upon one leg, as they use to do when they are sleeping ; whereupon, showing them quickly to Messer Currado, he said : "Now, sir. yourself may see whether I told you true yester-night or no. I am sure a crane hath but one thigh and one leg, as all here present are apparent witnesses, and I have been as good as my promise."

Messer Currado, looking on the cranes, and well understanding the knavery of his man, replied : "Stay but a little while, sirrah, and I will show thee that a crane hath two thighs and two legs." Then riding somewhat nearer to them, he cried out aloud, "Shough, shough !" which caused them to set down their other legs, and all fled away, after they had made a few paces against the wind for their mounting. So going unto Chichibio, he said : "How now, you lying knave ; hath a crane two legs or no ?" Chichibio, being well-near at his wits' end, not knowing now what answer he should make, but even as it came suddenly in his mind, said : "Sir, I perceive you are in the right ; and if you would have done as much yester-night, and have cried 'Shough!' as here you did, questionless, the crane would then have set down the other leg, as these here did ; but if, as they, she had fled away too, by that means you might have lost your supper."

This sudden and unexpected answer, coming from such a loggerheaded lout, and so seasonably for his own safety, was so pleasing to Messer Currado that he fell into a hearty laughter, and, forgetting all anger, said : "Chichibio, thou hast quitted thyself well and to my contentment, albeit I advise thee to teach me no more such tricks hereafter." Thus Chichibio, by his sudden and merry answer, escaped a sound beating, which otherwise his master had inflicted upon him.

THE FIFTH NOVEL.

Messer Forese da Rabatta and Maestro Giotto, a painter by his profession, coming together from Mugello, scornfully reprehended one another for their deformity of body.

So soon as Neifile sat silent, the ladies having greatly commended the pleasant answer of Chichibio, Pamfilo, by command from the Queen, spake in this manner:

Worthy ladies, it cometh to pass oftentimes that like as fortune is observed divers ways to hide under vile and contemptible arts, the great and invaluable treasures of virtue, as not long since was well discoursed unto us by Pampinea, so in like manner hath appeared that Nature hath infused very singular spirits into most misshapen bodies of men, as hath been noted in two of our own citizens. The one of them was named Messer Forese da Rabatta, a man of little and low person, but yet deformed in body, with a flat nose, like a terrier or beagle, very ugly to behold. But notwithstanding all his deformity, he was so singularly experienced in the laws, that no man was his equal, but reputed him as a treasury of civil knowledge. The other man, being named Giotto, had a spirit of such great excellency as there was nothing in Nature, the workmistress of all, by continual motion of the heavens, but he by his brush could perfectly portrait, shaping them all so truly alike, that they were taken for the real matters indeed; and whether they were present or no, there was hardly any possibility of their distinguishing. So that many times it happened that by the variable devices he made, the visible sense of men became deceived in crediting those things to be natural which were but painted. By which means he reduced that singular art to light which long time before had lain buried, under the gross error of some who, in the mystery of painting delighted more to content the ignorant than to please the wise, he justly deserving to be termed one of the Florentine's most glorious lights. And so much the rather, because he performed all his actions in true humility; for while he lived, and was a master in his art above all other painters, yet he refused any such title, which shined the more majestical in him, as appeared by such who knew much less than he, yet his knowledge was much desired of them.

Now, notwithstanding all this excellency in him, he was not a jot the handsomer a man than was our fore-named lawyer, Messer Forese, therefore my novel concerneth them both. Understand, fair assembly, the possessions of Messer Forese and Giotto lay in Mugello; wherefore, when holidays were celebrated by order of Court, and in the summer time upon the admittance of so apt a vacation, Forese rode thither upon a very unsightly jade. The like did Giotto the painter, as ill-fitted every way as the other; and having despatched their business there, they both returned back towards Florence, and neither of them could boast which was the best mounted.

Riding on a softly pace, because their horses could go no faster, and they being well entered into years, it fortuned that a sudden shower of rain overtook them, for avoiding whereof they made all possible haste to a poor man's cottage, well known to them both. Having continued there an indifferent while, and the rain unlikely to cease, to prevent all further protraction of time, and to arrive at Florence in due season, they borrowed two old cloaks of the poor man, of overworn and ragged country grey, as also two hoods of the like complexion, which did more misshape them than their own ugly deformity, and made them flouted and scorned of all that saw them.

After they had ridden some distance of ground, much moiled and bemired with their shuffling jades, flinging the dirt everywhere about them, that well they might be termed two filthy companions, the rain gave over, and the evening being somewhat clear, they began to confer familiarly together. Forese riding a lofty French trot, every step being ready to hoist him out of his saddle, hearing Giotto's answers to every idle question he made, began to survey him even from the foot to the head, and perceiving him to be greatly deformed, in his opinion, without any consideration of his own misshaping as bad, or rather more unsightly than he, in a scoffing laughing humour he said : " Giotto, dost thou imagine that a stranger who had never seen thee before, and should now happen into our company, would believe thee to be the best painter in the world, as indeed thou art ? " Presently Giotto, without any further meditation, returned him this answer : " Signior Forese, I think he might then believe it when, beholding you, he could imagine that you had learned your A B C." Which when Forese heard, he knew his own error, and saw his payment returned in such coin as he sold his wares for.

THE SIXTH NOVEL.

A young ingenious scholar being unkindly reviled and smitten by his ignorant father, and through the procurement of an unlearned vicar, afterward attained to be doubly revenged on him.

THE ladies smiled very heartily at the ready answer of Giotto, until the Queen charged Fiammetta that she should next succeed in order, whereupon thus she began :

The very greatest infelicity that can happen to a man, and most insupportable of all other, is ignorance ; a word, I say, which hath been so general, as under it is comprehended all imperfections whatsoever. Yet notwithstanding, whosoever can cull grain by grain, the defects incident to human race, will and must confess that we are not all born to knowledge, but only such whom the heavens illuminating by their bright radiance, wherein consisteth the source and well-spring of all science, by little and little do bestow the influence of their bounty on such and so many as they please, who are to express themselves the more thankful for such a blessing. And although this grace doth lessen the misfortune of

many, which were over-mighty to be in all, yet some there are who
by saucy presuming on themselves, do bewray their ignorance by
their own speeches; setting such behaviour on each matter, and
soothing everything with such gravity, even as if they would make
comparison; or, to speak more properly, durst encounter in the
lists with great Solomon or Socrates. But let us leave them, and
come to the matter of our purposed novel.

[OMITTED.]

THE SEVENTH NOVEL.

Filippa being accused by her husband Rinaldo de' Pugliese, delivered herself,
    by a sudden witty and pleasant answer, and moderated a severe strict
    statute formerly made against women.

AFTER that Fiammetta had given over speaking, and all the
auditory had sufficiently applauded the scholar's honest revenge,
the Queen enjoined Filostrato to proceed on next with his novel,
which caused him to begin thus.

[OMITTED.]

THE EIGHTH NOVEL.

Fresco da Celatico counselled and advised his niece Cesca, that if such as
    deserved to be looked on were offensive to her eyes, as she had often told
    him, she should forbear to look upon any.

ALL the while Filostrato was recounting his novel, it seemed that
the ladies who heard it found themselves much moved thereat, as
by their blood mounting up into their cheeks it plainly appeared.
But in the end, looking on each other with strange behaviour, they
could not forbear smiling, which the Queen, interrupting by a command of attention, turning to Emilia, willed her to follow next,
when she, puffing and blowing, as if she had been newly awaked
from sleep, began in this manner:

Fair beauties, my thoughts having wandered a great distance
hence, and further than I can easily collect them together again, in
obedience yet to our Queen, I shall report a much shorter novel
than otherwise perhaps I should have done, if my mind had been a
little nearer home. I shall tell you the gross fault of a foolish
damsel, well corrected by a witty reprehension of her uncle, if
she had been endued but with so much sense as to have understood it.

An honest man, named Fresco da Celatico, had a good fulsome
wench to his niece, who, for her folly and sqeamishness, was generally
called Cesca, or Nice Francesca. And although she had stature sufficient, yet she was none of the handsomest, with a good hard-favoured
countenance, nothing near such angelical beauties as we have seen.
Yet she was endued with such height of mind, and so proud an

opinion of herself, that it appeared as a custom bred in her, or rather a gift bestowed on her by Nature (though none of the best) to blame and despise both men and women, yea, whomsoever she looked on, without any consideration of herself, she being as unsightly, ill-shaped, and ugly-faced, as a worse was very hardly to be found.

Nothing could be done at any time to yield her liking or content. Moreover, she was so waspish, nice, and squeamish, that when she came into the Royal Court of France it was hateful and contemptible to her. Whensoever she went through the streets everything stunk and was noisome to her, so that she never did anything but stop her nose, as if all men or women she met withal, and whatsoever else she looked on were stinking and offensive. But let us leave all further relation of her ill conditions, being every way indeed so bad, and hardly becoming any sensible body, that we cannot condemn them so much as we should.

It chanced upon a day that she, coming home to the house where her uncle dwelt, declared her wonted scurvy and scornful behaviour, swelling, puffing, and pouting extremely, in which humour she sat down by her uncle, who, desiring to know who did displease her, said : "Why, how now, Francesca? what may the meaning of this be? This being a solemn festival day, what is the reason of your so soon returning home?" She, coyly biting the lip, and bridling her head, sprucely thus replied :

"Indeed, you say true, uncle. I am come very early; because, since the day of my birth, I never saw a city so pestered with unhandsome people, both men-and women, and worse this high holiday than ever I did observe before. I walked through some score of streets, and I could not see one proper man; and for the women, they are the most misshapen creatures that, if God had made me such an one, I should be sorry that ever I was born. And being no longer able to endure such unpleasing sights, you will not think, uncle, in what an anger I am come home." Fresco, to whom these qualities of his niece seemed so insufferable, that he could not with patience endure them any longer, thus short and quickly answered Francesca : "If all people of our city, both men and women, be so odious in thine eyes, and offensive to thy nose as thou hast often reported to me, be advised then by my counsel; stay still at home, and look upon none but thyself only, and then thou shalt be sure that they cannot displease thee." But she being as empty of wit as a pithless cane, and yet thought her judgment to exceed Solomon's, could not understand the least part of her uncle's meaning, but stood as senseless as a sheep, only she replied that she would resort to some other part of the country, which if she found as weakly furnished of handsome people as here she did, she would conceive better of herself than ever she had done before.

THE NINTH NOVEL.

Guido Cavalcanti, with a sudden and witty answer, repprehended the rash folly of certain Florentine gentlemen that thought to scorn and flout him.

WHEN the Queen perceived that Emilia was discharged of her novel, and none remained now to speak next, but only herself, his privilege always remembered who was to be last, she began in this manner :

Fair company, you have this day disappointed me of two novels at the least, whereof I had intended to make use. Nevertheless, you shall not imagine me so unfurnished, but that I have left one in store, the conclusion whereof may minister such instruction as will not be reputed impertinent ; but rather of such material consequence as better hath not this day past.

Understand then, most fair ladies, that in former time our city had many commendable customs in it, whereof we cannot say that poor one remaineth, such hath been the too much wealth and covetousness, the only supplanter of all good qualities. Among many, there was one of note that in many places of Florence, men of the best houses in every quarter had a sociable and neighbourly meeting, creating their company to consist of a certain number, such as were able to supply their expenses, as this day one, and to-morrow another ; and thus in a kind of friendly course each daily furnished the table for the rest of the company. Oftentimes they did honour to divers gentlemen and strangers upon their arrival in our city, by inviting them into their assembly, and many of our worthiest citizens besides, so that it grew to a customary use ; and one especial day in the year was appointed in memory of this so loving a meeting, when they would ride, triumphantly as it were, on horseback through the city, sometimes performing tilts, tourneys, and other martial exercises, but they were reserved for festival days.

Among which company there was one called Messer Betto Brunelleschi, who was earnestly desirous to procure Guido Cavalcanti to make one in their friendly society. And not without great reason, for over and beside his being one of the best logicians, as those times not yielded a better, he was also a most absolute natural philosopher, which worthy qualities were little esteemed among these honest meeters, a very friendly gentleman, singularly well spoken, and whatsoever else was commendable in any man, was no way wanting in him, being wealthy withal, and able to return equal honours where he found them to be duly deserved, as no man therein could go beyond him. But Messer Betto, notwithstanding his long-continued opportunity, could not draw him into their assembly, which made him and the rest of

his company conceive that the solitude of Guido, retiring himself always from familiar conversing with men, provoked him to
many curious speculations; and because he retained some part
of the Epicurean opinion, their vulgar judgment passed on him
· that his speculations tended to no other end, but only to find out, if
he could, that there was no God.

It chanced upon a day that Guido departing from the garden
of Saint Michael, and passing along by the Corso degli Adamari,
so far as to Saint John's Church, which evermore was his
customary walk; many goodly marble tombs were then about
the said church, as nowadays are at Saint Reparata, and divers
more beside. He entering among the columns of porphyry and
the other sepulchres being there, because the door of the church
was shut, Signior Betto and his company came riding from Saint
Reparata, and espying Signior Guido among the graves and tombs,
said : "Come, let us go make some jests to anger him." So
putting the spurs to their horses, they rode apace towards him,
and being upon him before he perceived them, one of them said :
"Guido, thou refusest to be one of our society, and seekest to
find that there is no God; when thou hast found it, tell us what
wilt thou have gained ?"

Guido, seeing himself round engirt with them, suddenly thus
replied : "Gentlemen, you may use me in your own house as you
please." And setting his hand upon one of the tombs, which
was somewhat great, he took his rising and leapt quite over it on
the further side, as being of an agile and sprightly body, and
being thus freed from them, he went away to his own lodging.
They stood all like men amazed, strangely looking one upon
another, and began afterward to murmur among themselves
that Guido was a man without any understanding, and the answer
which he had made unto them was to no purpose, neither savoured
of any discretion, but merely came from an empty brain, because
they had no more to do in the place where now they were than any
of the other citizens, and Guido himself as little as any of them ;
whereto Messer Betto thus replied :

"Alas, gentlemen, it is you yourselves that are void of understanding, for if you had but observed the answer which he made
unto us, he did honestly and, in very few words, not only notably
express his own wisdom, but also deservedly reprehend us.
Because, if we observe things as we ought to do, graves and tombs
are the houses of the dead, ordained and prepared to be the latest
dwellings. He told us moreover, that although we have here in
this life our habitations, they are tombs of the dead, containing us
in our stupidity. To let us know, and all other foolish indiscreet
and unlearned men, that we are dead men, in comparison of him
and other men equal to him in skill and learning ; and therefore,
while we are here where the dead have their dwelling, it may be
well be said that we are in our own houses."

Then every one could say that Messer Guido had spoken nothing
but the truth, and were much ashamed at their own folly and

shallow estimation which they made of Guido, desiring never more after to meddle with him so grossly; and thanking Messer Betto for so well reforming their ignorance by his much better apprehension.

THE TENTH NOVEL.

Friar Onyon promised certain honest people of the country to show them a wing feather of the Angel Gabriel. Instead whereof he found coals, which he avouched to be those very coals wherewith Saint Laurence was roasted.

WHEN all of them had delivered their novels, Dioneo knowing that it remained in him to relate the last for this day, without attending for any command, after he had imposed silence on them that could not sufficiently commend the witty reprehension of Guido, thus he began : Wise and worthy ladies, although by the privilege you have granted it is lawful for me to speak anything best pleasing to myself, yet notwithstanding, it is not any part of my meaning to vary from the matter and method whereof you have spoken to very good purpose. And therefore, following your footsteps, I intend to tell you how craftily and with a rampart suddenly raised in his own defence, a religious friar of Saint Anthony's Order shunned a shame which two wily companions had prepared for him. Nor let it offend you if I run into more large discourse than this day hath been used by any, for the apter completing of my novel ; because, if you will observe it, the sun is as yet in the midst of heaven, and therefore you may the better forbear me.

Certoldo, perhaps you know or have heard, is a village in the vale of Elsa, and under the command of our Florence, which although it be but small, yet in former times it hath been inhabited with gentlemen and people of especial respect. A religious friar of Saint Anthony's Order, named Friar Onyon, had long time used thither to receive the benevolent alms which those charitably affected people in simplicity gave him, and chiefly at divers days of the year, when their bounty and devotion would extend themselves more largely than at other seasons. And so much the rather because they thought him to be a good pastor, of holy life in outward appearance, and carried a name of much greater matter than remained in the man indeed ; beside, that part of the country yielded far more plentiful abundance of onions than all other in Tuscany elsewhere— a kind of food greatly affected by those friars, as men always of hungry and good appetite. This Friar Onyon was a man of little stature, red hair, a cheerful countenance, and the world afforded not a more crafty companion than he. Moreover, albeit he had very little knowledge, wit, or learning, yet he was so prompt, ready, and voluble of speech, uttering often he knew not what himself, that such as were not well acquainted with his qualities, supposed him to be a singular rhetorician, excelling either Cicéro or Quintilian themselves ; and he was a gossip, friend, dearly affected by every one dwelling in these parts.   According to his wonted custom, one time he went thither in the month of August, and on a Sunday morning, when all the dwellers thereabout were present to hear mass, and in the chiefest church above all the rest.   When the friar saw time convenient for his purpose, he advanced himself, and began to speak in this manner :

"Gentlemen and gentlewomen, you know you have kept a commendable custom in sending yearly to the poor brethren of our Lord Baron Saint Anthony, both of your corn and other provision, some more, some less, all according to their power, means, and devotion, to the end that blessed Saint Anthony should be the more careful of your oxen, sheep, asses, swine, pigs, and other cattle.   Moreover, you have used to pay—especially such as have their names registered in our fraternity—those duties which annually you send unto us ; for the collection whereof I am sent by my superior—namely, our Lord Abbot—and therefore, with God's blessing, you may come after noon hither, when you shall hear the bells of the church ring, then will I make a predication to you ; you shall kiss the cross, and beside, because I know you all to be most devout servants to our Lord Baron Saint Anthony, in especial grace and favour, I will show you a most holy and goodly relic, which I myself, long since, brought from the Holy Land beyond the seas.   If you desire to know what it is, let me tell you that it is one of the feathers of the Angel Gabriel left with the Virgin Mary at the Annunciation."   And having thus spoken, he became silent, returning back to hear mass.   While he delivered these and the like speeches, among the other people then in the church, there were two shrewd and crafty companions, the one named Giovanni del Bragoniera, and the other Biagio Pizzini.   These subtle fellows, after they had heard the report of Friar Onyon's relic, although they were his intimate friends, and came thither in his company, yet they concluded between themselves to show him a trick of legerdemain, and to steal the feather from him.   When they had intelligence of Friar Onyon's dining that day at the castle with a worthy friend of his, no sooner was he set at the table, but away went they in all haste to the inn where the friar frequented, with this determination, that Biagio should hold conference with the friar's boy, while his fellow ransacked the wallet, to find the feather and carry it away with him, for a future observation, what the friar would say unto the people, when he found the loss of the feather, and could not perform his promise to them.

The friar's boy, whom some called Guccio Balena, some Guccio Imbratta, and others Guccio Porco, was such a knavish lad, and had so many bad qualities as Lippo Topo, the cunning painter, or the most curious poetical wit, had not any ability to describe them. Friar Onyon himself did often observe his behaviour, and would make this report among his friends.   "My boy," quoth he, "hath nine rare qualities in him, and such they are as if Solomon, Aristotle, or Seneca, had only but one of them, it were sufficient to torment and trouble all their virtue, all their senses, and all their sanctity ·

Consider, then, what manner of man he is like to be, having nine
such varieties, yet void of all virtue, wit, or goodness." And when
it was demanded of Father Onyon what these nine rare conditions
were, he having them all ready by heart, and in rhyme, thus
answered :

> " Boys I have known and seen,
> And heard of many ;"

but

> " For lying, loitering, laziness,
> For facing, filching, filthiness,
> For careless, graceless, all unthriftiness,
> My boy excelleth any."

" But truly he is a notable servant to me, for I cannot speak with
any one, and in never so great secresy, but he will be sure to hear
his part ; and when any question is demanded of me, he stands in
such awe and fear of my displeasure that he will be sure to make
the first answer, yea or no, according as he thinketh it most convenient."

Now, to proceed where we left, Friar Onyon having left this
serviceable youth at his lodging, to see that nobody should meddle
with his commodities, especially his wallet, because of the sacred
things therein contained, Guccio Imbratta, who as earnestly affected
to be in the kitchen as birds to hop from branch to branch, having
carelessly left Friar Onyon's chamber door open, and all the holy
things so much to be neglected, although it was then the month of
August, when heat is in the highest predominance, yet he would
needs sit down by the fire, and began to confer with an amiable
creature, who was called by the name of Nuta.

Our former named crafty companions, seeing Guccio Porco so
seriously employed about Nuta, were therewith not a little contented
because their intended labour was now more than half ended. And
perceiving no contradiction to cross their proceeding, into Friar
Onyon's chamber entered they, finding it ready open for their
purpose, where the first thing that came into their hand in search
was the wallet. When they had opened it, they found a small
cabinet wrapped in a great many foldings of rich taffeta ; and
having unfolded it, a fine formal key was hanging thereat ; wherewith having unlocked the cabinet, they found a fair feather of
a parrot's tail, which they supposed to be the very same that he
meant to show the people of Certaldo. And truly, in those days, it
was no hard matter to make them believe anything, because the idle
vanities of Egypt and those remoter parts had not, as yet, been
seen in Tuscany, as since then they have been in great abundance,
to the utter ruin almost of Italy.

And although they might be known to very few, yet the inhabitants of the country generally understood little or nothing at all
of them. For there, the pure simplicity of their ancient predecessors still continuing, they had not seen any parrots, or so much
as heard any speech of them. Wherefore the crafty consorts, not a
little joyful of finding the feather, took it thence with them, and

because they would not leave the cabinet empty, espying charcoals
lying in a corner of the chamber, they filled it with them, wrapping
it up again in the taffeta, and in as demure manner as they found it.
So away came they with the feather, neither seen nor suspected by
any one, intending now to hear what Friar Onyon would say upon
the loss of his precious relic, and finding the coals were placed
instead thereof.

The simple men and women of the country, who had been at
morning mass in the church, and heard what a wonderful feather
they should see in the afternoon, returned in all haste to their
houses, where one telling this news to another, and gossip with
gossip consulting there, they made the shorter dinner, and afterwards flocked in main troops to the castle, contending who should
first get entrance, such was their devotion to see the holy feather.
Friar Onyon having dined and reposed a little after his wine, he
arose from the table to the window, where, beholding what multitudes
came to see the feather, he assured himself of good store of money.
Hereupon he sent to his boy Guccio Imbratta, that upon the bells
ringing, he should come and bring the wallet to him ; which, with
much ado, he did, so soon as his quarrel was ended in the kitchen
with the amiable chambermaid Nuta.   Away then he went with
his holy commodities, where he was no sooner arrived, but because
he was ready to burst with drinking water, he sent him to the
church to ring the bells, which not only would warm the cold water
within him, but likewise make him run as gaunt as a greyhound.

When all the people were assembled in the church together, Friar
Onyon, never mistrusting any injury offered to him, or that his close
commodities had been meddled withal, began his predication, uttering a thousand lies to fit his purpose.   And when he came to show
the feather of the Angel, having first in great devotion finished the
conclusion, he caused two goodly torches to be lighted, and ducking
down his head three several times before he would so much as touch
the taffeta, he opened it with much reverence.   So soon as the
cabinet came to be seen, off went his hood, lowly he bowed down his
body, and uttering especial praises of the Angel and sacred
properties of the wonderful relic, the cover of the cabinet being lifted
up, he saw the same to be full of coals.   He could not suspect his
villain boy to do the deed, for he knew him not to be endued with
so much wit, only he cursed him for keeping it no better, and cursed
himself also for reposing trust in such a careless knave, knowing
him to be slothful, disobedient, negligent, and void of all honest
understanding or grace.   Suddenly, without blushing, lest his loss
should be discerned, he lifted his looks and hands to Heaven,
speaking out so loud as every one might easily hear him, thus : " O
thou omnipotent Providence, for ever let thy power be praised."
Then making fast the cabinet again, and turning himself to the
people with looks expressing admiration, he proceeded in this
manner :

" Lords, ladies, and you the rest of my worthy auditors : you are
to understand, that I, being then very young, was sent by my

superior into those parts where the sun appeareth at his first rising. And I had received charge by express command that I should seek for, so much as consisted in my power to do, the especial virtues and privileges belonging to porcelain, which although the boiling thereof be worth but little, yet it is very profitable to any but us. In regard whereof, being upon my journey, and departing from Venice, passing along the Borgo de' Greci, I proceeded thence, on horseback, through the realm of Garbo, so to Baldacca, till I came to Parione ; from whence, not without great extremity of thirst, I arrived in Sardinia.

"But why do I trouble you with the repetition of so many countries? I coasted on still, after I had passed Saint George's Arm, into Truffia, and then into Buffia, which are countries much inhabited, and with great people. From thence I went into Lieland, where I found store of the brethren of our religion, and many other beside, who shunned all pain and labour, only for the love of God, and cared as little for the pains and travails which others took, except some benefit arised thereby to them ; nor spend they any money in this country but such as is without stamp. Thence I went into the land of Abruzzi, where the men and women go in galoches over the mountains, and make them garments of their swines' guts. Not far from thence, I found people that carried bread in their staves, and wine in satchels ; when parting from them I arrived among the mountains of Bacchus, where all the waters run down with a deep fall, and in short time I went on so far, that I found myself to be in India Pastinaca, where I swear to you by the holy habit which I wear on my body, that I saw serpents fly, things incredible, and such as was never seen before.

" But because I would be loth to lie, so soon as I departed thence, I met with Maso del Saggio, who was a great merchant there, and whom I found cracking nuts and selling cockles by retail. Nevertheless, all this while I could not find what I sought for, and therefore I was to pass from hence by water if I intended to travel thither, and so in returning back, I came into the Holy Land, where cool fresh bread is sold for fourpence, and the hot is given away for nothing. There I found the venerable Father Blame-me-not-I-beseech-you, the most worthy Patriarch of Jerusalem, who for the reverence due to the habit that I wear, and love to our Lord Baron Saint Anthony, would have me to see all the holy relics which he had there under his charge ; whereof there were so many, as if I should recount them all to you, I never could come to a conclusion. But yet, not to leave you discomforted, I will relate some few of them to you.

" First of all, he showed me the finger of the Holy Ghost, so whole and perfect as ever it was. Next, the nose of the cherubim which appeared to Saint Francis, with the paring of the nails of a seraphim, and one of the ribs of Verbum Caro, fastened to one of the windows, covered with the garments of the holy Catholic faith. Then he took me into a dark chapel, where he showed me divers beams of the star that appeared to the three Kings in the East ; also a vial of

Saint Michael's sweat when he combated with the devil, and the jaw-bone of dead Lazarus, with many other precious things beside. And because I was liberal to him, giving him two of the plains of Monte Morello, in the vulgar edition, and some of the chapters Del Capretio, which he had long laboured in search of, he bestowed upon me some of his relics.

" First he gave me one of the eye-teeth of Santa Crux, and a little vial filled with some part of the sound of those bells which hung in the sumptuous Temple of Solomon. Next he gave me the feather of the Angel Gabriel, as before I told you, and one of the wooden pattens which the good Saint. Gherardo da Villa Magna used to wear in his travels, and which I gave not long since to Gherardo di Bonsi at Florence, where it is respected with great devotion ; moreover, he gave me a few of those coals wherewith the holy Saint Laurence was roasted—all which things I brought away thence with me. Now, most true it is, that my superior would never suffer me to show them anywhere until he was faithfully certified whether they were the same precious relics or no ; but perceiving, by sundry miracles which they have wrought, and letters of sufficient credence received from the reverend patriarch that all is true, he hath granted me permission to show them, and because I would not trust any one with matters of such moment, I myself brought them hither with me.

" Now, I must tell you that the feather of the Angel Gabriel I conveyed into a small cabinet or casket, because it should not be bent or broken, and the coals wherewith the holy Laurence was roasted I put into another casket, in all respects so like to the former that many times I have taken one for another, as now at this instant it hath been my fortune ; for, imagining that I brought the casket with the feather, I mistook myself, and brought the other with the coals ; wherein, doubtless, I have not offended, because I am certain that we of our Order do not anything but it is ordered by Divine direction and our blessed patron the Lord Baron Saint Anthony. And so much the rather because, about a sennight hence, the fe? it of Saint Laurence is to be solemnized, against the preparation whereof, and to kindle your zeal with the greater fervency, he put the casket with the coals into my hand, meaning to let you see the feather at some fitting season ; and therefore, my blessed sons and daughters, put off your bonnets, and come hither with devotion to look upon them. But first let me tell you that, whosoever is marked by any of these coals with the sign of the Cross, he or she shall live all this year happily, and no fire whatsoever shall come near to touch or hurt them." So, singing a solemn anthem in the praise of Saint Laurence, he unveiled the casket and showed the coals openly.

The simple multitude having, with great admiration and reverence, a long while beheld them, they thronged in crowds to Friar Onyon, giving him far greater offerings than before they had, and entreating him to mark them each after other. Whereupon he, taking the coals in his hand, began to mark their garments of white and the veils on the women's heads with crosses of no mean extendure, affirming to them that the more the coals wasted with making those great crosses the more they still increased in the casket, as often before he had made trial.

In this manner, having crossed all the Certaldesi to his great benefit and their abuse, he smiled at his sudden and dexterous device in mockery of them who thought to have made a scorn of him by dispossessing him of the feather; for Brogeniera and Pizzini, being present at his learned predication, and having heard what a cunning shift he found to come off cleanly without the least detection, and all delivered with such admirable protestations, they were fain to forsake the church lest they should burst with laughing. But when all the people were departed and gone they met Friar Onyon at his inn, where closely they discovered to him what they had done, delivering him his feather again, which the year following did yield him such money as now the coals had done.

This novel afforded equal pleasing to the whole company, Friar Onyon's sermon being much commended, but especially his long pilgrimage and the relics he had both seen and brought home with him. Afterward, the Queen perceiving that her reign had now the full expiration, graciously she arose, and taking the crown from off her own head placed it on the head of Dioneo, saying: "It is high time, Dioneo, that you should take part of the charge and pain which poor women have felt and undergone in their sovereignty and government; wherefore, be you our King, and rule us with such awful authority that the ending of our dominion may yield us all contentment." Dioneo being thus invested with the crown, returned this answer:

"I make no doubt, bright beauties, but you many times have seen a better king among the chessmen than I am; but yet of a certainty, if you would be obedient to me as you ought in duty unto a true king, I should grant you a liberal freedom of that wherein you take the most delight, and without which our choicest desires can never be complete. Nevertheless, I mean that my government shall be according to mine own mind." So, causing the Master of the Household to be called for, as all the rest were wont to do for conference with him, he gave him direction for all things fitting the time of his regiment, and then proceeded:

"Honest ladies, we have already discoursed of variable devices and so many several manners of human industry concerning the business wherewith Licisca came to acquaint us, that her very words have ministered me matter sufficient for our morrow's conference, or else I stand in doubt that I could not have devised a more convenient theme for us to talk on. In which respect my will is, seeing Licisca hath given us so good an occasion, that our discoursing to-morrow may only concern such sly cunning and deceits as women have heretofore used for satisfying their own appetites and beguiling their own husbands without their knowledge or suspicion, and cleanly escaping with them or no."

This argument seemed not very pleasing to the ladies, and therefore they urged an alteration thereof to some matter better suiting with the day and their discoursing; whereto thus he answered :

"Ladies, I know as well as yourselves why you would have this instant argument altered, but to change me from it you have no power; considering the season is such as shielding all, both men and women, from meddling with any dishonest action, it is lawful for us to speak of what we please. And know you not that, through the sad occasion of the time which now overruleth us, the judges have forsaken their venerable benches, the laws, both divine and human, ceasing, granting ample license to every one to do what best agreeth with the conservation of life? Therefore, if your honesties do strain themselves a little both in thinking or speaking, not for prosecution of any immodest deed, but only for familiar and blameless intercourse, I cannot devise a more convenient ground, at least that carrieth apparent reason, for reproof of perils to ensue by any of you. Moreover, your company, which hath been most honest since the first day of our meeting to this instant, appeareth not any jot to be disgraced by anything either said or done, neithe shall be, I hope, in the meanest degree.

"And what is he, knowing your choice and virtuous dispositions, so powerful in their own prevailing that wanton words cannot misguide your ways—no, nor the terror of death itself—that dare insinuate a distempered thought? But admit that some slight or shallow judgments, hearing you, perhaps sometimes, talk of such amorous follies, should therefore suspiciously imagine you to be faulty, or else you would be more sparing of speech; their wit and censure are both alike, savouring rather of their own vile nature, who would brand others with their base-bred imperfections. Yet there is another consideration beside, of some great injury offered to my honour, and I know not how you can acquit yourselves.

"I that have been obedient to you all and borne the heavy load of your business, having now, with full consent, created me your King, you would wrest the law out of my hands and dispose of my authority as you please. Forbear, gentle ladies, all frivolous suspicions, more fit for them that are full of bad thoughts than you, who have true virtue shining in your eyes; and, therefore, let every one freely speak their mind according as their humours best please them."

When the ladies heard this they made answer that all should be answerable to his mind. Whereupon the King gave them all leave to dispose of themselves till supper-time. And because the sun was yet very high, in regard all the recounted novels had been so short, Dioneo went to play at the tables with another of the young gentlemen, and Elisa, having withdrawn the ladies aside, thus spake unto them : "During the time of our being here I have often been desirous to let you see a place somewhat near at hand, which I suppose you have never seen, it being called The Valley of Ladies. Till now I could not find any convenient time to bring you thither, but the sun being still high, you have apt leisure, and the sight, I am sure, can no way discontent you."

The ladies replied they were ready to walk with her thither ; and calling one of their women to attend on them, they set on, without speaking a word to any of the men.   And within the distance of half a mile they arrived at The Valley of Ladies, whereinto they entered by a straight passage at the one side, from whence there issued forth a clear running river.   And they found the said valley to be so goodly and pleasant, especially in that. season, which was the hottest of all the year, as all the world was nowhere able to yield the like.   And, as one of the said ladies since then related to me, there was a plain in the valley so directly round as if it had been formed by a compass, yet rather it resembled the workmanship of Nature than to be made by the hand of man, containing in circuit somewhat more than the quarter of a mile, environed with six small hills, of no great height, and on each of them stood a little palace, shapen in the fashion of castles.

The ground plots descending from those hills or mountains grew less and less by variable degrees, as we observe at entering into our theatres, from the highest part to the lowest, succinctly to narrow the circle by order.   Now, concerning these ground plots, or little meadows, those which the sun southward looked on were full of vines, olive-trees, almond-trees, cherry-trees, and fig-trees, with divers other trees beside, so plentifully bearing fruits as you could not discern a hand's-breadth of loss. The other mountains, whereon the northern winds blow, were curiously covered with small thickets or woods of oaks, ashes, and other trees, so green and straight, as it was impossible to behold fairer.   The goodly plain itself, not having any other entrance but where the ladies came on, was planted with trees of fir, cypress, laurel, and pines, so singularly growing in formal order, as if some artificial or cunning hand had planted them, the sun hardly piercing through their branches from the top to the bottom, even at the highest or any part of his course.

All the whole field was richly spread with grass, and such variety of delicate flowers as Nature yielded out of her plenteous store-house.   But that which gave no less delight than any of the rest, was a small running brook descending from one of the valleys that divided two of the little hills, and fell directly through a vein of the entire rock itself, that the fall and murmur thereof was most delight-ful to hear, seeming all the way in the descent like quicksilver, weaving itself into artificial works, and, arriving in the plain be-neath, it was there received into a small channel, swiftly running through the midst of the plain, to a place where it stayed, and shaped itself into a lake or pond, such as our citizens have in their orchards or gardens when they please to make use of such a commodity.

This pond was no deeper than to reach the breast of a man, and having no mud or soil in it the bottom thereof showed like small beaten gravel, with pretty pebble-stones intermixed. which some, that had nothing else to do, would sit down and count

as they lay, as very easily they might.   And not only was the
bottom thus apparently seen, but also such plenty of fishes swimming every way that the mind was never to be wearied in looking
on them.   Nor was this water bounded in with any banks, but only
the sides of the meadow, which made it appear the more sightly as
it arose in swelling plenty.   And always as it superabounded in
this course, lest it should overflow disorderly, it fell into another
channel, which conveying it along the lower valley, ran forth to
water other needful places.

When the ladies were come into this goodly valley, and upon
advised viewing of it, had sufficiently commended it, in regard the
heat of the day was great, the place tempting, and the pond free
from the sight of any, they resolved there to bathe themselves.
Wherefore they sent the waiting gentlewoman to have a diligent
eye on the way where they entered, lest any one should chance to
steal upon them.   All seven of them being stripped stark-naked,
into the water they went, which hid their delicate white bodies, like
as a clear glass concealeth a damask rose within it.   So they being
in the pond, and the water nothing troubled by their being there,
they found much pretty pastime together, running after the fishes
to catch them with their hands, but they were over-quick and cunning for them.   After they had delighted themselves there to their
own contentment, and were clothed with their garments as before,
thinking it fit time for their returning back again, lest their over-long
stay might give offence, they depart thence in an easy pace, doing
nothing else all the way as they went but extolling The Valley of
Ladies beyond all comparison.

At the palace they arrived in a due hour, finding the three
gentlemen at play, as they left them, to whom Pampinea pleasantly
thus spake : " Now trust me, gallants, this day we have very cunningly beguiled you."   " How now ? " answered Dioneo ; " begin
you first to act before you speak ? "   " Yes, truly, sir," replied
Pampinea, relating to him at large from whence they came, what
they had done there, the beauty of the place, and the distance
thence.   The King, upon her excellent report, being very desirous
to see it, suddenly commanded supper to be served in, which was
no sooner ended, but they and their three servants, leaving the
ladies, walked on to the valley, which, when they had considered,
no one of them having ever been there before, they thought it had
been the Paradise of the world.

They bathed themselves there likewise, as the ladies formerly had
done, and being re-vested returned home to their lodgings, because
dark night drew on apace ; but they found the ladies dancing to a
song which Fiammetta sang.   When the dance was ended, they
entertained the time with no other discourse but only concerning
The Valley of Ladies, whereof they all spake liberally in commendations. Whereupon the King called the Master of the Household,
giving him command that on the morrow dinner should be ready
betimes, and bedding to be thence carried, if any desired to rest at
mid-time of the day.

All this being done, variety of pleasing wines were brought, banqueting stuff, and other dainties, after which they fell to dancing. And Pamfilo, having received command to begin a special dance, the King turned himself to Elisa, speaking thus : " Fair lady, you have done me so much honour this day as to deliver me the crown ; in regard whereof be you this night the Mistress of the Song, and let it be such as best may please yourself." Whereupon Elisa, with a modest blush arising in her face, replied that his will should be fulfilled, and then, with a delicate voice, she began in this manner :

THE SONG.

The CHORUS *sung by all.*

Love, if I 'scape you free, from forth thy hold,
    Believe it for a truth,
Never more shall thy falsehood me enfold.

When I was young I entered first thy fights,
Supposing them to be a solemn peace ;
I threw off all my arms, and with delights
Fed my poor hopes, that still they did increase.
But like a tyrant, full of rancorous hate,
    Thou took'st advantage,
And I sought refuge, but it was too late.
        Love, if I 'scape you free, &c.

But being thus surprisèd in thy snares,
With bitter tears, to her thou gav'st me slave,
Born for my death, who fed me with despairs,
And kept me dying in a living grave ;
For I saw nothing daily 'fore mine eyes
    But racks and tortures,
From which I could not get in any wise.
        Love, if I 'scape you free, &c.

My sighs and tears I vented to the wind,
For none would hear or pity my complaints.
My torments still increasèd in this kind,
And more and more I felt these sharp restraints.
Release me now at last from forth this hell ;
    Assuage thy rigour,
Delight not thus in cruelty to dwell.
        Love, if I 'scape you free, &c.

If this thou wilt not grant, be yet so kind,
Release me from those worse than servile bands,
Which new vain hopes have bred, wherein I find
Such violent fears as comfort quite withstands.
Be now, at length, a little moved to pity ;
    Be it never so little,
Or in my death listen my swan-like ditty.
Love, if I 'scape you free, from forth thy hold,
    Believe it for a truth,
Never more shall thy falsehood me enfold.

After that Elisa had made an end of her song, which she sealed up with a heart-breaking sigh, they all sate amazedly wondering at her moans, not one among them being able to conjecture what should be the reason of her singing in this manner. But the King being in a good and pleasing temper, calling Tindaro, commanded him to bring his bagpipe, by the sound whereof they danced divers dances, and a great part of the night being spent in this manner, they all gave over and departed to their chambers.

THE SEVENTH DAY.

When the assembly being met together and under the regiment of Dioneo, the discourses are directed for the discovery of such policies and deceits as women have used for beguiling of their husbands, either in respect of their love, or for the prevention of some blame or scandal, escaping without sight, knowledge, or otherwise.

INDUCTION.

ALL the stars were departed out of the East, but only that which we commonly call bright Lucifer, or the Day Star, gracing the morning very gloriously, when the Master of the Household being risen, went with all the provision to The Valley of Ladies, to make everything in due and decent readiness, according as his lord overnight had commanded him. After which departure of his, it was not long before the King arose, being awaked with the noise which the carriages made ; and when he was up, the other two gentlemen and the ladies were quickly ready soon after. On they set towards the valley, even as the sun was rising, and all the way as they went, never before had they heard so many sweet nightingales and other pretty birds melodiously singing as they did this morning, which keeping them company throughout the journey, they arrived at The Valley of Ladies, where it seemed to them that infinite quires of delicate nightingales, and other sweet singing birds, had purposely made a meeting, even as it were to give them a glad welcome thither.

Divers times they walked about the valley, never satisfied with viewing it from one end to the other ; because it appeared far more pleasing unto them than it had done the preceding day, and because the day's splendour was much more conform to the beauty thereof. After they had broken their fast with excellent wines and banqueting stuff, they began to tune their instruments and sing, because therein the sweet birds should not excel them, the valley, with delicate echoes, answering all their notes. When dinner-time drew near, the tables were covered under the spreading trees, and by the goodly pond's side, where they sate down orderly by the King's direction, and all dinner-while they saw the fishes swim by huge shoals in the pond, which sometimes gave them occasion to talk as well as gaze on them.

When dinner was ended, and the tables withdrawn, in as jocund manner as before, they renewed again their harmonious singing. In divers places of this pleasant valley were goodly field-beds readily furnished, according as the Master of the Household gave instruction, enclosed with pavilions of costly stuffs such as are sometimes brought out of France. Such as were disposed, were licensed by the King to take their rest, and they that would not, he permitted them to their wonted pastime, each according to their minds. But when they were risen from sleep, and the rest from their other exercises, it seemed to be more than half time that they should prepare for talk and conference. So sitting down on Turkey carpets, which were spread abroad upon the green grass, and close by the place where they.had dined, the King gave command that Emilia should first begin, whereto she willingly yielded obedience, and expecting such silent attention as formerly had been observed, thus she began.

THE FIRST NOVEL.

Gianni Lotteringhi heard one knock at his door in the night-time, whereupon he awaked his wife Monna Tessa. She made him believe that it was a spirit which knocked at the door, and so they arose, going both together to conjure the spirit with a prayer; and afterwards they heard no more knocking.

MY gracious lord, quoth Emilia, it had been a matter highly pleasing me that any other,. rather than myself, should have begun to speak of this argument, which it hath pleased you to appoint. But seeing it is your highness's pleasure that I must make a passage of assurance for all the rest, I will not be irregular, because obedience is our chief article. I shall therefore, gracious ladies, strive to speak something which may be advantageable to you hereafter, in regard, that if other women be as fearful as we, especially of spirits, of which all our sex have generally been timorous—although, upon my credit, I know not what they are, nor never could meet with any to tell me what they be—you may by the diligent observation of my novel, learn a wholesome and holy prayer, very available and of precious power to conjure and drive them away whensoever they shall presume to assault you in any place.

[OMITTED.]

THE SECOND NOVEL.

Peronella hid a young man, her friend and lover, under a great brewing tub, upon the sudden returning home of her husband, who told her that he had sold the said tub, and brought him that bought it to carry it away. Peronella replied that she had formerly sold it unto another, who was underneath it to see whether it were whole or sound, or no. Whereupon he being come forth from under it, she caused her husband to make it neat and clean, and so the last buyer carried it away.

NOT without much laughter and good liking was the tale of Emilia listened unto, and both the prayers commended to be sound and sovereign ; but it being ended, the King commanded Filostrato that he should follow next in order, whereupon thus he began.

[OMITTED.]

THE THIRD NOVEL.

Friar Rinaldo, falling in love with a gentlewoman, wife to a man of good account, found a means to become her gossip. Afterward he conferring with her, and her husband coming suddenly thither, she made him believe that he came thither for no other end but to cure his godson by a charm, of a dangerous disease which he had by worms.

FILOSTRATO told not his tale so covertly, concerning Lazaro's simplicity and Peronella's witty policy, but the ladies found a knot in the rush, and laughed not a little at his quaint manner of discoursing it. But upon the conclusion, the King looking upon Elisa, willed her to succeed next, which as willingly she granted, and thus began :

Pleasant ladies, the charm or conjuration wherewith Emilia laid her night-walking spirit maketh me to remember a novel of another enchantment, which although it carrieth not commendation equal to the other, yet I intend to report it, because it suiteth to our present purpose, and I cannot suddenly be furnished with another answerable thereto in nature.

[OMITTED.]

THE FOURTH NOVEL.

Tofano in the night season did lock his wife out of his house, and she not prevailing to get entrance again by all the entreaties she could possibly use, made him believe that she had thrown herself into a well by casting a great stone into the same well. Tofano hearing the fall of the stone into the well, and being persuaded that it was his wife indeed, came forth of his house, and ran to the well s side. In the meanwhile his wife got into the house, made fast the door against her husband, and gave him many reproachful speeches.

So soon as the King perceived that the novel reported by Elisa was finished, he turned himself to Lauretta, and told her that it was his pleasure that she should now begin the next, whereto she yielded in this manner :

O Love ! What and how many are thy prevailing forces? How strange are thy foresights ! And how admirable thine attempts ! Where is, or ever was, the philosopher or artist that could instruct the wiles, escapes, preventions, and demonstrations, which suddenly thou teachest such as are thy apt and understanding scholars indeed ? Certain it is, that the documents and eruditions of all other whatsoever are of weak or of no worth in respect of thine, as hath notably appeared by the demonstrations already past, and whereto, worthy ladies, I will add another of a simple woman, who taught her husband such a lesson as she never learned of any but Love himself.

[OMITTED.]

THE FIFTH NOVEL.

A jealous man, clothed with the habit of a priest, became the confessor to his own wife, who made him believe that she was deeply in love with a priest, by means of which confession while her jealous husband watched the door of his house, to surprise the priest when he came; she that meant to do amiss had the company of a secret friend, who came over the top of the house to visit her, while her foolish husband kept the door.

LAURETTA having ended her novel, every one commended the woman for fitting Tofano in his kind, and as his jealousy and drunkenness justly deserved. The King, to prevent all loss of time, turned to Fiammetta, commanding her to follow next, whereupon, very graciously, she began in this manner.

[OMITTED.]

THE SIXTh NOVEL.

Isabella delighting in the company of her affected friend named Lionetto, and she likewise beloved by Messer Lambertuccio; at the same time as she had entertained Lionetto, she was also visited by Lambertuccio. Her husband returning home in the very instant, she caused Lambertuccio to run forth with a drawn sword in his hand, and, by that means, made an excuse sufficient for Lionetto to her husband.

WONDROUSLY pleasing to all the company was the reported novel of Fiammetta, every one applauding the woman's wisdom, and that she had done no more than as the jealous fool her husband justly deserved. But she having ended, the King gave order unto Pampinea that now it was her turn to speak, whereupon thus she began:

There are no mean store of people who say (though very falsely and foolishly) that love maketh many to be out of their wits, and that such as fall in love do utterly lose their understanding. To me this appeareth a very idle opinion, as already it hath been approved by the related discourses, and shall also be made manifest by another of mine own.

[OMITTED.]

THE SEVENTH NOVEL.

Lodovico discovered to Madonne Beatrice how he was affected to her. She cunningly sent Egano, her husband, into his garden in all respects disguised like herself, while friendly Lodovico conferred with her in the meanwhile. Afterward Lodovico pretendeth anger at his mistress, who would wrong his honest master, and instead of her beateth Egano soundly in the garden.

THIS so sudden dexterity of wit in Isabella, related in very modest manner by Pampinea, was not only admired by all the company, but likewise passed with as general approbation. But yet Filomena, whom the King had commanded next to succeed, peremptorily said :

Worthy ladies, if I am not deceived, I intend to tell you another tale presently, as much to be commended as the last.

[OMITTED.]

THE EIGHTH NOVEL.

Arriguccio Berlinghieri became immeasurably jealous of his wife Sismonda, who fastened a thread about her great toe for to serve as a signal when her friend should come to visit her. Arriguccio findeth the fallacy, and while he pursueth the friend, she causeth her maid to take her place against his return, whom he beateth extremely, cutting away the locks of her hair, thinking he had done all this violence to his wife Sismonda, and afterward fetcheth her mother and her brethren to shame her before them, and so be rid of her. But they finding all his speeches to be false, and reputing him to be a jealous fool, all the blame and disgrace falleth upon himself.

IT seemed to the whole assembly that Beatrice dealt somewhat strangely in the manner of beguiling her husband ; but when the King perceived that Filomena sate silent, he turned to Neifile, willing her to supply the next place, who, modestly smiling, thus began :

Fair ladies, it were a heavy burthen imposed on me, and a matter much surmounting my capacity, if I should vainly imagine to content you with so pleasing a novel as those have already done, by you so singularly praised. Nevertheless, I must discharge my duty in obeying my Sovereign, and take my fortune as it falleth out, albeit I hope to find you merciful.

[OMITTED.]

THE NINTH NOVEL.

Lydia, a lady of great beauty, birth, and honour, being wife to Nicostratus, Governor of Argos, falling in love with a gentleman named Pyrrhus, was requested by him, as a true testimony of her unfeigned affection, to perform three several actions of herself. She did accomplish them all, and embraced and kissed Pyrrhus in the presence of Nicostratus, by persuading him that whatsoever he saw was merely false.

THE novel delivered by Neifile seemed so pleasing to all the ladies, as they could not refrain from hearty laughter, beside much liberality of speech, albeit the King did oftentimes urge silence, and commanded Pamfilo to follow next. So, when attention was admitted, Pamfilo began in this manner:

I am of opinion, fair ladies, that there is not any matter, how uneasy or doubtful soever it might seem to be, but the man or woman that affecteth fervently dare boldly attempt and effectually accomplish. And this persuasion of mine, although it hath been sufficiently approved by many of our past novels, yet, notwithstanding, I shall make it much more apparent to you by a present discourse of mine own, wherein I have occasion to speak of a lady to whom fortune was more favourable than either reason or judgment could give direction. In which regard I would not advise any of you to entertain so high an imagination of mind as to track her footsteps of whom I am now to speak, because fortune containeth not always one and the same disposition, neither can all men's eyes be blinded after one manner. And so proceed we to our tale.

[OMITTED.]

THE TENTH NOVEL.

Two citizens of Siena, the one named Tingoccio Mini, and the other Meucio di Tura, affected both one woman called Monna Mitai, to whom one of them was a gossip. The gossip died, and appeared afterward to his companion, according as he had formerly promised him to do, and told him what strange wonders he had seen in the other world.

NOW there remained none but the King himself last of all to recount this novel, who, after he heard the ladies' complaints indifferently pacified for the rash felling down of such a precious peartree, thus he began:

Fair ladies, it is a case more than manifest that every king who will be accounted just and upright should first of all, and rather than any other, observe those laws which he himself hath made, otherwise to be reputed as a servant, worthy punishment, and no king, into which fault and reprehension I, your King, shall well near be constrained to fall ; for yesterday I enacted a law, upon the former of our discoursing with full intent, that this day I would not use any part of my privilege ; but being subject, as you all are, to the same law, I should speak of that argument which already you have done.

Wherein you ·have not only performed more than I could wish upon a subject so suitable to my mind, but in every novel such variety of excellent matter, such singular illustrations and delicate eloquence hath flown from you all, as I am utterly unable to invent anything (notwithstanding the most curious search of my brain), apt or fit for the purpose, to paragon the meanest of them already related ; and, therefore, seeing I must needs sin in the law established by myself, I tender my submission as worthy of punishment, or what amends else you please to enjoin me.   Now, as returned to my wonted privilege, I say that the novel recounted by Elisa, of the friar godfather and his gossip Agnesia, as also the sottishness of the Siennese, her husband, hath wrought in me, worthy ladies, to such effect as—forbearing to speak any more of these wily pranks which witty wives exercise on their simple husbands—I am to tell you a pretty short tale, which, though there is matter enough in it not worthy the crediting, yet partly it will be pleasing to hear.

[OMITTED.]

By this time the gentle blast of Zephyrus began to blow because the sun grew near his setting, wherewith the King concluded his novel ; and none remaining more to be thus employed, taking the crown from off his own head, he placed it on Lauretta's, saying : " Madam, I crown you with your own crown as Queen of our company.   You shall henceforth command as lady and mistress on such occasions as shall be to your liking and for the contentment of us all ; " with which words he sate him down.   And Lauretta being now created Queen, she caused the Master of the Household to be called, to whom she gave command that the tables should be prepared in the pleasant valley, but at a more convenient hour than formerly had been, because they might with better ease return back to the palace.   Then she took order likewise for all such other necessary matters as should be required in the time of her regiment ; and then, turning herself to the whole company, she began in this manner :

" It was the will of Dioneo yester-night that our discourses for this day should concern the deceits of wives to their husbands ; and were it not to avoid taxation of a splenitive desire to be revenged, like the dog that being bitten biteth again, I could command our to-morrow's conference to touch men's treacheries towards their wives. But because I am free from any such fiery humour, let it be your general consideration to speak of such quaint beguilings as have heretofore past, either of the woman to the man or the man to the woman, or of one man to another ; and I am of opinion that they will yield us no less delight than those related this day have done."

When she had thus spoken she rose, granting them all liberty to go recreate themselves until supper-time.

The ladies being thus at their own disposing, some of them bared their legs and feet to wash them in the cool current. Others, not so minded, walked on the green grass and under the goodly spreading trees; Dioneo and Fiammetta, they sate singing together the love-war between Arcite and Palamon. And thus, with diversity of disports in choice delight and much contentment, all were employed till supper drew near. When the hour was come, and the tables covered by the pond's side, we need not question their diet and dainties, infinite birds sweetly singing about them as no music in the world could be more pleasing; beside calm winds fanning their faces from the neighbouring hill, free from flies or the least annoyance, made a delicate addition to their pleasure.

No sooner were the tables withdrawn and all risen but they fetched a few turnings about the valley, because not as yet quite set. Then in the cool evening, according to the Queen's appointment, in a soft and gentle pace, they walked homeward, devising on a thousand occasions, as well those which the day's discourses had yielded, as others of their own inventing beside. It was almost dark night before they arrived at the palace, where, with variety of choice wines and abounding plenty of rare banqueting, they outwore the little toil and weariness which the long walk had charged them withal. Afterward, according to their wonted order, the instruments being brought and played on, they fell to dancing about the fair fountain, Tindaro intruding now and then the sound of his bagpipe, to make the music seem more melodious. But in the end the Queen commanded Filomena to sing; whereupon, the instruments being tuned fit for the purpose, thus she began:

THE SONG.

The CHORUS *sung by the whole Company.*

Wearisome is my life to me
Because I cannot once again return
Unto the place which made me first to mourn :
Nothing I know, yet feel a powerful fire
    Burning within my breast,
    Through deep desire
To be once more where first I felt unrest
    Which cannot be exprest.
O my sole good ! O my best happiness !
    Why am I thus restrained ?
Is there no comfort in this wretchedness?
Then let me live content, to be thus pained.
    Wearisome is my life to me, &c.

I cannot tell what was that rare delight
    Which first enflamed my soul
    And gave command in spite,
That I should find no ease by day or night
    But still live in control.

I see, I hear, and feel a kind of bliss,
    Yet find no form at all.
Others in their desire feel blessedness,
But I have none, nor think I ever shall.
    Wearisome is my life to me, &c.

Tell me if I may hope in following days,
    To have but one poor sight
    Of those bright sunny rays,
Dazzling my sense, that overcome me quite,
    Say "Soon;" let the delays
Be short before the time when I may prove
    Abiding of thy grace,
Through years made happy with the light of love!
Why should I live despised in every place?
    Wearisome is my life to me, &c.

Methinks mild favour whispers in my ear,
    And bids me not despair.
    There will a time appear
To quell and quite confound consuming care,
    Joy will surmount all fear.
In hope that gracious time will come at length,
    To end my long dismay,
My spirits reassume your former strength,
And never doubt to see that joyful day!
    Wearisome is my life to me,
Because I cannot once again return
Unto the place which made me first to mourn.

This song gave occasion to the whole company to imagine that some new and pleasing apprehension of love constrained Filomena to sing in this manner. And because by discourse thereof it plainly appeared that she had felt more than she saw, she was so much the more happy, and the like was wished also by all the rest. Wherefore after the song was ended the Queen, remembering that the next day following was Friday, turning herself graciously to them all, thus she spake :

"You know, noble ladies, and you likewise, most noble gentlemen, that to-morrow is the day consecrated to the Passion of our Blessed Lord and Saviour, which, if you have not forgotten it, as easily you cannot, we devoutly celebrated, when Neifile was Queen. We ceased from all our pleasant discoursing, as we did the like on the Saturday following, sanctifying the sacred Sabbath in due regard of itself. Wherefore being desirous to imitate precedent good examples, which in worthy manner she began to us all, I hold it very decent and necessary that we should abstain to-morrow and the day ensuing from recounting any of our pleasant novels, but recall to our memories what was done, as on those days, for the salvation of our souls." This holy and religious motion, made by the Queen, was commendably allowed by all the assembly ; and therefore, humbly taking their leave of her, and an indifferent part of the night being already spent, severally they betook themselves to their chambers.

THE EIGHTH DAY.

Wherein all the discourses pass under the rule and government of Lauretta, and the argument imposed is concerning such witty deceivings as have or may be put in practice by wives to their husbands, husbands to their wives, or one man towards another.

INDUCTION.

EARLY in the morning, Aurora showing herself bright and lovely, the sun's golden beams began to appear on the tops of the adjoining mountains, so that herbs, plants, trees, and all things else, were very evidently to be discerned. The Queen and her company being all come forth of their chambers, and having walked a while abroad in the goodly green meadows to taste the sweetness of the fresh and wholesome air, they returned back again into the palace, because it was their duty so to do.

Afterward, between the hours of seven and eight they went to hear mass in a fair chapel near at hand, and thence returned to their lodgings. When they had dined merrily together, they fell to their wonted singing and dancing; which being done, such as were so pleased, by license of the Queen first obtained, went either to their rest, or such exercises as they took most delight in. When midday and the heat thereof was well overpast, so that the air seemed mild and temperate, according as the Queen had commanded, they were all seated again about the fountain, with intent to prosecute their former pastime. And then Neifile, by the charge imposed on her as first speaker for this day, began as followeth.

THE FIRST NOVEL.

Gulfardo made a match or wager with the wife of Gasparruolo, for the obtaining of her favour in regard of a sum of money first to be given her. The money he borrowed of her husband, and gave it in payment to her, as in case of discharging him from her husband's debt. After his return home from Genoa, Gulfardo told him in presence of his wife, how he had paid the whole sum to her, with charge of delivering it to her husband, which she confessed to be true, albeit greatly against her will.

SEEING it is my fortune, gracious ladies, that I must give beginning to this day's discoursing, by some such novel which I think expedient, as duty bindeth me, I am therewith well contented. And because the deceits of women to men have been at large and liberally related, I will tell you a subtle trick of a man to a woman.

H

Not that I blame him for the deed, or think the deceit not well fitted to the woman, but I speak it in a contrary nature, as commending the man, and condemning the woman very justly ; as also to show how men can as well beguile those crafty companions which least believe any such cunning in them as in those that stand most on their artificial skill.

[OMITTED.]

THE SECOND NOVEL.

A youthful priest of Varlungo fell in love with Monna Belcolore. He left his cloak as a pledge of further payment with her. By subtle sleight afterward, he made means to borrow a mortar of her, which when he sent home again in the presence of her husband, he demanded to have his cloak sent him, as having left it in pawn for the mortar. To pacify her husband, offended that she did not lend the priest the mortar without a pawn, she sent him back his cloak again, albeit greatly against her will.

BOTH the gentlemen and ladies gave equal commendations of Gulfardo's quaint beguiling the Milanese gentlewoman, and wishing all other of her mind might always be so served. Then the Queen smiling on Pamfilo, commanded him to follow next, whereupon thus he began.

[OMITTED.]

THE THIRD NOVEL.

Calandrino, Bruno, and Buffalmacco, all of them being painters by profession, travelled to the plain of Mugnone to find the precious stone called Elitropia. Calandrino persuading himself that he had found it, returned home to his house heavily laden with stones. His wife rebuking him for his absence, he groweth into anger, and shrewdly beateth her. Afterward, when the case is debated among his other friends Bruno and Buffalmacco, all is found to be mere foolery.

PAMFILO having ended his novel, whereat the ladies laughed exceedingly, so that very hardly they could give over, the Queen gave charge to Elisa that she should next succeed in order, when being scarcely able to restrain from smiling, thus she began :

I know not, gracious ladies, whether I can move you to as hearty laughter, and with a brief novel of mine own, as Pamfilo did with his ; yet I assure you it is both true and pleasant, and I will relate it in the best manner I can.

In our city, which evermore hath contained all sorts of people, not long since there dwelt a painter named Calandrino, a simple man, yet as much addicted to matter of novelty as any man whatsoever could be. The most part of his time he spent in the company of two other painters, the one called Bruno and the other Buffalmacco, men of very recreative spirits, and indifferent good capacity, often resorting to the said Calandrino, because they took delight in his honest simplicity and pleasant behaviour. At the same time likewise there dwelt in Florence a young gentleman of singular disposition to every witty conceit, as the world did not yield a better companion, he being named Maso del Saggio, who having heard somewhat of Calandrino's silliness, determined to jest him in merry manner, and to suggest his longing humours after novelties with some conceit of extraordinary nature.

He happening on a day to meet him in the Church of St. John, and seeing him seriously busied in beholding the rare pictures and the curious carved tabernacle which, not long before, was placed on the high altar in the said church, considered with himself that he had now fit place and opportunity to effect what he had long time desired. And having imparted his mind to a very intimate friend how he intended to deal with simple Calandrino, they went both very near him where he sate all alone, and making show as if they saw him not, began to consult between themselves concerning the rare property of precious stones, whereof Maso discoursed as exactly as if he had been a most skilful lapidary, to which conference of theirs Calandrino lent an attentive ear, in regard it was a matter of singular rarity.

Soon after Calandrino started up, and perceiving by their loud speaking that they talked of nothing which required secret counsel, he went into their company, the only thing which Maso desired, and holding on still the former argument, Calandrino would needs request to know in what place these precious stones were to be found, which had such excellent virtues in them? Maso made answer that the most of them were to be had in Berlinzone, near to the city of Bascha, which was in the territory of a country called Bengodi, where the vines were bound about with sausages, a goose was sold for a penny, and the goslings freely given in to boot. There was also a high mountain, wholly made of parmesan, grated cheese, whereon dwelt people who did nothing else but make maccaroni and ravivuoli, boiling them with broth of capons, and afterward hurled them all about to whosoever can or will catch them. Near to this mountain runneth a fair river, the whole stream being pure white wine, none such was ever sold for any money, and without one drop of water in it.

"Now trust me, sir," said Calandrino, "that is an excellent country to dwell in, but I pray you tell me, sir, what do they with the capons after they have boiled them?" "The Baschanes," quoth Maso, "eat them all." "Have you, sir," said Calandrino, "at any time been in that country?" "How?" answered Maso, "do you demand if I have been there? Yes, man, above a thousand times at the least." "How far, sir, I pray you," quoth Calandrino, "is that worthy country from this our city?" "In troth," replied Maso, "the miles are hardly to be numbered; for the most part of them we travel when we are nightly in our beds, and if a man dream right he may be there upon a sudden."

"Surely, sir," said Calandrino, "it is further hence than to

H 2

Abruzzi?"   "Yes; questionless," replied Maso, "but to a willing mind no travel seemeth tedious."

Calandrino well noting that Maso delivered all these speeches with a steadfast countenance, no sign of smiling or any gesture to urge the least mislike, he gave such credit to them as to any matter of apparent and manifest truth, and upon this confidence he said : "Believe me, sir, the journey is over far for me to undertake ; but if it were nearer I could afford to go in your company, only to see how they make maccaronies and to fill my belly with them. "But now we are in talk, sir, I pray you pardon me to ask whether any such precious stones as you speak of are to be found in that country or no?"   "Yes, indeed," replied Maso, "there are two kinds of them to be found in those territories, both being of very great virtue.   One kind are gritty stones of Stignetano and of Montisci, by virtue of which places when as any millstones or grindstones are to be made, they knead the sand as they use to do meal, and so make them of what bigness they please.   In which respect they have a saying there that Nature maketh common stones, but Montisci millstones.   Such plenty are there of these millstones, so slenderly here esteemed among us, as emeralds are with them, whereof they have whole mountains, far greater than our Monte Morello, which shine most gloriously at midnight.   And how meanly soever we account of their millstones, yet they drill them, and enchase them in rings, which afterward they send to the great Soldan, and have whatsoever they will demand for them.

"The other kind is a most precious stone indeed, which our best lapidaries call the Elitropia, the virtue whereof is so admirable as whosoever beareth it about him so long as he keepeth it, it is impossible for any eye to discern him because he walketh merely invisible."   "O Lord, sir," quoth Calandrino, "those stones are of rare virtue indeed ; but where else may a man find that Elitropia?"   Whereto Maso thus answered, "That country only doth not contain the Elitropia, for they be many times found upon our plain of Mugnone."   "Of what brightness, sir," quoth Calandrino. . "is the stone, and what colour?"   "The Elitropia," answered Maso, "is not always of one quality, because some are big, and others less ; but all are of one colour—namely, black."

Calandrino committing all these things to respective memory, and pretending to be called thence by some other especial affairs, departed from Maso, concluding resolvedly with himself to find this precious stone, if possibly he could, yet intending to do nothing until he had acquainted Bruno and Buffalmacco therewith, whom he loved dearly ; he went in all haste to seek them, because, without any longer trifling the time, they three might be the first men that should find out this precious stone, spending almost the whole morning before they were all three met together.   For they were painting at the monastery of the Sisters of Faenza, where they had very serious employment, and followed their business diligently. There, having found them, and saluting them in such kind manner, as continually he used to do, thus he began :

"Loving friends, if you were pleased to follow mine advice, we three will quickly be the richest men in Florence, because by information from a gentleman, well deserving to be credited, on the plain of Mugnone there is a precious stone to be found which, whosoever carrieth it about him, walketh invisible, and is not to be seen by any one. Let us three be the first men to go and find it, before any other hear thereof, and go about it, and assure ourselves that we shall find it, for I know it, by description, so soon as I see it. And when we have it, who can hinder us from bearing it about us? Then will we go to the tables of our bankers or money-changers, which we see daily with plenty of gold and silver, where we may take so much as we list, for they, nor any, are able to descry us. So, in short time, we shall all be wealthy, never needing to drudge any more, or paint muddy walls, as hitherto we have done, and as many of our poor profession are forced to do."

Bruno and Buffalmacco hearing this began to smile, and, looking merrily each on other, they seemed to wonder thereat, and greatly commended the counsel of Calandrino, Buffalmacco demanding how the stone was called. Now it fortuned that Calandrino, who had but a gross and blockish memory, had quite forgot the name of the stone, and therefore said : "What need have we of the name, when we know and are assured of the stone's virtue? Let us make no more ado, but, setting aside all other business, go seek it where it is to be found." "Well, my friend," answered Bruno, "you say we may find it ; but how, and by what means?"

"There are two sorts of them," quoth Calandrino, "some big, others smaller, but all carry a black colour; therefore, in my opinion, let us gather all such stones as are black, so shall we be sure to find it among them without any further loss of time."

Buffalmacco and Bruno liked and allowed the counsel of Calandrino, which when they had, by several commendations, given him assurance of, Bruno said : "I do not think it a convenient time now for us to go about so weighty a business; for the sun is yet in the highest degree, and striketh such a heat on the plain of Mugnone as all the stones are extremely dried, and the very blackest will now seem whitest. But in the morning, after the dew is fallen, and before the sun shineth forth, every stone retaineth his true colour. Moreover, there be many labourers now working on the plain about such business as they are severally assigned, who seeing us in so serious a search, may imagine what we seek for, and partake with us in the said inquisition, by which means they may chance to speed before us, and so we may lose both our trot and amble. Wherefore, by my consent, if your opinion jump with mine, this is an enterprise only to be performed in an early morning, when the black stones are to be distinguished from the white, and a festival day were the best of all other, for then there will be none to discover us."

Buffalmacco applauded the advice of Bruno, and Calandrino did no less, concluding altogether that Sunday morning, next ensuing, should be the time, and then they all three would go seek the stone. But Calandrino was very earnest with them that they should not reveal it to any living body, because it was told him as an especial secret, disclosing further to them what he had heard concerning the country of Bengods, maintaining, with solemn oaths and protestations, that every part thereof was true.   Upon this agreement, they parted from Calandrino, who hardly enjoyed any rest at all, either by night or day, so greedy he was to be possessed of the stone.   On the Sunday morning he called upon his companions before break of day, and going forth at St. Gall's gate, they stayed not till they came to the plain of Mugnone, where they searched all about to find this strange stone.

Calandrino went stealing before the other two, and verily persuading himself that he was born to find the Elitropia, and, looking on every side about him, he rejected all other stones but the black, whereof first he filled his bosom, and afterwards both his pockets.   Then he took off his large painting apron, which he fastened with his girdle in the manner of a sack, and that he filled full of stones likewise.   Yet not so satisfied, he spread abroad his cloak, which being also full of stones, he bound it up carefully, for fear of losing the very least of them.   All which Buffalmacco and Bruno still observing—the day growing on, and hardly he could reach home by dinner-time—according as merrily they had concluded, and pretending not to see Calandrino, albeit he was not far from them : "What is become of Calandrino?" said Buffalmacco. Bruno, gazing strangely everywhere about him, as if he were desirous to find him, replied : "I saw him not long since, for then he was hard by before us.   Questionless, he hath given us the slip, is privily gone home to dinner, and making stark fools of us, hath left us to pick up black stones upon the parching plain of Mugnone." "Well," quoth Buffalmacco, "this is but the trick of a hollow-hearted friend, and not such as he protested himself to be to us. Could any but we have been so sottish, to credit his frivolous persuasions, hoping to find any stone of such virtue, and here on the fruitless plain of Mugnone?   No, no ; none but we would have believed him."

Calandrino, who was close by them, hearing these words, and seeing the whole manner of their wondering behaviour, became constantly persuaded that he had not only found the precious stone, but also had some store of them about him, by reason he was so near them, and yet they could not see him, therefore he walked before them.   Now was his joy beyond all compass of expression ; and being exceeding proud of so happy an adventure, did not mean to speak one word to them, but, heavily laden as he was, to steal home fair and softly before them ; which indeed he did, leaving them to follow after if they would.   Bruno perceiving his intent, said to Buffalmacco . "What remaineth now for us to do?   Why should not we go home as well as he?"   "And reason too," replied Bruno. "It is in vain to tarry any longer here.   But I solemnly protest Calandrino shall no more make an ass of me ; and were I now as near him as not long since I was, I would give him such a remembrance on the heel with this flint-stone as should stick by him this month, to teach him a lesson for abusing his friends."

He threw the stone, and hit him shrewdly on the heel therewith ; but all was one to Calandrino, whatsoever they said or did, as thus they still followed after him. And though the blow of the stone was painful to him, yet he mended his pace so well as he was able, in regard of being overladen with stones, and gave them not one word all the way, because he took himself to be invisible, and utterly unseen of them. Buffalmacco, taking up another flint-stone, which was indifferent heavy and sharp, said to Bruno. "Seest thou this flint?" Casting it from him, smote Calandrino on the back therewith, saying: "O that Calandrino had been so near as I might have hit him on the back with the stone." And thus all the way on the plain of Mugnone they did nothing else but pelt him with stones even so far as the gate of St. Gallo, where they threw down what other stones they had gathered, meaning not to molest him any more, because they had done enough already.

There they stepped before him into the gate, and acquainted the warders with the whole matter, who laughing heartily at the jest, and the better to uphold it, would seem not to see Calandrino in his passage by them, but suffered him to go on, sore wearied with his burden, and sweating extremely. Without resting himself in any place, he came home to his house, which was near to the corner of the mills, fortune being so favourable to him in the course of this mockery that as he passed along the river's side, and afterward through part of the city, he was neither met nor seen by any, in regard they were all in their houses because it was dinner-time.

Calandrino, every minute ready to sink under the weighty burthen, entered into his own house, where, by great ill luck, his wife, being a comely and very honest woman, and named Monna Tessa, was standing aloft on the stairs-head. She being somewhat angry for his so long absence, and seeing him come in grunting and groaning, frowningly said : "I thought that the devil would never let thee come home ; all the whole city hath dined, and yet we must remain without our dinner." When Calandrino heard this, and perceived that he was not invisible to his wife, full of rage and wrath, he began to rail, saying : "Ah, thou wicked woman, where art thou ? Thou hast utterly undone me ; but, as I live, I will pay thee soundly for it." Up the stairs he ascended into a small par-lour, where when he had spread all his burthen of stones on the floor, he ran to his wife, catching her by the hair of the head, and throwing her at his feet, giving her so many spurns and cruel blows as she was not able to move either arms or legs, notwithstanding all her tears and humble submission.

Now Buffalmacco and Bruno, after they had spent an indifferent while with the warders at the gate in laughter, in a fair and gentle pace they followed Calandrino home to his house, and being come to the door they heard the harsh bickering between him and his wife, and seeming as if they were newly arrived they called out aloud to him. Calandrino being in a sweat, stamping and raving still at his wife, looking out of the window, entreated them to ascend up to him, which they did, counterfeiting grievous displeasure against him. Being come into the room, which they saw all covered over with stones, his wife sitting in a corner, all the hair well near torn off her head, her face broken and bleeding, and all her body cruelly beaten, on the other side Calandrino standing unbraced and ungirded, struggling and wallowing like a man out of breath, after a little pausing, Bruno thus spake :

"Why, how now, Calandrino ! What may the meaning of this matter be ? What art thou preparing for building that thou hast provided such plenty of stones ? How sitteth thy poor wife ? how hast thou misused her ? Are these the behaviours of a wise or honest man ? " Calandrino, utterly overspent with travel, and carrying such a huge burthen of stones, as also the toilsome beating of his wife (but much more impatient and offended for that high good fortune which he imagined to have lost), could not collect his spirits together to answer them one ready word, whereupon he sat fretting like a madman. Whereupon Buffalmacco thus began to him : " Calandrino, if thou be angry with any other, yet thou shouldst not have made such a mockery of us as thou hast done, in leaving us, like a couple of coxcombs, on the plain of Mugnone, whither thou leadest us with thee to seek a precious stone called Elitropia.   And couldst thou steal home, never bidding us so much as farewell? How can we but take it in very evil part that thou shouldst abuse two honest neighbours ? Well, assure thyself this is the last time that ever thou shalt serve us so."

Calandrino by this time being somewhat better come to himself, with a humble protestation of courtesy, returned them this answer : " Alas ! my good friends, be not you offended. The case is far otherwise than you imagine. Poor unfortunate man that I am, I found the rare precious stone that you spake of ; and mark me well if I do not tell you the truth of all. When you asked one another the first time what was become of me, I was hard by you—at the most within the distance of two yards' length, and perceiving that you saw me not, being still so near and always before you, I went on smiling to myself to hear you brabble and rage against me."

So, proceeding on in his discourse, he recounted every accident as it happened, both what they had said and did unto him, concerning the several blows with the two flint-stones, the one hurting him grievously in the heel and the other paining him as extremely in the back, with their speeches used then and his laughter, notwithstanding he felt the harm of them both, yet being proud that he did so invisibly beguile them. " Nay more," quoth he, " I cannot forbear to tell you that when I passed through the gate I saw you standing with the warders, yet, by virtue of that excellent stone, undiscovered of you all. Beside, going along the streets, I met many of my gossips, friends, and familiar acquaintances, such as used daily to converse with me and drinking together in every tavern ; yet not one of them spake to me, neither used any courtesy

or salutation, which indeed I did the more freely forgive them because they were not able to see me.

" In the end of all, when I was come home into mine own house,
this devilish and accursed woman, being aloft upon my stairs-head,
by much misfortune chanced to see me, in regard, as it is not unknown to you, that women cause all things to lose their virtue. In
which respect I, that could have styled myself the only happy man
in Florence, am now made most miserable. Therefore did I justly
beat her so long as she was able to stand against me ; and I know
no reason to the contrary why I should not yet tear her in a thousand pieces, for I may well curse the day of our marriage, to hinder
and bereave me of such an invisible blessedness."

Buffalmacco and Bruno, hearing this, made show of very much
marvelling thereat, and many times maintained what Calandrino
said, being well-near ready to burst with laughter, considering how
confidently he stood upon it, that he had found the wonderful stone
and lost it by his wife's speaking only to him. But when they saw
him rise in fury once more, with intent to beat her again, then they
stepped between them, affirming that the woman had no way
offended in this case, but rather he himself, who knowing that
women cause all things to lose their virtue, had not therefore expressly commanded her not to be seen in his presence all that day
until he had made full proof of the stone's virtue. And, questionless, the consideration of a matter so available and important was
quite taken from him, because such an especial happiness should
not belong to him only, but in part to his friends whom he had
acquainted therewith, drew them to the plain with him in company,
where they took as much pains in search of the stone as possibly
he did or could, and yet dishonestly he would deceive them and bear
it away covetously for his private benefit.

After many other as wise and wholesome persuasions, which he
constantly credited because they spake them, they reconciled him
to his wife and she to him, but not without some difficulty in him,
who falling into wonderful grief and melancholy, for loss of such
an admirable precious stone, was in danger to have died within less
than a month after.

THE FOURTH NOVEL.

The Provost belonging to the Church of Fiesole, fell in love with a gentlewoman, being a widow, and named Piccarda, who hated him as much as
he loved her. He imagining that he was with her, by the gentlewoman's
brethren, and the Bishop under whom he served, was taken with her maid,
an ugly, foul, deformed slut.

ELISA having concluded the novel, not without infinite commendations of the whole company, the Queen, turning her looks to
Emilia, gave her such an express sign as she must needs follow next
after Elisa, whereupon she began in this manner.

[OMITTED.]

THE FIFTH NOVEL.

Three pleasant companions played a merry prank with a judge at Florence, at such time as he sat on the bench and hearing criminal causes.

No sooner had Emilia finished her novel, wherein the excellent wisdom of Piccarda, for so worthily punishing the old Provost, had general commendations of the whole assembly, but the Queen looking on Filostrato said, " I command you next to supply the place." Whereto he made answer, that he was both ready and willing, and then thus began :

Honourable ladies, the merry gentleman, so lately remembered by Elisa, being named Maso del Saggio, causeth me to pass over an intended tale which I had resolved on when it came to my turn, to report another concerning him and two men more, his friendly companions; which although it may appear to you somewhat unpleasing in regard of a little gross and unmannerly behaviour, yet it will move merriment without any offence, and that is the main reason why I relate it.

[OMITTED.]

THE SIXTH NOVEL.

Bruno and Buffalmacco stole a young brawn from Calandrino, and for his recovery thereof they used a pretended kind of conjuration with pills, by means whereof they made him believe that he had robbed himself; and for fear they should report this theft to his wife, they made him to go buy another brawn.

FILOSTRATO had no sooner ended his novel, and the whole assembly laughed heartily thereat, but the Queen gave command to Filomena that she should follow next in order, whereupon thus she began :

Worthy ladies, as Filostrato by calling to memory the name of Maso del Saggio, hath contented you with another merry novel concerning him, in the same manner must I entreat you to remember once again Calandrino and his subtle consorts by a pretty tale which I mean to tell you, how they were revenged on him for going to seek the invisible stone.

[OMITTED.]

THE SEVENTH NOVEL.

A young gentleman being a scholar fell in love with a lady named Helena, she being a widow and addicted in affection to another gentleman.   One whole night in cold winter she caused the scholar to expect her coming in an extreme frost and snow.   In revenge whereof, by his imagined art and skill, he made her stand naked on the top of a tower the space of a whole day, and in July, to be sunburnt and bitten with wasps and flies.

GREATLY did the ladies commend Filomena's novel, laughed heartily at poor Calandrino, yet grieving withal that he should be so knavishly cheated, not only of his brawn, but two couple of capons and a flagon of wine beside. But the whole discourse being ended, the Queen commanded Pampinea to follow next with her novel, and presently she thus begun.

[OMITTED.]

THE EIGHTH NOVEL.

Two near-dwelling neighbours—the one being named Spinelloccio Tanvena, and the other Zeppa di Mino—frequenting each other's company daily together; Spinelloccio disgraced Zeppa, who repaid in kind.

GRIEVOUS and full of compassion appeared the hard fortunes of Helena to be, having much discontented and well-near wearied all the ladies in hearing them recounted. But because they were justly inflicted upon her, and according as in equity she had deserved, they were the more moderate in their commiseration; howbeit, they reputed the scholar not only over-obstinate, but also too strict, rigorous and severe. Wherefore, when Pampinea had finished her novel, the Queen gave command to Fiammetta that she should follow next with her discourse, whereto she showing obedience, thus began.

[OMITTED.]

THE NINTH NOVEL.

Master Simon, an idle-headed doctor of physic, was thrown by Bruno and Buffalmacco into a common ley-stall of filth, the physician fondly believing that in the night-time he should be made one of a new created company, and there in the ley-stall they left him.

AFTER that the ladies had a while considered on the communication between the two wives of Sienna, and the falsehood in friendship of their husbands, the Queen, who was the last to recount her novel, without offering injury to Dioneo, began to speak thus:
   The reward for a precedent wrong committed, which Zeppa

retorted upon Spinelloccio, was answerable to his desert, and no more than equity required, in which respect I am of opinion that such men ought not to be over-sharply reproved, as do injury to him that seeketh for it, and justly should have it, although Pampinea not long since avouched the contrary. Now it evidently appeareth that Spinelloccio well deserved what was done to him, and I purpose to speak of another who needs would seek after his own disgrace. The rather to confirm my former speeches, that they which beguile such wilful foolish men, are not to be blamed but rather commended. And he unto whom the shame was done was a physician, who came from Bologna to Florence, and returned thither again like unto a beast, notoriously baffled and disgraced.

[OMITTED.]

THE TENTH NOVEL.

Jancofiore, by her subtle policy deceived a young merchant called Salabietto, of all his money he had taken for his wares at Palermo. Afterward he making show of coming thither again with far richer merchandises than before, made the means to borrow a great sum of money of her, leaving her so base a pawn as well requited her for her former cosenage.

NEEDLESS it were to question whether the novel related by the Queen, in divers passages thereof, moved the ladies to hearty laughter, and likewise to tears, as mirth made their eyes water. But the discourse being ended, Dioneo, who knew it was his office to be last speaker every day, after silence was commanded, began in this manner :

Worthy ladies, it is a matter very manifest that deceits do appear so much more pleasing when by the self-same means the subtle deceiver is jestingly deceived. In which respect, though you all have reported very singular deceits, yet I mean to tell you one that may prove as pleasing to you as any of your own. And so much the rather because the woman deceived was a great and cunning mistress in beguiling others, equalling, if not excelling, any of your former beguilers.

[OMITTED.]

So soon as Dioneo had ended his novel, Lauretta also knew that the conclusion of her regiment was come ; whereupon, when the counsel of Canigiano had passed with general commendation, and the wit of Salabietto no less applauded for fitting it with such an effectual prosecution, she took the crown of laurel from her own head and set it upon Emilia's, speaking graciously in this manner : " Madam, I am not able to say what a Queen we shall have of you, but sure I am that we shall enjoy a fair one ; let matters therefore be so carried fections ;" which words were no sooner delivered but she sat down in her mounted seat.

Emilia being somewhat bashful, not so much of her being created Queen, as to hear herself thus publicly praised, with that which women do most of all desire ; her face then appearing like the open-ing of the damask rose in the goodliest morning. But after she had a while dejected her looks, and the vermilion blush was vanished away, having taken order with the Master of the Household for all needful occasions befitting the assembly, thus she began :

' Gracious ladies, we behold it daily that those oxen which have laboured in the yoke most part of the day for their more convenient feeding, are let forth at liberty and permitted to wander abroad in the woods. We see, moreover, that gardens and orchards, being planted with variety of the fairest fruit-trees, are equalled in beauty by woods and forests, in the plentiful enjoying of as goodly spread-ing branches. In consideration whereof, remembering how many days we have already spent, under the severity of laws imposed, shaping all our discourses to a form of observation, I am of opinion that it will not only well become us, but also prove beneficial for us, to live no longer under such restraint, and like enthralled people, desirous of liberty, we should no more be subjected to the yoke, but recover our former strength in walking freely.

"Wherefore, concerning our pastime purposed for to-morrow, I am not minded to use any restriction, or tie you unto any par-ticular ordination ; but rather do liberally grant that every one shall devise and speak of arguments agreeing with your own dispositions.

"Besides, I am verily persuaded that variety of matter uttered so freely will be much more delightful than restraint to one kind of purpose only. Which being thus granted by me, whosoever shall succeed me in the government may (as being of more power and pre-eminence) restrain all back again to the accustomed laws." And having thus spoken, she dispensed with their any longer attendance until it should be supper-time.

Every one commended the Queen's appointment, allowing it to relish of good wit and judgment, and being all risen, fell to such exercises as they pleased. The ladies made nosegays and chaplets of flowers, the men played on their instruments, singing divers sweet ditties to them, and thus were busied until supper-time. Which being come and they supping about the beautiful fountain, after supper they fell to singing and dancing. In the end the Queen, to imitate the order of her predecessors, commanded Pam-filo that, notwithstanding all the excellent songs formerly sung, he should now sing one, whereunto dutifully obeying, thus he began :

THE SONG.

The CHORUS *sung by all.*

Love, I find such felicity
And joy in thy captivity,
As I before did never prove,
And think me happy being in love.

Comfort abounding in my heart,
          Joy and delight
          In soul and sight
Can be imprisoned in no part
Fill all, flow out, flash free :
          Shines in the face
          Love's day of grace :
          O, proud in place.
Thy happy thrall to be.
          Love, I found such felicity, &c.

My song wants power to relate
          The sweets of mind
          Which now I find
In that most blissful state !
O sovereign love, from thee
          No sad despair
          Or killing care
          Infects this air ;
Still thou didst comfort me.
          Love, I found such felicity, &c.

I hate all such as do complain,
          Blaspheming thee
          With cruelty
And sleights of coy disdain.
O sovereign love, to me
          Thou hast been kind ;
          If others find
          Thee worse inclined,
Yet I will honour thee.
          Love, I find such felicity
          And joy in thy captivity,
          As I before did never prove,
          And think me happy being in love.

Thus the song of Pamfilo ended, whereto all the rest as a chorus answered with their voices, yet every one particularly, according as they felt their love-sick passions, made a curious construction thereof, perhaps more than they needed, yet not divining what Pamfilo intended. And although they were transported with variety of imaginations, yet none of them could arrive at his true meaning indeed. Wherefore the Queen perceiving the song to be fully ended, as also the young gentlemen willing to go take their rest, she commanded them severally to their chambers.

THE NINTH DAY.

Wherein, under the government of Emilia, the argumeut of each several discourse is not limited to any one peculiar subject, but every one reinaineth at liberty to speak of whatsover themselves best pleaseth.

INDUCTION.

FAIR Aurora, from whose bright and cheerful looks, the dusky dark night flyeth as an utter enemy, had already reached so high as the eighth heaven, converting it all into an azure colour, and the pretty flowrets began to spread open their leaves, when Emilia, being risen, caused all her female attendants, and the young gentlemen likewise, to be summoned for their personal appearance. Who being all come, the Queen leading the way, and they following her majestic pace, walked into a little wood, not far off distant from the place.

No sooner were they there arrived, but they beheld store of wild beasts, as hinds, hares, goats, and such like ; so safely secured from the pursuit of huntsmen, by reason of the violent pestilence then reigning, that they stood gazing boldly at them, as dreadless of any danger, or as if they were become tame and domestic.

Approaching nearer them, first to one, then unto another, as if they purposed to play gently with them, they then began to skip and run, making them such pastime with their pretty tripping, that they conceived great delight in beholding of them.

But when they beheld the sun to exalt itself, it was thought convenient to return back again, shrouding themselves under the trees' spreading arms, their hands full of sweet flowers and odoriferous herbs, which they had gathered in their walking. So that such as chanced to meet them could say nothing else, but that death knew not by what means to conquer them, or else they had set down an absolute determination to kill him with their jovial disposition.

In this manner, singing, dancing, or prettily prattling, at length they arrived at the palace, where they found all things readily prepared, and their servants duly attending for them. After they had reposed themselves for a while, they would not, as yet, sit down at the table, until they had sung half a dozen of canzonets, some more pleasant than another, both the women and men together.

Then they fell to washing hands, and the Master of the Household caused them to sit down, according as the Queen had appointed, and dinner was most sumptuously served in before them. Afterward, when the tables were withdrawn, they all took hands to dance a roundelay ; which being done, they played on their instruments a while ; and then such as so pleased took their rest. But when the accustomed hour was come, they all repaired to the place of discoursing, where the Queen, looking on Filomena, gave her the honour of beginning the first novel for that day : whereto she dutifully condescending, began as followeth.

THE FIRST NOVEL.

Francesca, a widow of Pistoya, being affected by two Florentine gentlemen, the one named Rinuccio Palermini, and the other Alessandro Chiarmontesi, and she bearing no good will to either of them, ingeniously freed herself from both their importunate suits. One of them she caused to lie as dead in a grave, and the other to fetch him from thence ; so neither of them accomplishing what they were enjoined, failed of their expectation.

MADAM, it can no way discontent me, seeing it is your most gracious pleasure, that I should have the honour to break the first staff of freedom in this fair company, according to the injunction of your Majesty, for liberty of our own best liking arguments : wherein I dismay not, if I can speak well enough, but to please you all as well as any other that is to follow me. Nor am I so oblivious, worthy ladies, but full well I remember, that many times hath been related in our passed demonstrations, how mighty and variable the powers of love are : and yet I cannot be persuaded that they have all been so sufficiently spoken of, but something may be added, and the bottom of them never dived into, although we should sit arguing a whole year together. And because it hath been already approved, that lovers have been led into divers accidents, not only inevitable dangers of death, but also have entered into the very houses of the dead, thence to convey their amorous friends : I purpose to acquaint you with a novel, beside them which have been discoursed, whereby you may not only comprehend the power of love, but also the wisdom used by an honest gentlewoman, to rid herself of two importunate suitors, who loved her against her own liking, yet neither of them knowing the other's intent or affection.

[OMITTED.]

THE SECOND NOVEL.

Of Usimbalda, lady abbess of a monastery of nuns in Lombardy.

BY this time Filomena sat silent, and the wit of Francesca in free-ing herself from them whom she could not fancy was generally commended; as also, on the contrary, the bold presumption of the two amorous suitors was reputed not to be love but merely folly. And then the Queen, with a gracious admonition, gave way for Elisa to follow next; who presently thus began.

[OMITTED.]

THE THIRD NOVEL.

Master Simon, the physician, by the persuasions of Bruno and Buffalmacco, and a third named Nello, made Calandrino believe that he was conceived with child. And having physic ministered to him for the disease, they got both good fat capons and money of him, and so cured him, without any other manner of deliverance.

AFTER that Elisa had concluded her novel, and every one of the company gave thanks to Fortune for delivering poor Isabella, the fair young nun, from the bitter reprehensions of the as faulty abbess, as also the malice of her envious sisters . the Queen gave command unto Filostrato, that he should be the next in order, and he, with-out expecting any other warning, began in this manner:
  Fair ladies, the paltry judge of the Marquesate, whereof yester-day I made relation to you, hindered me then of another novel, concerning silly Calandrino, wherewith I purpose now to acquaint you. And because whatsoever hath already been spoken of him, tended to no other end but matter of merriment, he and his com-panions duly considered, the novel which I shall now report, keepeth within the self-same compass, and aimeth also at your contentment. according to the scope of imposed variety.

[OMITTED.]

THE FOURTH NOVEL.

Francesco Fortarrigo played away all that he had at Buonconvento, and likewise the money of Francesco Angiolieri, being his master. Then running
after him in his shirt, and avouching that he had robbed him, he caused
him to be taken by peasants of the country, clothed himself in his master's
wearing garments, and mounted on his horse rode thence to Sienna,
leaving Angiolieri in his shirt, and walking barefooted.

THE ridiculous words given by Calandrino to his wife, all the whole
company laughed at, but Filostrato ceasing, Neifile, as it pleased
the Queen to appoint, began to speak thus :

Virtuous ladies, if it were not more hard and more uneasy for
men to make good their understanding and virtue, than apparent
publication of their disgrace and folly, many would not labour in vain
to curb in their idle speeches with a bridle, as you have manifestly
observed by the weak wit of Calandrino ; who need no such
fantastic circumstance to cure the strange disease which he
imagined, by sottish persuasions, to have ; had he not been so
lavish of his tongue, and accusing his wife of over-mastering
him. Which maketh me to remember a novel, quite contrary to
this last related—namely, that one man may strive to surmount
another in malice, yet he to sustain the greater harm, that had at
the first the most advantage of his enemy, as I will presently
declare unto you.

[OMITTED.]

———

THE FIFTH NOVEL.

Calandrino became extraordinarily enamoured of a young damsel, named
Niccolosa. Bruno prepared a charm or writing for him, avouching constantly to him, that so soon as he touched the damsel therewith she should
follow him whithersoever he would have her. She being gone to an
appointed place with him, he was found there by his wife, and dealt withal
according to his deserving.

BECAUSE the novel reported by Neifile was so soon concluded,
not without much laughter or commendation of the whole company,
the Queen turned herself towards Fiammetta, enjoining her to
succeed in apt order, and she being as ready as suddenly commanded, began as followeth :

Most gracious ladies : I am persuaded of your opinion in
judgment with mine, that there is not anything which can be spoken
pleasingly, except it be conveniently suited with apt time and place,

in which respect, when ladies and gentlemen are bent in discoursing, the due election of them both are necessarily required. And therefore I am not unmindful that our meeting here, aiming at nothing more than to outwear the time with our general contentment, should tie us to the course of our pleasure and recreation, to the same convenience of time and place, not sparing, though some have been nominated oftentimes in our passed arguments; yet, if occasion serve, and the nature of variety be well considered, we may speak of the self-same persons again.

Now, notwithstanding the actions of Calandrino have been indifferently canvassed among us, yet remembering what Filostrato not long since said, "That they intended to nothing more than matter of mirth," I presume the bolder to report another novel of him beside them already past. And were I willing to conceal the truth, and clothe it in more circumstantial manner, I could make use of contrary names, and paint it in a poetical fiction, perhaps more probable, though not so pleasing. But because wandering from the truth of things doth much diminish, in relation, the delight of the hearers, I will build boldly on my fore-alleged reason, and tell you truly how it happened.

[OMITTED.]

THE SIXTH NOVEL.

Two young gentlemen, the one named Pinuccio and the other Adriano, lodged one night in a poor inn.

CALANDRINO, whose mishaps had so many times made the assembly merry, and this last passing among them with indifferent commendations, upon a general silence commanded, the Queen gave order to Pamfilo that he should follow, as indeed he did, beginning thus.

[OMITTED.]

THE SEVENTH NOVEL.

Talano di Molese dreamed that a wolf tore his wife's face and throat. Which dream he told to her, with advice to keep her out of danger; which she refusing to do, received what followed.

BY the conclusion of Pamfilo's novel, wherein the woman's ready wit at a time of such necessity, carried deserved commendations, the Queen gave command to Pampinea that she should next begin with hers, and so she did, in this manner:

In some discourses, gracious ladies, already past among us, the truth of apparitions in dreams hath partly been approved, whereof very many have made a mockery. Nevertheless, whatsoever hath heretofore been said, I purpose to acquaint you with a very short novel of a strange accident happening unto a neighbour of mine, in not crediting a dream which her husband told her.

I cannot tell whether you knew Talano di Molese or no, a man of very much honour, who took to wife a young gentlewoman named Margharita, as beautiful as the best, but yet so peevish, scornful, and fantastical, that she disdained any good advice given her ; neither could anything be done to cause her contentment ; which absurd humours were highly displeasing to her husband, but in regard he knew not how to help it, constrainedly he did endure it. It came to pass that Talano being with his wife at a summer-house of his own in the country, he dreamed one night that he saw his wife walking in a fair wood, which adjoined near unto his house, and while she thus continued there, he seemed to see issue forth from a corner of the same wood a great and furious wolf, which leaping suddenly on her caught her by the face and throat, drawing her down to the earth, and offering to drag her thence. But he crying out for help, recovered her from the wolf, yet having her face and throat very pitifully rent and torn.

In regard of this terrifying dream, when Talano was risen in the morning, and sate conversing with his wife, he spake thus unto her : "Woman, although thy froward wilful nature be such as hath not permitted me one pleasing day with thee since we became man and wife, but rather my life hath been most tedious to me, fearing still some mischief should happen unto thee, yet let me now in loving manner advise thee to follow my counsel, and this day not to walk abroad out of this house." She demanded a reason for this advice of his. He related to her every particular of his dream, adding withal these speeches :

"True it is, wife," quoth he "that little credit should be given to dreams ; nevertheless, when they deliver advertisement of harms to ensue, there is nothing lost by shunning and avoiding them." She fleering in his face, and shaking her head at him, replied : "Such harms as thou wishest, such thou dreamest of. Thou pretendest much pity and care of me, but all to no other end, but what mischiefs thou dreamest happening unto me, so wouldest thou see them effected on me. Wherefore, I will well enough look to myself both this day, and at all times else, because thou shalt never make thyself merry with any such misfortune as thou wishest unto me."

"Well, wife," answered Talano, "I knew well enough before what thou wouldest say ; an unsound head is soon scratched with the very gentlest comb ; but believe as thou pleasest. As for myself, I speak with a true and an honest meaning soul, and once again I do advise thee to keep within our doors all this day ; at least, wife, beware that thou walk not into our wood, be it but in regard of my dream." "Well, sir," quoth she scoffingly, "once you shall say I followed your counsel ; " but within herself she fell to this murmuring. " Now I perceive my husband's colouring, and why I must not walk this day into our wood ; he hath made a compact with some common quean, and is afraid lest I should take them tardy.   Belike he would have me feed among blind folk, and I were worthy to be thought a stark fool if I should not prevent a manifest treachery being intended against me.   Go thither, therefore, I will, and tarry there all the whole day long ; but I will meet with him in his merchandise, and see the pink wherein he adventures.'

After this her secret consultation, her husband was no sooner gone out of one door, but she did the like at another, yet so secretly as possibly she could devise to do, and without delay she went to the wood, wherein she hid herself very closely among the thickest of the bushes, yet could discern every way about her if anybody should offer to pass by her.   While she kept herself in this concealment, suspecting other mysterious matters as her idle imaginations had tutored her, rather than the danger of the wolf, out of a braky thicket by her suddenly rushed a huge and dreadful wolf, as having found her by the scent, mounting up, and grasping her throat in his mouth, before she saw him or could call to Heaven for mercy.

Being thus seized of her, he carried her as lightly away as if she had been no heavier than a lamb, she being by no means able to cry, because he held her so fast by the throat, and hindered any helping of herself.   As the wolf carried her thus from thence, he had quite strangled her, if certain shepherds had not met him, who with their outcries and exclaims at the wolf, caused him to let her fall and haste away to save his own life.   Notwithstanding the harm done to her throat and face, the shepherds knew her, and carried her home to her own house, where she remained a long while after, carefully attended by physicians and chirurgeons.

Now although they were very expert and cunning men all, yet could they not so perfectly cure her, but both her throat and part of her face were so blemished that, whereas she seemed a rare creature before, she was now deformed and much unsightly.   In regard of which strange alteration, being ashamed to show herself in any place where formerly she had been seen, she spent her time in sorrow and mourning, repenting her insolent and scornful carriage, as also her rash running into danger upon a foolish and jealous surmise, believing her husband's dreams the better for ever after.

THE EIGHTH NOVEL.

Biondello, in a merry manner, caused Ciacco to beguile himself with a good dinner, for which deceit Ciacco became cunningly revenged by procuring Biondello to be unreasonably beaten and misused.

IT was a general opinion in the whole jovial company that whatsoever Talano saw in his sleep was not any dream, but rather a vision, considering every part thereof fell out so directly, without the least failing ; but when silence was enjoined, then the Queen gave out by evident demonstration that Lauretta was next to succeed, whereupon she thus began :

As all they, judicious hearers, which have this day spoken before me, derived the ground in project of their novels from some other argument spoken of before, even so the cruel revenge of the scholar, yesterday discoursed at large by Pampinea, maketh me remember another tale of like nature somewhat grievous to the sufferer, yet not in such cruel manner inflicted, as that on Helena.

There dwelt sometime in Florence, one that was generally called by the name of Ciacco, a man being the greatest gourmand and grossest feeder as ever was seen in any country, all his means and procurements merely unable to maintain expenses for filling his stomach. But otherwise he was of sufficient and commendable carriage, fairly demeaned, and well discoursing on any argument, yet not as a curious and spruce courtier, but rather a frequenter of rich men's tables, where choice of good cheer is seldom wanting, and such should have his company, albeit not invited, he had the courage to bid himself welcome.

At the same time, and in our city of Florence also, there was another man, named Biondello, very low of stature, yet comely formed, quick-witted, more neat and brisk than a butterfly's, always wearing a wrought silk cap on his head, and not a hair standing out of order, but the tuft flourishing above the forehead, and he such another trencher-fly for the table as our fore-named Ciacco was. It so fell out on a morning in the Lent time that he went into the fish-market, where he bought two goodly lampreys for Messer Vieri de Cierchi, and was espied by Ciacco, who, coming to Biondello, said : " What is the meaning of this cost, and for whom is it ? " Whereto Biondello thus answered : " Yester-night, three other lampreys, far fairer than these, and a whole sturgeon, were sent unto Messer Corso Donati, and being not sufficient to feed divers gentlemen whom he hath invited this day to dine with him, he caused me to buy these two beside ; dost not thou intend to make one of them ? " " Yes, I warrant thee," replied Ciacco, " thou knowest I can invite myself thither without any other bidding."

So parting, about the hour of dinner-time Ciacco went to the house of Messer Corso, whom he found sitting and talking with certain of his neighbours, but dinner was not as yet ready, neither were they come thither to dinner. Messer Corso demanded of Ciacco what news with him, and whither he went. "Why, sir," said Ciacco, "I come to dine with you and your good company." Whereto Messer Corso answered that he was welcome ; and his other friends being gone, dinner was served in, none else thereat present but Messer Corso and Ciacco, all the diet being a poor dish of pease, a little piece of tunny, and a few small fishes fried, without any other dishes to follow after. Ciacco seeing no better fare, but being disappointed of his expectation, as longing to feed on the lampreys and sturgeon, and so to have made a full dinner indeed, was of a quick apprehension, and apparently perceived that Biondello had merely gulled him in a knavery, which did not a little vex him, and made him vow to be revenged on Biondello, as he could compass occasion afterward.

Before many days were past, it was his fortune to meet with Biondello, who having told his jest to divers of his friends, and much good merriment made thereat, he saluted Ciacco in a kind manner, saying : "How didst thou like the fat lampreys and sturgeon which thou feddest on at the house of Messer Corso?" "Well, sir," answered Ciacco, "perhaps before eight days pass over my head thou shalt meet with as pleasing a dinner as I did." So, parting away from Biondello, he met with a porter, such as are usually sent on errands, and hiring him to do a message for him, gave him a glass bottle, and bringing him near to the hall-house of Cavicciuli, showed him there a knight, called Signior Filippo Argenti, a man of huge stature, very choleric, and sooner moved to anger than any other man. "To him thou must go with this bottle in thy hand, and say thus to him : 'Sir, Biondello sent me to you, and courteously entreateth you that you would erubinate this glass bottle with your best claret wine, because he would make merry with a few friends of his.' But beware he lay no hand on thee, because he may be easily induced to misuse thee, and so my business be disappointed." "Well, sir," said the porter, "shall I say anything else unto him ?" "No," quoth Ciacco, "only go and deliver this message, and when thou art returned, I'll pay thee for thy pains." The porter being gone to the house, delivered his message to the knight, who being a man of no great civil breeding, but very furious, presently conceived that Biondello, whom he knew well enough, sent this message in mere mockage of him ; and starting up with fierce looks, said : "What erubination of claret should I send him? and what have I to do with him or his drunken friends? Let him and thee go hang yourselves together." So he stepped to catch hold on the porter, but he being nimble, and escaping from him, returned to Ciacco, and told him the answer of Filippo. Ciacco, not a little contented, paid the porter, tarried in no place till he met with Biondello, to whom he said : "When wast thou at the hall of Cavicciuli ?" "Not a long while," answered Biondello ; "but why dost thou ask such a question ?" "Because," quoth Ciacco, "Messer Filippo hath sought about for thee, yet know not I what he would have with thee." "Is it so?" replied Biondello, "then I will walk thither presently to understand his pleasure."

When Biondello was thus parted from him, Ciacco followed not far off behind him, to behold the issue of this angry business; and Messer Filippo, because he could not catch the porter, continued much distempered, fretting and fuming because he could not comprehend the meaning of the porter's message, but only surmised that Biondello, by the procurement of somebody else, had done this in scorn of him. While he remained thus deeply discontented, he espied Biondello coming towards him, and meeting him by the way, he stepped close to him, and gave him a cruel blow on the face, causing his nose to fall out a-bleeding. "Alas, sir!" said Biondello, "wherefore do you strike me?" Messer Filippo, catching him by the hair of the head, trampled his cap in the dirt, and his cloak also, when, laying many violent blows on him, he said: "Villainous traitor as thou art, I'll teach thee what it is to crubinate with claret either thyself or any of thy cupping companions. Am I a child to be jested withal?"

Nor was he more furious in words than in strokes also, beating him about the face, hardly leaving any hair on his head, and dragging him along in the mire, spoiling all his garments, and he not able, from the first blow given, to speak a word in defence of himself. In the end, Messer Filippo, having extremely beaten him, and many people gathering about them, to succour a man so much misused, the matter was at large related, and manner of the message sending; for which they all did greatly reprehend Biondello, considering he knew what kind of man Filippo was, not any way to be jested withal. Biondello in tears maintained that he never sent any such message for wine, or intended it in the least degree; so when the tempest was more mildly calmed, and Biondello, thus cruelly beaten and dirtied, had gotten home to his own house, he could then remember that, questionless, this was occasioned by Ciacco.

After some few days were passed over, and the hurts in his face indifferently cured, Biondello beginning to walk abroad again, chanced to meet with Ciacco, who laughing heartily at him, said: "Tell me, Blondello, how dost thou like the erubinating claret of Messer Filippo?" "As well," quoth Biondello, "as thou didst the sturgeon and lampreys at Messer Corso Donati's." "Why, then," said Ciacco, "let these tokens continue familiar between thee and me, when thou wouldest bestow such another dinner on me, then will I erubinate thy nose with a bottle of the same claret." But Biondello perceived to, his cost, that he had met with the worser bargain, and Ciacco got cheer without any blows, and therefore desired a peaceful atonement, each of them, always after, abstaining from flouting one another.

THE NINTH NOVEL.

Two young gentlemen—the one named Melisso, born in the city of Laiazzo, and the other Giosefo of Antioch—travelled unto Solomon. The one desiring to learn what he should do whereby to compass and win the love of men; the other craved to be instructed by what means he might reclaim a headstrong and unruly wife. And what answers the wise king gave unto them both before they departed away from him.

UPON the conclusion of Lauretta's novel, none remained to succeed next in order, but only the Queen herself, the privilege reserved, granted to Dioneo, wherefore, after they had all smiled at the folly of Biondello, with a cheerful countenance, thus the Queen began :

Honourable ladies, if with advised judgment, we do duly consider the order of all things, we shall very easily perceive that the whole universal multiplicity of women, by nature, custom, and laws, are and ought to be subject to men, yea, and to be governed by their discretion. Because every one desiring to enjoy peace, repose, and comfort with them, under whose charge they are, ought to be humble, patient, and obedient, over and beside her spotless honesty, which is the crown and honour of every good woman ; and although those laws which respect the common good of all things, or rather use and custom, as our wonted saying is, the powers whereof are very great and worthy to be reverenced, should not make us wise in this case, yet Nature hath given us a sufficient demonstration, in creating our bodies more soft and delicate, yea, and our hearts timorous, fearful, benign, and compassionable, our strength feeble, our voices pleasing, and the motion of our members sweetly pliant, all which are apparent testimonies that we have need of others' government.

Now it is not to be denied that whosoever hath need of help, and is to be governed, merely reason commandeth that they should be subject and obedient to their governor. Who then should we have for our helps and governors if not men ? Wherefore we should be entirely subject to them in giving them due honour and reverence ; and such a one as shall depart from this rule, she, in mine opinion, is not only worthy of grievous reprehensions, but also severe chastisements beside. And to this exact consideration—over and above divers other important reasons—I am the rather induced by the novel which Pampinea so lately reported, concerning the froward and wilful wife of Talano, who had a heavier punishment inflicted on her than her husband could devise to do ; and therefore it is my peremptory sentence that all such women as will not be gracious, benign and pleasing, do justly deserve, as I have already said, rude, rough, and harsh handling, as both nature, custom and laws have commanded.

In those ancient and reverend days whereof I am now to speak, the high renowned and admirable wisdom of Solomon, King of Jerusalem, was most famous throughout all parts of the world for answering all doubtful questions and demands whatsoever, that possibly could be propounded to him. So that many resorted to him, from the most remote and furthest-off countries, to hear his miraculous knowledge and experience, yea, and to crave his counsel in matters of greatest importance. Among the rest of them which repaired thither was a rich young gentleman, honourably descended, named Melisso, who came from the city of Laiazzo, where he was both born and dwelt.

In his riding towards Jerusalem, as he passed by Antioch, he overtook another young gentleman, a native of Antioch, and named Giosefo, whose journey lay the same way as the other's did. Having ridden in company some few days together, as it is a custom commonly observed among travellers, to understand one another's country and condition, as also to what part his occasions call him, so happened it with them, Giosefo directly telling him that he journeyed towards the wise King Solomon, to desire his advice, what means he should observe in the reclaiming of a wilful wife, the most froward and self-willed woman that ever lived ; whom neither fair persuasions nor gentle courtesies could in any manner prevail withal. Afterward he demanded of Melisso, to know the occasion of his travel, and whither.

"Now trust me, sir," answered Melisso, "I am a native of Laiazzo, and as you are vexed with one great misfortune, even so am I offended at another. I am young, wealthy, well derived by birth, and allow liberal expenses for maintaining a worthy table in my house, without distinguishing persons by their rank and quality, but make it free for all comers, both of the city and all places else. Notwithstanding all which bounty and honourable entertainment, I cannot meet with any man that loveth me. In which respect I journey to the same place as you do, to crave the counsel of so wise a King what I should do, whereby I might procure men to love me." Thus like two well-met friendly companions, they rode on together, until they arrived in Jerusalem, where, by the means of a noble Baron's attending on the King, they were brought before him. Melisso delivered his mind in a very few words, whereto the King made no other answer but this : "Learn to love." Which was no sooner spoken but Melisso was dismissed from the King's presence.

Giosefo also relating wherefore he came thither, the King replied only thus : "Go to the Goose Bridge ;" and presently Giosefo had also his dismission from the King. Coming forth, he found Melisso attending for him, and revealed in what manner the King had answered him : whereupon they consulted together concerning both their answers, which seemed either to exceed their comprehension or else was delivered in mere mockery, and therefore, more than half discontented, they returned homeward again.

After they had ridden on a few days together they came to a

river, over which was a goodly bridge, and because a great company of horses and mules (heavily laden, and after the manner of a
caravan of camels in Egypt) were first to pass over the said bridge,
they gladly stayed to permit their pass.   The greater number of
them being already passed over, there was one shy and skittish
mule (belike subject to timid starting, as oftentimes we see horses
have the like ill quality) that would not pass over the bridge by any
means, wherefore one of the muleteers took a good cudgel and smote
her, at the first gently, as hoping so to procure her passage.   Notwithstanding, starting one while backward, then again forward,
sideways, and every way indeed, but the direct roadway she would
not go.

Now grew the muleteer extremely angry, giving her many cruel
strokes on the head, sides, flanks, and all parts else, but yet they
proved to no purpose, which Melisso and Giosefo seeing, and
being by this means hindered of their passage, they called to the
muleteer, saying : "Foolish fellow, what dost thou ? Intendest thou
to kill the mule ?   Why dost thou not lead her gently, which is the
likelier course to prevail by than beating and misusing her as thou
doest ?"   "Content yourselves, gentlemen," answered the muleteer,
"you know your horses' qualities as I do my mule's, let me deal with
her as I please."   Having thus spoken, he gave her so many violent
strokes on head, sides, hips, and everywhere else, as made her at
last pass over the bridge quietly, so that the muleteer won the
mastery of his mule.

When Melisso and Giosefo had passed over the bridge, where
they intended to part each from other, a sudden motion happened
into the mind of Melisso, which caused him to demand of an aged
man, who sat craving alms of passengers at the bridge-foot, how
the bridge was called : "Sir," answered the old man, "this is called
the Goose Bridge."   Which words when Giosefo heard, he called
to mind the saying of King Solomon, and therefore immediately
said to Melisso : "Worthy friend and partner in my travel, I dare
now assure you that the counsel given me by King Solomon may
fall out most effectual and true ; for I plainly perceive that I knew
not how to handle my self-willed wife until the muleteer did instruct
me."   So, requesting still to enjoy the other's company, they journeyed
on, till at length they came to Laiazzo, where Giosefo retained
Melisso still with him, for some repose after so long a journey, and
entertained him very honourably.

One day Giosefo said to his wife : "Woman, this gentleman is my
intimate friend, and hath borne me company in all my travel; such
diet as thou wilt welcome him withal, I would have it ordered, in
dressing, according to his direction."   Melisso perceiving that Giosefo
would have it so, in few words directed her such a course as for ever
might be to her husband's contentment.   But she, not altering a jot
from her former disposition, but rather far more froward and tempestuous, delighting to vex and cross, doing everything quite contrary to the order appointed : which Giosefo observing, angerly he
said unto her : "Was it not told you by my friend in what manner

he would have our supper dressed?" She turning fiercely to him replied: "Am I to be directed by him or thee? Supper must and shall be dressed as I will have it; if it pleaseth me I care not who doth dislike it; if thou wouldst have it otherwise, go seek both your suppers where you may have it according to your liking."

Melisso marvelling at her froward answer, rebuked her for it in very kind manner; whereupon Giosefo spake thus to her: "I perceive, wife, you are the same woman as you were wont to be; but believe me, on my word, I shall quite alter you from this curst complexion." So turning to Melisso, thus he proceeded: "Noble friend, we shall try anon whether the counsel of King Solomon be effectual or no, and I pray you let it not be offensive to you to see it; but rather hold all to be done in merriment. And because I would not be hindered by you, do but remember the answer which the muleteer gave us, when he took compassion on his mule." "Worthy friend," replied Melisso, "I am in your own house, where I will not impeach whatsoever you do."

Giosefo having provided a good holly-wand, went into the chamber, where his wife sate railing, and despitefully grumbling, where taking her by the hair of the head, he threw her at his feet, beating her extremely with the wand. She crying, then cursing. next railing, lastly fighting, biting and scratching, when she felt the cruel smart of the blows, and that all her resistance served to no end; then she fell on her knees before him, and desired mercy for charity sake. Giosefo fought still more and more on head, arms, shoulders, sides, and all parts else, pretending as if he heard not her complaints, but wearied himself well-near out of breath, so that, to be brief, she that never felt his fingers before, perceived and confessed it was now too soon. This being done, he returned to Melisso and said: "To-morrow we shall see a miracle, and how available the counsel is of going to the Goose Bridge" So sitting a while together, after they had washed their hands and supped, they withdrew to their lodgings.

The poor beaten woman could hardly raise herself from the ground, which yet with much ado she did, and threw herself upon the bed, where she took such rest as she could; but arising early the next morning, she came to her husband, and making him a very low courtesy, demanded what he pleased to have for his dinner; he smiling heartily thereat, with Melisso, told her his mind. And when dinner-time came, everything was ready according to the directions given, in which regard they highly commended the counsel, whereof they made such a harsh construction at the first.

Within a while after, Melisso being gone from Giosefo, and returned home to his own house, he acquainted a wise and reverend man with the answer which King Solomon gave him, whereto he received this reply: " No better or truer advice could possibly be given you; for well you know that you love not any man, but the bountiful banquets you bestow on them is more in respect of your vainglory, than any kind affection you bear to them. Learn then to love men, as Solomon advised, and you shall be beloved of them again." Thus our unruly wife became mildly reclaimed, and the young gentleman, by loving others, found the fruits of reciprocal affection.

————

THE TENTH NOVEL.

Gianni di Barolo, at the instance and request of his gossip, Pietro da Tresanti, made an enchantment to have his wife become a mule.

THIS novel reported by the Queen, caused murmuring among the ladies, albeit the men laughed heartily thereat ; but after they were all grown silent, Dioneo began in this manner :

Gracious beauties, among many white doves, one black crow will seem more sightly than the very whitest swan can do. In like manner, among a multitude of wise men, sometimes one of much less wisdom and discretion shall not only increase the splendour and majesty of their maturity, but also give an addition of delight and great solace.

In which regard, you all being modest and discreet ladies, and myself much more defective in brain, than otherwise able, in making your virtues shine gloriously, through the evident appear-ance of mine own weakness, you should esteem the better of me, by how much I seem the more cloudy and obscure, and conse-quently I hope to have the larger scope of liberty, by plainly ex-pressing what I am, and be the more patiently endured by you all, in saying what absurdly I shall, than I should be if my speeches favoured of absolute wisdom. I will therefore tell you a tale, which shall not be of any great length, whereby you may comprehend how carefully such things should be observed, which are commanded by them as can effect matters by the power of enchantment, and how little delayance also ought to be in such as would not have an en-chantment to be hindered.

[OMITTED.]

Although there was much laughing at this novel, the ladies under-standing it better than Dioneo intended that they should have done, yet himself scarcely smiled. But the novels being all ended, and the sun beginning to lose his heat, the Queen also knowing that the full period of her government was come, dispossessing herself of the crown, she placed it on the head of Pamfilo, who was the last of all to be honoured with this dignity, wherefore, with a gracious smile, thus she spake to him :

"Sir, it is no mean charge which you are to undergo in making amends perhaps for all the faults committed by myself and the rest, who have gone before you in the same authority, and may it prove as prosperous unto you as I was willing to create you our

King." Pamfilo, having received the honour with a cheerful mind, thus answered : " Madam, your sacred virtues, and those beside remaining in my other subjects, will no doubt work so effectually for me, that, as the rest have done, I shall deserve your general good opinion." And having given order to the Master of the House-hold, as all his predecessors had formerly done, for every necessary occasion, he turned to the ladies, who expected his gracious favour, and said :

" Bright beauties, it was the discretion of your late Sovereign and Queen, in regard of ease and recreation unto our tired spirits, to grant you free liberty for discoursing on whatsoever yourselves best pleased. Wherefore, having enjoyed such a time of rest, I am of opinion that it is best to return once more to our law, in which respect I would have every one to speak in this manner to-morrow—namely, of those men or women who have done anything bountifully or magnificently, either in matters of amity or otherwise. The relation of such worthy arguments will doubtless give an addition to our best desires, for a free and forward inclination to good actions, whereby our lives, how short soever they be, may perpetuate an ever-living renown and fame, after that our mortal bodies are con-verted into dust, which otherwise are no better than those of brute beasts, reason only distinguishing this difference, that as they live to perish utterly, so we respire to reign in eternity."

The theme was exceedingly pleasing to the whole company, who, being all risen, by permission of the new King, every one fell to their wonted recreations as best agreed with their own disposition, until the hour of supper came, wherein they were served very sump-tuously. But being risen from the table they began their dances, among which many sweet sonnets were interlaced, with such delicate tunes, as moved admiration. Then the King commanded Neifile to sing a song in his name, or how herself stood best affected. And immediately, with a clear and rare voice, thus she began :

THE SONG.

The CHORUS *sung by all the Company.*

In the spring season,
Maids have best reason
    To dance and sing ;
With chaplets of flowers
To deck up their bowers,
    And all in honour of the spring.

I heard a nymph that sate alone
    By a fountain side,
Much her hard fortune to bemoan,
    For still she cried :   .
" Ah, who will pity her distress ?
That finds no foe like fickleness ;
    For truth lives not in men,
    Poor soul why live I then ? "
      In the spring season, &c.

Ah, how can mighty love permit
   Such a faithless deed,
And not in justice punish it,
   As treason's meed?
I am undone through perjury,
Although I love constantly.
     But truth lives not in men ;
     Poor soul why live I then?
       In the spring season, &c.

When I did follow Dian's train
   As a loyal maid,
I never felt oppressing pain,
   Nor was dismayed.
But when I listened Love's alluring,
Then I wand'red from assuring.
     For truth lives not in men ;
     Poor soul, why live I then?
       In the spring season, &c.

Adieu to all my former joys,
   When I lived at ease!
And welcome now those sad annoys,
   Which do most displease!
And let none pity her distress,
That fell not but by fickleness.
     For truth lives not in men ;
     Alas! why live I then?
       In the spring season, &c.

The song, most sweetly sung by Neifile,* was especially commended both by the King and all the rest of the ladies ; which, being fully finished, the King gave order that every one should repair to their chambers, because a great part of the night was already spent.

* This song is substituted by the old translator for Neifile's song in Boccaccio.

THE TENTH (AND LAST) DAY.

Whereon, under the government of Pamfilo, the several arguments do concern such persons, as either by way of liberality or in magnificent manner, performed any worthy action for love, favour, friendship, or any other honourable occasion.

INDUCTION.

ALREADY began certain small clouds in the west to blush with a vermilion tincture, while those in the east, having reached to their full height, looked like bright burnished gold, by splendour of the sunbeams drawing near unto them, when Pamfilo being risen, caused the ladies and the rest of his honourable companions to be called. When they were all assembled, and had concluded together on the place whither they should walk for the morning's recreation, the King led on the way before, accompanied with the two noble ladies, Filomena and Fiammetta, all the rest following after them, devising, talking, and answering to divers demands, both what that day was to be done, as also concerning the proposed imposition.

After they had walked an indifferent space of time, and found the rays of the sun to be over-piercing for them, they returned back again to the palace, as fearing to have their blood immoderately heated. Then rinsing their glasses in the cool, clear running current, each took their morning's draught, and then walked into the mild shades about the garden until they should be summoned to dinner. This was no sooner overpast, and such as slept returned waking, than they met together again in their wonted place, according as the King had appointed, where he gave command unto Neifile that she should for that day begin the first novel, which she humbly accepting, thus began.

———

THE FIRST NOVEL.

A Florentine knight, named Signior Ruggieri de Figiovanni, became a servant to Alfonso, King of Spain, who, in his opinion, seemed but slightly to respect and reward him, in regard whereof, by a notable experiment, the King gave him a manifest testimony that it was not through any defect in him, but only occasioned by the knight's ill-fortune, most bountifully recompensing him afterward.

I DO accept it, worthy ladies, as no mean favour that the King hath given me the first place, to speak of such an honourable argument as bounty and magnificence is, which precious jewel, even as the sun is the beauty or ornament and bright glory of all Heaven, so is bounty and magnificence the crown of all virtues. I shall then re-count to you a short novel, sufficiently pleasing in mine own opinion, and I hope, so much I dare rely on your judgments, both profitable and worthy to be remembered.

[OMITTED.]

THE SECOND NOVEL.

Ghinotto di Tacco took the Lord Abbot of Cligni as his prisoner, and cured him of a most grievous disease which he had in his stomach, and afterward set him at liberty. The same Lord Abbot when he returned to the Court of Rome, reconciled Ghinotto to Boniface, who made him a Knight and Lord Prior of a goodly hospital.

THE magnificence and royal bounty which King Alfonso bestowed on the Florentine knight, passed through the whole assembly with no mean applause, and the King, who gave it the greatest praise of all, commanded Elisa to take the second turn in order; where-upon thus she began :
Fair ladies, if a King showed himself magnificently minded, and expressed his liberal bounty to such a man as had done him good and honourable services : it can be termed no more than a virtuous deed well done, and becoming a King. But what will we say when we hear that a Prelate of the Church showed himself wondrously magnificent, and to such a one as was his enemy : can any malicious tongue speak ill of him ? Undoubtedly, no other answer is to be made, but the action of the King was merely virtue, and that of the Prelate no less than a miracle : for how can it be otherwise, when prelates are more greedily covetous than women, and deadly enemies to all liberality ? And although every man naturally desireth

I

revenge for injuries and abuses done unto him, yet men of the Church, in regard that they daily preach patience, and command, above all things else, remission of sins, it would appear a mighty blemish in them to be more froward and furious than other men. But I am to speak of a revered Prelate of the Church, as also concerning his magnificent bounty to one that was his enemy, and yet became his reconciled friend, as you shall perceive by my novel.

Ghinotto di Tacco, for his insolent and stout robberies, became a man very far famed, who being banished from Sienna, and an enemy to the Counts of Santa Fiore, prevailed so by his bold and headstrong persuasion, that the town of Radicofani rebelled against the Church of Rome ; wherein he remaining, all passengers whatsoever, travelling any way thereabout, were robbed and rifled by his thieving companions. At the time whereof I now speak, Boniface the Eighth governed as Pope at Rome, and the Lord Abbot of Cligni, accounted to be one of the richest Prelates in the world, came to Rome, and there either by some surfeit, excess of feeding, or otherwise, his stomach being grievously offended and pained, the physicians advised him to travel to the baths at Sienna, where he should receive immediate cure. In which respect, his departure being licensed by the Pope, he set onward thither, with great and pompous carriages, of horses, mules, and a goodly train, without hearing any rumour of the thievish consorts.

Ghinotto di Tacco, being advertised of his coming, spread about his scouts and nets, and without missing so much as one page, shut up the Abbot with all his train and baggage, in a place of narrow restraint, out of which he could by no means escape. When this was done, he sent one of his most sufficient attendants, well accompanied, to the Lord Abbot, who said to him in his master's name, that if his lordship were so pleased, he might come and visit Ghinotto at his castle. Which the Abbot hearing, answered cholericly, that he would not come thither, because he had nothing to say to Ghinotto : but meant to proceed on his journey, and would fain see who durst presume to hinder his pass. To which rough words the messenger thus mildly answered : " My lord," quoth he, " you are arrived in such a place where we fear no other force but the all-controlling power of Heaven, clearly exempted from the Pope's thundercracks of maledictions, interdictions, or whatsoever else : and therefore it would be much better for you if you pleased to do as Ghinotto adviseth you."

During the time of this their interparlance, the place was suddenly round engirt with strong armed thieves, and the Lord Abbot perceiving that both he and all his followers were surprised, took his way, though very impatiently, towards the castle, and likewise all his company and carriages with him. Being dismounted, he was conducted, as Ghinotto had appointed, all alone into a small chamber of the castle, it being very dark and uneasy, but the rest of his train, every one according to his rank and quality, were all well lodged in the castle, their horses, goods, and all things else delivered into secure keeping without the least touch of injury or prejudice. All which being orderly done, Ghinotto himself went to the Lord Abbot, and said : "My lord, Ghinotto, to whom you are a welcome guest, requesteth that it might be your pleasure to tell him, whither you are travelling, and upon what occasion ?"

The Lord Abbot being a very wise man, and his angry distemper more moderately qualified, revealed whither he went, and the cause of his going thither. Which when Ghinotto had heard, he departed courteously from him, and began to consider with himself how he might cure the Abbot, yet without any bath. So, commanding a good fire to be kept continually in his small chamber, and very good attendance on him, the next morning he came to visit him again, bringing a fair white napkin on his arm, and in it two slices or toasts of fine manchet, a goodly clear glassful of the purest white bastard of Corniglia, but indeed of the Abbot's own provision brought thither with him, and then he spake to him in this manner :

"My lord, when Ghinotto was younger than now he is he studied physic, and he commanded me to tell you that the very best medicine he could ever learn against any disease in the stomach was this which he had provided for your lordship as an especial preparative, and which you should find to be very comfortable." The Abbot, who had a better stomach to eat than any will or desire to talk, although he did it somewhat disdainfully, yet he ate up both the toasts and roundly drank off the glass of bastard. Afterward divers other speeches passed between them, the one still advising in physical manner and the other seeming to care little for it, but moving many questions concerning Ghinotto, and earnestly desiring to see him. Such speeches as savoured of the Abbot's discontentment and came from him in passion were clouded with courteous acceptance, and not the least sign of any mislike, but assuring his lordship that Ghinotto intended very shortly to see him, and so they parted for that time.

Nor returned he any more till the next morning with the like two toasts of bread and such another glass of white bastard as he had brought him at the first, continuing the same course for divers days after, till the Abbot had eaten (and very hungerly too) a pretty store of dried beans which Ghinotto purposely, yet secretly, had hidden in the chamber. Whereupon he demanded of him, as seeming to be so enjoined by his pretended master, in what temper he found his stomach now ? "I should find my stomach well enough," answered the Lord Abbot, "if I could get forth of thy master's fingers, and then have some good food to feed on ; for his medicines have made me so soundly stomached that I am ready to starve with hunger."

When Ghinotto was gone from him he then prepared a very fair chamber for him, adorning it with the Abbot's own rich hangings, and also his plate and other moveables, such as were always used for his service. A costly dinner he prepared likewise, whereto he invited divers of the town and many of the Abbot's chiefest followers. Then going to him again the next morning, he said :

I 2

" My lord, seeing you do feel your stomach so well, it is time you should come forth of the infirmary." And taking him by the hand he brought him to the prepared chamber, where he left him with his own people, and went to give order for the dinner's serving in, that it might be prepared in magnificent manner.

The Lord Abbot recreated himself a while with his own people, to whom he recounted the course of his life since he saw them, and they likewise told him how kindly they had been entreated by Ghinotto. But when dinner-time was come, the Lord Abbot and all his company were served with costly viands and excellent wines, without Ghinotto's making himself known to the Abbot, till after he had been entertained some few days in this order. Into the great hall of the castle Ghinotto caused all the Abbot's goods and furniture to be brought, and likewise into a spacious court, whereon the windows of the same court gazed, all his mules and horses, with their sumpters, even to the very silliest of them; which being done, Ghinotto went to the Abbot, and demanded of him how he felt his stomach now, and whether he would serve him to venture on horseback as yet or no? The Lord Abbot answered that he found his stomach perfectly recovered, his body strong enough to endure travel, and all things well, so he were delivered from Ghinotto.

Hereupon he brought him into the hall where his furniture was, as also all his people, and, commanding a window to be opened whereat he might behold his horses, he said : " My lord, let me plainly give you to understand that neither cowardice nor baseness of mind induced Ghinotto di Tacco, which is myself, to become a lurking robber on the highways, an enemy to the Pope, and so consequently to the Roman Court, but only to save his own life and honour, knowing himself to be a gentleman cast out of his own house, and having beside infinite enemies. But because you seem to be a worthy lord, I will not, although I have cured your stomach disease, deal with you as I do to others, whose goods, when they fall into my power, I take such part of as I please ; but rather am well contented that, my necessities being considered by yourself, you spare me out a portion of the things you have here, answerable to your own liking, for all are present here before you, both in this hall and in the court beneath, free from any spoil or the least im-pairing. Wherefore, give a part or take all, if you please, and then depart hence when you will, or abide here still, for now you are at your own free liberty."

The Lord Abbot wondered not a little that a robber on the highways should have such a bold and liberal spirit, which did very well please him, and instantly his former hatred and spleen against Ghinotto became converted into cordial love and kindness, so that, embracing him in his arms, he said : " I protest, upon my vow made to religion, that to win the love of such a man, as I plainly perceive thee to be, I would undergo far greater injuries than those which I have received at thy hands Accursed be cruel destiny that forced thee to so base a kind of life, and did not bless thee with a fairer fortune." After he had thus spoken, he left there the greater part of all his goods, and returned back again to Rome with fewer horses and a meaner train.

During these past accidents the Pope had received intelligence of the Lord Abbot's surprisal, which was not a little displeasing to him; but when he saw him returned, he demanded what benefit he received at the baths? Whereto the Abbot, merrily smiling, thus replied : " Holy Father, I met with a most skilful physician nearer hand, whose experience is beyond the power of the baths, for by him I am perfectly cured ; " and so discoursed all at large. The Pope, laughing heartily, and the Abbot continuing on still his report, moved with a high and magnificent courage, he demanded one gracious favour of the Pope, who, imagining that he would request a matter of greater moment than he did, freely offered to grant whatsoever he desired.

" Holy Father," answered the Lord Abbot, "all the humble suit which I make to you is, that you would be pleased to receive into your grace and favour Ghinotto di Tacco, my physician, because amongst all the virtuous men deserving to have special account made of them, I never met with any equal to him, both in honour and honesty. Whatever injury he did to me, I impute it as a greater infortune than any way he deserveth to be charged withal ; which wretched condition of his, if you were pleased to alter, and bestow on him some better means of maintenance, to live like a worthy man, as he is no less, I make no doubt but in very short time he will appear as pleasing to your holiness as, in my best judgment, I think him to be."

The Pope, who was of a magnanimous spirit, and one that highly affected men of virtue, hearing the commendable motion made by the Abbot, returned answer that he was as willing to grant it as the other desired it, sending letters of safe conduct for his coming thither.

Ghinotto, receiving such assurance from the Court of Rome, came thither immediately, to the great joy of the Lord Abbot ; and the Pope, finding him to be a man of valour and worth, upon reconciliation, remitted all former errors, creating him knight and lord prior of the very chiefest hospital in Rome, in which office he lived long time after, as a loyal servant to the Church and an honest friend to the Lord Abbot of Cligni.

———

THE THIRD NOVEL.

Mithridanes, envying the life and liberality of Nathan, and travelling thither with a settled resolution to kill him, chanced to confer with Nathan unknown. And being instructed by him in what manner he might best perform the bloody deed according as he gave direction, he meeteth him in a small thicket or wood, where knowing him to be the same man that taught him how to take away his life, confounded with shame, he acknowledgeth his horrible intention and becometh his loyal friend.

IT appeared to the whole assembly that they had heard a matter of marvel for a Lord Abbot to perform any magnificent action, but their admiration ceasing in silence, the King commanded Filostrato to follow next, who forthwith thus began :

Honourable ladies, the bounty and magnificence of Alfonso, King of Spain, was great indeed, and that done by the Lord Abbot of Cligni a thing perhaps never heard of in any other. But it will seem no less marvellous to you when you hear how one man, in expression of great liberality to another man, that earnestly desired to kill him, should secretly dispose him to give the life, which had been lost, if the other would have taken it, as I purpose to acquaint you withal in a short novel.

Most certain it is, at least, if faith may be given to the report of certain Genoese, and other men resorting to those remote parts, that in the country of Cathay there lived sometimes a gentleman, rich beyond comparison, and named Nathan. He having his living adjoining to a common roadway, whereby men travelled from the east to the west, as they did the like from the west unto the east, as having no other passage. And being of a bountiful and cheerful disposition, which he was willing to make known by experience, he summoned together many master masons and carpenters, and there erected, in a short time, one of the greatest and goodliest and most beautiful houses, in manner of a prince's palace, that ever was seen in all those quarters.

With moveables and all kinds of furnishment befitting a house of such outward appearance, he caused it to be plentifully stored, only to receive, entertain, and honour all gentlemen, or other travellers whatsoever, as had occasion to pass that way ; being not unprovided also of such a number of servants as might continually give attendance on all comers and goers. Two-and-fifty several gates stood alway wide open, and over each of them in great golden characters was written " Welcome, welcome," and they gave free admission to all comers whatsoever. In this honourable order, observed as his estated custom, he persevered so long while, as not only the east parts, but also those in the west, were everywhere acquainted with his fame and renown. Being already well stepped into years, but yet not weary of his great charge and liberality, it fortuned that the rumour of his noble hospitality came to the ear of another gallant gentleman, named Mithridanes, living in a country not far off from the other.

The gentleman, knowing himself no less wealthy than Nathan, and enviously repining at his virtue and liberality, determined in his mind to dim and obscure the other's bright splendour by making himself far more famous. And having built a palace answerable to that of Nathan's, with like winding of gates, and Welcome inscriptions, he began to extend immeasurable courtesies to all such as were disposed to visit him, so that in a short while he grew very famous in infinite places.

It chanced on a day, as Mithridanes sate all alone within the goodly court of his palace, a poor woman entered at one of the gates craving an alms of him, which she had; and returned in again at a second gate, coming also to him, and had a second alms; continuing so still a dozen times, but in the thirteenth returning, Mithridanes said to her: "Good woman, you go and come very often, and still you are served with alms." When the old woman heard these words, she said: "O the liberality of Nathan! how honourable and wonderful is that? I have passed through two-and-thirty gates of his palace, even such as are here, and at every one I received an alms without any knowledge taken of me, either by him, or any of his followers, and here I have passed but through thirteen gates, and am there both acknowledged and taken. Farewell to this house, for I never mean to visit it any more." With which words she departed thence, and never after came thither again.

When Mithridanes had a while pondered on her speeches, he waxed much discontented, as taking the words of the old woman to extol the renown of Nathan, and darken and eclipse his glory, whereupon he said to himself: "Wretched man as I am, when shall I attain to the height of liberality and perform such wonders as Nathan doth? In seeking to surmount him, I cannot come near him in the very meanest. Undoubtedly I spend all my endeavour, but in vain, except I rid the world of him, which, seeing his age will not make an end of him, I must needs do with mine own hands." In which bloody determination, without revealing his intent to any one, he mounting on horseback, with few attendants in his company, and after three days' journey, arrived where Nathan dwelt. He gave order to his men to make no show of being his servants, or any way to acknowledge him, but to provide themselves of convenient lodgings until they heard other tidings from him.

About evening, and in this manner alone by himself, near to the palace of Nathan, he met him solitarily walking, not in pompous apparel whereby to be distinguished from a meaner man, and, because he knew him not, neither had heard any relation of his description, he demanded of him if he knew where Nathan then was? Nathan, with a cheerful countenance, thus replied: "Fair sir, there is no man in these parts that knoweth better how to show you Nathan than I do; and therefore, if you be so pleased, I will bring you to him." Mithridanes said: "Therein he should do him a great

kindness : albeit, if it were possible, he would be neither known nor
seen of Nathan." "And that," quoth he, "can I also do sufficiently
for you, seeing it is your will to have it so, if you will go along with
me."

Dismounting from his horse, he walked on with Nathan, diversely
discoursing, until they came unto the palace, where one of the
servants taking Mithridanes' horse, Nathan rounded the fellow
in the ear that he should give warning to all in the house for revealing to the gentleman that he was Nathan, as accordingly it was performed.   No sooner were they within the palace, but he conducted
Mithridanes into a goodly chamber, where none as yet had seen him
but such as were appointed to attend on him reverently ; yea, and
he did himself greatly honour him, as being loth to leave his
company.

While thus Mithridanes conversed with him, he desired to know,
albeit he respected him much for his years, what he was. "In troth,
sir," answered Nathan, "I am one of the meanest servants to Nathan,
and from my childhood have made myself thus old in his service,
yet never hath he bestowed any other advancement on me than as
you see ; in which respect, howsoever other men may commend
him, yet I have no reason at all to do it."   These words gave some
hope to Mithridanes that, with a little more counsel, he might
securely put in execution his wicked determination.   Nathan likewise demanded of him, but in very humble manner, of whence and
what he was, as also the business inviting him thither, offering him
his utmost aid and counsel in whatsoever consisted in his power.

Mithridanes sate an indifferent while meditating with his thoughts
before he would return any answer, but at the last, concluding to
repose confidence in him, in regard of his pretended discontentment,
with many circumstantial persuasions, first for fidelity, next for constancy, and lastly for counsel and assistance, he declared to him truly
what he was, the cause of his coming thither, and the cause urging
him thereto.   Nathan hearing these words, and the detestable deliberation of Mithridanes, became quite changed in himself, yet
wisely making no outward appearance thereof, with a bold courage
and settled countenance, thus he replied :

"Mithridanes, thy father was a noble gentleman, and in virtuous
qualities inferior to none, from whom, as now I see, thou desirest
not to be degenerate, having undertaken so bold and high an enterprise, I mean, in being liberal and bountiful unto all men.   I do
greatly commend the envy which thou bearest to the virtue of
Nathan ; because if there were many more such men, the world,
that is now wretched and miserable, would become good and conformable.   As for the determination which thou hast disclosed to
me, I have sealed it up secretly in my soul, wherein I can better give
thee counsel than any especial help or furtherance ; and the
course which I would have thee to observe followeth thus in few
words.   This window which we now look forth at, showeth thee
a small wood or thicket of trees, being little more than a quarter of
a mile distant hence, whereto Nathan usually walketh every morn-

ing, and there continueth time long enough. There mayest thou very easily meet him, and do whatsoever thou intendest to him. If thou killest him, because thou mayest with safety return home unto thine own abiding, take not the same way which guided thee thither, but another lying on the left hand, and directing speedily out of the wood, as being not so much frequented as the other, but rather free from all resort, and surest for visiting thine own country after such a dismal deed is done."

When Mithridanes had received this instruction, and Nathan was departed from him, he secretly gave intelligence to his men (who likewise were lodged, as welcome strangers, in the same house), at what place they should stay for him the next morning. Night being passed over, and Nathan risen, his heart altered not a jot from his counsel given to Mithridanes, much less changed from any part thereof; but all alone by himself, walked on to the wood, the place appointed for his death. Mithridanes also being risen, taking his bow and sword (for other weapons had he none), mounted on horseback, and so came to the wood, where, somewhat far off, he espied Nathan walking, and no creature with him. Dismounting from his horse, he had resolved, before he would kill him, not only to see, but also to hear him speak; so stepping roughly to him, and taking hold of the bonnet of his head, his face being then turned from him, he said : " Old man, thou must die ! " Whereunto Nathan made no other answer but thus : " Why then, belike, I have deserved it."

When Mithridanes heard him speak, and looked advisedly on his face, he knew him immediately to be the same man that had entertained him so lovingly, conversed with him so familiarly, and counselled him so faithfully ; all which overcoming his former fury, his harsh nature became merely confounded with shame. So throwing down his drawn sword, which he held readily prepared for the deed, he prostrated himself at Nathan's feet, and in tears spake in this manner : " Now do I manifestly know, most loving father, your admirable bounty and liberality, considering with what industrious providence you made the means for your coming hither, prodigally to bestow your life on me, which I have no right unto, although you were so willing to part with it. But those high and supreme powers, more careful of my duty than I myself, even at the very instant, and when it was most needful, opened the eyes of my better understanding, which infernal envy had closed up before, and therefore look how much you have been forward to pleasure me, so much the more shame and punishment I confess my heinous transgression hath justly deserved. Take therefore on me, if you please, such revenge as you think, in justice, answerable to my sin."

Nathan lovingly raised Mithridanes from the ground ; then kissing his cheek, and tenderly embracing him, he said : " Son, thou needest not to ask, much less to obtain pardon for any enterprise of thine, which thou canst not yet term to be good or bad ; because thou soughtest not to bereave me of my life for any hatred thou bearest me, but only in coveting to be reputed the worthier man. Take, then, this assurance of me, and believe it constantly that there is no man living whom I love and honour as I do thee ; considering the greatness of thy mind, which consisteth not in the heaping up of money, as wretched and miserable worldlings make it their only felicity, but contending in bounty to spend what is thine, didst hold it for no shame to kill me, thereby to make thyself so much the more worthily famous.

"Nor is it any matter to be wondered at, in regard that emperors and the greatest kings had never made such extendure of their dominions, and consequently of their renown, by any other art than killing ; yet not one man only, as thou wouldest have done, but infinite numbers, burning whole countries, and making desolate huge towns and cities, only to enlarge their dominion, and further spreading of their fame. Wherefore, if for the increasing of thine own renown, thou wast desirous of my death, it is no matter of novelty, and therefore deserving the less marvel, seeing men are slain daily, and all for one purpose or other."

Mithridanes, excusing no further his malevolent deliberation, but rather commending the honest defence which Nathan made on his behalf, proceeded so far in after discoursing as to tell him plainly that it did wondrously amaze him, how he durst come to the fatal appointed place, himself having so exactly plotted and contrived his own death : whereunto Nathan returned this answer :

" I would not have thee, Mithridanes, to wonder at my counsel or determination ; because since age hath made me master of mine own will, and I resolved to do that wherein thou hast begun to follow me, never came any man to me whom I did not content, if I could, in anything he demanded of me. It was thy fortune to come for my life, which, when I saw thee so desirous to have it, I resolved immediately to bestow it on thee ; and so much the rather, because thou shouldest not be the only man that ever departed hence without enjoying whatsoever he demanded. And to the end thou mightest the more assuredly have it, I gave thee that advice, lest by not enjoying mine thou shouldest chance to lose thine own. I had the use of it full fourscore years, all this while, with the consummation of all my delights and pleasures ; and well I know that, according to the course of nature (as it fares with other men, and generally with all things else), it cannot be long before it must leave me.

" Wherefore I hold it much better for me to give it away freely, as I have always done my goods and treasure, than be curious in keeping it, and suffer it to be taken away from me, whether I will or no, by nature. A small gift it is, if time make me up the full sum of a hundred years ; how miserable it is then to stand beholding for four or five, and all of them vexation too? Take it then. I entreat thee, if thou wilt have it ; for I never met with any man before but thyself that did desire it, nor, perhaps, shall find any other to request it ; for the longer I keep it. the worse it will be esteemed, and before it grow contemptible, take it, I pray thee."

Mithridanes, being exceedingly confounded with shame, bashfully said: "Fortune forefend that I should take away a thing so precious as your life is, or once to have so vile a thought of it, as lately I had ; but rather than I would diminish one day thereof, I could wish that my time might more amply enlarge it." Forthwith answered Nathan, saying : "Wouldest thou, if thou couldest, shorten thine own days, only to lengthen mine ? Why then thou wouldest have me to do that to thee, which, as yet, I never did unto any man—namely, rob thee to enrich myself. I will instruct thee in a far better course, if thou wilt be advised by me. Lusty and young, as now thou art, thou shalt dwell here in my house, and be called by the name of Nathan. Aged and spent with years, as thou seest I am, I will go live in thy house, and be called by the name of Mithridanes. So both the name and place shall illustrate thy glory, and I live contentedly without the very least thought of envy."

"Dear father," answered Mithridanes, "if I knew so well how to direct mine own actions as you do, and always have done, I would gladly accept your most liberal offer ; but because I plainly perceive that my very best endeavours must remain darkened by the bright renown of Nathan, I will never seek to impair that in another which I cannot by any means increase in myself, but, as you have worthily taught me, live contented with mine own condition."

After these and many more like loving speeches had passed between them, according as Nathan very instantly requested, Mithridanes returned back with him to the palace, where many days he highly honoured and respected him, comforting and counselling him to persevere always in his honourable determination. But in the end, when Mithridanes could abide there no longer, because necessary occasions called him home, he departed thence with his men, having found, by good experience, that he could never go beyond Nathan in liberality.

THE FOURTH NOVEL.

Messer Gentile de Carisendi, being come from Modena, took a gentlewoman, named Catarina, forth of a grave, wherein she was buried for dead, which act he did in regard of his former honest affection to the said gentlewoman. Catarina remaining there afterward and delivered of a goodly son, was by Messer Gentile delivered to her own husband, named Messer Niccoluccio Caccianimico, and the young infant with her.

By judgment of all the assembly, it was reputed wonderful that a man should be so bountiful as to give away his own life, and to his hateful enemy. In which respect it passed with general affirmation, that Nathan, in the virtue of liberality, had exceeded Alfonso, King of Spain, but especially the Abbot of Cligni. So after every one had delivered their opinion, the King, turning himself to

Lauretta, gave her such a sign as well instructed her understanding, that she should be the next in order, whereto she gladly yielding, began in this manner :

Youthful ladies, the discourses already passed, have been so worthy and magnificent, yea, reaching to such a height of glorious splendour, as methinks there remaineth no more matter for us that are yet to speak, whereby to enlarge so famous an argument, and in such manner as it ought to be : except we lay hold on the actions of love, wherein is never any want of subject, it is so fair and spacious a field to walk in. Wherefore, as well in behalf of the one as advancement of the other, whereto our instant age is most of all inclined, I purpose to acquaint you with a generous and magnificent act of an amorous gentleman, which when it shall be duly considered on, perhaps will appear equal to any of the rest ; at least, if it may pass for current, that men will give away their treasures, forgive mighty injuries, and lay down life itself, honour and renown, which is far greater, bearing infinite dangers, only to attain possession of the one beloved.

[OMITTED.]

THE FIFTH NOVEL.

Dianora, the wife of the rich Gilberto, being immodestly affected by Messer Ansaldo, to free herself from his tedious importunity, she appointed him to perform, in her judgment, an act of impossibility—namely, to give her a garden as plentifully stored with fragrant flowers in January as in the flourishing month of May. Ansaldo by means of a bond which he made to a magician, performed her request. Messer Gilberto, the lady's husband, gave consent that his wife should fulfil her promise made to Ansaldo ; who hearing the bountiful mind of her husband released her of her promise, and the magician likewise discharged Ansaldo, without taking aught of him.

Not any one in all the company but extolled the worthy act of Signior Gentile to the skies ; till the King gave command to Emilia, that she should follow next with her tale, who boldly stepping up, began in this order :

Gracious ladies, I think there is none here present among us, but, with good reason, may maintain that Messer Gentile performed a magnificent deed ; but whosoever saith it is impossible to be more, perhaps is ignorant in such actions, as can and may be done, as I mean to make good unto you by a novel not over-long or tedious.

[OMITTED.]

THE SIXTH NOVEL.

Victorious King Charles, surnamed The Aged, and first of that name, fell in
love with a young maiden, named Ginevra, daughter to an ancient knight,
called Neri degli Uberti.   And waxing ashamed of his amorous folly,
caused both Ginevra and her fair sister Isotta to be joined in marriage
with two noble gentlemen ; the one named Messer Maffeo da Palazzi, and
the other Messer Guilielmo della Magna.

WHO is able to express ingenuously the diversity of opinions which
happened among the ladies in censuring on the act of Dianora, and
which of them was most liberal, either Messer Gilberto the
husband, Lord Ansaldo the importunate suitor, or the magician,
expecting to be bountifully rewarded.   Surely it is matter beyond
my capacity, but after the King had permitted their disputation a
long while, looking on Fiammetta, he commanded that she should
report her novel to make an end of their controversy, and she,
without any further delaying, thus began.

[OMITTED.]

THE SEVENTH NOVEL.

Lisa, the daughter of a Florentine apothecary, named Bernardo Puccini,
being at Palermo, and seeing Pietro King of Aragon run at the tilt, fell so
affectionately enamoured of him that she languished in an extreme and long
sickness.   By her own device and means of a song, sung in the hearing of
the King, he vouchsafed to visit her, and giving her a kiss, terming himself
also to be her knight for ever after, he honourably bestowed her in marriage
on a young gentleman, who was called Perdicone, and gave him liberal
endowments with her.

FIAMMETTA being come to the end of her novel, and the great
magnificence of King Charles much commended, howbeit some of
the company affecting the Ghibelline faction, were otherwise minded,
Pampinea, by order given from the King, began in this manner.

[OMITTED.]

THE EIGHTH NOVEL.

Sophronia thinking herself to be the married wife of Gisippus, was indeed the wife of Titus Quintus Fulvius, and departed thence with him to Rome. Within a while after, Gisippus also came thither in very poor condition, and thinking that he was despised by Titus, grew weary of his life, and confessed that he had murdered a man, with full intent to die for the fact. But Titus, taking knowledge of him and desiring to save the life of Gisippus, charged himself to have done the bloody deed. Which the murderer himself (standing then among the multitude) seeing, truly confessed the deed. By means whereof all three were delivered by the Emperor Octavius, and Titus gave his sister in marriage to Gisippus, giving them also the most part of his goods and inheritances.

By this time Filomena, at command of the King, Pampinea ceasing, prepared to follow next in order, whereupon thus she began :

What is it, gracious ladies, that kings cannot do if they list, in matters of greatest importance, as especially unto such as most they should declare their magnificence? He then that performeth what he ought to do when it is within his own power doth well. But it is not so much to be admired, neither deserveth half the commendations, as when one man doth good to another, when least it is expected, as being out of his power, and yet performed. In which respect, because you have so extolled King Pietro as appearing not meanly meritorious in your judgments, I make no doubt but you will be much more pleased when the actions of our equals are duly considered, and I shall parallel any of the greatest kings. Wherefore I purpose to tell you a novel, concerning an honourable courtesy of two worthy friends.

At such time as Octavius Cæsar (not as yet named Augustus, but only in the office of the Triumvirate) governed the Roman Empire, there dwelt in Rome a gentleman named Publius Quintus Fulvius, a man of singular understanding, who, having one son named Titus Quintus Fulvius, of towardly years and apprehension, sent him to Athens to learn philosophy, but with letters of familiar commendation to a noble Athenian gentleman named Chremes, being his ancient friend of long acquaintance. This gentleman lodged Titus in his own house as a companion to his son, named Gisippus, both of them studying together, under the tutoring of a philosopher called Aristippus. These two young gentlemen, living thus in one city, house and school, it bred between them such a brotherhood and amity, as they could not be severed from one another but only by the accident of death, nor could either of them enjoy any content but when they were both together in company.

Being each of them endued with gentle spirits and having begun their studies together, they arose, by degrees, to the glorious height of philosophy, to their much fame and commendation. In this manner they lived to the no mean comfort of Chremes, hardly distinguishing the one from the other for his son, and thus the scholars continued the space of three years. At the ending whereof, as it happeneth in all things else, Chremes died, whereat both the young gentlemen conceived such hearty grief, as if he had been their common father; nor could the kindred of Chremes discern which of the two had most need of comfort, the loss touched them so equally.

It chanced within some two months after that the kindred of Gisippus came to see him, and, before Titus, advised him to marriage, and with a young gentlewoman of singular beauty derived from a most noble house in Athens, and she named Sophronia, aged about fifteen years. This marriage drawing near, Gisippus on a day entreated Titus to walk along with him thither, because as yet he had not seen her. Coming to the house, and she sitting in the midst between them, Titus, making himself a considerator of beauty, and especially on his friend's behalf, began to observe her very judiciously, and every part of her seemed so pleasing in his eye, that giving them all a private praise, yet answerable to their due deserving, he became so inflamed with affection to her as never any lover could be more violently surprised, so suddenly doth beauty beguile our best senses.

After they had sat an indifferent while with her, they returned home to their lodging, while Titus, being alone in his chamber, began to bethink on her whose perfections had so powerfully pleased him, and the more he entered into this consideration, the fiercer he felt his desires inflamed, which being unable to quench, by reasonable persuasions, after he had vented forth infinite sighs, thus he questioned :

" Most unhappy Titus as thou art, whither doest thou transport thine understanding, love and hope ? Dost thou not know as well by the honourable favours which thou hast received of Chremes and his house, as also the entire amity between thee and Gisippus, unto whom fair Sophronia is the affianced friend, that thou shouldst hold her in the reverent respect as if she were thy true born sister ? Darest thou presume to fancy her ? Whither shall beguiling love allure thee, and vain imagining hopes carry thee ? Open the eyes of thy better understanding and acknowledge thyself to be a most miserable man, give way to reason, bridle thine intemperate appetites, reform all irregular desires, and guide thy fancy to a place of better direction. Resist thy wanton and lascivious will in the beginning, and be master of thyself while thou hast opportunity, for what thou aimest at is neither reasonable nor honest. And if thou wert assured to prevail upon this pursuit, yet thou oughtest to avoid it if thou hast any regard of true friendship and the duty therein justly required. What wilt thou do, then, Titus ? Fly from this inordinate affection if thou wilt be reputed to be a man of sensible judgment."

After that he had thus discoursed with himself, remembering Sophronia, and converting his former allegations into a quite contrary sense in utter detestation of them, and guided by his idle appetite, thus he began again : " The laws of love are of greater force than any other whatsoever, they not only break the bands of friendship, but even those also of more divine consequence. How many times it hath been noted the father to affect his own daughter, the brother his sister, and the stepmother her son-in-law, matters far more monstrous than to see one friend love the wife of another, a case happening continually ? Moreover, I am young, and youth is wholly subjected to the passions of love ; is it reasonable then, that those should be barred from me which are fitting and pleasing to love ? Honest things belong to men of more years and maturity than I am troubled withal, and I can covet none but only those wherein love is director. The beauty of Sophronia is worthy of general love, and if I that am a young man love her, what man living can justly reprove me for it ? Should I not love her because she is affianced to Gisippus ? That is no matter to me, I ought to love her because she is a woman, and women were created for no other occasion but to be loved. Fortune hath sinned in this case, and not I, in directing my friend's affection to her, rather than any other, and if she ought to be loved, as her perfections do challenge, Gisippus understanding that I affect her, may be the better contented that it is I, rather than any other."

With these and the like intercourses he often mocked himself, falling into the contrary, and then to this again, and from the contrary into another kind of alteration, wasting and consuming himself, not only this day and the night following, but many more afterward, till he lost both his feeding and his sleep, so that through debility of body he was constrained to keep his bed. Gisippus, who had divers days noted his melancholy disposition, and now his falling into extremity of sickness, was very sorry to behold it, and with all means he could devise to use, he both questioned the cause of this strange alteration, and essayed every way how he might best comfort him, never ceasing to demand a reason why he should be thus sad and sickly. But Titus after infinite importuning (which still he answered with idle and frivolous excuses, far from the truth indeed, and to the no mean affliction of his friend), when he was able to use no more contraditions, at length, in sighs and tears, thus he replied :

" Gisippus, were the gods so well pleased, I could more gladly yield to die than continue any longer in this wretched life, considering that fortune hath brought me into such an extremity, as proof is now to be made of my constancy and virtue, both which I find conquered in me, to my eternal confusion and shame. But my best hope is that I shall shortly be requited as I have in justice deserved—namely, with death, which will be a thousand times more welcome to me than a loathed life with remembrance of my base dejection in courage ; which because I can no longer conceal from thee, not without blushing shame, I am well contented for to let thee know it."

Then began he to recount the whole occasion of this strange conflict in him, what a main battle he had with his private thoughts, confessing that they got the victory, causing him to die hourly for

the love of Sophronia, and affirming withal, that in due acknowledgment, how greatly he had transgressed against the laws of
friendship, he thought no other penance sufficient for him, but only
death, which he willingly expected every hour, and with all his
heart would gladly bid welcome.

Gisippus hearing this discourse, and seeing how Titus bitterly
wept, in agonies of moving afflictions, sate an indifferent while sad
and pensive, as being wounded with affection to Sophronia, but yet
in a well-governed and temperate manner. So without any long
delaying he concluded with himself, that the life of his friend
ought to be accounted much more dear than any love he could bear
to Sophronia, and in this resolution the tears of Titus forcing his
eyes to flow forth like the fountains, and running down his cheeks,
thus he replied :

"Titus, if thou hadst not need of comfort, as plainly I see thou
hast, I would justly complain of thee to myself, as of the man who
hath violated our friendship, in keeping thy extremity so long time
concealed from me, which hath been over-tedious for thee to
endure. And although it might seem to thee a dishonourable case,
and therefore kept from the knowledge of thy friend, yet I plainly
tell thee that dishonest courses in the league of amity deserve no
more concealment than those of the honestest nature. But leaving
these impertinent wanderings, let us come to them of much greater
necessity.

"If thou doest earnestly love fair Sophronia, who is betrothed
and affianced to me, it is no matter for me to marvel at ; but I
should rather be much abashed, if thou couldst not entirely affect
her, knowing how beautiful she is, and the nobility of your mind
being abler to sustain passion as the thing pleasing is fuller of
excellency. And look how reasonably thou fanciest Sophronia, as
unjustly thou complainest of thy fortune, in ordaining her to be my
wife, although thou doest not speak it expressly, as being of an opinion
that thou mightest with more honesty love her if she were any
other's than mine. But if thou art so wise as I have always held
thee to be, tell me truly upon thy faith, to whom could fortune
better guide her, and for which thou oughtest to be more thankful,
than in bestowing her on me ? Any other that had enjoyed her,
although thy love was never so honest, yet he would better affect
her himself, than for thee ; which thou canst not in like manner look
for from me, if thou doest account me for thy friend and as constant
now as ever.

"Reason is my warrant in this case, because I cannot remember,
since first our entrance into friendship, that ever I enjoyed anything
but it was as much thine as mine. And if our affairs had such an
equal course before, as otherwise they could not subsist, must they
not now be kept in the same manner ? Can anything more particularly appertain to me, but thy right therein is as absolute as mine ?
I know not how thou mayest esteem of my friendship, if in anything
concerning myself, I can plead my privilege to be above thine.
True it is, that Sophronia is affianced to me, and I love her dearly

daily expecting when our nuptials shall be celebrated. But seeing thou dost more fervently affect her, as being better able to judge of the perfection, remaining in so excellent a creature as she is, than I do : assure thyself, and believe it constantly, that she shall come to my bed, not as my wife, but only thine. And therefore leave these despairing thoughts, shake off this cloudy disposition, reassume thy former jovial spirit with comfort, and what else can content thee ; in expectation of the happy hour, and the just requital of thy long, loving, and worthy friendship, which I have always valued as mine own life."

Titus hearing this answer of Gisippus, look how much the sweet hope of that which he desired gave him pleasure, as much both duty and reason affronted him with shame, setting before his eyes this due consideration, that the greater the liberality of Gisippus was, far greater and unreasonable it appeared to him in disgrace, if he should unmannerly accept it. Wherefore, being unable to refrain from tears, and with such strength as his weakness would give leave, thus he replied :

" Gisippus, thy bounty and firm friendship suffereth me to see apparently, what, on my part, is no more than ought to be done. All the gods forbid, that I should receive as mine, her whom they have adjudged to be thine, by true respect of birth and desert. For if they had thought her a wife fit for me, do not thou or any else imagine that ever she should have been granted to thee. Use freely therefore thine own election, and the gracious favour wherewith they have blessed thee : leave me to consume away with tears, a mourning garment by them appointed for me, as being a man unworthy of such happiness : for either I shall conquer this disaster, and that will be my crown ; or else it will vanquish me, and free me from all pain." Whereto Gisippus presently thus answered :

" Worthy Titus, if our amity would give me so much license, as but to contend with myself in pleasing thee with such a thing as I desire, and could also induce thee therein to be directed : it is the only end whereat I aim, and I am resolved to pursue it. In which regard, let my persuasions prevail with thee, and thereto I conjure thee, by the faith of a friend, suffer me to use mine authority, when it extendeth both to mine own honour and thy good, for I will have Sophronia to be only thine. I know sufficiently how far the forces of love do extend in power, and am not ignorant also how, not once or twice, but very many times, they have brought lovers to unfortunate ends, as now I see thee very near it, and so far gone, as thou art not able to turn back again, nor yet to conquer thine own tears, but proceeding on further in this extremity, thou wilt be left vanquished, sinking under the burden of Love's tyrannical oppression, and then my turn is next to follow thee. And therefore, had I no other reason to love thee, yet because this life is dear to me, in regard of my own depending thereon, I stand the nearer thereto obliged. For this cause, Sophronia must and shall be thine, for thou canst not find any other so conform to thy fancy. Albeit I who can easily convert my liking to another wife, but never to have the like friend again, shall hereby content both thee and myself.

"Yet perhaps this is not a matter so easily done, or I to express such liberality therein, if wives were to be found with the like difficulty, as true and faithful friends ; but, being able to recover another wife, though never such a worthy friend, I rather chose to change, I do not say lose her, for in giving her to thee, I lose her not myself, and by this change, make that which was good before ten times better, and so preserve both thee and myself. To this end therefore, if my prayers and persuasions have any power with thee, I earnestly entreat thee, that by freeing thyself out of this affliction, thou wilt, in one instant, make us both truly comforted, and dispose thyself, living in hope, to embrace that happiness which the fervent love thou bearest to Sophronia hath justly deserved."

Now although Titus was confounded with shame to yield consent that Sophronia should be accepted as his wife, and used many obstinate resistances : yet, notwithstanding, love pleaded on the one side powerfully, and Gisippus as earnestly persuading on the other, thus he answered : "Gisippus, I know not what to say, neither how to behave myself in this election, concerning the fitting of my contentment, or pleasing thee in thy importunate persuasion. But seeing thy liberality is so great, as it surmounteth all reason or shame in me, I will yield obedience to thy more than noble nature. Yet let this remain for thine assurance, that I do not receive this grace of thine as a man not sufficiently understanding how I enjoy from thee, not only her whom most of all I do affect, but also do hold my very life of thee. Grant then, you greatest gods, if you be the patrons of this mine unexpected felicity, that with honour and due respect I may hereafter make apparently known how highly I acknowledge this thy wonderful favour, in being more merciful to me than I could be to myself."

"For abridging of all further circumstances," answered Gisippus, "and for easier bringing this matter to full effect, I hold this to be our only way. It is not unknown to thee, how after much discourse had between my kindred and those belonging to Sophronia, the matrimonial conjunction was fully agreed on, and therefore if now I shall fly off and say, I will not accept her as my wife, great scandal would arise thereby, and make much trouble among our friends, which could not be greatly displeasing to me, if that were the way to make her thine. But I rather stand in fear, that if I forsake her in such peremptory sort, her kindred and friends will bestow her upon some other, and so she is utterly lost, without all possible means of recovery.

"For prevention therefore of all sinister accidents, I think it best, if thy opinion jump with mine, that I still pursue the business as already I have begun, having thee always in my company, as my dearest friend and only associate. The nuptials being performed with our friends, in secret manner at night, as we can cunningly enough contrive it, thou shalt be to her even as if she were thine own wife. Afterward, in apt time and place, we will publicly make known what is done ; if they take it well, we will be as jocund as they : if they frown and wax offended, the deed is done over-late to be recalled, and so perforce they must rest contented."

You may well imagine this advice was not a little pleasing to Titus, whereupon Gisippus received home Sophronia into his house, with public intention to make her his wife, according as was the custom then observed ; and Titus being perfectly recovered, was present at the feast very ceremonially observed. When night was come, the ladies and gentlewomen conducted Sophronia to the bride-chamber, where they left her in her husband's bed, and then departed all away.

The chamber wherein Titus used to lodge, joined close to that of Gisippus, for their easier access each to the other at all times whensoever they pleased ; and Gisippus being alone in the bride-chamber, preparing as if he were coming to bed : extinguishing the light, he went softly to Titus, willing him to go to his wife ; which Titus hearing, overcome with shame and fear, became repentant, and denied to go.

But Gisippus being a true entire friend indeed, and confirming his words with actions, after a little lingering dispute, sent him to the bride, and as soon as he was in the bed with her, taking Sophronia gently by the hand, softly he moved the usual question to her, if she were willing to be his wife.

She believing verily that he was Gisippus, modestly replied : " Sir, I have chosen you to be my husband, reason requires then that I should be willing to be your wife." At which words a costly ring, which Gisippus used daily to wear, he put upon her finger, saying : " With this ring I confess myself to be your husband, and bind you for ever my spouse and wife." No other kind of marriage was observed in those days, and so he continued all the night with her, she never suspecting him to be any other than Gisippus : and thus was the marriage consummated between Titus and Sophronia, albeit the friends on either side thought otherwise.

By this time Publius, the father of Titus, was departed out of this mortal life, and letters came to Athens that with all speed he should return to Rome, to take order for occasions there concerning him, wherefore he concluded with Gisippus about his departure, and taking Sophronia thither with him, which was no easy matter to be done until it were first known how occasions had been carried among them. Whereupon, calling her one day into her chamber, they told her entirely how all had passed, which Titus confirmed substantially by such direct passages between themselves as exceeded all possibility of denial, and moved in her much admiration ; looking each on other very discontentedly, she heavily weeping and lamenting, and greatly complaining of Gisippus for wronging her so unkindly.

But before any further noise was made in the house, she went to her father, to whom, as also to her mother, she declared the whole treachery, how much both they and their other friends were wronged by Gisippus, avouching herself to be the wife of Titus and not of

Gisippus, as they supposed. These news were highly displeasing to the father of Sophronia, who with her kindred, as also those of Gisippus, made great complaints to the Senate—very dangerous troubles and commotions arising daily between them, drawing both Gisippus and Sophronia into harsh reports, he being generally reputed not only worthy of all bitter reproof, but also the severest punishment. Nevertheless, he maintained publicly what he had done, avouching it for an act both of honour and honesty, wherewith Sophronia's friends had no reason to be offended, but rather to take it in very thankful part, having married a man of far greater worth and respect than himself was or could be.

On the other side, Titus, hearing these uncivil acclamations, became much moved and provoked at them ; but knowing it was a custom observed among the Greeks to be so much the more hurried away with rumours and threatenings until they find them to be answered, and when boldly met they show themselves not humble only, but rather as base men and of no courage, he resolved with himself that their braveries were no longer to be endured without some bold and manly answer. And having a Roman heart, as also an Athenian understanding, by politic persuasions he caused the kindred of Gisippus and Sophronia to be assembled in a temple, and himself coming thither accompanied with none but Gisippus only, he began to deliver his mind before them all, in this manner following :

The Oration uttered by Titus Quintus Fulvius, *in the hearing of the Athenians, being the kindred and friends to Gisippus and Sophronia.*

" Many philosophers do hold opinion that the actions performed by mortal men do proceed from the disposing and ordination of the immortal gods. Whereupon some do maintain that things which be done, or never are to be done, proceed of necessity ; albeit some others do hold that this necessity is only referred to things done. Both which opinions, if they be considered with mature judgment, do most manifestly approve that they who reprehend anything which is irrevocable, do nothing else but show themselves as if they were wiser than the gods who, we are to believe, that with perpetual reason, and void of any error, do dispose and govern both us and all our actions ; in which respect how foolish and beast-like a thing it is presumptuously to check or control their operations, you may very easily consider, and likewise how justly they deserve condign punishment who suffer themselves to be transported in so temarious a manner.

" In which notorious transgression I understand you all to be guilty, if common fame speak truly concerning the marriage of myself and Sophronia, whom you imagined as given to Gisippus ; for you never remember that it was so ordained from eternity, she to be mine, and nowise to Gisippus, as at this instant is made manifest by full effect. But because the kind of speaking concerning divine providence and intention of the gods may seem a difficult matter to many, and somewhat hard to be understood, I am content to presuppose that they meddle not here with anything of ours, and will only stay myself on human reasons; and in this nature of speech I shall be enforced to do two things quite contrary to my natural disposition. The one is to speak somewhat in praise and commendation of myself; and the other, justly to blame and condemn other men's seeming estimation. But because both in the one and the other I do not intend to swerve a jot from the truth, and the necessity of the present case in question doth not only require but also command it, you must pardon what I am to say.

"Your complaints do proceed rather from fury than reason, and with continual murmurings, or rather seditious slander, backbite and condemn Gisippus because, of his own free will and noble disposition, he gave her to be my wife who, by your election, was made his; wherein I account him most highly praiseworthy, and the reasons inducing me thereunto are these: The first, because he hath performed no more than what a friend ought to do; and the second, in regard he hath dealt more wisely than you did. I have no intention to display at this present what the secret law of amity requireth to be acted by one friend towards another, it shall suffice me only to inform you that the league of friendship, far stronger than the bond of blood and kindred, confirmed us in our election of either at the first to be true, loyal, and perpetual friends; whereas that of kindred cometh only by fortune or chance. And therefore, if Gisippus affected more my life than your benevolence, I being ordained for his friend, as I do now confess myself to be, none of you ought to wonder thereat, in regard it is no matter of marvel.

"But let us now come to our second reason, wherein with far greater instance I will show you, that he hath in this occasion shown himself to be much more wise than you have been; because it plainly appeareth that you have no feeling of the divine providence and much less knowledge in the effects of friendship. I say that your foresight, counsel, and deliberation gave Sophronia to Gisippus, a young gentleman and a philosopher; Gisippus likewise hath given her to a young gentleman and a philosopher, as himself is. Your discretion gave her to an Athenian; the gift of Gisippus is to a Roman. Yours to a noble and honest man; that of Gisippus, to one more noble by race and no less honest than himself. Your judgment hath bestowed her on a rich young man; Gisippus hath given her to one far richer. Your wisdom gave her to one who not only loved her not, but also one that desired not to know her; Gisippus gave her unto him who, above all felicity else —yea, more than his own life—both entirely loved and desired her.

"Now, for proof of that which I have said to be most true and infallible, and that his deed deserveth to be much more commended than yours, let it be duly considered on, point by point. That I am a young man and a philosopher, as Gisippus is, my years, face, and studies, without seeking after further proof, doth sufficiently testify. One self-same age is both his and mine; in like quantity of course have we lived and studied together. True it is that he is an Athenian, and I am a Roman. But if the glory of these two cities should be disputed on, then let me tell you that I am of a city that is frank and free, and he is of a tributary city. I say that I am of a city which is the chief lady and mistress of the whole world, and he is of a city subject to mine. I say that I am of a city that is strong in arms, empire, and study also ; whereas his can commend itself but for studies only. And although you seem here to be a scholar, in appearance mean enough, yet I am not descended from the simplest stock in Rome.

" My houses and public places are filled with the ancient statues of my predecessors, and the annals record the infinite triumphs of the Quintii, brought home by them into the Roman Capitol ; and years cannot eat out the glory of our name, but it will live and flourish to all posterity.

" Modest shame makes me silent in my wealth and possessions, my mind truly telling me that honest contented poverty is the most ancient and richest inheritance of our best and noblest Romans, which opinion, if it be condemned by the understanding of the ignorant multitude, and herein we shall give way to them by preferring riches and worldly treasures, then I can say that I am abundantly provided ; not as ambitious, nor greedily covetous, but sufficiently stored with the goods of fortune.

" I know well enough that you hold it as a desired benefit, Gisippus being a native of your city, should also be linked to you by alliance ; but I know no reason why I should not be as near and dear to you at Rome, as if I lived with you here. Considering, when I am there, you have a ready and well-wishing friend to stead you in all beneficial and serviceable offices, as careful and provident for your support, yea, a protector of you and your affairs, as well public as particular. Who is it then not transported with partial affection, that can in reason more approve your act than that which my friend Gisippus hath done ? Questionless not any one, as I think. Sophronia is married to Titus Quintus Fulvius, a noble gentleman by antiquity, a rich citizen of Rome, and, which is above all, the friend of Gisippus ; therefore such a one that thinks it strange, is sorry for it, or would not have it be, knoweth not what he doth.

" Perhaps there may be some who will say they do not so much complain that Sophronia is the wife to Titus, but of the manner whereby it was done, as being made his wife secretly and by theft, not any of her friends called thereto, no, not so much as advertised thereof. Why, gentlemen, this is no miraculous thing, but heretofore hath oftentimes happened, and therefore no novelty.

" I cannot count unto you how many there have been who, against the will of their father, have made choice of their husbands, nor of them that have fled away with their lovers into strange countries, being first friends, before they were wives ; nor of them who have sooner made testimony of marriage by their bellies, than those ceremonies due to matrimony, or publication thereof by the tongue, so that mere necessity and constraint hath forced the parents to yield consent, which hath not so happened to Sophronia, for she was given to me by Gisippus discreetly, honestly, and orderly.

" Others also may say that she is married to him to whom it belonged not to marry her. These complaints are foolish and womanish, proceeding from very little or no consideration at all. In these days of ours, fortune makes no use of novel or inconsiderate means whereby to bring matters to their determined effect. Why should it offend me if a cobbler, rather than a scholar, hath ended a business of mine, either in private or in public. if the end be well made? Well, I may take order if the cobbler be indiscreet, that he meddle no more with any matters of mine, yet I ought in courtesy to thank him for that which he did.

" In like manner, if Gisippus hath married Sophronia well, it is foolish and superfluous to find fault with the manner he used in her marriage. If you mislike his course in the case, beware of him hereafter, yet thank him because it is no worse.

" Nevertheless, you are to understand that I sought not by fraud or deceit, but only by wit, an opportunity whereby any way to sully the honesty and clear nobility of your blood, in the person of Sophronia ; for although in secret I made her my wife, yet I came not as an enemy to take perforce, nor, like a ravisher, wronged her virginity, to blemish your noble titles, or despising your alliance. But fervently inflamed by her bright beauty, and incited also by her unparalleled virtues, I shaped my course, knowing well enough that if I took the ordinary way of wiving, by moving the question to you. I should never win your consent, as fearing lest I would take her with me to Rome, and so convey out of your sight a jewel by you so much esteemed as she is.

" For this and no other reason did I presume to use the secret cunning which now is openly made known unto you ; and Gisippus disposed himself thereunto, which otherwise he never determined to have done, in contracting the marriage for me, and she consenting to me in his name.

" Moreover, albeit most earnestly I affected her, I sought to procure your union, not like a lover, but as a true husband, nor would I immodestly touch her, till first, as herself can testify, with the words becoming wedlock, and the ring also, I espoused her, demanding of her if she would accept me as her husband, and she answered me with her full consent. Wherein, if it may seem that she was deceived, I am not any way to be blamed, but she, for not demanding what and who I was.

" This then is the great evil. the great offence, and the great injury committed by my friend Gisippus, and by me as a lover ; that Sophronia is secretly become the wife of Titus Quintus Fulvius. And for this cause, like spies you watch him, threaten him daily, as if you intended to tear him in pieces. What could you do more, if he had given her to a man of the very vilest condition ? to a villain, to a slave ? What prisons, what fetters, or what torments are sufficient for this fact ? But leaving those frivolous matters, let us come to discourse of more moment, and better beseeming your attention.

"The time is come that I may no longer continue here, because Publius my father is dead, and I must needs return to Rome, wherefore being minded to take Sophronia thither with me, I was the more willing to acquaint you therewith, as also what else I have said, which otherwise had been concealed from you. Nor can you but take it in good part, if you be wise, and rest well contented with what is done, considering if I had any intention either to deceive, or otherwise wrong you, I could have basely left her, and made a scorn both of her and you, you not having any power to stay me here. But the gods will never permit that any courteous Roman should ever conceive so vile and degenerate a thought.

"Sophronia, by ordination of the gods, by force of human laws, and by the laudable consent of my friend Gisippus, as also the powerful command of love, is mine. But you perchance imagining yourselves to be wiser than the gods, or any other men whatsoever, may think ill of it, and more brutishly than beasts, condemn their working in two kinds, which would be offensive to me. The one is, the detaining of Sophronia from me, of whom you have no power but what pleaseth me. The other is your bitter threatenings against Gisippus, my dear friend, to whom you are in duty obliged. In both which cases, how unreasonable soever you carry yourselves, I intend not at this time to press any further. But rather let me counsel you like a friend, to cease your hatred and disdain, and suffer Sophronia to be delivered me, that I may depart contentedly from you as a kinsman, and, being absent, remain your friend, assuring you, that whether what is done shall please or else displease yon, if you purpose to proceed any otherwise, I will take Gisippus along with me, and when I come to Rome, take such sure order to fetch her hence, who in justice is mine, even in mere despite of you all ; and then you shall feel by sound experience, how powerful is the just indignation of the wronged Romans."

When Titus had thus concluded his oration, he rose up with a stern and discontented countenance and took Gisippus by the hand, plainly declaring that he made small account of all the rest that were in the temple, and shaking his head at them, rather menaced than any otherwise seemed to care, or stand in fear of them.

They which tarried when they were gone, considering partly of the reasons alleged by Titus, and partly terrified by his latest speeches, became induced to like well of his alliance and amity as, with common consent, they concluded, that it was much better to accept Titus as their kinsman, seeing Gisippus had made manifest refusal thereof, than to lose the kindred of the one and procure the hatred of the other. Wherefore they went to seek Titus, and said unto him, they were very well contented that Sophronia should be his wife, he their dear and loving kinsman, and Gisippus to remain their much respected friend. And embracing one another, making a solemn feast, such as in the like cases is necessarily required, they departed from him, presently sending Sophronia to him, who making a virtue of necessity, converted her love in short time

after to Titus in as effectual manner as formerly she had done to
Gisippus, and so was sent away with him to Rome, where she was
received and welcomed with very great honour.

Gisippus remaining still at Athens, in small regard of either
theirs or his own friends, not long after, by means of sundry
troublesome citizens, and partialities happening among the common
people, was banished from Athens, and he, as also all his family,
condemned to perpetual exile ; during which tempestuous time,
Gisippus was become not only wretchedly poor, but wandered abroad
as a common beggar, in which miserable condition he travelled to
Rome to try if Titus would take any acknowledgment of him.
Understanding that he was living, and one most respected among
the Romans as being a great commander and a senator, he inquired
for the place where he dwelt, and going to be near about his house,
stayed there so long till Titus came home, yet not daring to manifest
himself, or speak a word to him in regard of his poor and miserable
estate, but strove to have him see him to the end, that he might
acknowledge and call him by his name ; notwithstanding, Titus
passed by him without either speech or looking on him. Which
when Gisippus perceived, and making full account that, at the least,
he would remember him, in regard of former courtesies done to him,
confounded with grief and desperate thoughts, he departed thence,
never meaning to see him any more.

Now, in regard it was night, he had eaten nothing all that day,
nor provided of one penny to buy him any food, wandered he knew
not whither, desiring rather to die than live. He came at last to
an old ruinous part of the city, overspread with briars and bushes,
and seldom resorted unto by any, where, finding a hollow cave or
vault, he entered it, meaning there to wear away the comfortless
night, and, laying him down on the hard ground, almost stark-naked,
and without any warm garments, over-wearied with weeping, at
last he fell into a sleep.

It fortuned that two men who had been abroad the same night,
committing thefts and robberies together, somewhat very early in
the morning came to the same cave, intending there to share and
divide their booties ; and differences happening between them
about it, he that was the stronger person slew there the other, and
then went away with the whole purchase.

Gisippus having heard and seen the manner of this accident, was
not a little joyful, because he had now found a way to death, without laying any violent hand on himself ; for life being very loath-
some to him, it was his only desire to die. Wherefore he would not
budge from the place, but tarried there so long till the sergeants and
officers of justice (by the information of him that did the deed) came
thither well attended, and furiously led Gisippus thence to prison.
Being examined concerning this bloody fact, he plainly confessed
that he himself had committed the murder, and afterward would
not depart from the cave, but purposely stayed for apprehension, as
being truly touched with compunction for so foul an offence, upon
which peremptory confession Marcus Varro, being then Prætor, gave

sentence that he should be crucified on a cross, as it was the usual manner of death in those days. Titus, chancing to come at the same time into the Prætorium, advisedly beholding the face of the condemned man, as he sate upon the bench, knew him to be Gisippus, not a little wondering at this strange accident, the poverty of his estate, and what occasion should bring him thither, especially in the questioning for his life, and before the tribunal of justice.

His soul earnestly thirsting by all possible means to help and defend him, and no other course could be now taken for safety of his life but by accusing himself, to excuse and clear the other of the crime; he stepped from off the judgment bench, and crowding through the throng to the bar, called out to the Prætor in this manner : " Marcus Varro, recall thy sentence given on the condemned man sent away, because he is truly guiltless and innocent. With one bloody blow have I offended the gods, by killing that wretched man whom the sergeants found this morning slain ; wherefore, noble Prætor, let no innocent man's blood be shed for it, but only mine, that have offended."

Marcus Varro stood like a man confounded with admiration, being very sorry for that which the whole assistants had both seen and heard, and yet he could not, with honour, desist from what must needs be done, but would perform the law's severe injunction ; and sending for condemned Gisippus back again, in the presence of Titus thus he spake to him :

"How camest thou so madly incensed as, without any torment inflicted on thee, to confess an offence by thee never committed? Art thou weary of thy life? Thou chargest thyself falsely to be the person who this last night murdered the man in the cave, and there is another that voluntarily also doth confess his guiltiness."

Gisippus lifting up his eyes, and perceiving it was Titus, conceived immediately that he had done this only for his deliverance, as one that remembered him sufficiently, and would not be ungrateful for former kindnesses received. Wherefore the tears flowing abundantly down his cheeks, he said to Judge Varro : " It was none but I that murdered the man ; wherefore I commiserate the case of this noble gentleman, Titus, who speaks now too late for the safety of my life." Titus, on the other side, said : " Noble Prætor, this man, as thou seest, is a stranger here, and was found without any weapon, fast asleep by the dead body. Thou mayest then easily perceive that merely the miserable condition wherein he is hath made him desperate, and he would make mine offence the occasion of his death. Absolve him, and send me to the cross, for none but I only have deserved to die for this notorious fact."

Varro was amazed to observe with what earnest instance each of them strove to excuse the other, which half persuaded him in his soul that they were both guiltless. And as he was starting up with full intent to acquit them, a young man, who had stood there all this while, and observed the hard pleading on either side, he crowded into the bar, being named Publius Ambastus, a fellow of

lewd life and utterly out of hopes, as being debauched in all his fortunes, and known amongst the Romans to be a notorious thief, who
verily had committed the murder. Well knew his conscience that
none of them were guilty of the crime wherewith each so wilfully
charged himself, being therefore truly touched with remorse, he
stepped before Marcus Varro, saying :
"Honourable Prætor, mine own horrid and abominable actions
have induced me thus to intrude myself for clearing the strict contention between these two persons. And, questionless, some god
or greater power hath tormented my wretched soul, and so com-
punctually solicited me, as I cannot choose but make open confession of my sin. Here therefore I do apparently publish that neither
of these men is guilty of the offence, wherewith so wilfully each
chargeth himself. I am the villain who this morning murdered the
man in the cave, one of no greater honesty than myself ; and seeing
this poor man lie there sleeping, while we were dividing the stolen
booties between us, I slew my companion because I would be the
sole possessor. As for noble Lord Titus, he had no reason thus to
accuse himself, because he is a man of no such base quality. Let
them both be delivered, and inflict the sentence of death on me."

Octavius Cæsar, to whom tidings were brought of this rare
accident, commanding them all three to be brought before him,
would needs understand the whole history in every particular as all
had happened, which was substantially related to him ; whereupon
Octavius quitted them all three ; the two noble friends because
they were innocent, and the third for openly revealing the very
truth.

Titus took home with him his friend Gisippus, and after he had
sharply reproved him for his distrust and cold credence of his
friendship, he brought him to Sophronia, who welcomed him as
lovingly as if he had been her natural-born brother, bemoaning
his hard and disastrous fortune, and taking especial care to convert all passed distresses into a happy and a comfortable change,
fitting him with garments and attendants beseeming his degree in
nobility and virtue. Titus, out of his honourable bounty, imparted
half his lands and rich possessions to him, and afterward gave him
in marriage his own sister, a most beautiful lady, named Fulvia,
saying to him beside : "My dear friend Gisippus, it remaineth now
in thine own election whether thou wilt live here still with me, or
return back to Athens with all the wealth which I have bestowed
on thee." But Gisippus being one way constrained by the sentence
of banishment from his native city, and then again, in regard of
the constant love which he bare to so true and thankful a friend as
Titus was, concluded to live there as a loyal Roman, where he
with his Fulvia, and Titus with his fair Sophronia, lived long after
together in one and the same house, augmenting daily, if possible
it might be, their amity beyond all other equalizing.

A most sacred thing therefore is cordial amity, worthy not only
of singular reverence, but also to be honoured with eternal commendation, as being the only wise mother of all magnificence and

honesty, the sister of charity and gratitude, the enemy to hatred and avarice, and which is always ready, without waiting to be requested, to extend all virtuous actions to others which she would have done to herself. Her rare and divine effects, in these contrary times of ours, are turned into shame for the miserable covetousness of men who, respecting nothing but only their particular benefit, have banished true amity to the utmost confines of the whole earth, and sent her into perpetual exile.

What love, what wealth, or affinity of kindred, could have made Gissipus feel, even in the innermost part of his soul, the fervent compassion, the tears, the sighs of Titus, and with such efficacy as plainly appeared, to make him consent that his fair elected spouse, by him so dearly esteemed, should become the wife of his companion, but only the precious league of friendship? What laws, what threatenings, what fears, could cause the young arms of Gisippus to abstain embraces, betaking himself to solitary walks, and obscure places, when in his own home he might have enjoyed so matchless a beauty—who perhaps desired it so much as himself—but only the title of friendship? What greatness, what merits, or precedence, could cause Gisippus not to care for the loss of his kindred—those of Sophronia, yea, of Sophronia herself—not respecting the dishonest murmurings of base-minded people, their vile and contemptible language, scorns, and mockeries, and all to content and satisfy a friend, but only divine friendship?

Come now likewise to the other side. What occasions could compel noble Titus, so promptly and deliberately to procure his own death, to rescue his friend from the cross, and inflict the pain and shame upon himself, pretending not to see or know Gisippus at all, had it not been wrought by powerful friendship? What cause else could make Titus so liberal in dividing, with such willingness, the larger part of his patrimony to Gisippus, when fortune had dispossessed him of his own, but only heaven-born friendship? What else could have procured Titus, without any further dilation, fear, or suspicion, to give his sister Fulvia in marriage to Gisippus, when he saw him reduced to such extreme poverty, disgrace, and misery, but only infinite friendship? To what end do men care then to covet and procure great multitudes of kindred, store of brethren, numbers of children, and to increase, with their own moneys, plenty of servants, when by the least loss and damage happening, they forget all duty to father. brother, or master? Amity and true friendship is of a quite contrary nature, satisfying, in that sacred bond, the obligation due to all degrees, both of parentage and all alliances else.

THE NINTH NOVEL.

Saladin the great Soldan of Babylon, in the habit of a merchant, was honourably received and welcomed into the house of Messer Torello d'Istria, who travelling to the Holy Land, prefixed a certain time to his wife for to return back to her again, wherein if he failed it was lawful for her to take another husband. By clouding himself in the disguise of a falconer, the Soldan took notice of him, and did him many great honours. Afterward Torello falling sick, by magical art he was conveyed in one night to Pavia, when his wife was to be married on the morrow ; where making himself known to her, all was disappointed, and she went home with him to his own house.

FILOMENA having concluded her discourse, and the rare acknowledgment which Titus made of his esteemed friend Gisippus extolled justly as it deserved by all that company, the King reserving the last office to Dioneo—as it was at the first granted him—began to speak thus :

Without all question to the contrary, worthy ladies, nothing can be more truly said than what Filomena hath delivered concerning amity ; and her complaint in the conclusion of her novel is not without great reason, to see it so slenderly reverenced and respected nowadays among all men. But if we had met her in duty only for correcting the abuses of iniquity and the malevolent courses of this preposterous age, I could proceed further in this just cause of complaint. But because our end aimeth at matters of other nature, it cometh to my memory to tell you of a history, which, perhaps, may seem somewhat long, but altogether pleasant, concerning a magnificent act of great Saladin, to the end that by observing those things which you shall hear in my novel, if we cannot, by reason of our manifold imperfections, entirely compass the amity of any one, yet at least we may take delight in stretching our kindness, in good deeds, so far as we are able, in hope one day after some worthy reward will ensue thereon, as thereto justly appertaining.

Let me tell you then that, as it is affirmed by many, in the time of the Emperor Frederick, first of that name, the Christians, for the better recovery of the Holy Land, resolved to make a general voyage over the seas, which being understood by Saladin, a very worthy Prince, and then Soldan of Babylon, he concluded with himself that he would, in person, go see what preparation the Christian potentates made for the war, that he might the better provide for himself. Having settled all things orderly in Egypt for the business, and making an outward appearance as if he purposed a pilgrimage to Mecca, he set onwards on his journey, habited like a merchant, attended only with two of his most noble and wisest baschas and three waiting servants.

When he had visited many Christian provinces, and was riding

through Lombardy to pass the mountains, it fortuned in his jour-
neying from Milan to Pavia, and the day being very far spent, so
that night hastened speedily on him, he met with a gentleman,
named Messer Torello d'Istria, but dwelling at Pavia, who with
his men, hawks, and hounds, went to a house of his, seated in a
pleasant place, and on the river of Tesino. Signior Torello seeing
such men making towards him, presently imagined that they were
some gentle strangers, and such he desired to respect with honour.
    Wherefore Saladin demanding of one of Torello's men how far,
as then, it was to Pavia, and whether they might reach thither by
such an hour as would admit their entrance into the city, Torello
would not suffer his servant to return the answer, but replied thus
himself: "Sir," quoth he, "you cannot reach Pavia, but night will
abridge you of any entrance there." "I beseech you then, sir,"
answered Saladin, "favour us so much, because we are all strangers
in these parts, as to tell us where we may be well lodged." "That
shall I, sir," said Torello, "and very gladly, too."
    "Even at the instant, sir, as we met with you, I had determined
in my mind to send one of my servants somewhat near to Pavia
about a business concerning myself. He shall go along with you,
and conduct you to a place where you will be very well entertained."
So, stepping to him who was of best discretion amongst his men,
he gave order to him what should be done, and sent him with them.
Himself making haste by a far nearer way, caused supper to be prepared in worthy manner, and the tables to be covered in his garden;
and all things being in good readiness, he sate down at his door to
attend the coming of the guests. The serving man, discoursing
with the gentleman on divers occasions, guided them by such
unusual passages as, before they could discern it, he brought him
to his master's house, where, so soon as Torello saw them
arrived, he went forth to meet them, assuring them all of most
hearty welcome.
    Saladin, who was a man of acute understanding, did well per-
ceive that this knight Torello misdoubted his going with him, if,
when he met him, he should have invited him; and, therefore,
because he would not be denied of entertaining him into his house,
he made choice of this kind and honourable course, which caused
him to return this answer: "Gentle sir, if courtesy from one man to
another do deserve condemning, then may we justly complain of
you, who, meeting us upon the way, which you have shortened by
your kindness, and which we are no way able to deserve, we are
constrained to accept, taking you to be the mirror of courtesy."
Torello, being a knight of ingenious apprehension and well lan-
guaged, replied thus:
    "Gentlemen, this courtesy, seeing you term it so, which you
receive of me, in regard of that justly belonging to you, as your
faces do sufficiently inform me, is matter of very slender account;
but assuredly, out of Pavia, you could not have any lodging deserving to be termed good. And therefore let it not be displeasing to
you, if you have a little gone forth of the common roadway, to have

your entertainment somewhat better, as many travellers are easily induced to do."

Having thus spoken, all the people of the house showed themselves in serviceable manner to the gentlemen, taking their horses as they dismounted, and Torello himself conducted the three gentlemen into three several fair chambers, which in costly manner were prepared for them, where their boots were plucked off, fair napkins with manchets lay ready, and delicate wines to refresh their wearied spirits, much pretty conference being intercoursed, till supper-time invited them thence.

Saladin and they that were with him spake the Latin tongue very readily, by which means they were the better understood ; and Torello seemed, in their judgment, to be the most gracious, complete, and best-spoken gentleman as ever they met with in all their journey. It appeared also, on the other side, to Messer Torello, that the guests were men of great merit, and worthy of much more esteem than there he could use towards them ; wherefore it did highly distaste him that he had no more friends there this night to keep them company, or himself better provided for their entertainment, which he intended on the morrow to recompense with larger amends at dinner.

Hereupon, having instructed one of his men with what he intended, he sent him to Pavia, which was not far off (and where he kept no door shut) to his wife, named Adalieta, a woman singularly wise and of a noble spirit, needing little or no direction, especially when she knew her husband's mind. As they were walking in the garden, Torello desired to understand of whence and what they were ; whereto Saladin thus answered : " Sir, we are Cyprian merchants, coming now from Cyprus, and are travelling to Paris about affairs of importance." " Now, trust me, sir," replied Torello, " I could heartily wish that this country of ours would yield such gentlemen as your Cyprus affordeth merchants." So, falling from one discourse unto another, supper was served in ; and look how best themselves pleased, so they sate at table, where, we need make no doubt, they were respected in honourable order.

So soon as the tables were withdrawn, Torello, knowing they might be weary, brought them again to their chambers, where, committing them to their good rest, himself went to bed soon after. The servant sent to Pavia delivered the message to his lady, who, not like a woman of ordinary disposition, but rather truly royal, sent Torello's servants into the city to make preparation for a feast indeed, and with lighted torches, because it was somewhat late, they invited the very greatest and noblest persons of the city, all the rooms being hanged with the richest arras, cloths of gold-work, velvet, silks, and all other rich adornments, in such manner as her husband had commanded and answerable to her own worthy mind, being no way to learn in what manner to entertain strangers.

On the morrow morning the gentlemen rose, and mounting on horseback with Signior Torello, he called for his hawks and hounds, brought them to the river, where he showed two or three fair flights ; but Saladin desiring to know which was the fairest hostelry in all Pavia, Torello answered : "Gentlemen, I will show you that myself, in regard that I have occasion to ride thither ;" which they believing, were the better contented, and rode on directly unto Pavia. Arriving there about nine of the clock, and thinking he guided them to the best inn, he brought them to his own house, where fifty of the worthiest citizens stood ready to welcome the gentlemen, embracing them as they lighted from their horses ; which Saladin and his associates perceiving, they guessed as it was indeed ; and Saladin said : "Believe me, worthy Torello, this is not answerable to my demand. You did too much yester-night, and much more than we could desire or deserve ; wherefore you might well be the sooner discharged of us, and let us travel on our journey."

"Noble gentlemen," replied Torello, "for in mine eye you seem no less, that courtesy which you met with yester-night I am to thank fortune for more than you, because you were then straitened by such necessity as urged your acceptance of my poor country house. But now this morning I shall account myself much behold-ing to you, as the like will all these worthy gentlemen here about you, if you do but answer kindness with kindness, and not to refuse to take a homely dinner with them."

Saladin and his friends being conquered with such potent per-suasions, and already dismounted from their horses, saw that all denial was merely in vain, and therefore thankfully condescending, after some few ceremonious compliments were overpast, the gentle-men conducted them to their chambers, which were most sump-tuously prepared for them, and having laid aside their riding garments, being a little refreshed with cakes and wine, they after a while descended into the dining-hall, the pomp whereof I am not able to report.

When they had washed and were seated at the tables, dinner was served in most magnificent sort, so that if the emperor himself had been there he could not have been more sumptuously served ; and although Saladin and his baschas were noble lords and wanted to see matters of admiration, yet could they do no less now but rather exceed in marvel, considering the quality of the knight, whom they knew to be a citizen, and no prince or great lord. Dinner being ended, and divers familiar conferences passing between them, because it was exceeding hot, the gentlemen of Pavia, as it pleased Torello to appoint, went to repose themselves a while, and he, keeping company with his three guests, brought them into a goodly chamber, where, because he would not fail in the least scruple of courtesy, or conceal from them the richest jewel which he had, he sent for his lady and wife, because as yet they had not seen her.

She was a lady of extraordinary beauty, tall stature, very sump-tuously attired, and having two sweet sons resembling angels, she came with them waiting before her, and graciously saluted her

K

guests. At her coming they arose, and having received her with great reverence, they seated her in the midst, kindly cherishing the two children. After some gracious language passed on either side, she demanded of whence and what they were ; which they answered in the same kind as they had done before to her husband. Afterward, with a modest smiling countenance, she said : " Worthy gentlemen, let not my weak womanish discretion appear distastable in desiring to crave one especial favour from you—namely, not to refuse or disdain a small gift wherewith I purpose to present you. But considering first that women, according to their simple faculty, are able to bestow but silly gifts, so you would be pleased to respect more the person that is the giver than the quality or quantity of the gift."

Then causing to be brought for each of them two goodly gowns or robes, made after the Persian manner, the one lined through with cloth of gold, and the other with the costliest fur, not after such fashion as citizens and merchants used to wear, but rather beseeming lords of greatest account; and three light under-wearing cassocks or mandilions of carnation satin, richly embroidered with gold and pearls, and lined through with white taffety; presenting these gifts to them she said : " I desire you, gentlemen, to receive these mean trifles, such as my husband wears the like, and these other beside, considering you are so far from your wives, having travelled a long way already, and many miles more yet to overtake ; also merchants, being excellent men, affect to be comely and handsome in their habits ; although these are of slender value, yet in necessity they may do you service."

Now were Saladin and his baschas half astonished with admiration at the magnificent mind of Messer Torello, who would not forget the least part of courtesy towards them, and greatly doubted, seeing the beauty and riches of the garments, lest they were discovered by Torello. Nevertheless, one of them thus answered the lady : " Believe me, madam, these are rich gifts, not lightly either to be given or received, but in regard of your strict imposition we are not able to deny them." This being done with most gracious and courteous demeanour, she departed from them, leaving her husband to keep them still company, who furnished their servants also with divers worthy necessaries fitting for their journey.

Afterward Torello, by very much importunity, won them to stay with him all the rest of the day ; wherefore, when they had rested themselves a while, being arrayed in their newly given robes, they rode on horseback through the city. When supper-time came they supped in most honourable and worthy company, being afterwards lodged in most fair and sumptuous chambers ; and being risen in the morning, in exchange of their horses, over-wearied with travel, they found three other very richly furnished, and their men also in like manner provided, which, when Saladin had perceived, he took his baschas aside, and spake in this manner :

" By our greatest gods, I never met with any man more complete in all noble perfections, more courteous and kind, than Torello is. If all the Christian kings, in the true and heroical nature of kings, do deal so honourably as I see this knight doth, the Soldan of Babylon is not able to endure the coming of one of them, much less so many, as we see preparing to make head against us." But beholding that both refusal and acceptation was all one in the mind of Torello, after much kind language had been intercoursed between them, Saladin and his attendants mounted on horseback.

Messer Torello, with a number of his honourable friends, to the number of a hundred horse, accompanied them a great distance from the city, and although it grieved Saladin exceedingly to leave the company of Torello, so dearly was he affected to him, but necessity, which controlleth the power of all laws whatsoever, must needs divide them, yet requesting his return again that way, if possibly it might be granted, which Saladin promised, but did not perform. "Well, gentlemen," quoth Torello at parting, "I know not what you are, neither against your will do I desire it; but whether you be merchants or no, remember me in your kindness, and so to the heavenly powers I commend you." Saladin having taken his leave of all of them that were with Torello, returned him this answer: "Sir, it may one day hereafter so happen, as we shall let you see some of our merchandises, for the better confirmation of your belief and our profession."

Thus parted Messer Torello and his friends from Saladin and his company, who verily determined in the height of his mind if he should be spared with life, and the war which he expected concluded, to requite Torello with no less courtesy than he had already declared to him, conferring a long while after with his baschas, both of him and his beauteous lady, not forgetting any of their courteous actions, but gracing them all with deserved commendation.

But after they had, with very laborious pains, surveyed most of the western parts, they all took shipping and returned into Alexandria, sufficiently informed what preparation was to be made for their own defence, and Signior Torello being come back again to Pavia, consulted with his private thoughts many times after what these three travellers should be, but came far short of knowing the truth till, by experience, he became better informed.

When the time was come that the Christians were to make their passage, and wonderful great preparations in all places performed, Messen Torello, notwithstanding the tears and entreaties of his wife, determined to be one in so worthy and honourable a voyage, and having made his provision ready, nothing wanting but mounting on horseback to go where he should take shipping to his wife, whom he most entirely affected, thus he spake: "Madam, I go as thou seest in this famous voyage, as well for mine honour as also the benefit of my soul: all our goods and possessions I commit to thy virtuous care, and because I am not certain of my return back again, in regard of a thousand accidents which may happen in such

K 2

a country as I go unto, I desire only but one favour of thee, whatsoever dangers may befall me—namely, when any certain tidings
shall be brought thee of my death, to stay no longer before thy second
marriage, but one year, one month, and one day, to begin on this
day of my departing from thee." The lady, who wept exceedingly,
presently thus answered : " Alas ! sir, I know not how to carry myself in such extremity of grief as now you leave me ; but if my life
surmount the fortitude of sorrow, and whatsoever shall happen to
you for certainty, either life or death, I will live and die the wife of
Torello, and make my obsequies in his memory only."

" Not so, madam," replied her husband, " not so ; be not over-rash
in promising anything, albeit I am well assured that so much as
consisteth in thy strength I make no question of thy performance ;
but consider withal, dear heart, thou art a young woman, beautiful,
of great parentage, and no way thereto inferior in the blessing of
fortune.

" Thy virtues are many and universally both divulged and known ;
in which respect, I make no doubt, but divers and sundry great
lords and gentlemen, if but the least rumour of my death be noised,
will make suit for thee to thy parents and brethren, from whose
violent solicitings wouldest thou never so resolutely make resistance,
yet thou canst not be able to defend thyself, but whether thou wilt
or no, thou must yield to please them, and this is the only reason
why I would tie thee to this limited time, and not one day or
minute longer."

Adalieta, sweetly hugging him in her arms, and melting herself
in kisses, sighs, and tears on his face, said : " Well, sir, I will do so
much as I am able in this your most kind and loving imposition,
and when I shall be compelled to the contrary, yet rest thus constantly assured that I will not break this your charge so much as in
thought, praying ever heartily to the heavenly powers that they
will direct your course home again to me, before your prefixed
date, or else I shall live in continual languishing." In the knitting
up of this woful parting, embracing and kissing each other infinite
times, the lady took a ring from off her finger, and giving it to her
husband, said : " If I chance to die before I see you again,
remember me when you look on this." He receiving the ring, and
bidding all the rest of his friends farewell, mounted on horseback
and rode away well attended.

Being come to Genoa, he and his company boarded a galley, and
in few days after arrived at Acre, where they joined themselves
with the Christian army, wherein there happened a very dangerous
mortality, during which time of so sharp visitation, the cause unknown whence it proceeded, whether through the industry or rather
the good fortune of Saladin, well-near all the rest of the Christians,
which escaped death, were surprised his prisoners, without a blow
strucken, and sundered and imprisoned in divers towns and cities,
amongst the which number of prisoners it was Signior Torello's
chance to be one, and walked in bonds to Alexandria, where

being unknown, and fearing lest he should be discovered, constrained thereto merely by necessity, he showed himself in the condition of a falconer, wherein he was very excellently experienced, and by which means his profession was made known to Saladin, he delivered out of prison, and created the Soldan's falconer.

Torello, whom the Soldan called by no other name than the Christian, neither of them knowing the other, sadly now remembered his departure from Pavia, devising and practising many times how he might escape thence, he could not compass it by any possible means. Wherefore certain ambassadors being sent by the Genoese to redeem divers citizens of theirs, there detained as prisoners, and being ready to return home again; he purposed to write to his wife that he was living, and would repair to her so soon as he could, desiring the still continual remembrance of her limited time. By close and cunning means he wrote the letter, earnestly entreating one of the ambassadors, who knew him perfectly, but made no outward appearance thereof, to deal in such sort for him, that the letter might be delivered to the hands of the Abbot of San Pietro in Ciel d'Oro, who was indeed his uncle.

While Torello remained in this his falconer's condition, it fortuned upon a day that Saladin, conversing with him about his hawks, Torello chanced to smile, and used such a kind of gesture or motion with his lips, which Saladin, when he was in his house at Pavia, had heedfully observed, and by this note instantly he remembered Signior Torello, and began to eye him very respectively, persuading himself that he was the same man. And therefore falling from the former kind of discoursing : "Tell me, Christian," quoth Saladin, "what countryman art thou of the west?" "Sir," answered Signior Torello, "I am by country a Lombard, born in a city called Pavia, a poor man, and of as poor condition."

So soon as Saladin had heard these words, becoming assured in that which, but now, he doubted, he said within himself : "Now the gods have given me time, wherein I may make known to this man how thankfully I accepted his kind courtesy, and cannot easily forget it." Then, without saying anything else, causing his wardrobe to be set open, he took him with him thither, and said: "Christian, observe well all these garments, and quicken thy remembrance, in telling me truly whether thou hast seen either of them before now or no." Signior Torello looked on them all advisedly, and espied those two especial garments which his wife had given one of the strange merchants ; yet he durst not credit it, or that possibly it could be the same ; nevertheless he said : "Sir, I do not know any of them, but true it is, that these two do resemble two such robes as I was wont to wear myself, or the like were given to three merchants that happened to visit my poor house."

Now could Saladin contain no longer, but embracing him joyfully in his arms, he said : "Signior Torello d'Istria, and I am one of those three merchants to whom your wife gave these robes, and

now the time is come to give you credible intelligence of my merchandise, as I promised at my departing from you, for such a time,
I told you, would come at length." Torello was both glad and
bashful together ; glad, that he had entertained such a guest; and
bashfully ashamed, that his welcome had not exceeded in more
bountiful manner. "Torello," replied Saladin, "seeing the gods
have sent you so happily to me ; account you yourself to be solely
lord here, for I am now no more than a private man."

I am not able to express their counterchange of courtesy ; Saladin commanding him to be clothed in royal garments, and brought
in presence of his very greatest lords, where having spoken liberally
in his due commendation, he commanded them to honour him as
himself, if they expected any grace and favour from him, which
every one did immediately, but, above all the rest, those two baschas
which accompanied Saladin at his house. The greatness of this
pomp and glory, so suddenly thrown on Messer Torello, made him
half forget all matters of Lombardy ; and so much the rather,
because he had no doubt at all but that his letters were safely come
to the hands of his uncle.

Here I am to tell you, that in the camp or army of the Christians,
on the day when Saladin made his surprisal, there was a pro-
vincial gentleman, dead and buried, who was Messer Torello di
Dignes, a man of very honourable and great esteem, in which
respect Messer Torello d'Istria, known throughout the army by
his nobility and valour, whosoever heard that Messer Torello was
dead, believed it to be Torello d'Istria, and not he of Dignes, so
that Torello d'Istria's unknown surprisal and thraldom made it
also to pass for an assured truth.

Beside many Italians returning home, and carrying this report
or credible, some were so audaciously presumptuous, as they
avouched upon their oaths, that not only they saw him dead, but
were present at his burial likewise. Which rumour coming to the
ear of his wife, and likewise to his kindred and hers, procured a
great and grievous mourning among them, and all that happened
to hear thereof.

Over tedious time it would require to relate at large the public
grief and sorrow with the continual lamentations of his wife, who,
within some few months after, became tormented with new marriage
solicitings, before she had half sighed for the first ; the very
greatest persons of Lombardy making the motion, being daily
followed and furthered by her own brothers and friends. Still,
drowned in tears she returned denial, till in the end when no contradiction could prevail, to satisfy her parents, and the importunate
pursuers, she was constrained to reveal the charge imposed on her
by her husband, which she had vowed infallibly to keep, and till
that very time she could in nowise consent.

While wooing for a second wedding with Adalieta, proceeding
in this manner at Pavia, it chanced on a day that Signior Torello
had espied a man in Alexandria, whom he saw with the Genoese

ambassadors, when they set thence towards Genoa with their galleys. And causing him to be sent for, he demanded of him the success of the voyage, and when the galleys arrived at Genoa; whereto he returned him this answer : "My lord, our galleys made a very fatal voyage, as it is already too well known in Crete, where my dwelling is. For when we drew near to Sicily, there suddenly arose a very dangerous north-west wind, which drove us on the quicksands of Barbary, where not any man escaped with life, only myself excepted, but in the wreck two of my brethren perished."

Messer Torello, giving credit to the man's words, because they were most true indeed, and remembering also that the time limited to his wife drew near, expiring within very few days, and no news now possible to be sent thither of his life, his wife would question-less be married again ; he fell into such a deep conceited melancholy, as food and sleep forsook him, whereupon he kept his bed, setting down his peremptory resolution for death. When Saladin, who dearly loved him, heard thereof, he came in all haste to see him, and having, by many earnest persuasions and entreaties, understood the cause of his melancholy and sickness, he very severely reproved him because he would no sooner acquaint him therewith. Many kind and comfortable speeches he gave him, with constant assur-ance, that if he were so minded, he would so order the business for him, as he should be at Pavia by the same time as he had appointed to his wife, revealed to him also the manner how.

Torello verily believed the Soldan's promise, because he had often heard the possibility of performance, and others had effected as much divers times elsewhere ; whereupon he began to comfort himself, soliciting the Soldan earnestly that it might be accom-plished, Saladin sent for one of his sorcerers, of whose skill he had formerly had experience, to take a direct course how Messer Torello should be carried in one night to Pavia, and being in his bed. The magician undertook to do it, but, for the gentleman's more ease, he must first be possessed with an entranced dead sleep. Saladin being then assured of the deed's full effecting, he came again to Torello, and finding him to be settled for Pavia, if possible it might be accomplished by the determined time, or else no other expectation but death, he said unto him as follows :

"Messer Torello, if with true affection you love your wife, and misdoubt her marriage to some other man, I protest unto you by the supreme powers that you do deserve no reprehension in any manner whatsoever. For of all the ladies that ever I have seen, she is the only woman whose carriage, virtues, and civil speaking, setting aside beauty, which is but a fading flower, deserveth most graciously to be respected, much more to be effected in the highest degree. It were to be no mean favour of our gods, seeing fortune directed your course so happily hither, that for the short or long time we have to live, we might reign equally together in these kingdoms under my subjection. But if such grace may not be granted me, yet seeing it stands mainly upon the peril of your life, to be at Pavia again by your own limited time, it is my chiefest comfort that I am therewith acquainted, because I intended to have you conveyed thither, yea, even into your own house, in such honourable order as your virtues do justly merit, which in regard it cannot be so conveniently performed but as I have informed you, and as the necessity of the case urgently commandeth, accept it as it may be best accomplished."

"Great Saladin," answered Torello, "effects, without words, have already sufficiently warranted your gracious disposition towards me, far beyond any requital remaining in me ; your word only being enough for my comfort in this case, either dying or living. But in regard you have taken such order for my departure hence, I desire to have it done with all possible expedition, because to-morrow is the very last day that I am to be absent." Saladin protested that it should be done, and the same evening in the great hall of his royal palace, commanded a rich and costly bed to be set up, the mattrass formed after the Alexandrian manner, of velvet and cloth of gold ; the quilts, counterpoints, and coverings, sumptuously embroidered with orient pearls and precious stones, supposed to be of inestimable value, and two rarely wrought pillows, such as best beseemed so stately a bed, the curtains and vallance every way equal to the other pomp.

Which being done, he commanded that Torello, who was indifferently recovered, should be attired in one of his own sumptuous Saracen robes, the very fairest and richest that ever was seen, and on his head a majestical turban, after the manner of his own wearing ; and the hour appearing to be somewhat late, he, with many of his baschas, went to the chamber where Torello was, and sitting down a while by him, in tears thus he spake : "Messer Torello, the hour for sundering you and me is now very near ; and because I cannot bear you company in regard of the business you go about, and which by no means will admit it, I am to take my leave of you in this chamber, and therefore I am come to do it. But before I bid you farewell, let me entreat you by the love and friendship confirmed between us, to be mindful of me, and to take such order, your affairs being fully finished in Lombardy, that I may once more enjoy the sight of you here, for a mutual solace and satisfaction of our minds, which are now divided by this urgent haste. Till which may be granted, let me want no visitation of your kind letters, commanding thereby of me whatsoever here can be possibly done for you ; assuring yourself no man living can command me as you do." Messer Torello could not forbear weeping, but being much hindered thereby, answered in few words, that he could not possibly forget his gracious favours and extraordinary benefits used towards him, but would accomplish whatsoever he commanded, according as Heaven did enable him. Hereupon Saladin embracing him, and kissing his forehead, said : "All my gods go with you, and guard you from any peril ;" departing so out of the chamber weeping, and his baschas, having likewise taking their leaves of Thorello, fol-

lowed Saladin into the hall, whereas the bed stood readily prepared. Because it waxed very late, and the magician also there
attending for his despatch, the physician went with the potion to
Torello, and persuading him, in the way of friendship, that it was
only to strengthen him after his great weakness, he drank it off,
being thereby immediately entranced, and so presently sleeping
was, by Saladin's command, laid on the sumptuous and costly
bed, whereon stood an imperial crown of infinite value, appearing,
by a description engraven on it, that Saladin sent it to Adalieta,
the wife of Torello. On his finger he put a ring, wherein was
enchased an admirable carbuncle, which seemed like a flaming
torch, the value thereof not to be estimated. By him likewise he
laid a rich sword, with the girdle, hangers, and other furniture, such
as seldom can be seen the like. Then he laid a jewel on the pillow
by him, so sumptuously embellished with pearls and precious
stones as might have beseemed the greatest monarch in the world
to wear. Last of all, on either side of them he set two great basons
of pure gold, full of double ducats, many cords of orient pearls,
rings, girdles, and other costly jewels, over-tedious to be recounted,
and kissing him once more as he lay in his bed, commanded the
magician to despatch and be gone.

Instantly, the bed and Torello in it, in the presence of Saladin,
was invisibly carried thence, and while he sat conferring with his
baschas, the bed, Signior Torello, and all the rich jewels about
him, was transported, and set in the Church of San Pietro in Ciel
d'Oro in Pavia—according to his own request, and soundly sleeping—being placed directly before the high altar. Afterward, when
the bells rung to matins, the sexton entering the church with a light
in his hand, where he beheld a light of greater splendour, and suddenly espied the sumptuous bed there standing, not only was he
smitten into admiration, but he ran away also very fearfully. When
the abbot and the monks met him thus running into the cloister,
they became amazed, and demanded the reason why he ran in such
haste, which the sexton told them. "How," quoth the abbot,
"thou art no child, or a new-come-hither, to be so easily affrighted
in our holy church, where spirits can have no power to walk. God
and Saint Peter, we hope, are stronger for us than so ; wherefore
turn back with us, and let us see the cause of thy fear."

Having lighted many torches, the abbot and his monks entered
with the sexton into the church, where they beheld the wonderful
rich bed, and the knight lying fast asleep in it. While they stood
all in amazement, not daring to approach near the bed, whereon lay
such costly jewels, it chanced that Signior Torello awaked, and
breathed forth a most vehement sigh. The monks and the abbot
seeing him to stir, ran all away in fear, crying out aloud : "God and
Saint Peter defend us."

By this time Torello had opened his eyes, and looking round
about him, perceiving that he was in the place of Saladin's promise, whereof he was not a little joyful, Wherefore sitting up in

the bed, and particularly observing all the things about him, albeit he knew sufficiently the magnificence of Saladin, yet now it appeared far greater to him, and imagined more largely thereof, than he could do before. But yet without any other ceremony, seeing the flight of the monks, hearing their cry, and perceiving the reason, he called the abbot by his name, desiring him not to be afraid, for he was his nephew Torello, and no other.

When the abbot heard this, he was ten times more affrighted than before, because, by public fame, he had been so many months dead and buried; but receiving by true arguments better assurance of him, and hearing him still calling him by his name, blessing himself with the sign of the cross, he went somewhat nearer to the bed, when Torello said: "My loving uncle, and religious holy father, whereof are you afraid? I am your nephew, newly returned from beyond the seas." The abbot, seeing his beard to be grown long, and his habit after the Arabian fashion, yet did collect some resemblance of his former countenance, and being better persuaded of him, took him by the hand, saying:

"Son, thou art happily returned, yet there is not any in our city but doth verily believe thee to be dead, and therefore do not much wonder at our fear. Moreover, I dare assure thee that thy wife Adalieta, being conquered by the controlling command and threatenings of her kindred, but much against her own mind, is this very morning to be married to a new husband, and the marriage-feast is solemnly prepared in honour of this second nuptials."

Torello arising out of the bed, gave gracious salutations to the abbot and his monks, entreating earnestly of them all that no word might be spoken of his return until he had completed an important business. Afterward, having safely secured the bed and all the rich jewels, he fully acquainted the abbot with all his past fortunes, whereof he was immeasurably joyful, and having satisfied him concerning the new-elected husband, Torello said unto the abbot: "Uncle, before any rumour of my return, I would gladly see my wife's behaviour at this new briding-feast; and although men of religion are seldom seen at such jovial meetings, yet, for my sake, do you so order the matter that I, as an Arabian stranger, may be a guest under your protection:" whereto the abbot very gladly and joyfully condescended.

In the morning he sent to the bridegroom, and advertised him that he, with a stranger newly arrived, intended to dine with him, which the gentleman accepted in thankful manner. And when dinner-time came, Torello in his strange disguise went with the abbot to the bridegroom's house, where he was looked on with admiration of all the guests, but not known or suspected by any one, because the abbot reported him to be a Saracen, and sent by the Soldan, in embassage, to the King of France. Torello was seated at a by-table, but directly opposite to the new bride, whom he much delighted to look on, and easily collected by her sad countenance that she was scarcely well pleased with this new nuptials. She likewise beheld him very often, not in regard of any knowledge she took of him, for the bushiness of his beard, strangeness of habit, but most of all, firm belief of his death, was the main prevention.

At such a time as Torello thought it convenient to approve how far he was fallen out of her remembrance, he took the ring which she gave him at his departure, and calling a young page that waited on none but the bride, said to him in Italian : " Fair youth, go to the bride, and saluting her from me, tell her it is a custom in my country that when any stranger, as I am here, sitteth before a new-married bride, as now she is, in sign that he is welcome to her feast she sendeth the same cup wherein she drinketh herself, full of the best wine, and when the stranger hath drunk so much as him pleaseth, the bride then pledgeth him with all the rest." The page delivered the message to the bride, who being a woman of honourable disposition, and reputing him to be a noble gentleman, to testify that his presence there was very acceptable to her, she commanded a fair cup of gold, which stood directly before her, to be neatly washed, and when it was filled with excellent wine, caused it to be carried to the stranger, and so it was done presently according as she commanded.

Torello, having drunk a hearty draught to the bride, conveyed the ring into the cup before that any person could perceive it, and having left but small store of wine in it, covered the cup and sent it again to the bride, who received it very graciously, and to honour the stranger in the country's custom, drank up the rest of the wine, and, espying the ring, she took it forth undescried by any. Knowing it to be the same ring which she gave Messer Torello at his parting from her, she fixed her eyes often upon it, and as often on him, whom she thought to be a stranger, the cheerful blood mounting up into her cheeks and returning again with remembrance to her heart, that, howsoever thus disguised, he only was her husband.

Like one in Bacchus' throes, up furiously she started, and throwing down the table before her, cried out aloud : " This is my lord and husband ! this truly is my lord Torello !" So, running to the table where he sate, without regard of all the riches thereon, down she threw it likewise, and, clasping her arms about his neck, hung so mainly on him—weeping, sobbing, and kissing him—as she could not be taken off by any of the company, nor showed any moderation in this excess of passion till Torello spake, and entreated her to be more patient, because this extremity was over-dangerous for her. Thus was the solemnity much troubled, but every one there very glad and joyful for the recovery of such a famous and worthy knight, who entreated them all to vouchsafe him silence, and so related all his fortunes to them, from the time of his departure to the instant hour ; continuing withal that he was no way offended with the new bridegroom, who, upon the so constant report of his death, deserved no blame in making election of his wife.

The bridegroom, albeit his countenance was somewhat cloudy to see his hope thus disappointed, yet granted freely that Adalieta was Torello's wife in equity, and he could not lay any claim to her. She also resigned the crown and rings which she had so lately received of her new spouse, and put that on her finger which she found in the cup, and that crown was set upon her head in honour sent her from great Saladin. In which triumphant manner she left the new bridegroom's abiding, and repaired home to Torello's house with such pomp and magnificence as never had the like been seen in Pavia before, the citizens esteeming it as a miracle that they had so happily recovered Messer Torello again.

Some part of the jewels he gave to him who had been at cost with the marriage feasting, and some to his uncle the abbot, beside a bounty bestowed on the monks. Then he sent a messenger to Saladin, with letters of the whole success, and confessing himself for ever his obliged servant, living many years after with his wife Adalieta, and using greater courtesy to strangers than ever before he had done.

In this manner ended the troubles of Signior Torello and the afflictions of his dearly affected lady, with due recompense to their honest and ready courtesies. Many strive in outward show to do the like, who, although they are sufficiently able, do perform it so basely as it rather redoundeth to their shame than honour. And therefore, if no merit ensue thereon, but only such disgrace as justly should follow, let them lay the blame upon themselves.

THE TENTH NOVEL.

The Marquess of Saluzzo, named Gualtieri, being constrained by the importunate soliciting of his lords, and other inferior people, to join himself in marriage, took a woman according to his own liking, called Griselda, she being the daughter of a poor countryman named Giannuculo, by whom he had two children, which he pretended to be secretly murdered. Afterward they being grown to years of more stature, and making show of taking in marriage another wife more worthy of his high degree and calling, made a seeming public liking of his own daughter, expulsing his wife Griselda poorly from him. But finding her incomparable patience more dearly than before, he received her into favour again, brought her home to his own palace, where, with her children, he caused her and them to be respectively honoured in despite of all her adverse enemies.

QUESTIONLESS, the King's novel did not so much exceed the rest in length, but it proved as pleasing to the whole assembly, and passed with their general approbation, till Dioneo, in a merry, jesting humour, said : "The plain, honest, simple man, that stood holding the candle to see the setting on of his mule's tail, deserved twopennyworth of more praise than all our applauding of Messer Torello." And knowing himself to be left for the last speaker, thus he began :

Mild and modest ladies, for aught I can perceive to the contrary, this day was dedicated to none but kings, soldans, and great potentates, not in favour of any inferior or meaner persons. And therefore, because I would be loth to disrank myself from the rest, I purpose to speak of a Lord Marquess, not any matter of great magnificence, but rather in a more humble nature, and forced to an honest end ; which yet I will not advise any to imitate, because perhaps they cannot so well digest it, as they did whom my novel concerneth. Thus then I begin :

It is a great while since, when among those that were Lord Marquesses of Saluzzo, the very greatest and worthiest man of them all was a young noble lord, named Gualtieri, who having neither wife nor child, spent his time in nothing else but hawking and hunting. Nor had he any mind of marriage, or to enjoy the benefit of children, wherein many did repute him the wiser. But this being distasteful to his subjects, they very often solicited him to match himself with a wife, to the end that he might not decease without an heir, nor they be left destitute of a succeeding lord, offering themselves to provide him of such a one, so well descended by father and mother as not only should confirm their hope, but also yield him high contentment, whereto the Marquess thus answered :

"Worthy friends, you would constrain me to the thing wherewith I never had any intent to meddle, considering how difficult a case it is to meet with such a woman, who can agree with a man in all his conditions. And how great the number is of them who daily happen on the contrary ! but most, and worst of all the rest, how wretched and miserable proves the life of that man who is bound to live with a wife not fit for him ! And in saying you can learn to understand the custom and qualities of children by behaviour of the fathers and mothers, and so to provide me of a wife, it is a mere argument of folly ; for neither shall I comprehend, or you either, the secret inclinations of parents—I mean of the father, and much less the complexion of the mother. But admit it were within compass of power to know them, yet it is a frequent sight, and observed every day, that daughters do resemble neither father nor mother, but that they are naturally governed by their own instinct.

"But because you are so desirous to have me fettered in the chains of wedlock, I am contented to grant what you request. And because I would have no complaint made of any but myself, if matters should not happen answerable to expectation, I will make mine own eyes my electors, and not see by any other sight. Giving you this assurance before, that if she whom I shall make choice of be not of you honoured and respected as your lady and mistress, it will ensue to your detriment, how much you have displeased me, to take a wife at your request and against mine own will."

The noblemen answered that they were well satisfied, provided that he took a wife.

Some indifferent space of time before the beauty, manners, and well-seeming virtues of a poor countryman's daughter, dwelling in no far distant village, had appeared very pleasing to the Lord Marquess, and gave him full persuasion that with her he should lead a comfortable life. And therefore without any farther search or inquisition he absolutely resolved to marry her, and having conferred with her father, agreed that his daughter should be his wife. Whereupon the Marquess made a general convocation of all his lords, barons, and other of his especial friends, from all parts of his dominion, and when they were assembled together he then spake to them in manner as followeth :

"Honourable friends, it appeared pleasing to you all, and yet, I think, you are of the same mind, that I should dispose myself to take a wife, and I thereto condescended, more to yield you content-ment than for any particular desire in myself. Let me now remem-ber you of your solemn made promise, with full consent to honour and obey her whomsoever as your sovereign lady and mistress, that I shall elect to make my wife ; and now the time is come for my exacting the performance of that promise, and which I look you must constantly keep. I have made choice of a young virgin, answerable to mine own heart and liking, dwelling not far off hence, whom I intend to make my wife, and within few days to have her brought home to my palace. Let your care and diligence then extend so far as to see that the feast may be sumptuous and her entertainment to be most honourable, to the end that I may receive as much contentment in your promise performed as you shall perceive I do in my choice."

The lords and all the rest were wonderfully joyful to hear him so well inclined, expressing no less by their shouts and jocund suffrages, protesting cordially that she should be welcomed with pomp and majesty, and honoured of them all as their liege lady and sovereign. Afterward they made preparation for a princely and magnificent feast, as the Marquess did the like, for a marriage of extraordinary state and quality, inviting all his kindred, friends, and acquaintances in all parts and provinces about him. He made also ready most rich and costly garments, shaped by the body of a comely young gentlewoman, whom he knew to be equal in propor-tion and stature to her of whom he had made his election.

When the appointed nuptial day was come the Lord Marquess, about nine of the clock in the morning, mounted on horseback, as all the rest did, who came to attend him honourably, and having all things in due readiness with them, he said : "Lords, it is time for us to fetch the bride." So on he rode with his train to the same poor village whereat she dwelt, and when he was come to her father's house, he saw the maiden returning very hastily from a well, where she had been to fetch a pail of water, which she set down, and stood, accompanied with other maidens, to see the passage of the Lord Marquess and his train. Gualtieri called her by her name, which was Griselda, and asked her where her father was, who bashfully answered him, and with an humble courtesy, saying, " My gracious lord, he is in the house."

Then the Marquess dismounted from his horse, commanding every one to attend him, then all alone he entered into the poor cottage, where he found the maid's father, being named Giannuculo, and said unto him : " God speed, good father, I am come to espouse thy daughter Griselda, but first I have a few demands to make, which I will utter to her in thy presence." Then he turned to the maid and said :

" Fair Griselda, if I make you my wife, will you do your best endeavour to please me in all things, which I shall do or say ? will you be also gentle, humble and patient ? " with divers other the like questions, whereto she still answered that she would, so near as Heaven with grace should enable her.

Presently he took her by the hand, so led her forth of the poor man's homely house, and in the presence of all his company, with his own hands he took off her mean wearing garments, smock and all, and clothed her with those robes of state which he had purposely brought thither for her, and plaiting her hair over her shoulders, he placed a crown of gold on her head. Whereat every one standing as amazed, and wondering not a little, he said, " Griselda, wilt thou have me to thy husband ? " Modestly blushing and kneeling on the ground, she answered, " Yes, my gracious lord, if you will accept so poor a maiden to be your wife." " Yes, Griselda," quoth he, " with this holy kiss I confirm thee for my wife ; " and so espoused her before them all. Then mounting her on a milk-white palfrey, brought thither for her, she was thus honourably conducted to her palace.

Now concerning the marriage-feast and triumphs, they were performed with no less pomp than if she had been daughter to the King of France. And the young bride apparently declared that, with her garments, her mind and behaviour were quite changed. For indeed she was, as it were shame to speak otherwise, a rare creature, both of person and perfections, and not only was she absolute for beauty, and so sweetly amiable, gracious and goodly, as if she were not the daughter of poor Giannuculo, and a country shepherdess, but rather of some noble lord, whereat every one wondered that formerly had known her. Beside all this, she was so obedient to her husband, so fervent in all dutiful offices, and patient, without the very least provoking, as he held himself much more than contented, and the only happy man that lived in the world.

In like manner, towards the subjects of her lord and husband she showed herself always so benign and gracious, as there was not any one but the more they looked on her the better they loved her, honouring her voluntarily and praying to the Heavens for her health, dignity and welfare's long continuance, speaking now quite contrary to their former opinion of the Marquess, honourably and worthily, that he had shown himself a singular wise man in the election of his wife, which few else but he in the world would ever have done, because their judgment might fall far short of discerning those great and precious virtues, veiled under a homely habit, and obscured in a poor country cottage. To be brief, in very short time not only the Marquisate itself, but all neighbouring provinces round about, had no other common talk but of her rare course of life, devotion, charity, and all good actions else whatsoever, quite quailing all sinister constructions of her husband, before he had received her in matrimony.

About four or five years after the birth of her daughter she conceived with child again, and at the limited hour of deliverance had a goodly son, to the no little liking of the Marquess. Afterward a strange humour entered into his brain—namely, that by a long continued experience, and courses of an intolerable quality, he would needs make proof of his fair wife's patience. First he began to provoke her by injurious speeches, showing fierce and frowning looks to her, intimating that his people grew displeased with him, in regard of his wife's base birth and education, and so much the rather because she was likely to bring children who, by her blood, were no better than beggars, and murmured at the daughter already born. Which words, when Griselda heard, without any alteration of countenance, or the least distemperature in any appearing action, she said :

" My honourable and gracious lord, dispose of me as you think best for your own dignity and contentment, for I shall therewith be well pleased, as she that knows herself far inferior to the meanest of your people, much less worthy of the honour whereto you liked to advance me."

This answer was very welcome to the Marquess, as apparently perceiving hereby that the dignity whereto he had exalted her, or any particular favours beside, could not infect her with any pride, coyness or disdain. Not long after having told her in plain and open speeches that her subjects could not endure the daughter born of her, he instructed and despatched to her one of his servants, who, sorry, sad, and much perplexed in mind, said : " Madam, except I intend to lose my own life, I must accomplish what my lord hath strictly enjoined me, which is, to take this your young daughter, and then——" He said no more. The lady hearing these words, and noting his frowning looks, remembering also what the Marquess himself had formerly said, imagined that he had commanded his servant to kill the child. Suddenly therefore she took it out of the cradle, and having sweetly kissed, and bestowed her blessing on it, albeit her heart throbbed with the inward affection of a mother, without any alteration of countenance, she tenderly laid it in the servant's arms and said : " Here, friend, take it, and do with it as thy lord and mine hath commanded thee ; but leave it in no rude place where birds or savage beasts may devour it, except it be his will."

The servant departing from her with the child, and reporting to the Marquess what his lady had said, he wondered at her incomparable constancy. Then he sent it by the same servant to Bologna, to an honourable lady his kinswoman, requesting her, without revealing whose child it was, to see it both nobly and carefully educated.

At time convenient afterward, being with child again, and delivered of a princely son, than which nothing could be more joyful to the Marquess, yet all this was not sufficient for him, but with far ruder language than before, and looks expressing harsh intentions, he said unto her : " Griselda, though thou pleasest me wonderfully by the birth of this princely boy, yet my subjects are not therewith contented, but blunder abroad maliciously that the grandchild of Giannuculo, a poor country peasant, when I am dead and gone, must be their sovereign lord and master. Which makes me stand in fear of their expulsion, and to prevent that, I must be rid of this child, as well as the other, and then send thee away from hence, that I may take another wife more pleasing to them."

Griselda, with a patient sufferent soul, hearing what he had said, returned no other answer but this : " Most gracious and honourable lord, satisfy and please your own royal mind, and never use any respect of me, for nothing is precious or pleasing to me, but what may agree with your good liking." Within a while after, the noble Marquess in the like manner as he did before for his daughter, so he sent the same servant for his son, and seeming as if he had sent it to have been slain, conveyed it to be nursed at Bologna, in company of his sweet sister. Whereat the lady showed no other discontentment in any kind than formerly she had done for her daughter, to the no mean marvel of the Marquess, who protested in his soul that the like woman was not in all the world beside. And were it not for his heedful observation, how loving and careful she was of her children, prizing them as dearly as her own life ; rash opinion might have persuaded him that she had no more in her than a carnal affection, not caring how many she had so she might thus easily be rid of them ; but he knew her to be a truly virtuous mother, and wisely liable to endure his severest impositions.

His subjects believing that he had caused his children to be slain, blamed him greatly, thought him to be a most cruel man, and did highly compassionate the lady's case, who when she came in company of other gentlewomen, which mourned for their deceased children, would answer nothing else but that they could not be more pleasing to her than they were to the father that begot them.

Within certain years after the birth of these children, the Marquess purposed with himself to make his last and final proof of fair Griselda's patience, and said to some near about him that he could no longer endure to keep Griselda as his wife, confessing he had done foolishly, and according to a young giddy brain when he was so rash in the marriage of her. Wherefore he would send to the Pope and purchase a dispensation from him to repudiate Griselda and take another wife. Wherein, although they greatly reproved him, yet he told them plainly it must needs be so.

The lady hearing this news, and thinking she must return again to her poor father's house and estate, and perhaps to her old occupation of keeping of sheep, as in her younger days she had done ; understanding withal that another must enjoy him whom she dearly loved and honoured, you may well think, worthy ladies, that her patience was now put to the main proof indeed. Nevertheless, as with an invincible true virtuous courage, she had overstood all the other injuries of fortune, so did she constantly settle her soul to bear this with an undaunted countenance and behaviour.

At such time as was prefixed for the purpose, counterfeit letters came to the Marquess, as sent from Rome, which he caused to be publicly read in the hearing of his subjects, that the Pope had dispensed with him to leave Griselda, and marry with another wife ; wherefore, sending for her immediately, in presence and before them all, thus he spake to her : "Woman, by concession sent me from the Pope, he hath dispensed me to make choice of another wife, and to free myself from thee. And because my predecessors have been noblemen and great lords in this country, thou being the daughter of a poor country clown, and their blood and mine notoriously imbased by my marriage with thee, I intend to have thee no longer for my wife, but will return thee home to thy father's house with all the rich dowry thou broughtest me ; and then I will take another wife, with whom I am already contracted, better beseeming my birth, and far more contenting and pleasing to my people."

The lady hearing these words, not without much pain and difficulty, restrained her tears, quite contrary to the natural inclination of women, and thus answered : "Great Marquess, I never was so empty of discretion, but did always acknowledge that my base and humble condition could not in any manner suit with your high blood and nobility, and my being with you, I ever acknowledged to proceed from Heaven and you, not any merit of mine, but only as a favour lent me, which you being now pleased to recall back again, I ought to be pleased, and so am, that it be restored. Here is the ring wherewith you espoused me : here, in all humility, I deliver it to you. You command me to carry home the marriage dowry which I brought with me ; there is no need of a treasurer to repay it me, neither any new purse to carry it in, much less any sumpter to be laden with it. For, noble lord, it was never out of my memory that you took me stark-naked, and if it shall seem sightly to you that this body that hath borne two children, begotten by you, must again be seen naked, willingly must I depart hence naked. But I humbly beg of your excellency, in recompense of my virginity which I brought you blameless, so much as in thought, that I might have but one of my wedding smocks, only to conceal the shame of nakedness, and then I shall depart rich enough."

The Marquess, whose heart wept bloody tears, as his eyes would likewise gladly have yielded their natural tribute, covered all with a dissembling angry countenance, and starting up, said : "Go, give her a smock only, and so send her gadding." All there present then entreated him to let her have a petticoat, because it might not be said that she who had been his wife thirteen years and more was sent away so poorly in her smock ; but all their persuasions prevailed not with him. Naked in her smock, without hose or shoes, bareheaded, and not so much as a cloth or rag about her neck, to the great grief and mourning of all that saw her, she went home to her own father's house.

· And he, good man, never believing that the Marquess would long keep his daughter as his wife, but rather expecting daily what now happened, had safely laid up the garments whereof the Marquess despoiled her the same morning when he espoused her. Wherefore he delivered them to her, and she fell to her father's household business, according as formerly she had done, sustaining with a great and unconquerable spirit all the cruel assaults of her enemy, Fortune.

About such time also, as suited with his own disposition, the Marquess made publicly known to his subjects that he meant to join in marriage again with the daughter to one of the Counts of Panago, and causing preparation to be made for a sumptuous wedding, he sent for Griselda, and she being come, thus he spake to her : "The wife that I have made new election of is to arrive here within very few days, and at her first coming I would have her to be most honourably entertained. Thou knowest I have no woman in my house that can deck up the chambers and set all requisite things in due order befitting so solemn a feast, and therefore I sent for thee, who knowing better than any other all the parts, provision, and goods in the house, mayest set everything in such order as thou shalt think necessary.

"Invite such ladies and gentlewomen as thou wilt, and give them welcome as if thou wert the lady of the house, and when the marriage is ended return then home to thy father again."

Although these words pierced like wounding daggers the heart of the poor but noble patient Griselda, as being unable to forget the unequalled love she bare the Marquess, though the dignity of her former fortune more easily slipped out of her remembrance, yet nevertheless thus she answered :

"My gracious lord, I am glad that I can do you any service wherein you shall find me both willing and ready." In the same poor garments as she came from her father's house, although she was turned out in her smock, she began to sweep and make clean the chambers, rub the stools and benches in the hall, and ordered everything in the kitchen, as if she were the worst maid in all the house, never ceasing or giving over, till all things were in due and decent order, as best beseemed in such a case. After all which was done, the Marquess having invited all the ladies of the country to be present at so great a feast, when the marriage day was come,

Griselda in her gown of country grey, gave them welcome in honourable manner, and graced them all with very cheerful countenance.

Gualtieri the Marquess, who had caused his two children to be nobly nourished at Bologna with a near kinswoman of his, who had married with one of the Counts of Panago, his daughter being now aged twelve years old and somewhat more, as also his son about six or seven, he sent a gentleman expressly to his kindred to have them come and visit him at Saluzzo, bringing his daughter and son with them, attended in very honourable manner, and publishing everywhere as they came along that the young virgin, known to none but himself and them, should be the wife to the Marquess, and that only was the cause of her coming. The gentleman was not slack in the execution of trust reposed in him, but having made convenient preparation, with the kindred, son, daughter, and a worthy company attending on them, arrived at Saluzzo about dinner-time, where wanted no resort, from all neighbouring parts round about, to see the coming of the Lord Marquess's new spouse.

By the lords and ladies she was joyfully entertained, and coming into the great hall, where the tables were ready covered, Griselda, in her homely country habit, humbled herself before her, saying, "Gracious welcome to the new-elected spouse of the Lord Marquess."

All the ladies there present, who had very earnestly importuned Gualtieri, but in vain, that Griselda might better be shut up in some chamber, or else to lend her the wearing of any other garments which formerly had been her own, because she should not so poorly be seen among strangers; being seated at the tables, she waited on them very serviceably. The young virgin was observed by every one, who spared not to say that the Marquess had made an excellent change; but, above them all, Griselda did most commend her, and so did her brother likewise, as young as he was, yet not knowing her to be his sister.

Now was the Marquess sufficiently satisfied in his soul that he had seen so much as he desired concerning the patience of his wife, who in so many heart-grieving trials was never noted so much as to alter her countenance; and being absolutely persuaded that this proceeded not from any want of understanding in her, because he knew her to be singularly wise, he thought it high time now to free her from all these afflicting oppressions, and give her such assurance as she ought to have. Wherefore, commanding her into his presence, openly before all his assembled friends, smiling on her, he said: "What thinkest thou, Griselda, of our new-chosen spouse?" "My lord," quoth she, "I like her exceeding well; and if she be so wise as she is fair, which verily I think she is, I make no doubt but you shall live with her as the only happy man of the world. But I humbly entreat your honour, if I have any power in me to prevail by, that you would not give her such cutting and unkind language as you did to your other wife, for I cannot think her armed with such patience as should indeed support them; as well in regard she is much younger, as also her more delicate breeding and education, whereas she whom you had before was brought up in continual toil and travail."

When the Marquess perceived that Griselda believed verily this young daughter of hers should be his wife, and answered him in so honest and modest manner, he commanded her to sit down by him, and said: "Griselda, it is now more than fit time that thou shouldest taste the fruit of thy long admired patience, and that they who have thought me cruel, harsh, and uncivil-natured, should at length observe that I have done nothing at all basely or unadvisedly. For this was a work premeditated before for instructing thee what it is to be a married wife, and to let them know, whosoever they be, how to take and keep a wife; which hath begotten to me perpetual joy and happiness so long as I have a day to live with thee, a matter whereof I stood before greatly in fear, and which in marriage I thought would never happen to me.

"It is not unknown to thee, in how many kinds, for my first proof, I gave thee harsh and unpleasant speeches, which drew no discontentment from thee, either in looks, words, or behaviour, but rather such comfort as my soul desired, and so in my other succeeding afterward. In one minute now I purpose to give thee that consolation which I bereft thee of in my tempestuous storms, and make a sweet restoration for all thy former sour sufferings. My fair and dear affected Griselda, she whom thou supposest for my new-elected spouse, with a glad and cheerful heart embrace for thine own daughter, and this also her brother, being both of them thy children and mine, in common opinion of the whole vulgar multitude imagined to be, by my command, long since slain. I am thy honourable lord and husband, who doth and will love thee far above all women else in the world; giving thee justly this deserved praise and commendation, that no man living hath the like wife as I have."

So sweetly kissing her infinitely, and hugging her joyfully in his arms, the tears now streaming like new-let loose rivers down her fair face, which no disaster before could force from her, he brought her and seated her by her daughter, who was not a little amazed at so rare an alteration. She having, in zeal of affection, kissed and embraced them both, all else present being clearly resolved from the former doubt, which too long deluded them, the ladies arose jocundly from the tables, and attending on Griselda to her chamber, in sign of a more successful augury to follow, took off her poor contemptible rags, and put on such costly robes which, as Lady Marchioness, she used to wear before.

Afterward they waited on her into the hall again, being their sovereign lady and mistress, as she was no less in her poorest garments; where all rejoicing for the new-restored mother and happy recovery of so noble a son and daughter, the festival continued many months after. Now, every one thought the Marquess to be a noble and a wise prince, though somewhat sharp and unsufferable in the severe experience made of his wife; but above all they reputed Griselda to be a most wise, patient, and virtuous lady. The Count of Panago, within few days after, returned back to Bologna; and the Lord Marquess fetching home old Giannuculo from his country drudgery, to live with him as his father-in-law in his princely palace, gave him honourable maintenance, wherein he long continued and ended his days. Afterward he matched his daughter in a noble marriage, he and Griselda living long time together in the highest honour that possible could be.

What can now be said to the contrary, but that poor country cottages may yield as divine and excellent spirits as the most stately and royal mansions, which breed and bring up some more worthy to be hog-rubbers than hold any sovereignty over men? Where is any other beside Griselda who, not only without a wet eye, but emboldened by a valiant and invincible courage, could suffer the sharp rigours, and never the like heard-of proofs, made by the Marquess? Perhaps he might have met with another who would have quitted him in a contrary kind, and for thrusting her forth of doors in her smock, could have found better succour somewhere else, rather than walk so nakedly in the cold streets.

Dioneo having thus ended his novel, and the ladies delivering their several judgments according to their own fancies—some holding one conceit, others leaning to the contrary; one blaming this thing, and another commending that; the King lifting up his eyes to Heaven, and seeing the sun began to fall low, by rising of the evening star, without arising from his seat, spake as followeth: "Discreet ladies, I am persuaded you know sufficiently that the sense and understanding of us mortals consisteth not only, as I think, by preserving in memory things past or knowledge of things present; but such as both by the one and other know how to foresee future occasions, are worthily thought wise, and of no common capacity.

"It will be to-morrow fifteen days since we departed from the city of Florence, to come hither for our pastime and comfort, the conservation of our lives, and support of our health, by avoiding those melancholies, griefs, and anguishes which we beheld daily in our city since the pestilential visitation began there. Wherein, by my judgment, we have done well and honestly, albeit some light novels, perhaps attractive to a little wantonness, as some say, and jovial feasting, with good cheer, singing, and dancing, may seem matters inciting to incivility, especially in weak and shallow understandings. But I have neither seen, heard, nor known any act, word, or whatsoever else, either on your part or ours, justly deserving to be blamed; but all has been honest, as in a sweet and harmonious concord, such as might well beseem the community of Brethren and Sisters. This assuredly, as well in regard of you as us, hath much contented me.

"And therefore, lest by over-long consuetude something should

take life which might be converted into a bad construction, and by
a bad construction and by our country retirement for so many
days, some captious conceit may wrest out an ill imagination, I am
of opinion, if yours be the like, seeing each of us hath had the
honour which now remaineth still on me, that it is very fitting for
us to return thither from whence we came. And so much the
rather, because these sociable meetings of ours, which already hath
won the knowledge of many dwellers here about us, should now grow
to such an increase as might make our purposed pastime offensive
to us. In which respect, if you allow of my advice, I will keep
the crown till our departing hence, the which I intend shall be to-
morrow ; but if you determine otherwise, I am the man ready to
make my resignation."

Many imaginations passed among the ladies, and likewise the
men, but yet in the end they reputed the King's counsel to be the
best and wisest, concluding to do as he thought convenient.
Whereupon he called the Master of the Household, and conferred
with him of the business belonging to the next morning, and gave
the company leave to rise. The ladies and the rest, when they
were risen, fell some to one kind of recreation, and others as their
fancies served them, even as before they had done. And when
supper-time came they despatched it in very loving manner.
They began to play on instruments, sing, and dance ; and Lauretta leading the dance, she commanded Fiammetta to sing a
song, which pleasantly she began in this manner :

THE SONG.

The CHORUS *sung by all the rest of the Company.*

If Love were free from jealousy,
　　No lady living
　　Had less heart-grieving,
Or lived so happily as I.

If gallant youth
In a fair friend a woman could content,
　　If virtue's prize, valour and hardiment,
Wit, carriage, purest eloquence,
Could free a woman from impatience,
　　Then I am she can vaunt, if I were wise,
All these in one fair flower,
　　Are in my power ;
And yet I boast no more but truth.
　　If Love were free from jealousy, &c.

But I behold
That other women are as wise as I,
　　Which kills me quite ;
Fearing false surquedry.
For when my fire begins to flame,
　　Other desires misguide my aim,

And so bereave me of secure delight ;
    Only through fond mistrust Love is unjust.
Thus are my comforts hourly hot and cold.
    If Love were free, &c.

If in my friend
I found like faith as manly mind, I know
    Mistrust were slain,
But fresh griefs still will grow,
By sight of such as do allure ;
    So I can think none true, none sure,
But all would rob me of my golden gain.
    Lo, thus I die in jealousy,
For loss of him on whom I mind.
    If Love were free, &c.

Let me advise
Such ladies as in love are bravely bold,
    Not to wrong me ; I scorn to be controll'd.
If any one I chance to find,
By winks, words, smiles, in crafty kind
    Seeking for that which only mine should be,
Then I protest to do my best,
    And make them know that they are scarcely wise.
    If Love were free, &c.

So soon as Fiammetta had ended her song, Dioneo, who sat by her, smiling, said : " Truly, madam, you may do us a great courtesy to let him be known to us all, lest through ignorance you be deprived of your possession, when you ought not to be so offended." After the song was past, divers others were sung beside, and it now drawing well-near midnight, by the King's command they all went to bed. And when new day appeared, and all the world awaked out of sleep, the Master of the Household having sent away the carriages, they returned, under the conduct of their discreet King, to Florence, where the three gentlemen left the seven ladies at the Church of Santa Maria Novella, from whence they went with them at the first. And having parted with kind salutations, the gentlemen went whither themselves best pleased, and the ladies repaired home to their houses.

THE END.

PRINTED BY BALLANTYNE, HANSON AND CO.
LONDON AND EDINBURGH

CPSIA information can be obtained at www.ICGtesting.com
Printed in the USA
BVOW011510270513

321662BV00005B/74/A